Heidegger and Music

New Heidegger Research

Series Editors: Gregory Fried, Professor of Philosophy, Boston College, USA and Richard Polt, Professor of Philosophy, Xavier University, USA

The New Heidegger Research series promotes informed and critical dialogue that breaks new philosophical ground by taking into account the full range of Heidegger's thought, as well as the enduring questions raised by his work.

Titles in the Series
Heidegger and Jewish Thought, edited by Micha Brumlik and Elad Lapidot
Heidegger and the Environment, by Casey Rentmeester
Heidegger and the Global Age, edited by Antonio Cerella and Louiza Odysseos
Heidegger Becoming Phenomenological: Preferring Dilthey to Husserl, 1916–25, by Robert C. Scharff
Heidegger in Russia and Eastern Europe, edited by Jeff Love
Heidegger's Gods: An Ecofeminist Perspective, by Susanne Claxton
Making Sense of Heidegger, by Thomas Sheehan
Proto-Phenomenology and the Nature of Language, by Lawrence J. Hatab
Heidegger in the Islamicate World, edited by Kata Moser, Urs Gösken and Josh Michael Hayes
Time and Trauma: Thinking Through Heidegger in the Thirties, by Richard Polt
Contexts of Suffering: A Heideggerian Approach to Psychopathology, by Kevin Aho
Heidegger's Phenomenology of Perception: An Introduction, Volume I, by David Kleinberg-Levin
Confronting Heidegger: A Critical Dialogue on Politics and Philosophy, edited by Gregory Fried
Proto-Phenomenology, Language Acquisition, Orality and Literacy: Dwelling in Speech II, by Lawrence J. Hatab
Transcending Reason: Heidegger on Rationality, edited by Matthew Burch and Irene McMullin
The Fate of Phenomenology: Heidegger's Legacy, by William McNeill
Agency, Freedom, and Responsibility in the Early Heidegger, by Hans Pedersen
Heidegger's Phenomenology of Perception: Learning to See and Hear Hermeneutically, Volume II, by David Kleinberg-Levin
Towards a Polemical Ethics: Between Heidegger and Plato, by Gregory Fried
Thought Poems: A Translation of Heidegger's Verse, by Martin Heidegger, translated by Eoghan Walls
Correspondence: 1919–1973, by Martin Heidegger and Karl Löwith, translated by J. Goesser Assaiante and S. Montgomery Ewegen
Heidegger and the Holy, edited by Richard Copabianco
Heidegger and Music, edited by Casey Rentmeester and Jeff R. Warren

Heidegger and Music

Edited by
Casey Rentmeester and Jeff R. Warren

ROWMAN & LITTLEFIELD
Lanham • Boulder • New York • London

Published by Rowman & Littlefield
An imprint of The Rowman & Littlefield Publishing Group, Inc.
4501 Forbes Boulevard, Suite 200, Lanham, Maryland 20706
www.rowman.com

86-90 Paul Street, London EC2A 4NE

Copyright © 2022 Selection and Editorial Matter, Jeff R. Warren and Casey Rentmeester

All rights reserved. No part of this book may be reproduced in any form or by any electronic or mechanical means, including information storage and retrieval systems, without written permission from the publisher, except by a reviewer who may quote passages in a review.

British Library Cataloguing in Publication Information Available

Library of Congress Cataloging-in-Publication Data

Names: Rentmeester, Casey, editor. | Warren, Jeff R., 1977- editor.
Title: Heidegger and music / edited by Casey Rentmeester and Jeff R. Warren.
Description: Lanham : Rowman & Littlefield, 2021. | Includes bibliographical references and index.
Identifiers: LCCN 2021046371 (print) | LCCN 2021046372 (ebook) |
  ISBN 9781538154137 (cloth) | ISBN 9781538154151 (paperback) |
  ISBN 9781538154144 (ebook)
Subjects: LCSH: Music—Philosophy and aesthetics. | Music and philosophy. | Heidegger, Martin, 1889-1976.
Classification: LCC ML3800 .H315 2021 (print) | LCC ML3800 (ebook) |
  DDC 781.1/7—dc23
LC record available at https://lccn.loc.gov/2021046371
LC ebook record available at https://lccn.loc.gov/2021046372

Contents

Acknowledgments   vii

Introduction: Music, Being, Thinking   ix
Casey Rentmeester and Jeff R. Warren

PART I: MUSIC AND BEING-HUMAN

1. Rocking Heidegger: Musical Experience between Technology and Ontology   3
   Frederik Pio

2. Heidegger on the Slopes and Musical Mountain Biking Multimedia   19
   Jeff R. Warren and John Reid-Hresko

3. Distracted Dasein?   37
   Anthony Gritten

4. Rilke and the "Tone of Death": Music and Word in Heidegger   53
   Babette Babich

PART II: MUSICAL TRADITIONS OF THE WORLD

5. Grand Style, Heidegger, Nietzsche: Elaborations of a Concept   75
   Erik Wallrup

6. Heidegger, *Iki*, and Musical Resistance to *Gestell*   91
   J. P. E. Harper-Scott

7 The "Silent Music" in Ancient Chinese Thought and Heidegger's
   Sound of Stillness   109
   Qinghua Zhu

8 Heidegger's *Musik-Sprache* or Silence and Bells in the Music
   of Arvo Pärt   127
   Peter Trawny and Agamenon de Morais

9 We Live Therefore We Are: African Musical Aesthetics
   Challenge Heidegger's Forgetfulness   143
   Eve Ruddock

PART III: MUSICAL CREATION AND PERFORMANCE

10 Improvising the Round Dance of Being: Reading Heidegger
   from a Musical Perspective   163
   Sam McAuliffe and Jeff Malpas

11 Meditative Thinking in Jazz and the Challenge of the Technical 179
   Trevor Thwaites

12 Musical Performance as Poetic Thinking   195
   Goetz Richter

13 Being-with in Music   213
   Justin Christensen and Janeen Loehr

PART IV: THE POWER OF MUSIC

14 Somewhere between Plato and Pinker: A Heideggerian
   Ontology of Music   235
   Casey Rentmeester

15 Touched by Music: Affective Expression as Measure-Taking   253
   Roger W. H. Savage

16 Remembering Air in Schilingi's Generative Music:
   Heideggerian Reflections on *Argo* and *Terra*   271
   Jill Drouillard

17 The Working of Aural Being in Electronic Music   289
   Gerry Stahl

Index   309

About the Contributors   317

Acknowledgments

I thank the late Charles Guignon for showing me how to read Heidegger and my parents, Handel and Diane Rentmeester, for inspiring a love of music. Personally, I owe a debt of gratitude to Mark Bake for granting me the flexibility in terms of my duties at Bellin College to accomplish my portion of this volume and especially to my wife, Cassie, for taking on more than her fair share of family responsibilities during the late stages of the editing process. Finally, I thank Amelia, Bennett, and Cash, who are traversing their own philosophical and musical journeys and serve as steady inspirations in my life.

Casey Rentmeester

I acknowledge that I live, work, and play on the traditional, ancestral, and unceded territories of the Skwxwú7mesh (Squamish) peoples. I am grateful to the professors, colleagues, and students who have read and re-read Heidegger alongside me. Each of you helped me learn something new. I am also thankful to the musicians I have played with who—even if they have never read Heidegger—helped my philosophical inquiry more than they know. Thanks to my wife Melissa for being an incredible partner, and my daughters Ella and Ara for allowing me to learn alongside their inquisitive minds.

Jeff R. Warren

Special thanks go to Richard Polt, Gregory Fried, and Frankie Mace for their help in editing this volume, as well as Monica Sukumar for overseeing the production of the book.

Introduction

Music, Being, Thinking

Casey Rentmeester and Jeff R. Warren

Perhaps the most famous quote from a philosopher on music comes from Friedrich Nietzsche, who states, "Without music, life would be an error."[1] Martin Heidegger, it seems, didn't exactly feel that way, as he directed very little explicit philosophical attention to music. Thus, one might think that those interested in both philosophy and music should look to philosophers other than Heidegger—canonical figures like Plato or Nietzsche, perhaps—for a philosophical analysis of music. However, even though Heidegger did not have much to say about music proper, the breadth and richness of his thought have inspired philosophical thinking in various fields that go beyond the ideas that commonly garnered his attention. Indeed, the range of topics that have been covered thus far in the *New Heidegger Research* series is a testament to this, as the series has showcased highly original and creative engagements with Heidegger's thought in the realms of politics, ethics, environmentalism, health, psychopathology, globalism, and others, many of which were not explicit targets of philosophical analysis on the part of Heidegger. This volume seeks to continue this tradition by showcasing a wide range of thinkers from various backgrounds who think through the relationship between Heidegger's philosophy and music.

One of the great strengths in this volume lies in the variety of its contributors, which comes in many forms. Regarding geographical location, the authors stem from ten different countries and the diversity of their interpretations of Heidegger reflects this variance. In terms of intellectual background, the authors span across disciplines including philosophy, musical performance, music education, musicology, sociology, psychology, and information science. Thus, it is safe to say that this volume is truly interdisciplinary in nature. Moreover, some of the contributors are musicians and composers themselves, which adds a practical element to the volume. Finally, the chapter content is wide-ranging not only in terms of engagements with various musical traditions of the world, musical styles, or specific musicians and composers, but also in terms of the overarching topics covered in the volume, including the relationship between music and what it means to be human, the creation and performance of music, the role of hearing, and the threats that accompany our current digital age of music, among others.

This volume was conceived by Josh Spier, a pianist and composer who was formerly a research associate at Flinders University in Australia. Spier found Heidegger's philosophy to be insightful in attempting to understand how Heidegger's thoughts on the age of modern technology could help to explain the changes that have occurred in the work of piano composers in the contemporary era. He had an intuition that much could be learned from a philosophical analysis of music from a Heideggerian lens, and thus put together the initial workings of this volume. In editing the volume, we are indebted to Spier's initial work.

As editors, we have prioritized the autonomy of the authors with the hope of generating as diverse a spectrum of perspectives as possible and have done this for two overarching reasons. First, as noted previously, Heidegger had very little to say directly about music, so it takes some creativity to extrapolate Heidegger's philosophical concepts to the realm of music. Giving authors leeway to explore this topic broadly allowed for unique creativity to flourish in which Heidegger's philosophy is used as a theoretical overlay to interpret the work of musicians as various as Arvo Pärt, an Estonian Orthodox Christian composer, to Jacopo Baboni Schilingi, an Italian composer working at the cutting edge of the contemporary generative and interactive musical movement. Second, given the limited secondary literature on the topic of Heidegger and music, we hoped that such an approach would lead to new conceptual terrain that had previously not been traveled. We were lucky enough to solicit chapters from intellectuals who already have written on Heidegger and music in the past. In those cases, the authors used their previous analyses as springboards for novel perspectives. We think that, as a result of prioritizing the autonomy of our authors, the reader will find a variety of new avenues from which to understand the philosophy of music from a Heideggerian lens. The volume is organized into four parts, each of which is briefly summarized below.

Part I of the volume is titled "Music and Being-Human." In the first chapter, Frederik Pio discusses how Heidegger's philosophy can help us understand the importance of music education in a contemporary context that reflects but updates some of his thoughts in his coedited volume *Philosophy of Music Education Challenged: Heideggerian Inspirations*.[2] Pio uses Heideggerian concepts to help us understand why we as humans are invigorated by musical experience due to our inherent need for the phenomena of beauty in our lives.

This chapter is followed by Jeff R. Warren who expands upon his insights on Heidegger and music from his book *Music and Ethical Responsibility*.³ In chapter 2, Warren partners with sociologist John Reid-Hresko to explore musical multimedia and mountain biking culture from a Heideggerian perspective, arguing that that ski and mountain biking films are tools of dwelling. In chapter 3, Anthony Gritten examines the consequences of the observation that Dasein hears. Gritten uses Heidegger's ideas to develop a phenomenology of sonic distraction, with particular focus on the ends of sounds, the sound of Dasein's being-toward-death. The last chapter of this section, by Babette Babich, examines sound and death from another angle. Beginning with Heidegger's reading of the poet Rilke, Babich draws out the importance of tone and sound in Heidegger's ideas, showing the important role the acoustic and music play in Heidegger's philosophy.

Part II is titled "Musical Traditions of the World." The first chapter of this section is by Erik Wallrup, who thoughtfully applied the Heideggerian concept of *Stimmung* (attunement) to music in his book *Being Musically Attuned*.⁴ In his chapter, Wallrup looks specifically at the ways in which Heidegger's understanding of art as world-transformative can extend Nietzsche's aesthetics by looking primarily at European musical works in the grand style. Next, J. P. E. Harper-Scott focuses specifically on the relationship between the later Heidegger's aesthetics and the *iki* aesthetics of the Japanese philosopher Kuki Shūzō, who studied under Heidegger in the late 1920s, wrote the first book-length study on Heidegger in Japanese, and is explicitly referenced by Heidegger in the 1959 work *On the Way to Language*.⁵ Harper-Scott views the English composer Benjamin Britten's later music, that is, the music that followed his engagement with Japan, as a focal practice (in Albert Borgmann's sense of the term)⁶ that is able to provide an example of musical resistance to *Gestell*, that is, the age of modern technology wherein everything shows up as mere resources. Chapter 7 takes the reader west across the East China Sea from Japan to China—conceptually, at least. In this chapter, Qinghua Zhu shows us how Heidegger's philosophy of art can help us to better understand ancient Chinese music and particularly the importance of silence in that tradition. The next chapter is a collaboration between Peter Trawny and Agamenon de Morais and continues the conversation on the significance of silence. Trawny and de Morais provide a highly creative chapter by juxtaposing Heidegger's thoughts on silence with the musical works of the Orthodox Christian Estonian composer Arvo Pärt, who invented the compositional technique known as tintinnabula, a minimalist technique influenced by Pärt's mystical experiences with chant music. In the final chapter of this section, Eve Ruddock contrasts Heidegger's philosophy with John Murungi's phenomenological exploration of African musical aesthetics. In particular, Ruddock tries to highlight potential elements of "forgetfulness" in

Heidegger's thinking not only in terms of music but in terms of non-German traditions.

"Musical Creation and Performance," which is the title of Part III of the volume, contains chapters that deal more explicitly with the practice of creating and performing music. In chapter 10, Sam McAuliffe and Jeff Malpas look specifically at improvisation from a Heideggerian philosophical perspective. The authors examine the ways that Heidegger's ideas of equipmentality, dwelling, and the event (*Ereignis*) relate to improvised musical performance. They argue that Heidegger can provide insight into musical improvisation, and also argue that musical improvisation can illuminate elements of Heidegger's thought. Chapter 11 features the work of Trevor Thwaites, who continues the conversation on improvisation by looking at its role in jazz performance. A jazz musician himself, Thwaites thinks through the ways in which the digitization of jazz has eroded traditional methods of sound production but finds hope in Heidegger's concept of meditative thinking, a practice Heidegger describes during a speech at the commemorative celebration of the 175th birthday of the composer Conradin Kreutzer, who hailed from Heidegger's hometown of Messkirch, Germany.[7] In chapter 12, Goetz Richter also finds inspiration in Heidegger's concept of meditative and poetic thinking, which is thinking that requires a mode of openness on the part of the thinker. In contrasting this form of thinking with calculative thinking, which is inherently restrictive, Richter argues that Heidegger's poetic thinking can help us understand musical thinking, and that understanding musical performance as a form of poetic thinking provides a resolution for musical performers who often think in dualistic concepts. The final chapter of this section is a collaboration between Justin Christensen and Janeen Loehr, who are both researchers in the realm of psychology. Christensen and Loehr employ the psychological concept of joint agency, that is, a sense of shared control over actions and their consequences, and combine it with Heidegger's concept of being-with in order to understand how musicians are able to interact synchronously in the act of performing music.

The last section of the book is titled "The Power of Music." In chapter 14, Casey Rentmeester attempts to build a Heideggerian ontology of music that lies "somewhere between" the views of Plato and Steven Pinker. Rather than a dangerous force to be censored (as Plato thought)[8] or a mere pleasantry to the senses (as Pinker has argued),[9] Rentmeester utilizes Woodstock to show how music's true significance from a Heideggerian perspective lies in its ability to gather together meanings and open up new worlds for people but also how the digital era of music threatens this world-building capacity. In the following chapter, Roger W. H. Savage also thinks through the ontological significance of music. Savage draws upon his insights in his book *Music, Time, and Its Other*,[10] to analyze the ways in which both Heidegger's philosophy and the phenomenological hermeneutics of Paul Ricoeur can help us understand what it means to be touched by music. In chapter 16, Jill Drouillard draws upon Heidegger's ideas in providing an interpretation of the works of the Italian composer Jacopo Baboni Schilingi. Keeping in mind Luce Irigaray's argument of Heidegger's "forgetting of air,"[11] Drouillard shows us how Schilingi's generative music makes air visible in his interactive musical compositions, *Argo* and *Terra*, in such a way that can teach us how to dwell before "the music stops," that is, before death. In the last chapter, Gerry Stahl discusses Heidegger's philosophy in the context of electronic music as it emerged in the 1960s. He combines Heidegger's idea of the revelatory nature of art with a Marxian understanding of the production of art being mediated through technological means to demonstrate how electronic music is able to open new sonic worlds.

This diverse collection of essays on Heidegger and music interacts with and responds to a wide range of existing scholarship that considers Heidegger and music, from the mid-twentieth-century interest in the phenomenology of music to the growth of interest in Heidegger and music (and music and philosophy more generally) over the past decade. We hope that this volume continues these discussions and provides new ways to continue considering the relationship between Heidegger's ideas and music.

NOTES

1. Friedrich Nietzsche, *Twilight of the Idols or How to Philosophize with the Hammer*, trans. Richard Polt (Indianapolis and Cambridge: Hackett Publishing Company, 1997), 10.

2. *Philosophy of Music Education Challenged: Heideggerian Inspirations*, eds. Frederik Pio and Øivind Varkøy (Dordrecht: Springer, 2015).

3. Jeff R. Warren, *Music and Ethical Responsibility* (Cambridge and New York: Cambridge University Press, 2014).

4. Erik Wallrup, *Being Musically Attuned: The Act of Listening to Music* (London and New York: Routledge, 2015).

5. Martin Heidegger, *On the Way to Language*, trans. Peter D. Hertz (New York: Harper & Row, 1971).

6. Albert Borgmann, *Technology and the Character of Contemporary Life: A Philosophical Inquiry* (Chicago: University of Chicago Press, 1984).

7. Martin Heidegger, "Memorial Address," in *Discourse on Thinking*, trans. John M. Anderson and E. Hans Freund (New York: Harper & Row, 1966), 43–57.

8. Cf. Plato, *Republic*, trans. G. M. A. Grube and C. D. C. Reeve (Indianapolis and Cambridge: Hackett Publishing Company, 1992).

9. Steven Pinker, *How the Mind Works* (New York: W. W. Norton & Company, 1997).

10. Roger W. H. Savage, *Music, Time, and Its Other: Aesthetic Reflections on Finitude, Temporality, and Alterity* (Abingdon, Oxon: Routledge, 2018).

11. Cf. Luce Irigaray, *The Forgetting of Air in Martin Heidegger*, trans. Mary Beth Mader (Austin: University of Texas Press, 1999).

BIBLIOGRAPHY

Borgmann, Albert. *Technology and the Character of Contemporary Life: A Philosophical Inquiry*. Chicago: University of Chicago Press, 1984.
Heidegger, Martin. "Memorial Address." In *Discourse on Thinking*, translated by John M. Anderson and E. Hans Freund, 43–57. New York: Harper & Row, 1966.
Heidegger, Martin. *On the Way to Language*. Translated by Peter D. Hertz. New York: Harper & Row, 1971.
Irigaray, Luce. *The Forgetting of Air in Martin Heidegger*. Translated by Mary Beth Mader. Austin: University of Texas Press, 1999.
Nietzsche, Friedrich. *Twilight of the Idols or How to Philosophize with the Hammer*. Translated by Richard Polt. Indianapolis and Cambridge: Hackett Publishing Company, 1997.
Philosophy of Music Education Challenged: Heideggerian Inspirations. Edited by Frederik Pio and Øivind Varkøy. Dordrecht: Springer, 2015.
Pinker, Steven. *How the Mind Works*. New York: W. W. Norton & Company, 1997.
Plato. *Republic*. Translated by G. M. A. Grube and C. D. C. Reeve. Indianapolis and Cambridge: Hackett Publishing Company, 1992.
Savage, Roger W. H. *Music, Time, and Its Other: Aesthetic Reflections on Finitude, Temporality, and Alterity*. Abingdon, Oxon: Routledge, 2018.
Wallrup, Erik. *Being Musically Attuned: The Act of Listening to Music*. London and New York: Routledge, 2015.
Warren, Jeff R. *Music and Ethical Responsibility*. Cambridge and New York: Cambridge University Press, 2014.

Part I

MUSIC AND BEING-HUMAN

Chapter 1

Rocking Heidegger

Musical Experience between Technology and Ontology

Frederik Pio

Drawing on Heidegger's reading of the German poet Friedrich Hölderlin, I aim to develop an understanding of the experiential relation between music and world by offering an existential approach aligned with Heidegger's ontology. In this understanding, the phenomenon of beauty cannot be solely encapsulated within a contemplative, aesthetical discourse. Rather, musical experience as existential experience is contrarily shown to situate the listener in a lived world. I begin by introducing Heidegger's notion of technique (*die Technik*) and the broader cultural critique that aligns with this concept. I then develop eight critical points regarding the technical, digital revolution of musical experience that has taken place in the last twenty years. But the skeptical perspectives formulated in these eight points are shown not to be a full reflection of Heidegger's notion of the technical order of the world. To be more precise, in Heidegger's philosophical analysis of being (*Sein*), the notion of *die Technik* plays a crucial double role as it is simultaneously pregnant with a dangerous threat as well as a saving possibility. When this perspective is connected to the particular developments in digital technology in the last twenty years, then music somehow takes up a peculiar and quite central role. It seems to a large extent to be a musical experience that today brings to life the significant mediation between technology and art, for which Heidegger's philosophy paid so much attention. Again and again, it is the marriage of art and technology that comes into focus when Heidegger talks about a possible emergence of a new understanding of being (designated as *the Ereignis*). I try to show how Heidegger's perspective allows us to perform an ontological analysis of our technical age with an eye toward musical sensitivity.

ON OUR NEED FOR BEAUTY

Through the unavoidable experiences of loss and the wear we impose on each other from day to day, a part of our lives is potentially imposed with a sense of fear, resistance, and potential chaos. For us to endure this, we also at times have an option to comprehend our lives through something quite different than the unavoidable conflicts and brutality we may meet in everyday life. Here we can turn to sensuous musical experiences of beauty available to us through melodic, harmonious, and rhythmic phenomena. When we let ourselves be absorbed by grooves, beautiful tonal structures, and imaginative narratives of harmonic process, we are fascinated, as these musical experiences help to nurture meaning in our lives. With that, the experience of something beautiful in life becomes a significant factor for the maintenance of our connection with meaning and viability.

Such experience, however, cannot exclusively be reduced to a private, inner mental and aesthetic contemplation. Rather, any such experience imprints itself in the world of meaning we share with each other. Such musical experience can help us to understand what one's life "is all about," as our meeting with the music becomes a sensuous prism for a fundamental being-in-the world. It discloses a mood that is imaginative, pre-theoretical, as well as non-discursive. In this mood, we access a holistic understanding of our world that cannot be realized in any other obvious way (for instance, by paragraphs, principles, or theories). This is an experience that exclusively concerns the domain of art. And here music constitutes a most peculiar means of expression.

MUSICAL EXPERIENCE AS AESTHETIC EXPERIENCE AND EXISTENTIAL EXPERIENCE

From a Heideggerian perspective, beauty (of, say, music) is not only about a worldless, uninterested *aesthetic* contemplation. Rather, there is another dimension because, at the same time, a depth of being in the experience of musical or poetical beauty is disclosed. This depth of being situates us into a lived, existential world: "What if, the hearable (die *Hörigkeit*) is not the only and not the authentic way of listening?"[1] For Heidegger, art is a privileged escape hatch to being. More specifically, Heidegger perceives the artwork as a prism for the being that constitutes Dasein. Dasein designates our being-in-the-world as a "there" (*Da*) constituted by being (*Sein*). According to Heidegger, Dasein refers to the experience that you are standing out of being, which you have not created, but rather have received, that maintains what you are.[2] The poetical sphere of art and music is significant to Dasein, as art has the ability to summarize our background understanding of the lifeworld, that is, our tacit sense of being-in-it. When Heidegger talks about the relation between art and being (for instance, in his discussions on the ontology of the artwork), he is referring to the artwork as a condensed manifestation of that cultural comprehension of being in which it is rooted. Heidegger's interpretations of Van Gogh's painting of peasant shoes or the Greek temple are famous examples of this.[3] Below I will look into how his readings of the German Romantic poet Hölderlin provide crucial insight into how Heidegger perceives this relation between art and being. From that discussion, light can be shed upon how music still plays an important part even in our modern society. This importance has to do with the fact that our need for beauty as mentioned is not merely aesthetically founded but also ontologically founded. This ontological dimension of musical experience is, however, to a high extent covered over and ignored, especially in the educational system of music teaching today.[4] We must thus ask ourselves if we have generally impaired our ability to connect with music as a life-orienting force due to the current model of music education wherein it is treated as an "unnecessary luxury" by the higher echelons of our dominant decision-makers in public life, namely politicians. This is a symptom of the current societal ambivalence toward music.

But what is meant when Heidegger claims that our experience of aesthetic phenomena can potentially disclose ontological significance? In my interpretation, artistic-poetical phenomena can obtain a high affinity with the experience of what "one's place in the world" is all about. Heidegger states, "The poetical grounds the humans towards the earth, and thus leads us into dwelling."[5] The same goes for our listening, attuned way of being-in-the-world when we respond to the complexities of music. In our listening, we are drawn into a belonging to the world. We cannot remove our listening connection with the world since our hearing draws us into it. In fact, we are fundamentally listening beings. We hear, because in our *Hören* (*hearing*) lies a fundamental *Ge-hören*, which means "belonging." Listening (as *Hören*) is for Heidegger about reaching back toward that part of our tradition that makes us belong. Indeed, Heidegger explicitly links his conception of "belonging to being" with listening.[6] In the depth of what we hear, our Dasein resonates with a world in which we belong. We cannot remove our hearing from an undesirable sound the way we remove our gaze from something that we do not want to look at. As listening beings, we belong in a world that constantly makes itself known through an auditory character of sound with which we are familiar. We hear a door slamming. We hear the wife downstairs scolding her husband. We never primarily hear an acoustic sound or just neutral auditory data. Rather, we immediately hear a world constantly happening in our vicinity.[7] Without our listening sensibility, we are cut off from a proper being-in-the-world. Listening pulls us into an interaction with the world. Our listening way of belonging to the world is so basic that it is a precondition for playing music. From this perspective, listening is "an activity of a [person]—defined by the history of its life—that includes this life history in the musical learning process."[8]

The world of phenomena has a being that Heidegger mentions as "a center" (*Mitte*) that is claimed to be "unheard" (*Unerhört*), which he refers to as "the unheard center of beingness (*das Seiende*)."[9] This holy chaos of unheard world-sound has a sort of affinity with a phenomenon from antiquity and the Middle Ages: *the music of the spheres*, that is, the idea that the heavenly bodies in the cosmos are aligned to each other through harmonic proportions that resonate with each other, thus creating a music of the cosmos.[10] This concept posits the question: what kind of sound emanates from the world? One could say that this sound has a basic tone that is unheard. It functions like an attunement to a collective tonality, an organ point of sociality. According to the Heidegger scholar Max van Manen, we must learn "to attune to the deep tonalities of language, that normally fall out of our accustomed range of hearing [and be] able to listen to the way the things of the world speak to us."[11] We dwell in the world when *grooves*, universes of timbre, or patterns of tone disclose a world we are already familiar with. According to Heidegger we should "open our ears, make space for that which addresses us in the recreated tradition of the being of beings. As we listen to this, we move closer to the possibility of corresponding."[12] Such "corresponding" (*Entsprechung*) is about finding ourselves attuned with each other in a mood of openness—created through this art of listening that is always already musical. The world is already there as something unheard (*unerhört*) in our belonging to it (our *Ge-hören*).[13] Our belonging to being is thus already given.[14] Indeed, as Heidegger states, "the emergence of being speaks, dependent on whether it is heard or overheard."[15] From this ontological delineation of listening as a musical way of being-in-the-world, Heidegger, however, launches a cultural critique.

HEIDEGGER'S CULTURAL CRITIQUE

Heidegger sees that the grounding essence of art seems to be compromised by what he calls *die Technik*, a "technique" dedicated to technical or technological rationality that reigns in modernity.[16] He argues that this peculiar way of making sense of the world (designated as *die Technik*) is double in nature, in accordance with his distinction between *Sein* (being) and *das Seiende* (beings). This means that *die Technik* has two dimensions. In terms of *das Seiende*, "the technical" is equal to concrete technologies, technical solutions, various apparatuses, chemical processes, machines, etc. But "the technical" also defines—at the level of *Sein*—how the world today appears to us in a way in which our being-in-it makes sense to us as something technical. *Die Technik* is here much more about what we can think of as a spiritual power that lets the world be recognized in a very narrow and distinct way only: a way that regulates the openness and closedness of the horizon in which we live.[17] Heidegger sees that our modern epoch has become wholly seized by this particular technical worldview that turns everything into resources to be optimized, which he refers to as *Bestand*.[18] This turn toward a generalized technical logic impacts everything, not least the human vision of modernity. In his commentary on this, Heidegger distinguishes between the human being as (i) *Lebewesen* (a purely rational and problem-solving organism) and (ii) Dasein (in the sense of "being-there" mentioned earlier): "The *Lebewesen* . . . are not in need of being; they do not endure the truth of being and do not safekeep that which emerges in its being. Thus they have no world . . . but only 'surroundings.'"[19] Thus a difference remains between understanding the world from a place you belong (*Heimat*), and then on the basis of logistics to have a preliminary place of residence somewhere.[20] Art has the potential ability to disclose significance in the world to Dasein. But at the same time there is a technical pressure on the artwork to reduce it to its surface, which we might—to paraphrase Heidegger—refer to as its so-called harmless exterior.[21] In such reduction, the artwork is, for instance, reduced to a communication of signs, that is, something that consists of a sender, content, and a recipient. But when such reductions are applied (for instance, in system theory), then artworks cease to open an understanding of being: "The technoscientific world is through and through . . . the consequential design of the metaphysical world conception . . . so that nature and art both disappear in this conception . . . and are dissolved into that which is today called culture."[22] Art thus becomes visual culture; drama becomes scenic information; music becomes auditive culture or acoustic semiotics. And new skill sets can thus be aligned to educational competence goals in relation to the handling of these new types of information.

From a Heideggerian perspective, we suffer from overload when there is too much of everything. When information expands into myriads of unmanageable chains of information or hyperlinks, "the more decisive a delusion will spread out together with a blindness to the phenomena."[23] Heidegger employs a peculiar metaphor for the concealment of the artwork when he talks about the "fleeing of the gods" from the world. A world disclosed by the modern technic-technological gaze is a world embossed by "the flight of the gods, the destruction of the earth, the massification of man, the hate and suspicion towards everything that is creative and free."[24] The ability of our epoch to gain insight into that which is fundamental (*Sein*) is thus potentially weakened by a current deluge of information. Heidegger puts the point the following way: "Mostly we only comprehend what is common (*Gangbar*) and its diversity, because we are not prepared to see that which is simple."[25] In such a scenario music decays into a status of purely aesthetic information (possibly purchased online for uninvolved pleasure).[26] When this occurs, an object is simply installed and supported by theories of culture, communication, or semiotics.[27]

The noise from these reductions of art fades, however, when one turns toward Heidegger, as he attempts to uncover the artwork as an ontological vortex (*Wirbel*).[28] We can understand this as that wherein being is uncovered. Heidegger speaks of it as "a vortex that captivatingly takes us somewhere."[29] Heidegger thus perceives art as a potential counter-movement (*Gegenbewegung*) to the modern, technical worldview of control, information, and endless optimization.[30] The artwork articulates a potential counter-movement because it constitutes an ontological "awakening . . . of the individual existence, through which the individual reaches back towards her own being-in-the-world. If everybody derives from this starting point, a true gathering of each individual into an authentic community has already happened."[31] The above-cited "awakening" (*Erweckung*) is about a shared being-in-the-world. Here we are listening from being to being in a continuous process, before being (*Sein*) is substantiated and thus made into beings (*das Seiende*), that is, into entities.[32] Our participation in such a poetical or musical *Wirbel* makes it possible for us to experience who we are (*wer wir sind*).[33] Art thus becomes "the constitutive ground of history."[34] But if a basic community disappears from a society or is weakened, then at the same time music decays. Because music constitutes a primal language of social cohesion, music offers an immediate form of experience in terms of a community's sense of itself. It institutes and vindicates a community's concrete way of making sense of its world.

According to Karl Heinrich Ehrenforth, Heidegger is here touching on an ancient theme that reaches back to the earliest high cultures outside Europe.[35] From this perspective, a paradigm shift occurs around 400 BCE in which the understanding of reality shifts from *mythos* to *logos*, that is, from myth-based narratives to rationality.[36] Right around this time, one sees a transition where the pre-Socratic, Greek horizon of *mythos* is gradually replaced by the dry *logos* of rationality and later through the expanding Roman Empire. It is here during this mighty transition—according to Ehrenforth—that music starts losing its "life-orienting force."[37] Consequences more or less derived from these events are even felt more than a millennium later, as Western music around the middle of the eighteenth century achieves autonomy when the major compositions predominantly move from the liturgical, ritualized space of the church into the secularized concert hall. However, this does not mean that music has "lost contact to the basic rootedness in *Mythos (myth)*. In the words and harmonies of the artforms, an experience of the bedrock (*Urgrund*) of the world rings out, without which we cannot live."[38] This background still resonates when the lifeworld of music is today described phenomenologically as a "faltering ground."[39] One can even raise the question as to whether music in this technical age has managed to maintain its ancient ability to gather us around something shared and meaningful in the world. Or rather, does our technical-scientific grid-segmentation of the world hold sway in a sovereign mastery of our being-in-the-world?

GOING ONLINE

If we take into account how young people today are typically having musical experiences, then it is a question as to whether the current digital online revolution can learn from Heidegger's above-mentioned philosophical critique of the technical-technological worldview. In other words, to what extent can Heidegger's analysis claim relevance today? Such a discussion also has to do with how in a musical sense we educate and socialize the younger generation with the obvious focal point here being the current symbiosis between music and technology. Below is summarized eight key points on this topic, triggered by Heidegger's thinking (*Denken*):

1. Music is today to a large extent de-situated as digital sound files. When music is mediated digitally as online information, it becomes fluid, flexible, and anonymous.
2. At the same time, the recipient of these files is often positioned as a consumer of these online services. In a calculative survey of relevance and quality of this distribution of information, the dominant measure for value easily becomes the number of "hits," "likes," or downloads that a given file can produce in the marketplace. One can discuss whether this could potentially promote an enhanced understanding of quality based on the lowest common denominator.
3. On the internet, every music information is distributed on the basis of equality and equal access so that an intended leveling is installed. The internet revolution does not *destroy* tradition and our history of music. Neither does it *conserve* any tradition. It rather *levels* any significance of musical meaning or tradition. Every music is placed on equal footing. Everything is of equal significance. No distinctions of hierarchy in any but the crudest form can be made. Any organization of cultural memory is blurred. Even the most terrible music can be showcased on the internet. And vice versa no music is good enough to achieve any highlighting.

4. How can we move from uninvolved consumers of sound files on the internet toward cultivating a musical commitment in Heidegger's sense, that is, where we translate music into lived experiences in the world? This is about the musical experience in the way it can possibly become absorbed into attuned, social feelings, disclosing a community's essential sense of itself. This is about avoiding the point at which a lived world is no longer mirrored in the digital files we access. The music psychologist John Sloboda points toward such a risk, as he states about our current use of music that "the valued outcomes are mainly self-referring, internal, even solipsistic. Music seems to be a ready source of conflict between people as much as it is something that draws them together."[40]
5. The logarithms of *Spotify*, for instance, relieve us from the difficult decision of where we need to direct our attention. The perfected soundscapes of global radio hits hold sway over the global ear when they reach us via *YouTube* carrying the titanic authority of a billion hits.
6. We are close to a scenario now where any conceivable music is available with a push of a button on a keyboard. But what does it mean that everything is distributed, segmented, made transparent, and accessible against the need for slow immersion and involvement? There is always "something more" available on the menu. We are always on our way toward the next kick (just click). Do we ultimately become nomads surfing the endless, glimmering, and seductive surfaces of the world wide web? Do we become the modern Odysseus with the net acting as the alluring mermaids?
7. Flawless, perfected digital music is present everywhere as unattainable soundscapes. Easy-play user platforms such as *GarageBand* demonstrate in practice that you don't really need to have any musical skills of hand to play and compose music. This technological conquest of our relation to music carries a potential problem in relation to young people's musical self-esteem and their motivation to risk themselves in actual scenarios of hand-played music. Here the fight is on, against installed notions of music that are unrealistic. We mirror ourselves in flawless tracks of unachievable perfection. We must make sure that we do not end up in a situation where we measure our practical exercise of music against the otherworldly sound images of the net that can never be properly imitated.
8. One could make the case that any education and pedagogy is made superfluous in such a gradually expanding online technological music culture where the listener is increasingly coincident with the customer. Music becomes something produced and consumed online in an endless circle. Do these digital arenas (of marketplaces, social media, file sharing) need any pedagogical influence at all? The young people make up their own minds as to what they need to know. The school hence becomes

of diminishing authority because it is on the net (not in the classroom) that the students encounter "the new" (whatever that might be). And the young do not hesitate to access any needed skills they need in online *YouTube* manuals, tutorials, or subscription services providing online lessons and other resources at specialized homepages (cf. guitarplayer.com).

So where does that leave the project of schooling in relation to the arts? In a wider sense, what are the historical backgrounds that have traditionally necessitated that our traditions of music are to be handled pedagogically as part of a school curriculum? Is the net gradually bringing an end to this? The ambition of this tradition has been about much more than just the distribution of as many music offerings to as many users as possible, on as many platforms as possible. Not so many decades ago, one could sense the still vibrant remnants of music, cultivated as a phenomenon, invigorated within the frames of a common, popular obligation toward a broader significance of life.[41] And what do we do in the wake of a breakdown of such a common binding obligation?

DIE TECHNIK AND BEING

The overly skeptical perspectives summarized above are not at all a full reflection of Heidegger's notion of the technic-technological order of the world. To be sure, Heidegger's analysis suggests the possibility that music education can be something more than an online, technical resource standby for application. Indeed, one could argue that Heidegger's perspective points beyond the modernity in which we live.[42] But nevertheless Heidegger cannot unambiguously be designated purely as a technology critic. His interpretation of "the technique" (*die Technik*) is ambivalent: a mixed bag of critique and potential. The technic-technological revolution makes our being-in-the-world one-dimensional, he says. It makes us into subjects so that we forget the *Dasein* we are. It blocks our natural, intuitive development of skill sets and replaces these skills with easy, uninvolved, technological solutions. But *die Technik* also contains a promise of something completely different. It is thus for Heidegger nothing less than a key to a new (non-technical) understanding of being (*Sein*).[43] We must see *die Technik* not primarily as technological machinery, but essentially as our understanding of being characterizing the current age. We thus have to keep in mind the above distinction between (a) technical, everyday equipment (beings, *das Seiende*) and (b) our technical understanding of being (*Sein*) as the background horizon on which the world becomes meaningful to us. Thus *die Technik* becomes the key for our time to experience our rootedness in being. Heidegger states, "modern man must first of all reach back into the width of his own existential reflection (*Wesensraum*)."[44] And here Heidegger sees the key to what he calls "the second beginning" or "the last god"[45] as a so-called exit strategy from our modernity. These metaphors represent a vision of a possible transgression (*Verwindung*) of our current technical understanding of being, toward a non-technical way of being-in-the-world.[46] In the vision of such *Verwindung* there is obviously still technology. But there is no longer any understanding of being that is purely technical. Heidegger thus points toward such transgression as a possibility in which "a new earth and ground become bestowed on man."[47]

Heidegger's approach to *die Technik* is thus double. On one side he is worried about it. Again and again, he emphasizes the danger connected with our technical understanding of being.[48] The danger lies in that "man could be denied access into a more authentic disclosure [of the world] and thus experience the bestowal of a more essential truth."[49] Our encounter with the essence of *die Technik* is for Heidegger a key to understanding the essential character of being as that unnoticed background that constitutes what we are. He states,

> When we make ourselves accessible to the essence of technology (*Technik*), we unexpectedly find ourselves drawn into a liberating expectation.... Accordingly we must address again the question of technology. Because . . . in the essence of technology the saving power is rooted and thrives.[50]

So, *die Technik* is simultaneously pregnant with a dangerous threat as well as a saving possibility. Heidegger reserves the concept of *Gelassenheit* for this necessity of simultaneously saying "yes" (in terms of *das Seiende*) and "no" (in terms of *Sein*) to *die Technik*.[51] He says that such suspension of being is the first step on the way to the arrival of being: "the avoidance (*Verweigerung*) is the first and highest bestowal of being, indeed it constitutes the emerging essence itself. The avoidance summons itself . . . in silence, in which the truth in accordance with its essence will be decided anew."[52] Regarding the dangerous aspect, one can say it contains the risk of an orderly recklessness. A phenomenon like music is here uncovered as a readily available resource, broken down into its underlying components and offered in the marketplace. These sound units are organized, made transparent, made accessible, compared, surveyed as information, and ultimately made fluid and flexible for maximum enjoyment. This is a seducing vision. But behind it thrives potentially barren instrumentalism, an anti-social will to frame and master open processes of life in terms of control technologies. Every commonsense life meaning is potentially dissolved into an individualized hedonism that calls forth the ego-consumer. In such an iron grip, all intensities of meaning will ultimately become surveyed, explicated, controlled, and ultimately optimized.

But *die Technik* in its healing, saving dimension is according to Heidegger never far away:

> In the center of the sheerest danger a graceful favor emerges, that is the favor that turns away from the oblivion of being into the truth of being. In the essence of danger, where it holds sway as risk, is the turn towards truthfulness, is truth itself, is the saving power of being.[53]

Technologically facilitated *musical experiences* could thus become an invitation to open ourselves for the full experience of the essence of *die Technik*. Only then can we realize our modern being as an oblivion of being.[54] However, if Heidegger is right, what does it mean that artworks in symbiosis with our technic-technological mastery of our lifeworld can facilitate a saving transgression beyond *die Technik*? Well, such an event would initially be coincident with a general recognition that what is meaningful and valuable in life is characterized by not being available for emulation into an available resource.

THE SAVING POSSIBILITY?

At this point, we may be left with more questions than answers. Will the meeting between music and its digital technologies turn out to disclose the essence of musical experience in a new way? Can our modern technical rationality through such a meeting achieve a saving dimension that points toward a new cultural sensibility, that is, where music contributes to the disclosure of new aspects of world? Will a new figuration of musical experience in the world be able to gather us and focus our practices around a common forward-looking sense of meaning? It is difficult to formulate *the right* question that is able to resonate with the openness of this situation.

Through the experience of the way in which we are absorbed by our technological being, a different space for togetherness and experience could emerge as a possibility if we listen to Heidegger. This could be a space in which there is of course still a development of ever more advanced technology, but where our background understanding of the practices that sustain us has become non-technical in nature. Through the way in which people are currently coping with music online, it is clear that musical experience here brings to life a significant mediation between that relation of technology and art for which Heidegger paid so much attention. When Heidegger talks about *die Technik* and art, he seems to always go on to talk about the metaphor of "gods." The symbiosis of technology and art thus becomes a key for the arrival of that which Heidegger calls the "artwork" or "the last god." These are obviously metaphors. But what is the name for this strange symbiosis between technology and music? And how will this artwork as "a last god" come to be? The theater of the world is currently being played out on the basis of a narrowed-down sense of being. The subject is framed as a resource to be optimized. The world is framed as an accumulation of raw materials to be harvested.[55] Evermore we are divided. Art constitutes for Heidegger a potential *escape hatch* out of this technical understanding of being. The question of whether the artwork in our modern time can become such an escape hatch is not answered by Heidegger. The phenomenon of art and the experiences it afford us, though, are never far away. The doubt on Heidegger's behalf has rather got to do with how we humans possibly will decide—or not decide—to act on this. Nobody knows the outcome of such a decision: "Nobody knows whether this highest possibility will be bestowed on art in the midst of the most urgent danger."[56] It is underlined that the change brought about by technology and music in terms of disclosing the world anew is not about psychology or feelings "but about an essential mood, wherein the historical being-in-the-world of a people and its judgement must take place."[57] What remains to be seen is the extent to which the hybrid of music and digital technology will be able to contribute to focus our cultural practices toward a new mood or atmosphere for all to share. Who knows? This might just leave us with the challenge to prepare for the arrival of an anonymous, online, poetical-musical artwork that can re-configure the way we understand ourselves in the world. For Heidegger, "art belongs neither to the performance-field of culture, neither does it represent an appearance of spirit—art belongs to the primary event in which the meaning of being . . . is decided."[58] Perhaps such an "event" (*Ereignis*) could emerge when such poetical-musical meaning through the net is distributed globally in a hitherto unforeseen way. Maybe it is somewhere here in such interaction between digital technology and the vibrant beauty of art that the hold of *die Technik* will start to dissolve into something new and still uncharted. But in this equation, human beings remain the vague and undecided question mark.

NOTES

1. Martin Heidegger, *Der Satz vom Grund* (Stuttgart: Verlag Günther Neske, 1997), 203. All translations of the German text are my own.
2. Martin Heidegger, *Beiträge zur Philosophie. Vom Ereignis* (Frankfurt am Main: Vittorio Klostermann, 2003), 242; Martin Heidegger, *Vorträge und Aufsätze* (Stuttgart: Verlag Günther Neske, 2000), 251.

3. Martin Heidegger, *Holzwege* (Frankfurt am Main: Vittorio Klostermann, 2003). For an analysis of Heidegger's interpretation of Van Gogh's shoes, see Rentmeester's chapter in this volume.

4. *Philosophy of Music Education Challenged: Heideggerian Inspirations*, eds. Frederik Pio and Øivind Varkøy (Dordrecht: Springer, 2015).

5. Heidegger, *Vorträge und Aufsätze*, 186.

6. Martin Heidegger, *Identität und Differenz* (Stuttgart: Klett-Cotta, 2002), 18.

7. Martin Heidegger, *Was heisst Denken?* (Tübingen: Max Niemeyer Verlag, 1997), 88–89.

8. Hermann J. Kaiser and Eckard Nolte, *Musikdidaktik* (Mainz: Schott, 2003), 59.

9. Heidegger, *Holzwege*, 294, 298.

10. Karl Heinrich Ehrenforth, *Geschichte der musikalischen Bildung* (Mainz: Schott, 2005). The music of the spheres dates back to Pythagoras in Greek antiquity. Roughly 2000 years after Pythagoras, this ancient philosophical concept influenced the astronomer Johannes Kepler around 1600 and was believed to be partially confirmed through his empirical findings.

11. Max van Manen, *Researching Lived Experience* (Ontario: State University of New York, 1990), 111.

12. Martin Heidegger, *Was ist das – die Philosophie* (Stuttgart: Klett-Cotta, 2003), 22.

13. Heidegger, *Der Satz vom Grund*, 101.

14. Heidegger, *Was heisst Denken?* 88–89.

15. Heidegger, *Was ist das – die Philosophie*, 23.

16. Martin Heidegger, *Erläuterungen zu Hölderlins Dichtung* (Frankfurt am Main: Vittorio Klostermann, 1996), 176.

17. Medard Boss, *Von der Spannweite der Seele* (Bern: Benteli Verlag, 1982), 61.

18. Martin Heidegger, *Die Technik und die Kehre* (Stuttgart: Klett-Cotta, 2002).

19. This statement from Heidegger is cited in Otto Pöggeler, *Der Denkweg Martin Heideggers* (Stuttgart: Verlag Günther Neske, 1994), 257–258.

20. Martin Heidegger, "Hölderlins Hymnen *Germanien* und *Der Rhein*," *Gesamtausgabe*, bd. 39 (Frankfurt am Main: Vittorio Klostermann, 1999), 105.

21. Heidegger, *Erläuterungen zu Hölderlins Dichtung*, 44–45.

22. Martin Heidegger, "Feldweg-Gespräche," *Gesamtausgabe*, bd. 77 (Frankfurt am Main: Vittorio Klostermann, 1975), 194.

23. Martin Heidegger, *Zollikoner Seminare* (Frankfurt am Main: Vittorio Klostermann, 2006), 96.

24. Martin Heidegger, *Einführung in der Metaphysik* (Tübingen: Max Niemeyer Verlag, 1953), 29.

25. Martin Heidegger, "Reden und andere Zeugnisse eines Lebensweges," *Gesamtausgabe*, bd. 16 (Frankfurt am Main: Vittorio Klostermann, 2000), 67.

26. I discuss this at greater length later in the chapter. Rentmeester also analyzes this phenomenon in chapter 14 of this volume.

27. John Sloboda, *Exploring the Musical Mind: Cognition, Emotion, Ability, Function* (Oxford: Oxford University Press, 2005), 334.

28. Heidegger, "Hölderlins Hymnen *Germanien* und *Der Rhein*," 135.

29. Heidegger, "Hölderlins Hymnen *Germanien* und *Der Rhein*," 45.
30. Heidegger, "Feldweg-Gespräche," 187.
31. Heidegger, "Hölderlins Hymnen *Germanien* und *Der Rhein*," 8.
32. Cf. Heidegger, *Identität und Differenz*, 37; Heidegger, *Vorträge und Aufsätze*, 166.
33. Heidegger, "Hölderlins Hymnen *Germanien* und *Der Rhein*," 58–59.
34. Heidegger, *Erläuterungen zu Hölderlins Dichtung*, 42.
35. Ehrenforth, *Geschichte der musikalischen Bildung*, 36–37.
36. The mythos horizon was marked by the Greek thought of Parmenides and Anaximander as well as the poetry of Homer narrating the diversity of gods intermingling with human affairs.
37. Ehrenforth, *Geschichte der musikalischen Bildung*, 81.
38. Karl Heinrich Ehrenforth, "Kultur – Schule – Musikalische Bildung oder Kulturpolitische Defizite der Bildungspolitik," in *Musikalische Bildung und Kultur*, ed. Wilfried Gruhn, 127–140 (Regensburg: Gustav Bosse Verlag, 1987), 135.
39. Jürgen Vogt, *Der schwankende Boden der Lebenswelt* (Würzburg: Königshausen & Neumann, 2001), 232, 254.
40. John Sloboda, *Exploring the Musical Mind*, 329.
41. Ehrenforth, *Geschichte der musikalischen Bildung*.
42. Michael A. Peters, "Introduction: Heidegger, Education, and Modernity," in *Heidegger, Education and Modernity*, ed. Michael A. Peters (Oxford: Rowman & Littlefield, 2002), 15–16.
43. Martin Heidegger, *Die Technik und die Kehre*, 46.
44. Heidegger, *Die Technik und die Kehre*, 39.
45. Cf. Martin Heidegger, "Only a God Can Save Us," *Philosophy Today* 20, no. 4 (1976): 267–285; Heidegger, *Beiträge zur Philosophie*.
46. Heidegger, *Identität und Differenz*, 25.
47. Martin Heidegger, *Gelassenheit* (Stuttgart: Verlag Günther Neske, 2002), 21.
48. Heidegger, *Die Technik und die Kehre*, 28, 37, 40; Heidegger, *Was heisst Denken?* 7.
49. Heidegger, *Die Technik und die Kehre*, 28.
50. Heidegger, *Die Technik und die Kehre*, 25, 29.
51. Heidegger, *Gelassenheit*, 22–23.
52. Heidegger, *Beiträge zur Philosophie*, 241.
53. Heidegger, *Die Technik und die Kehre*, 42.
54. Heidegger, *Was heisst Denken?* 20–21.
55. Martin Heidegger, "Die Seinsgeschichtliche Bestimmung des Nihilismus," in *Nietzsche II* (Stuttgart: Verlag Günther Neske, 1961), 316.
56. Heidegger, *Die Technik und die Kehre*, 35.
57. Heidegger, "Hölderlins Hymnen *Germanien* und *Der Rhein*," 116.
58. Heidegger, *Holzwege*, 73.

BIBLIOGRAPHY

Boss, Medard. *Von der Spannweite der Seele*. Bern: Benteli Verlag, 1982.

Ehrenforth, Karl Heinrich. *Geschichte der musikalischen Bildung*. Mainz: Schott, 2005.
Ehrenforth, Karl Heinrich. "Kultur—Schule—Musikalische Bildung oder Kulturpolitische Defizite der Bildungspolitik." In *Musikalische Bildung und Kultur*, edited by Wilfried Gruhn, 127–140. Regensburg: Gustav Bosse Verlag, 1987.
Heidegger, Martin. *Beiträge zur Philosophie. Vom Ereignis*. Frankfurt am Main: Vittorio Klostermann, 2003.
Heidegger, Martin. *Der Satz vom Grund*. Stuttgart: Verlag Günther Neske, 1997.
Heidegger, Martin. *Die Technik und die Kehre*. Stuttgart: Klett-Cotta, 2002.
Heidegger, Martin. *Einführung in der Metaphysik*. Tübingen: Max Niemeyer Verlag, 1953.
Heidegger, Martin. *Erläuterungen zu Hölderlins Dichtung*. Frankfurt am Main: Vittorio Klostermann, 1996.
Heidegger, Martin. *Feldweg-Gespräche: Gesamtausgabe 77*. Frankfurt am Main: Vittorio Klostermann, 1975.
Heidegger, Martin. *Gelassenheit*. Stuttgart: Verlag Günther Neske, 2002.
Heidegger, Martin. *Hölderlins Hymnen Germanien und Der Rhein: Gesamtausgabe 39*. Frankfurt am Main: Vittorio Klostermann, 1999.
Heidegger, Martin. *Holzwege*. Frankfurt am Main: Vittorio Klostermann, 2003.
Heidegger, Martin. *Identität und Differenz*. Stuttgart: Klett-Cotta, 2002.
Heidegger, Martin. *Nietzsche II: Die Seinsgeschichtliche Bestimmung des Nihilismus*. Stuttgart: Verlag Günther Neske, 1961.
Heidegger, Martin. "Only a God Can Save Us." *Philosophy Today* 20, no. 4 (1976): 267–285.
Heidegger, Martin. *Reden und andere Zeugnisse eines Lebensweges: Gesamtausgabe 16*. Frankfurt am Main: Vittorio Klostermann, 2000.
Heidegger, Martin. *Vorträge und Aufsätze*. Stuttgart: Verlag Günther Neske, 2000.
Heidegger, Martin. *Was heisst Denken?* Tübingen: Max Niemeyer Verlag, 1997.
Heidegger, Martin. *Was ist das—die Philosophie*. Stuttgart: Klett-Cotta, 2003.
Heidegger, Martin. *Zollikoner Seminare*. Frankfurt am Main: Vittorio Klostermann, 2006.
Kaiser, Hermann J. and Eckard Nolte. *Musikdidaktik*. Mainz: Schott, 2003.
Peters, Michael A. "Introduction: Heidegger, Education, and Modernity." In *Heidegger, Education and Modernity*, edited by Michael A. Peters, 1–26. Lanham, MA and Oxford: Rowman & Littlefield, 2002.
Philosophy of Music Education Challenged: Heideggerian Inspirations. Edited by Frederik Pio and Øivind Varkøy. Dordrecht: Springer, 2015.
Pöggeler, Otto. *Der Denkweg Martin Heideggers*. Stuttgart: Verlag Günther Neske, 1994.
Sloboda, John. *Exploring the Musical Mind: Cognition, Emotion, Ability, Function*. Oxford: Oxford University Press, 2005.
Van Manen, Max. *Researching Lived Experience*. Ontario: State University of New York, 1990.
Vogt, Jürgen. *Der schwankende Boden der Lebenswelt*. Würzburg: Königshausen & Neumann, 2001.

Chapter 2

Heidegger on the Slopes and Musical Mountain Biking Multimedia

Jeff R. Warren and John Reid-Hresko

In this chapter we use Heidegger's ideas to examine mountain sports musical multimedia, and also consider Heidegger's own relation to mountain sports. We focus on two mountain sports: mountain biking and skiing. We draw many musical examples from mountain biking, while looking at Heidegger's relationship with skiing. Skiing and the mountains were a recurring theme in Heidegger's life, from the skiing that accompanied the 1929 conference in Davos that increased his profile,[1] to making career decisions to remain living in the Black Forest Mountains.[2] According to philosopher and former student Hans-Georg Gadamer, Heidegger once began a lecture on skiing (while wearing his ski suit) with the claim that "one can learn to ski only on the slopes and for the slopes."[3] This chapter begins by using some of Heidegger's ideas to examine a recent development related to skiing: the filmed presentation of skiing and other mountain sports paired with music. From the 1950s onward, Warren Miller's production company produced ski films on an annual basis. One of the early mass market presentations of music and skiing was through James Bond films, where ski chases were a recurring segment in the films from 1969 onward. The growth of skiing's popularity and the advent of digital film distribution venues such as YouTube have given rise to a short form format often termed "edits."[4]

Over the past twenty years, another mountain sport has soared in popularity: mountain biking. Mountain biking joins skiing in having a growing influence on local economies, influencing land use policies, and being desirable recreation activities for those with the means to participate. Both activities also mimic each other in the production of bodily sensations and tonal feelings: as Lee, a twenty-nine-year-old white Canadian, told us,

In the winter I ski and in the summer I mountain bike. The two sports complement each other so well—both take you into beautiful landscapes, are about speed and grace, and work best when you find the flow—that moment where everything else melts away and you are just present.[5]

These activities have several parallels in terms of user groups, interactions with landscape, and multimedia representation. Skiing and mountain biking films usually feature athletes descending mountains paired with music. In other words, they are musical multimedia.[6]

This chapter argues that Heidegger—particularly through his concepts of tool usage and dwelling—provides useful ways to consider how these pieces of musical multimedia are co-constitutive of mountain sports experiences. In other words, in aiming to capture something of an experience, these films also *shape* the experiences of the viewers. This chapter begins with a general introduction to the role of music in ski and mountain bike films. We then look at the strengths (and limitations) of utilizing some of Heidegger's ideas to understand the ways musical multimedia reflects and creates experience. We follow Jean-Paul Sartre's application of Heidegger's concept of tool usage to skiing, showing how the perception of landscape is changed by the tools used to navigate it. We extend tool usage to mountain sports films, arguing that musical multimedia also shapes users' relationships to landscape. We then transition to Heidegger's ideas around dwelling, arguing these films are tools of dwelling. The application of Heidegger's work to understanding skiing and mountain biking musical multimedia is complemented by and tested against views from mountain bikers sourced from a set of interviews with mountain bikers from Squamish, British Columbia. To illustrate our points, we draw on interview data, collected in 2019, with white Canadian settler mountain bikers, who spoke about their embodied experiences and understandings of bike riding and the ways in which mountain bike-related media influenced and shaped their experiences of landscape and self. Their words add another level of richness to our understandings of portrayals of how these sports influence how participants engage with and understand recreation.

This analysis also provides a lens to question Heidegger's own complex relation to the mountains and to skiing. In his short text *Why Do I Stay in the Provinces?* Heidegger seems to see his own skiing as part of creating a deep connection to the land parallel to the work of peasants and is at the same time critical of the skiers from the city looking for entertainment.[7] It seems for Heidegger that to ski "for the slopes" requires a particular way of dwelling with the mountains. Yet Heidegger's own views seem to be reflective of a pernicious view of the mountains and the people who live there.

Taken together, then, this chapter aims to use Heideggerian concepts to examine musical multimedia and mountain sports, and at the same time reconsiders Heidegger's own relation to his preferred mountain sport of skiing.

MUSICAL MULTIMEDIA AND MOUNTAIN SPORTS

Before delving into the application of Heidegger's ideas, we provide a brief introduction to the characteristics and trends in the musical multimedia we are exploring. Skiing and biking can be included in what Belinda Wheaton terms "lifestyle sports."[8] The participants of these sports spend significant time and resources on these sports without direct financial incentive, and often their participation in the sport makes important links to other parts of their lives. In the book *Surfing about Music*, ethnomusicologist Timothy Cooley explores the lifestyle sport most conspicuously linked to music.[9] Cooley looks at the music listened to and created by surfers, as well as the popularization of genres of "surf music" featured in films about surfing. Following Cooley, in this chapter, we examine mountain biking and skiing musical multimedia's impact on their primary audience: those who participate in these sports.

Most generally, this media takes the form of short films, called "edits," which range from three to eight minutes, paralleling the length of most contemporary popular music. Despite the significant variety in these films, there are some repeated narrative arcs and uses of music. It is common to begin with some establishment of the context to frame the narrative. This might include waking up, having a coffee, or climbing up a trail before descending. Shorter videos may not have this sort of introduction but may instead begin with descending action. It is common to have contrasting music for an introductory segment and the beginning of the descent. The descent is often linked to higher intensity music. Longer form films are commonly built up from these shorter sequences or "edits" that are either played back-to-back or connected by a larger narrative with connecting segments.

Early mountain biking films presented the activity as "extreme" and rebellious partially through the use of high-energy guitar-driven music. For example, the Bjørn Enga's 1998 mountain biking film *Kranked 1: Live to Ride* features Senser's "What's going on?" in the opening segment that showcases riders descending slopes near Kamloops, British Columbia.[10] As a thirty-one-year-old white male settler respondent put it,

> When I saw the first Kranked film with crazy riding, slasher heavy metal music and an anti-establishment vibe, I felt like that film was made just for me. Here was all the crazy stuff we were trying to do being celebrated. I was so amped.

Music in this film might reflect the adrenaline of the rider or might aim to induce adrenaline in the viewer. The "DIY" (do it yourself) aesthetic of these early mountain biking videos was matched with the DIY aesthetic of the music chosen to accompany the videos. In contrast, the more mainstream Warren Miller ski productions often used more highly produced high-energy guitar music.

In the early 2010s, electronic music became more prominent in these films, perhaps most prominently featured in the 2011 snowboarding film "The Art of Flight." Electronic music "drops" provided opportunities to synchronize athletes landing jumps to the music. Steven, a twenty-six-year-old white settler, told us,

> Look, I'm not like a huge electronic music fan, but there have been times when I've like watched a piece of mountain bike media with electronic music where everything just aligns: the rider's spectacular visual stunts, the rhythm and shifts in the electronic beats, and the beauty of the landscape. It's almost like you are there.

Leveraging this compelling media, websites (such as pinkbike.com) and digital media channels, combined with increased access to filmmaking equipment and an increase of viewership, have widened the variety of form, music, and accessibility of mountain sport films. Many films retain high-energy music from guitar-driven rock to hip hop and other genres, but almost any music can now be found in mountain sports films. Music is often used to emphasize one element of the narrative, whether reflecting the athlete's experience, attempting to induce a mood in the viewer, or connecting to the landscape. For example, Stacy, a twenty-nine-year-old white Canadian, explained,

> The music used in edits is crucial. The right music helps the film to come alive. It draws you into the screen and triggers this sense of aliveness, of wanting to be there. I often imagine myself right there, flowing through the landscape, as if I were the rider.

In films, music might be considered a tool of the filmmaker and the viewer.

TOOLS AND MOUNTAIN SPORTS

One reading of Heidegger's claim that "one can learn to ski only on the slopes and for the slopes" is that skiing requires involvement. This echoes Hegel's metaphor of swimming.[11] Andrew Bowie states that Hegel's point is that "unless one goes in the water, one cannot learn to swim, in the same way as one cannot know without always already being involved with what is to be known."[12] There is a sense of being enveloped by and submitting to the water or the slopes, yet still actively responding to and shaping the water and slopes to achieve the desired outcome. These ideas seem to be related to the way that Heidegger's concept of "releasement" (*Gelassenheit*) has been taken up by skiers. According to Michael E. Zimmerman, the noted skier and alpinist Dolores LaChapelle claimed that releasement "was crucial to the practice of powder snow skiing" because the "skier could neither be active (imposing her will on the snowy slope), nor merely passive. Instead, the skier had to 'let the mountain be.'" LaChapelle also found that since Heidegger was himself a skier, "his notion of 'letting things be' was grounded in experience akin to her own."[13] Indeed, while referencing a different skiing subdiscipline, Lev Kreft traces how the term "releasement" became common in Slovenian ski jumping.[14]

In this section, we look at how in skiing and biking "for the slopes" the equipment we use becomes invisible but is crucial to traverse the landscape. We then expand this tool use concept from equipment to musical multimedia. While films are not equipment in the same ways as skis or bikes, we argue that they are signs that point to ways of interacting with the landscape that cocreate the experience of the slopes.

Graham Harman calls Heidegger's tool analysis "perhaps the greatest moment of twentieth-century philosophy."[15] Harman is so taken with this idea that he extends tool analysis beyond the interaction of people with things and applies it to all things in his version of object-oriented ontology.[16] In this chapter, we focus on human interaction with things. For Heidegger, tools usually function as equipment that hides from us. In his terminology, they are ready-to-hand (*Zuhanden*). When one is absorbed in skiing and focusing on the descent, the skis and even the snow surface become an extension of what the skier is working to achieve. This receding of tools contributes to what has been characterized both in research and our interview respondents as a state of flow.[17] Charles, a forty-two-year-old white Canadian mountain biker told us,

> When everything is working perfectly and you achieve the feeling of flow, it is like the bike disappears and you are just floating through the forest on an invisible magic carpet. It is one of the best feelings I have ever felt.

Flow can be quickly lost when equipment stops working. A broken binding or a rock hiding under the snow bring attention to the broken tool, and the skis become present-at-hand (*Vorhanden*). Bill, a forty-nine-year-old white Canadian quipped, "it is a total bummer when things aren't working like they should—a squealing brake, a bad shift, or a flat tire is all it takes to pull you out of the moment." For tools to work, they need to also be in the hands of an experienced user. The new mountain biker struggles to discover the appropriate amount of brake to apply. For the experienced rider in "flow," the brakes are invisible, linking to Heidegger's description of the absorption in taking care of things.[18] Experienced riders, however, still aim to challenge themselves, and in these situations the brakes reappear and the rider thinks about the amount of brake required to navigate a section of terrain. Put another way, equipment is not just present-at-hand when a tool is broken. Rather, throughout the iterative process of learning to use a tool and continued application—whether skis, a bike, or a musical instrument—the tool continuously recedes from and moves into the view of the user.[19] The world of equipment use is wider than a person and a tool, and involves a wider world applying the tool.

Near the end of *Being and Nothingness*, Jean-Paul Sartre writes an extended example about skiing in his chapter on "Doing and Having." Sartre argues that sport has an "appropriative component" that "is a free transformation of the worldly environment into the supporting element of the action," making sport "creative like art."[20] Yet the worldly environment provides resistance, and the resistance of snow is different for skis than for boots or bare hands.[21]

The ways that the slope is experienced or apprehended is related to the speed traveled. Sartre argues that the slope as a definite object is "entirely distinct from what it would be at another speed. The speed organizes the ensembles at will."[22] He makes his point about speed by asking the reader to compare the difference between seeing the geographical region of Provence on foot, by car, by train, or by bicycle.[23] Each speed apprehends the landscape in a different manner. For the sliding involved in skiing, speed both responds to the resistance of the snow and also appropriates it, actively making changes to the landscape.[24] In an earlier section, Sartre discussed the relation between freedom and resistance using examples from rock climbing and cycling. Sartre argues that one encounters "an obstacle only within the field of his freedom," leading to the "paradox of freedom: there is freedom only in a situation, and there is a situation only through freedom."[25]

Sartre's discussion helps to expand Heidegger's tool usage to include the landscape that skis and bikes traverse. Sartre also raises the appropriative element of skiing and biking that makes the landscape one's own. Heidegger reminds us that tool usage expands outwards even further, as tools and their significance are "not invented by Dasein in monkish solitude: equipment always belongs to a public world."[26] This is clear in the example of the tools of musical instruments, which are made by others and played in communities of interpretation including other players, genres, and listeners. The equipment of skiing and biking also participates in such communities, and this is where we return to the role of musical multimedia. We argue that these films not only portray the use of equipment but also shape the public world that influences both how the equipment is used and how the skier or biker relates to and appropriates the landscape.

The expansion of tools beyond equipment is also undertaken by Heidegger in a "special case of readiness-to-hand: signs and signals."[27] Heidegger uses the example of turn signals of cars. Unlike equipment that recedes from view, the signal remains visible as equipment while still pointing to something else. Heidegger also uses the example of someone who takes wind as a sign that rain is coming. Harman summarizes Heidegger's argument that the person "does not just feel a rush of air in his face and later add the judgment that 'rain must be coming.' Everything happens simultaneously."[28] The signal and the sign do not recede as much as equipment but seem to remain available to be both present-at-hand and ready-to-hand.

The example of the sound and feel of wind points us to consider sound as part of the feedback cycle of equipment use, from the sounds of musical instruments to the "tinking" of the hammer. Sound is part of the feedback that skiers use to adjust their technique, from the muted "whoomp" of a turn in deep powder, to the continuous scrape on ice, to the "rip" of a freshly groomed run. Similarly, bikers respond to the sound of tires on the trail surface. As Samantha, a forty-six-year-old white settler, explained,

> It is really important to be able to hear what is going on around you while riding. If something is going wrong with your bike, often your first clue is a change in sound. On top of that, the sound of tires ripping through fresh tacky dirt is divine. I chase that sound, the sound of speed when you know you are dancing with the forest.

Sounds are signs of equipment working, flow, and relation to landscape. This reinforces Heidegger's points that we hear sound in the "as-structure" of understanding.[29] That is, we hear the sound of something—Heidegger uses the example of a motorcycle—rather than process abstract sound and then index it to existing known sounds.[30] In this example of a motorcycle, we do not just hear a motorcycle. We hear power, or annoyance, or freedom, or interruption. How we hear is affected by the sound, our history, mood, and current context. And the same goes for music. The music in mountain sport films provides context for viewers to think about their own activities. Music is a sign of experience, at the same time portraying, influencing, and reinforcing ways of participating in these activities.

The sounds of skis, the snow, the bike, the interface of tire and trail all provide things to hear that affect the rest of the experience, and these sounds are present both when doing these activities and when heard in idealized form in video edits. Similarly, the music in these films provides ways of experiencing the trail and timing body movements. While some mountain bikers and skiers listen to music while doing their activity, others imagine music, linking particular parts of the mountain with particular music. Mark, a thirty-eight-year-old white Canadian, remarked,

> I never ride with music because I think it is unsafe. You need to be able to hear what is going on around you. But that doesn't mean I don't have a soundtrack in my mind while I ride. The harder, the faster I ride, the more aggressive that mental soundtrack becomes.

In this section, we have examined two tools of mountain sports: the interface of rider and equipment, and the sign of musical multimedia. We have begun looking at how each of these becomes part of the interpretation of the landscape, making the link between tool and dwelling. In the example of a hammer, Heidegger initially focuses on the experience of the tool. But the hammer—like the bike and ski—is a tool that shapes the landscape and shapes how we think about dwelling in the landscape.

SKIING DWELLING BIKING

In an article entitled "The Ethics and Politics of Dwelling," political scientist Nicholas Dungey counters criticisms of Heidegger's concept of dwelling to argue that it provides a helpful way to consider the ethical and political implications of dwelling.[31] In this section, we have the more modest aim of arguing that mountain biking and skiing—both the activities themselves and how films influence ways of thinking about the activities—are part of dwelling, setting up a framework to consider some ethical and political implications of these recreational activities. While much has been made of the differences between Heidegger's earlier and later work, Dungey argues that there is some continuity in Heidegger's thinking on dwelling.[32] Dungey summarizes the concept of dwelling in *Being and Time* by arguing that to "care for, and be involved with, one's life, others, and the world, are all manifestations of dwelling."[33] This framing of dwelling as care and involvement is expanded in Heidegger's essay "Building Dwelling Thinking."[34] Dungey summarizes: "dwelling entails the practical activity of building structures and cultivating the ontological relationships revealed in and through building."[35] Heidegger argues building and dwelling are necessarily intertwined, as "we attain to dwelling, so it seems, only by means of building. The latter, building, has the former, dwelling, as its goal."[36] This argument could be applied to skiing and biking by considering the building of recreational sites from ski resorts to mountain biking trails. In short, the built environment changes the ways that we think about and dwell in the landscape.

Heidegger uses the example of a bridge, which "does not just connect banks that are already there. The banks emerge as banks only as the bridge crosses the stream."[37] This example shows how buildings shape the thinking about how one might traverse space. Heidegger then takes the next step to argue that thinking applies not only to when we are crossing it but continues even at a distance. Using the example of "the old bridge in Heidelberg," Heidegger argues that "it belongs to the nature of our thinking *of* that bridge that *in itself* thinking gets through, persists through, the distance to that location."[38] Put another way, buildings are part of dwelling that continuously shapes our thinking. Trails and recreational areas shape our thinking beyond the time spent recreating.

Dungey links together Heidegger's discussions of dwelling and argues that the implications here are that "when we dwell we build these relations, cultivate a certain posture toward things and others."[39] And this, we argue, is the key link to musical multimedia: these films not only portray building and dwelling in the recreational landscape, but they present ways of thinking about the landscape and the people who currently dwell and have dwelt in the landscape.

At the end of the chapter, Heidegger claims that "enough will have been gained if dwelling and building have become worthy of questioning and thus have remained worthy of thought."[40] We hope that this chapter shows that the links between music, mountain sports, and dwelling are worthy of continued thought. It is also worth applying these insights derived from Heidegger back on to Heidegger's own relationship with the mountains.

HEIDEGGER ON THE SLOPES

So far, we have argued that Heidegger's tool analysis not only applies to skis and bikes, but also to musical multimedia about mountain sports. These images and music are co-constitutive of the thoughts and acts of dwelling in recreational landscapes. While building these arguments from Heidegger's ideas, they can also be used to turn a critical lens back on Heidegger's own views about mountain sports, recreation, and landscape. We begin with Heidegger at Davos in 1929, and then turn to Heidegger's short 1934 text "Why do I stay in the Provinces?"

Nestled in the Alps in Davos, Switzerland, the second International Davos Conference took place in March of 1929. It was an important event for Heidegger's prominence. Emmanuel Lévinas, attending as a student, wrote that in the debates between Heidegger and Ernst Cassirer, "a young student could have had the impression that he was witness to the creation and the end of the world."[41] The framing of the event perhaps influenced its eventual influence. The previous year featured Albert Einstein in attendance, and in 1929 there were several prominent scholars that attended the conference. Davos itself was also a draw as, by this time, Davos was already considered "a fashionable gathering sport for travellers and artists"—including Robert Louis Stevenson and Sir Arthur Conan Doyle—and had a "reputation as a 'Kurort,' or rest spa" influenced by "centuries-old folk belief that the Alpine air in the town held special curative powers."[42]

Gadamer reminds us that "how nature pleases us" is "determined by the artistic creativity of a particular time,"[43] and the draw to Davos needs to be contextualized in the reception of the history of nineteenth-century ideals of selfhood, music, the sublime, and the alpine landscape, perhaps most conspicuously embodied by Nietzsche's wandering in the Alps and his views of music.[44] Edward Dickinson summarizes this view: "mountains had a peculiar beauty, and that they therefore made people better."[45] These received ideas—many of which still hold sway today—influence the patterns of dwelling that influence Heidegger and others.

Although fond of the surrounding mountains, Heidegger was less taken by the town itself. In a letter home to his wife, Heidegger wrote that the town of Davos was "dreadful" as he noted the "boundless vulgarity in the architecture."[46] Heidegger was able to escape the town to go skiing during the conference, along with his student Kurt Riezler:

> Heidegger wrote to Elfriede on March 21 that he led a small band up the Parsenn mountain, climbing to 2,700 meters and skiing back into the valley. "At the beginning I was rather anxious how it would go," he confessed, "but after the first 100m. I realized that I was superior to them all, even Riezler, who has skied a lot in the Alps."[47]

Here Heidegger breaks his pretensions about the relation to the mountains and shows his nerves about how he is perceived in terms of physical prowess and skiing skill in relation to the rest of his skiing group. Heidegger reveals here that skiing is not just about being "for the slopes," but is also about conquering them. In an exploration of early twentieth-century skiing, Andrew Denning terms this tension "alpine modern."[48]

In 1934, Heidegger wrote a short essay entitled "Why do I stay in the Provinces?" In the essay, he makes several comments on skiing and relation to landscape. The core of his argument is that his place in the mountains and the activity he does there "is intimately rooted in and related to the life of the peasants" and is at odds with the "city-dweller."[49] He begins by describing the subalpine "small ski hut" where he spends much of his time. He claims that the reader of this description of his "work world" will be "seen through the eye of an observer: the guest or summer vacationer."[50] In contrast, Heidegger lives in this landscape rather than observes it: "strictly speaking I myself never observe the landscape. I experience its hourly changes."[51] While he claims that his experience is "not in forced movements of 'aesthetic' immersion or artificial empathy," he follows by saying that

> On a deep winter's night when a wild, pounding snowstorm rages around the cabin and veils and covers everything, that is the perfect time for philosophy.... The struggle to mold something into language is like the resistance of the towering firs against the storm.[52]

Heidegger seems to both renounce the Romanticism of visitors to the mountains and at the same time embraces it, echoing again the alpine modern tension.

The foil to Heidegger's "work world" is the "city-dweller," who is criticized by thinking "he has gone 'out among the people' as soon as he condescends to have a long conversation with a peasant" and who "gets 'stimulated' by a so-called stay in the country."[53] In the end, Heidegger argues that it is the city that seems to form this character: "the world of the city runs the risk of falling into a destructive error."[54] For the city-dweller, the "country" is entertainment, and the growing popularity of skiing is part of the problem:

> But nowadays many people from the city, the kind who know their way around and not least of all the skiers, often behave in the village or at a farmer's house in the same way they "have fun" at their recreation centres in the city. Such goings-on destroy more in one evening than centuries of scholarly teaching about folk-character and folklore could ever hope to promote.[55]

Heidegger develops a complex relationship between skiing, landscape, and those who dwell in the landscape. On the one hand, visiting skiers from the city are not considered as dwelling properly in the mountains but are presented as irresponsible and see the mountains as their playground. These views remain today. Local settler residents of popular mountain sport locations often complain about entertainment-seeking visitors from the city, sometimes using the portmanteau "citiots," that is, idiots from the city.

In this quotation, Heidegger also invokes "folk-character and folklore" as providing significant and valuable insights about dwelling that are in danger of being destroyed by visitors. Yet at the same time, he frames "scholarly teaching" as the holder and distributor of these ideas. This is a delicate balancing act of valuing folkways of knowing and dwelling and at the same time wrapping them within the control of academic expertise.

Historian Edward Dickinson argues that the "discovery" of the Alps as a recreational space was accompanied by the "discovery" of the people who lived there, in the process generating a growing interest "in the character and culture of the Alpler, the Indigenous people of the Alps."[56] The views of Alplers cut two ways. On the one hand, they lived in a place increasingly aligned with a national racial identity, but on the other were thought of as uncivilized or as "Europe's own noble savages."[57] Despite living in these places of supposed moral learning and German ideals, urban middle-class Germans considered Alplers "ignorant, backward, and even primitive."[58] These conflicting ideals remain prominent from ideals of authenticity to certain strands of ecological movements to views of Indigeneity. They are part of the veneration of "folk" from the writings of Johann Gottfried von Herder to composers ranging from Béla Bartók to Bob Dylan. In each case, the ideals linked with the "folk" are seemingly fulfilled by those who "discover," properly understand, and apply these ideas.

Heidegger attempts to integrate his own existence in the provinces to his academic work. Letters home from Davos reflected "Heidegger's familiar complaint: The deracinated urbanite was incapable of philosophy, only in the countryside was genuine reflection truly possible."[59] This view also influenced his choices about work. When contemplating a job offer in Berlin, Heidegger went to his cabin and claims that "I listened to what the mountains and the forest and the farmlands were saying," and then spoke to an old farmer whose wisdom confirmed that he should not take the posting.[60] Significant interest in the relation between Heidegger's philosophy and his life has been undertaken, especially around his support of Nazism.

For example, Adam Sharr's book *Heidegger's Hut* takes a closer examination of Heidegger's mountain dwelling. Sharr raises (but does not resolve) questions about whether Heidegger's provincial views of the mountains contributed to a "blood and soil" rhetoric linked with Heidegger's acceptance of Nazism:

> While any provincialism invites such questions, because of Heidegger's involvement with Nazism they haunt in a special way both his writings on dwelling and place and any appreciation of the hut at Todtnauberg. It has been argued that the philosophy that he claimed from the mountains, freighted with Hölderlinian providence and arguably imagined as a recovery of pre-Socratic Greece, predisposed Heidegger to the barbaric ideology of Nazism.[61]

It is worth continuing to consider how interactions with landscape reflect and develop ways of thinking. In the final sentence of the book, Sharr concludes that "Reflected in it [the hut], and its landscape, are some of Heidegger's remarks, his sense of his own existence, and conceptual elements structuring his thought."⁶² Just as we can ask critical questions of the role and influence of Heidegger's "work world," we should also ask them of our own musical and recreational worlds.

MOUNTAIN SPORT MUSICAL MULTIMEDIA AS TOOLS OF DWELLING

By way of conclusion, we briefly consider one final example of the role of musical multimedia as a tool of dwelling. In a recent article, we examined the rhetorical strategies of mountain bikers in British Columbia who ride on unceded Indigenous territory.⁶³ We asked how these rhetorical strategies either reinforce colonial views through what we term "recreational colonialism" or facilitate an opening toward reconciliation as described, for example, by Canada's Truth and Reconciliation Commission. In the article, we briefly examined Damien Vergez's 2018 short film *Mother Earth* as a rhetorical response, alongside rhetorical responses gathered through interviews of mountain bikers. In this chapter, we have developed ways of approaching the same phenomenon from a different direction, looking at how musical multimedia is a tool for dwelling, influencing how people recreate in the mountains.

Many mountain sports films do not even recognize the ancestral land that is being traversed, reflecting and performing the rhetorical strategy of ignorance to the history of the land. *Mother Earth*, in contrast, appreciates the history of the land by naming it and including the voices and music of Líl̓wat Nation members. The film features ways of dwelling in a landscape described, acted, and musically played by the Líl̓wat Nation members. Sonically and visually, however, these ways of dwelling are paralleled to the ways of dwelling of a mountain biker. The film seems to reflect and perform the tension that we identified in Heidegger, wherein the wisdom of Indigenous dwelling is brought to fruition by a settler who uses different tools to dwell in the landscape. Even as it admires Indigenous ways of dwelling, this piece of musical multimedia might be questioned as to whether it serves as a tool that contributes to or short circuits reconciliation.

We have done a significant amount of thinking and writing for this chapter in the woods, on the mountains, on days when we were skiing or mountain biking, and through watching and listening to the films that are shared in biking and skiing communities. This work has been part of the integration between our work as scholars and what we do in our leisure time. Through our critical application of Heidegger's ideas to musical multimedia and Heidegger's own views of skiing, we see how easy it is to unevenly apply our ideas to work and life. We hope this chapter not only contributes to the scholarship on Heidegger, music, and mountain sport films but is part of the critical engagement we all need to undertake about the ways that we use music as a tool to dwell.

NOTES

1. Peter E. Gordon, *Continental Divide: Heidegger, Cassirer, Davos* (Cambridge: Harvard University Press, 2010).
2. Martin Heidegger, "Why Do I Stay in the Provinces? (1934)," in *Heidegger: The Man and the Thinker*, ed. Thomas Sheehan (New York: Routledge, 1981), 27–30.
3. Hans-Georg Gadamer, *Heidegger's Ways* (Albany: State University of New York Press, 1994), 115.
4. For examples of edits, see this list of the top mountain biking edits of 2018 (https://www.pinkbike.com/news/the-ten-best-edits-of-2018.html) or this selection of best skiing edits from 2017 (https://unofficialnetworks.com/2017/05/21/our-pick-top-ski-edit-of-the-season/).
5. All interview data come from a set of interviews with mountain bikers from Squamish, British Columbia, collected in 2019.
6. Nicholas Cook, *Analysing Musical Multimedia* (Oxford: Oxford University Press, 1998).
7. Heidegger, "Why Do I Stay in the Provinces?"
8. Belinda Wheaton, *The Cultural Politics of Lifestyle Sports* (New York: Routledge, 2013).
9. Timothy J. Cooley, *Surfing about Music* (Berkeley: University of California Press, 2014).
10. Senser is an anti-establishment rap rock band that has been active since the late 1980s and is known for their high energy.
11. G. W. F. Hegel speaks of "the error of refusing to enter the water until you have learnt to swim," in *The Logic of Hegel*, trans. William Wallace (Oxford: Oxford University Press, 2017), 17.
12. Andrew Bowie, *German Philosophy: A Very Short Introduction* (Oxford: Oxford University Press, 2010), 47.
13. Michael E. Zimmerman, "Heidegger in the Mountains," *The Trumpeter* 24, no. 1 (2008): 3.
14. Lev Kreft, "Lost in Translation: Heidegger and Ski Jumping in Slovenia," *Physical Culture and Sport Studies and Research* 49 (2010): 13–20.
15. Graham Harman, *Heidegger Explained: From Phenomenon to Thing* (Chicago: Open Court, 2007), 63.
16. Graham Harman, *Tool-being: Heidegger and the Metaphysics of Objects* (Chicago: Open Court, 2011).
17. Jeanne Nakamura and Mihaly Csikszentmihalyi, "The Concept of Flow," in *Handbook of Positive Psychology*, eds. C. R. Snyder and Shane J. Lopez (Oxford: Oxford University Press, 2001): 89–105.

18. Martin Heidegger, *Being and Time*, trans. Joan Stambaugh (New York: State University of New York Press, 1996), 67.

19. The chapter in this volume by Samuel McAuliffe and Jeff Malpas applies Heidegger's idea of tool usage to playing a musical instrument, and parallel ideas are explored in music learning and performance in Jeff R. Warren, *Music and Ethical Responsibility* (Cambridge: Cambridge University Press, 2014); David Sudnow, *Ways of the Hand: The Organization of Improvised Conduct* (London: Routledge, 1978); and also in the practical learning of mountain biking in Brian Lopes and Lee McCormack, *Mastering Mountain Bike Skills* (Windsor: Human Kinetics, 2010).

20. Jean-Paul Sartre, *Being and Nothingness* (New York: Washington Square Press, 1984), 742.

21. Sartre, *Being and Nothingness*, 743.

22. Sartre, *Being and Nothingness*, 745.

23. Provence is a region in southeastern France known for its beautiful landscapes.

24. Sartre, *Being and Nothingness*, 745.

25. Sartre, *Being and Nothingness*, 628–629.

26. Harman, *Heidegger Explained*, 62.

27. Harman, *Heidegger Explained*, 63.

28. Harman, *Heidegger Explained*, 64.

29. See Gerry Stahl's chapter in this volume for discussion on the as-structure of hearing.

30. Heidegger, *Being and Time*, 153.

31. Nicholas Dungey, "The Ethics and Politics of Dwelling," *Polity* 39, no. 2 (2007): 234–258.

32. Steve Burgess and Casey Rentmeester argue that there is continuity between Heidegger's early notion of *Eigentlichkeit* (authenticity) and his later notion of dwelling in "Knowing Thyself in a Contemporary Context: A Fresh Look at Heideggerian Authenticity," in *Horizons of Authenticity in Phenomenology, Existentialism, and Moral Psychology: Essays in Honor of Charles Guignon*, eds. Hans Pedersen and Megan Altman (Dordrecht: Springer, 2015), 31–43.

33. Dungey, "The Ethics and Politics of Dwelling," 239.

34. Martin Heidegger, "Building Dwelling Thinking," in *Poetry, Language, Thought* (New York: Harper Perennial Modern Classics, 2001), 143–152.

35. Dungey, "The Ethics and Politics of Dwelling," 239.

36. Heidegger, "Building Dwelling Thinking," 143.

37. Heidegger, "Building Dwelling Thinking," 150.

38. Heidegger, "Building Dwelling Thinking," 154.

39. Dungey "The Ethics and Politics of Dwelling," 240.

40. Heidegger, "Building Dwelling Thinking," 158.

41. Gordon, *Continental Divide*, 2.

42. Gordon, *Continental Divide*, 87.

43. Hans-Georg Gadamer, "Aesthetics and Hermeneutics," in *The Continental Aesthetics Reader*, ed. C. Cazeaux (London: Routledge, 2000), 182.

44. For more on Nietzsche, hiking, and the alps, see John Kaag, *Hiking with Nietzsche: On Becoming Who You Are* (New York: Farrar, Straus, and Giroux, 2018).

For more on Romanticism, the sublime, and the mountains, see Paola Giacomoni, "Mountain landscape and the Aesthetics of the Sublime in Romantic Narration," in *Romantic Prose Fiction*, ed. Gerald Gillespie, Manfred Engel, and Bernard Dieterle (Amsterdam and Philadelphia: John Benjamins Publishing Company, 2008), 107–121. For more on links between music and nature, see Warren, *Music and Ethical Responsibility*, 59–60, 78–79.

45. Edward Dickinson, "Altitude and Whiteness: Germanizing the Alps and Alpinizing the Germans," *German Studies Review* 33, no. 3 (2010): 581.
46. Gordon, *Continental Divide*, 110.
47. Gordon, *Continental Divide*, 110.
48. Andrew Denning, "Alpine Modern: Central European Skiing and the Vernacularization of Cultural Modernism, 1900–1939," *Central European History* 46, no. 4 (2013): 850–890.
49. Heidegger, "Why Do I Stay in the Provinces?" 28.
50. Heidegger, "Why Do I Stay in the Provinces?" 27.
51. Heidegger, "Why Do I Stay in the Provinces?" 27.
52. Heidegger, "Why Do I Stay in the Provinces?" 28.
53. Heidegger, "Why Do I Stay in the Provinces?" 28.
54. Heidegger, "Why Do I Stay in the Provinces?" 29.
55. Heidegger, "Why Do I Stay in the Provinces?" 29.
56. Dickinson, "Altitude and Whiteness," 584–585.
57. Dickinson, "Altitude and Whiteness," 581.
58. Dickinson, "Altitude and Whiteness," 584.
59. Gordon, "Continental Divide," 112.
60. Heidegger, "Why Do I Stay in the Provinces?" 29.
61. Adam Sharr, *Heidegger's Hut* (Cambridge: The MIT Press, 2006), 109.
62. Sharr, *Heidegger's Hut*, 112.
63. John Reid-Hresko and Jeff R. Warren, "'A Lot of What We Ride is Their Land:' White Settler Canadian Understandings of Mountain Biking, Indigeneity, and Recreational Colonialism," *Sociology of Sport Journal* (2021): https://doi.org/10.1123/ssj.2020-0161.

BIBLIOGRAPHY

Bowie, Andrew. *German Philosophy: A Very Short Introduction.* Oxford: Oxford University Press, 2010.

Burgess, Steven and Casey Rentmeester. "Knowing Thyself in a Contemporary Context: A Fresh Look at Heideggerian Authenticity." In *Horizons of Authenticity in Phenomenology, Existentialism, and Moral Psychology: Essays in Honor of Charles Guignon*, edited by Hans Pedersen and Megan Altman, 31–43. Dordrecht: Springer, 2015.

Cook, Nicholas. *Analysing Musical Multimedia.* Oxford: Oxford University Press, 1998.

Cooley, Timothy J. *Surfing about Music.* Berkeley: University of California Press, 2014.

Denning, Andrew. "Alpine Modern: Central European Skiing and the Vernacularization of Cultural Modernism, 1900–1939." *Central European History* 46, No. 4 (2013): 850–890.
Dickinson, Edward. "Altitude and Whiteness: Germanizing the Alps and Alpinizing the Germans." *German Studies Review* 33, No. 3 (2010): 579–602.
Dungey, Nicholas. "The Ethics and Politics of Dwelling." *Polity* 39, No. 2 (Apr., 2007): 234–258.
Gadamer, Hans-Georg. "Aesthetics and Hermeneutics." In *The Continental Aesthetics Reader*, edited by C. Cazeaux, 181–186. London: Routledge, 2000.
Gadamer, Hans-Georg. *Heidegger's Ways*. Albany: State University of New York Press, 1994.
Giacomoni, Paola. "Mountain landscape and the Aesthetics of the Sublime in Romantic Narration." In *Romantic Prose Fiction*, edited by Gerald Gillespie, Manfred Engel, and Bernard Dieterle, 107–121. Amsterdam and Philadelphia: John Benjamins Publishing Company, 2008.
Gordon, Peter E. *Continental Divide: Heidegger, Cassirer, Davos*. Cambridge: Harvard University Press, 2010.
Harman, Graham. *Heidegger Explained: From Phenomenon to Thing*. Chicago: Open Court, 2007.
Harman, Graham. *Tool-being: Heidegger and the Metaphysics of Objects*. Chicago: Open Court, 2011.
Hegel, G. W. F. *The Logic of Hegel*. Translated by William Wallace. Oxford: Oxford University Press, 2017.
Heidegger, Martin. *Being and Time*. Translated by Joan Stambaugh. New York: State University of New York Press, 1996.
Heidegger, Martin, "Building Dwelling Thinking." In *Poetry, Language, Thought*, translated by Albert Hofstadter, 143–162. New York: Harper Perennial Modern Classics, 2001.
Heidegger, Martin. "Why Do I Stay in the Provinces? (1934)." In *Heidegger: The Man and the Thinker*, edited by Thomas Sheehan, 27–30. New York: Routledge, 1981.
Kaag, John. *Hiking with Nietzsche: On Becoming Who You Are*. New York: Farrar, Straus, and Giroux, 2018.
Kreft, Lev. "Lost in Translation: Heidegger and Ski Jumping in Slovenia." *Physical Culture and Sport Studies and Research* 49 (2010): 13–20.
Lopes, Brian and Lee McCormack. *Mastering Mountain Bike Skills*. Windsor: Human Kinetics, 2010.
Nakamura, Jeanne and Mihaly Csikszentmihalyi. "The Concept of Flow." In *Handbook of Positive Psychology*, edited by C. R. Snyder and Shane J. Lopez, 89–105. Oxford: Oxford University Press, 2001.
Reid-Hresko, John and Jeff R. Warren. "'A Lot of What We Ride is Their Land:' White Settler Canadian Understandings of Mountain Biking, Indigeneity, and Recreational Colonialism." *Sociology of Sport Journal* (2021): https://doi.org/10.1123/ssj.2020-0161.
Sartre, Jean-Paul. *Being and Nothingness*. New York: Washington Square Press, 1984.
Sharr, Adam. *Heidegger's Hut*. Cambridge: The MIT Press, 2006.

Sudnow, David. *Ways of the Hand: The Organization of Improvised Conduct.* London: Routledge, 1978.
Warren, Jeff R. *Music and Ethical Responsibility.* Cambridge: Cambridge University Press, 2014.
Wheaton, Belinda. *The Cultural Politics of Lifestyle Sports.* New York: Routledge, 2013.
Zimmerman, Michael E. "Heidegger in the Mountains." *The Trumpeter* 24, No. 1 (2008): 3–4.

Chapter 3

Distracted Dasein?

Anthony Gritten

Our ears are full of things that prevent us from hearing properly.
—Heidegger[1]

Distraction is ubiquitous within contemporary Western life, as any study of digital culture and urban society shows. It occupies a complex place, inspiring fear and excitement in equal measure. It is central to all modes of hearing, including musicking; in fact, it is essential. What distracts hearing is the sheer sound of sound: its sonic presence.

In this chapter I extrapolate a broadly Heideggerian phenomenology of sonic distraction, based on the four assumptions above. It is an extrapolation rather than a reconstruction, as I am unaware of studies configuring distraction as the center of Heideggerian phenomenology.[2] I begin unpacking the multiple sensory modalities of being implied in Heidegger's assertion that "the clearing, the open region, is not only free for brightness and darkness but also for resonance and echo, for sound and the diminishing of sound."[3] After all, if it is true that "To *let* unconcealment *show itself* [. . .] is perhaps the most succinct formulation of the task of Heidegger's thinking,"[4] then we must unpack all modalities of unconcealment together in order to let being resound and come into presence. In this chapter, I focus on a single modality: the sonic—the *sound* of Dasein's being-toward-death.

Three caveats are required. I make no claims about Heidegger's politics (the issue of National Socialism), no revisions to his historical understanding (the world has changed), and no differentiation between his earlier and later writings (*die Kehre*, i.e., the turn). These issues I leave to Heidegger scholars. My reading of Heidegger is mostly extrapolated from *An Introduction to Metaphysics*, given as a lecture course in 1935 and published in 1953. Working iteratively from world to sound to entropy and finally to distraction,

I simply wish to explore the sonic consequences of the assertion that Dasein *hears*.

DASEIN'S WORLD

Taking Heidegger's constitution of hearing seriously is not novel. The wider conjunctions between Heidegger and the performing arts[5] and between Heidegger and music[6] are fairly well-trodden. However, the vicariously sonic-musical registers of Dasein's being-toward-death are less familiar.[7] What I consider here are his claims about hearing and their position within his theory of Dasein's being-toward-death. I claim that they operate on two levels. First level: Heidegger is not writing as a musician and music is not central to his theory, but metaphors of "the sonic" and "the musical" recur frequently across his writing. Second level: any theory of Dasein's worldly presence needs to account for its embodiment,[8] and the sonic register is one component of this since it is the entire physical body that vibrates and resonates with sound, not just the ears.

Taking Heidegger's constitution of hearing seriously means considering the materiality of sound, and this drifts into his interpretation of the modern world in terms of *techne*. I do not address *techne* in detail here but note the essential points. According to Heidegger, the primary *telos* of the modern world is "the unreasonable demand [to nature] that it supply energy which can be extracted and stored as such."[9] Moreover, "The essential unfolding of technology threatens revealing, threatens it with the possibility that all revealing will be consumed in ordering and that everything will present itself only in the unconcealment of standing-reserve [*Bestand*]."[10] Perhaps unsurprisingly, the overriding mood of the modern world is boredom, with Dasein aimlessly "drifting here and there,"[11] and the tendency toward acceleration is the cause of multiple temporal pathologies.[12] The modern world remains broadly like this almost seventy years after Heidegger's technology essay. For this essay I extrapolate one phenomenon in particular: it is a *distracted* world.

The term "distraction" is not one that Heidegger uses particularly frequently except in relation to "everydayness," "fallenness," and "thrownness,"[13] though he does write about attention, which is a quasi-opposite to distraction. He uses "dispersion"/"dispersal" (the German constellation around *zerstreut* and *zerstreuung*) more frequently, arguing that "Dasein's facticity is such that its being-in-the-world has always dispersed itself or even split itself up into definite ways of being-in."[14] However, much of what Heidegger says about the modern world's clutter, techno-scientific development, and how human activity should (but preternaturally fails to) deal with the world are congruent with the theories of distraction. Sociological theories of distraction model how distraction structures the modern world, while cognitive theories model human activity within that world. Thus, extrapolating from *techne* to distraction helps to address two aspects of Heidegger's position on hearing: first, how hearing is constituted in relation to Dasein's project; and second, how such hearing as Dasein is capable of emerges within and engages with the world. Both aspects are inseparable, of course, because Dasein is co-constituted with the world, but they can be considered in turn. Dealing with distraction also addresses not just how, with appropriate effort and energetic investment, Dasein might overcome its fallen state and become what it is, but why this effort—and care—has to be consistent and continual rather than opportunistic and one-off, and why on Heidegger's own terms it is difficult.

Given the constitution of the distracted modern world as Heidegger interprets it, where does he stand on the relationships between sound, music, and hearing? Heidegger constitutes these terms variously, mostly at passing moments within broader theories of Dasein's being-toward-death, and he does not offer a systematic theory of sound–perception or of music (and I do not attempt to extrapolate either of those in this chapter). There are, however, many curious pointers to his assumptions about how Dasein's ears function. Perhaps the most important is his repeated claim that hearing is always hearing in the world.[15] For example, he writes in "The Origin of the Work of Art" that "in order to hear a bare sound we have to listen away from things, divert our ear from them, i.e., listen abstractly."[16] Similarly, in *An Introduction to Metaphysics* he writes that "it is difficult to describe even the pure sound, and we do not ordinarily do so, because it is *not* what we commonly hear. [From the standpoint of sheer sound] we always hear *more*."[17]

Hearing in the world, unlike the variously abstracted activities of hearing pure sound and hearing music (in the conventional folk psychological sense), is essential to Heidegger's theory of Dasein. What he terms the "call" of conscience[18] or the "appeal to the Self" requires a response from Dasein that turns it back toward the world. In *Being and Time* the issue is phrased thus:

> The appeal to the Self in the they-self does not force it inwards upon itself, so that it can close itself off from the "external world." The call passes over everything like this and disperses it, so as to appeal solely to that Self which, notwithstanding, is in no other way than being-in-the-world.[19]

Furthermore, the response to the call that Heidegger valorizes assumes a certain constitution of hearing as focused, committed, intensive, and driven; indeed, Dasein must not merely "take hold" of its possibilities of existence, as Macquarrie and Robinson translate *Being and Time*, but "seize" them, as Stambaugh translates it.[20] Such driven hearing, which Heidegger proposes is able to overcome Dasein's "fallenness," is driven by the sheer force of the call, and embodied in Dasein's "upsurgent presence."[21] There is effectively good and bad hearing, which for Heidegger maps onto "hearing" and "listening," though he does not deploy these terms systematically, translations notwithstanding. For example, "Mere hearing scatters and diffuses itself in what is commonly believed and said, in hearsay, in *doxa*, appearance."[22] And elsewhere: "Only where the being of the essent is heard does a mere casual listening become a hearing."[23] Either way, the idea that a certain type of auditory activity is vital to Dasein's being-toward-death is clear throughout his writings: "Indeed, hearing constitutes the primary and authentic way in which Dasein is open for its ownmost potentiality-for-being—as in hearing the voice of a friend whom every Dasein carries with it. Dasein hears, because it understands."[24] The musicological convention is that hearing, being merely physiological, is valued lower than listening, which has additional aesthetic registers. For ease of reading, I will refer in this essay to hearing, noting simply that really I am talking about the pair hearing–listening.

On the matter of other sensory modalities, it should be noted that Heidegger's theory of the "clearing" is predicated upon a visual logic—moreover, a broadly theatrical logic in which the clearing is a stage upon which a voice can be exercised.[25] He writes in the 1930s of how "the realm of emerging and abiding is intrinsically at the same time a shining appearing. The radicals *phy* and *pha* name the same thing. *Phyein*, self-sufficient emergence, is *phainesthai*, to flare up, to show itself, to appear,"[26] and he constitutes a visual theory of truth as unconcealment and un-hiddenness.[27] In *The Essence of Human Freedom*, he writes that "within the illumination which allows being to be understood as constant presence, the light which expends this illumination itself becomes visible. This light is *time* itself."[28] In the 1960s he writes of "*eidos, idea*: the outward appearance in which beings as such show themselves."[29] Juxtaposing these visual and sonic logics alongside each other affords a way of understanding the roles of the sensory modalities in Dasein's embodiment. The theory of distraction in this essay contributes to that understanding.

On the basis of this contextualization of the sensory modalities of Dasein's embodied presence, the rest of this chapter attempts to show how distraction and entropy are at work within hearing, with significant consequences for how we constitute Dasein's being-toward-death. Entropy affords me a way of exploring sonic decay and death, a tool to unpack the energetic shape and temporal profile of sound, and, in particular, how sound can be central— not just metaphorically, but physically—to Dasein's being-toward-death. Entropy is singular and one way, while distraction is multiple, but the point for understanding hearing as Heidegger deploys the term is that, paradoxically, while distraction depends on entropy, it is also undone by it.

DASEIN'S SONIC WORLD

Dasein's ears have two tasks. First, they must function cognitively *qua* embodiment. Second, they must afford Dasein access to the realm of being and overcome its fallenness and thrownness into the world. In this section, I consider the first task.

Sound and perception are mutually co-constituted; I should speak of the pair sound–perception rather than of separate terms. Nevertheless, I start here with sound, and constitute it around the concept of "disturbance."[30] What are sounds? Aesthetic theories separate sound from noise on the one hand and tone on the other.[31] Sounds are events that take time to unfold, but which do not last longer than the disturbance events that set them in motion. While sound is the periodic disturbing of one object by another, it is sound waves that move from the site of disturbance through a medium to ears, with more or less interference. How do sounds behave? Their behavior changes over time, according to factors including the nature of the medium and the nature of the originating disturbance. Being predicated upon the transmission of sound waves, sounds are sustained if energy continues to be invested in maintaining the original disturbance, but if energetic input stops then they decay, energy is lost and dissipated into the surrounding environment, and the sound waves die out. In this respect, what is most important about a sound is its acoustic envelope, the pattern of its energetic investment, continuation, and probable dispersal. The acoustic envelope of sound segments it into three parts: attack/onset, sustain/steady-state, and decay—just as chess is divided up into functionally different sections (opening, middlegame, endgame). Differences between acoustic envelopes determine differences between sounds: the blossoming of their individual timbres over time.

Of the theory of sound as disturbance, what is most important for my argument about the function of hearing in Dasein's being-toward-death is that sound is predicated upon energetic investment. Sound-generating disturbances are "events in which mechanical energy is transferred from one medium into another."[32] The energy profile of a sound determines how it is to start, continue, and end—as with life generally. This constitution of sound implies that sound may not *be* anything other than a process—an open process that Dasein can mistake for a finished object.

While this constitution of sound as part of the pair sound–perception seems initially to give sound an anthropomorphic motivation, it now needs to be complicated by one specific aspect of sound. This is in relation to "temporality" as the horizon for Dasein's being-in-the-world,[33] the "end" of hearing: both how long it lasts, and what it is for. It is the aspect of sound's "ruin" and "decay," to invoke architectural and thermodynamic terms respectively. Moving away from architecture toward thermodynamics, we need to displace building by hearing as we turn to the non-anthropomorphic empirical heart of sound. This is not to undermine the importance of sound's attack for sonic experience, but to situate Dasein's hearing within its decay.

DASEIN'S LOST SONIC WORLD

In the modern world, what is the fundamental mood as far as hearing sound is concerned? Primarily, it is loss and decay: this is the sonic register of the existential "anxiety" characterizing Dasein. Thus, as Heidegger states in *Being and Time*, "Busily losing *himself* in the object of his concern, he *loses his time* in it too."[34] The loss of sound—not just that Dasein is lost in sound, but that sound is lost to Dasein—is nothing more than its decay and the dispersal of its sound waves into the environment, but the consequences of this loss for Dasein's being-in-the-world are more than merely physical. So the immediate question is: How does loss ground anxiety? In this section, I consider first the loss of sound, followed by the loss to hearing (though fundamentally they are the same thing, namely a loss to Dasein).

Like energy transfer in the other sensory modalities, sound follows the second law of thermodynamics: entropy. Within science, entropy measures the relative degree of disorder in a system (how its parts are arranged) in relation to the transfer and dispersal of energy. In a system that is closed upon itself, entropy increases toward thermodynamic equilibrium and uncertainty decreases. Entropy works in two ways: first, it defines the limits of relationships between bodies, whether physical, virtual, aesthetic, organic, or inorganic, and second, it affords a way of plugging in a proposal for what should be valued in and by Dasein into the diagnosis of its physical fate. Given that entropy is energy's natural rhythm, its slowing down and decay, Heidegger's note that "unconcealment occurs only when it is achieved by work"[35] is an important one, embedding "work" at the heart of the energetic investments that constitute being-toward-death. When, on the following page, he acknowledges that "this struggle for unconcealment, which even in itself is continuous conflict, is at the same time a combat against concealment, disguise, false appearance,"[36] he can be read as leaving an open moment for unconcealment to be no more than temporary, and hence for entropy to take over. Schematically put, unconcealment requires work, work expends energy, energy becomes entropic.

Entropy is behind the dying out of sound waves, their echoing, fading, and general loss of sonic presence. If we are to understand Dasein's relation to sound, then we need to acknowledge this relentless process of loss and decay in terms of being-toward-death. Sound is not straightforwardly the sonic embodiment of Dasein (later invocations of sonic "subjectivity" are supervenient upon this fundamental level of sonic activity). The core of sound's phenomenological constitution, then, is its end, rather than its beginning (notwithstanding Heidegger's fundamental ontology of "inceptuality,"[37] awe and wonder,[38] and other modes of the opening of being and beings)— or, better, the beginning within the end, which is his angle in "The End of Philosophy and the Task of Thinking."[39]

The empirical loss of sound is its essential *qualia* and should thus be constituted as the primary determinant of Dasein's behavior; hearing is based neither solely on the presence of sound constituted as empirical plenitude and neurological activation, nor simply on a sense of engagement as "grasping."[40] Indeed, when Heidegger writes that "in order to be determinable being must be indeterminate,"[41] what this means is that a snapshot of being at any one point in time is measurable in principle, but the broader shape and trajectory of being is not (the uncertainty principle). In this context, the classical Husserlian position that time consciousness can be understood through musical melody[42] is only feasible on the back of a prior constitution of the temporality of hearing as governed by entropy, as governed by Dasein's perishing as the echo dies out and the energy driving the original sonic disturbance dissipates outwards into the world. Dasein's authentic being may require "the command of energies"[43] and "the original emergence and standing of energies,"[44] as well as the storing of energy,[45] but there is also an essential loss of energy, and this is both experienced (felt) and empirical (measurable).

The indeterminacy of entropy affects how we constitute Dasein's hearing. Of particular importance is that entropy is not heard as such; however, it does trace out sound's withdrawal from the auditory scene, and for Dasein this is the trajectory of being-toward-death: "that *possibility which is one's ownmost, which is non-relational, and which is not to be outstripped.*"[46] Configuring Dasein's hearing requires acknowledging that the entropy of sound cannot be "outstripped," and its direction of travel is away from a simplistic anthropomorphism of hearing (whereby the ears "grasp" sonic entities). Hearing is forever at the dynamic interface between its own sense making and the dying out of sound, the dissipation of vibrations, and the dispersal of resonance. As Heidegger says in the mid-1930s, "All violence shatters against *one* thing. That is death. It is an end beyond all consummation, a limit beyond all limits. Here there is no breaking-out or breaking-up, no capture or subjugation."[47] What he does not say is that death is "beyond consummation" because of its being overtaking by entropy. Thus when he claims that "To be a man means to *take* gathering *upon oneself*, to undertake a gathering apprehension of the being of the essent, the sapient incorporation of appearing in the work, and so to *administer* unconcealment, to *preserve* it against cloaking and concealment,"[48] this is overstating the matter: "gathering" risks slipping into mere "administering" at all times, but entropy—never mind Dasein's own futural self-projection—sees to it that "unconcealment" happens while energy disperses around the clearing (there are no walls in this proto-theatrical *agora* against which sound waves could reverberate and return). Entropy governs the "passage" of thought: "Only this openness grants to the movement of speculative thinking the passage through what it thinks."[49]

All modes of hearing, then, defer to entropy eventually. Hearing includes acknowledging that sound will always eventually drift away from Dasein. In fact, sound also drifts away from hearing itself; entropy guarantees that sound will have disappeared before hearing has finished apprehending it. The direction of travel is from multiple rhythmic objects (the basis of auditory representations in the brain) to a less differentiated flow of energy toward a singular silence. And this is the silence of "Original anxiety," which "can awaken in existence at any moment. It needs no unusual event to rouse it. Its sway is as thoroughgoing as its possible occasionings are trivial. It is always ready, though it only seldom springs, and we are snatched away and left hanging."[50] Although the dispersal of Dasein's sonic presence is a temporal phenomenon (it governs temporality as the horizon of understanding), Dasein's experience of the process, of living through hearing, is not psychological; it is not even really an "experience," in the sense of a ring-fenced activity undergone by a subject. The loss of hearing via the entropy of sound comes with a sting in its tail: Dasein ends up *"stretched along* between birth and death,"[51] "thrown" and "projected" ahead of itself into the future[52] toward the next sound–perception, and the next sound–perception, and so on.

DASEIN'S DISTRACTED LOST SOUND WORLD

Certain ways of configuring Dasein in relation to the sensory modalities of its embodiment, and in this chapter specifically in relation to sound–perception and hearing, do not work unless entropy is acknowledged as playing a role within being. Two examples suffice here: "truth" and "the clearing."

Constitutions of truth in terms of "what accords, the accordant"[53] lead, says Heidegger, only to an impoverished account of being, because they assume a position on being that has narrowed down its original, primary Greek meaning—as *physis* (discussed below)—to merely the correctness of correspondence between statement and reality, between knowledge and matter. In this reduced meaning of being as "the accomplishment of a pregiven directedness,"[54] the problem is that it is "pregiven." Entropy, however, which is entirely futural in its pull, all "occurrence," affords Dasein a different mode of access to truth. Heidegger unpacks this alternative in the following terms:

Truth *qua* unhiddenness never abides in and of itself, but [. . .] its nature is such that it *is* only as an occurrence, indeed as a fundamental occurrence in man as an existing being. That which occurs in man as primordial letting-become-unhidden is what we called *deconcealment*.[55]

Entropy also mediates between Heidegger's slightly black and white distinction between truth and untruth *qua* "self-dispersal"[56] so that dispersal can be recuperated positively and play an essential role in Dasein's sonic being-toward-death.

Regarding the clearing, Heidegger writes in "The End of Philosophy and the Task of Thinking" that "the quiet heart of the clearing is the place of stillness from which alone the possibility of the belonging together of being and thinking, that is, presence and apprehending, can arise at all."[57] Clearing is stillness, like a theatrical stage (a derivative mode of clearing) before a tragic performance. But it is more productive (as Heidegger himself seems to suggest a few pages earlier, though without providing detail) to constitute the clearing as a loud, bustling space within which a riot of sounds emerges, jostles for salience, and distracts Dasein, a space across which they drift, echo, and die. Entropy creates and sustains the clearing as a place for harnessing and relinquishing Dasein's energy.

These three examples are productively constituted around entropy. But their logic is that of distraction: energies are pulled away, sound decays, the fundamental mood is one of loss. What is distracted hearing? It is supervenient upon a core property of auditory perception, namely that we engage and process every sound within our hearing, whether or not it is salient to conscious perception (this is basically an evolutionary consequence of the fight-or-flight ability). Distracted hearing takes advantage of two of our auditory skills: first, to direct our attention onto one auditory event rather than another; second, to redirect attention to a new object swiftly and relatively accurately (configuring the process passively clarifies the stakes via the etymology of the word, which comes from the Latin *dis+trahere*, a drawing apart). Distracted hearing and attentive hearing (or cognates like concentration, absorption, and so on) are not opposites, popular beliefs notwithstanding. Rather, attentive hearing emerges from within distracted hearing, from the requirement that the brain engages with a new auditory event in a manner that overlaps with a previous event, and that interrupts the processing of the previous event. Distracted hearing is more reactive rather than proactive, and, in fact, to claim that hearing is more proactive would be to misinterpret the function of mental representations and cognitive schemata.

In this context of the mechanics of distracted hearing, truth and the clearing provide two examples of how entropy plays a productive role within Dasein's being-toward-death. Constituted more broadly, the lesson is that distracted hearing is the way for Dasein to embrace the entropy at work within sound (which is not to claim mastery over it but simply to acknowledge it) and to recuperate something positive from the modern world. Distracted hearing affords Dasein a means of acknowledging that sound makes claims upon its time, real claims that require a committed and embodied response if temporality as a horizon of understanding is to be a meaningful concept.

As will have become clear from the start, I have been reading Heidegger in an idiosyncratic manner, if not simply misreading him and taking concepts in strange directions, not in the routes already painstakingly planned out by Heidegger. Nevertheless, as this chapter nears its conclusion, it is worth pausing to consider the congruence between the argument about entropy and distraction that I have been rehearsing and Heidegger's argument about being *qua physis*.[58]

In a sense, this is the heart of the matter: how the transcendental meets the material, the ontological meets the ontic, the ears being Dasein's interface between ontic and ontological. Heidegger outlines a list of traits of being, reeling them off conveniently as follows: "The 'being' uttered in 'is' means: really present, permanently there, takes place, came from, belongs to, is made of, stays, succumbs to, stands for, has entered upon, has appeared."[59] And a little later, the second set of phrases is proposed:

> To be an essent—this comprises to come to light, to appear on the scene, to take one's place, to produce something. [. . .] The essence of appearing includes coming-on-the-scene and withdrawing, hither and thither in the truly demonstrative, indicative sense. Being is thus dispersed among the manifold essents. These display themselves as the momentary and close-at-hand.[60]

These lists constitute a constellation of phenomenological descriptions, a rich vocabulary of Dasein's being-in-the-world. In a late text Heidegger writes, in a similar vein, that

> Wherever the thinking of the Greeks gives heed to the presence of what is present, the traits of presence which we mentioned find expression: unconcealedness, the rising from unconcealedness, the entry into unconcealedness, the coming and the going away, the duration, the gathering, the radiance, the rest, the hidden suddenness of possible absenting.[61]

Other lists are possible. Notwithstanding terminological differences (these texts were written thirty years apart), what these lists have in common is a sense of being's tripartite constitution (the three temporal "ecstasies")—coming into presence, sustained in presence, and withdrawing from presence conceived in terms of motion—and of the energetic investment in being that grounds Dasein. Of particular interest here in relation to my argument about entropy and distraction—about distracted Dasein—is that there is nothing in these phenomenological motifs that resists entropy, nothing that takes Heidegger's argument in a direction contrary to the direction that entropy takes sound. Dasein can be everything that Heidegger says it is, and at the same time distracted, dispersed, and decaying on account of entropy being at work within it. Janus-faced Dasein is caught up in its being-toward-death, and its "striving for being, *qua* striving, is in its from-itself an away-from-itself and a toward-which"[62]—quaintly summarized in Heidegger's two diagrams at the end of *The Essence of Truth*.[63]

To focus on this point about Heidegger's phenomenological motifs in more detail, consider what Heidegger says about *physis*: "It denotes self-blossoming emergence (e.g., the blossoming of a rose), opening up, unfolding, that which manifests itself in such unfolding and preservers and endures in it; in short, the realm of things that emerge and linger on";[64] "*physis* means the emerging and arising, the spontaneous unfolding that lingers";[65] and later, "that which from out of itself stands and which moves and rests in itself: the self-standing. [. . .] to emerge, to be powerful, of itself to come to stand and remain standing, to dwell, to sojourn."[66] As Heidegger summarizes his argument mid-flow: "From the three stems we derive the three initial concrete meanings: to live, to emerge, to linger or endure."[67] What is interesting about this constitution of being *qua physis* is that what "emerges" and "lingers" does so on the back of investments of energy, on the back of Dasein's leap into being. But this is also an emergence and lingering that must at some point—because it is predicated upon entropy—disperse, decay, deteriorate, and die out. The question is, "linger or endure" for how long?

CONCLUSION

At several points in his voluminous oeuvre, Heidegger feigns a worry that both being and all his talk of being are nothing more than "vapor." To cite two instances: "Yet we must admit that the word 'to be' always dissipates like a vapor"[68] and "All the things we have named *are* and yet—when we wish to apprehend being, it is always as though we were reaching into the void. [. . .] unreal vapor."[69] Posturing apart, though, the embedding of a phrase about being as vapor from Nietzsche's *Twilight of the Idols* within these texts affords Heidegger a serious point.[70] This is clear from his investigations of the history of being, and in particular its forgetting: "the history of Western thought begins, not by thinking what is most thought-provoking, but by letting it remain forgotten. Western thought thus begins with an omission, perhaps even a failure."[71]

Another way of reading the idea drifting around Heidegger's Nietzsche—vaporous failure—is to extrapolate Heidegger's theory of Dasein to include its full range of sensory modalities. For distraction and entropy work through all modalities, not just the sonic at issue in this chapter, and to lose the sonic is to lose an essential mode of vibrating and resonating Dasein into being. This affords Dasein its proper body, physical as well as transcendental. On that basis, we can also say: being may indeed be a vapor, because it is shot through with distraction and entropy. But this does not make it a failure. The sonic dissipation of Dasein's being is an essential part of what it means to be human in the distracted modern world. And perhaps we should also add this: the world's musics, constituted as practices of sound-driven temporality, therefore have, through their material events and individual manners of entropic distraction, much to teach us about our being-toward-death and how we deal with this predicament in the contemporary world.

NOTES

1. Martin Heidegger, *An Introduction to Metaphysics*, trans. Ralph Manheim (New Haven: Yale University Press, 1959), 146.
2. Cf. Paul North, The Problem of Distraction (Stanford: Stanford University Press, 2012), 109–142.
3. Martin Heidegger, "The End of Philosophy and the Task of Thinking," in *Heidegger: Basic Writings*, ed. David Farrell Krell (New York: Routledge, 1977 repr. 2011), 319.
4. David Farrell Krell, "Introduction to 'On the Essence of Truth'," in *Heidegger: Basic Writings*, ed. David Farrell Krell (New York: Routledge, 1977 repr. 2011), 62.
5. E.g., Jon McKenzie, Perform or Else: From Discipline to Performance (New York: Routledge, 2001), 155–172.
6. E.g., Andrew Bowie, "Adorno, Heidegger and the Meaning of Music," *Thesis Eleven* 56 (February 1999): 1–23.
7. E.g., Jennifer Heuson, "Heidegger's Ears: Hearing, Attunement, and the Acoustic Shaping of *Being and Time*," *Contemporary Music Review* 31/5–6 (October–December 2012): 411–423; E.g., Martin Parker Dixon, "Dwelling and the Sacralisation of the Air: A Note on Acousmatic Music," *Organised Sound* 16, no. 2 (2011): 115–119. See also Drouillard's chapter in this volume.
8. Kevin Aho, "The Missing Dialogue between Heidegger and Merleau-Ponty: On the Importance of the Zollikon Seminars," *Body and Society* 11, no. 2 (2005): 1–23.
9. Martin Heidegger, "The Question concerning Technology," 223.
10. Heidegger, "The Question Concerning Technology," 236. *Bestand* is typically translated as "standing reserve" and can be understood as a mere resource on hand to

be manipulated or consumed. See the chapters by Harper-Scott and Rentmeester in this volume.

11. Martin Heidegger, "What is Metaphysics?" in *Heidegger: Basic Writings*, ed. David Farrell Krell (New York: Routledge, 1977 repr. 2011), 50.

12. Kevin Aho, "Acceleration and Time Pathologies: The Critique of Psychology in Heidegger's *Beiträge*," *Time and Society* 16, no. 1 (2007): 25–42.

13. E.g., Martin Heidegger, *Being and Time*, trans. John Macquarrie and Edward Robinson (Oxford: Blackwell, 1962), 264, 334ff, 387, 398, and 441–443.

14. Heidegger, *Being and Time*, 83.

15. E.g., Martin Heidegger, *What is Called Thinking?* trans. J. Glenn Gray (New York: Harper and Row, 1968), 129–130.

16. Martin Heidegger, "On the Origin of the Work of Art," in *Heidegger: Basic Writings*, ed. David Farrell Krell (New York: Routledge, 1977 repr. 2011), 95.

17. Heidegger, *An Introduction to Metaphysics*, 34.

18. E.g., Heidegger, *What is Called Thinking?* 161, 164; Heidegger, "The End of Philosophy and the Task of Thinking," 318; Heidegger, *Being and Time*, 318 and 357.

19. Heidegger, *Being and Time*, 318.

20. Respectively, Heidegger, *Being and Time*, 33. And: Martin Heidegger, "Introduction [to *Being and Time*]," trans. Joan Stambaugh, in *Heidegger: Basic Writings*, ed. David Farrell Krell (New York: Routledge, 1977 repr. 2011), 17.

21. Martin Heidegger, "On the Essence of Truth," in *Heidegger: Basic Writings*, ed. David Farrell Krell (New York: Routledge, 1977 repr. 2011), 73.

22. Heidegger, *An Introduction to Metaphysics*, 129.

23. Heidegger, *An Introduction to Metaphysics*, 132.

24. Heidegger, *Being and Time*, 206.

25. Heidegger, "The End of Philosophy and the Task of Thinking," 325. Cf. William Egginton, "Staging the Event: The Theatrical Ground of Metaphysical Framing," in *Being Shaken: Ontology and the Event*, eds. Michael Marder and Santiago Zabala (New York: Palgrave Macmillan, 2014), 177–185.

26. Heidegger, *An Introduction to Metaphysics*, 100–101.

27. Mark Wrathall, "Heidegger on Plato, Truth, and Unconcealment: The 1931–32 Lecture on *The Essence of Truth*," *Inquiry* 47 (2004): 443–463.

28. Martin Heidegger, *The Essence of Human Freedom: An Introduction to Philosophy*, trans. Ted Sadler (London: Continuum, 2002), 80.

29. Heidegger, "The End of Philosophy and the Task of Thinking," 320.

30. Casey O'Callaghan, *Sounds: A Philosophical Theory* (New York: Oxford University Press, 2007), 59ff.

31. Roger Scruton, *The Aesthetics of Music* (Oxford: Clarendon Press, 1997).

32. O'Callaghan, *Sounds*, 65.

33. Martin Heidegger, *The Basic Problems of Phenomenology*, trans. Albert Hofstadter (Bloomington: Indiana University Press, 1982), 227ff.

34. Heidegger, *Being and Time*, 463.

35. Heidegger, *An Introduction to Metaphysics*, 191.

36. Heidegger, *An Introduction to Metaphysics*, 192.

37. Martin Heidegger, *The Event*, trans. Richard Rojcewicz (Bloomington: Indiana University Press, 2013), 43ff.

38. Martin Heidegger, *Basic Questions of Philosophy: Selected 'Problems' of 'Logic,'* trans. Richard Rojcewicz and André Schuwer (Bloomington: Indiana University Press, 1994), 131ff.

39. Claudia Baracchi, "A Vibrant Silence: Heidegger and the End of Philosophy," in *Being Shaken: Ontology and the Event*, eds. Michael Marder and Santiago Zabala (New York: Palgrave Macmillan, 2014), 92–121.

40. Heidegger, *What is Called Thinking?* 211.

41. Heidegger, *An Introduction to Metaphysics*, 91.

42. Edmund Husserl, *On the Phenomenology of the Consciousness of Internal Time (1983-1917)*, trans. John Brough (Dordrecht: Kluwer Academic Publishers, 1991).

43. Heidegger, *An Introduction to Metaphysics*, 46, 47.

44. Heidegger, *An Introduction to Metaphysics*, 63.

45. Heidegger, "The Question Concerning Technology," 223ff.

46. Heidegger, *Being and Time*, 294.

47. Heidegger, *An Introduction to Metaphysics*, 158.

48. Heidegger, *An Introduction to Metaphysics*, 174.

49. Heidegger, "The End of Philosophy and the Task of Thinking," 319.

50. Heidegger, "What is Metaphysics?" 54.

51. Heidegger, *Being and Time*, 374.

52. Stephen Mulhall, *Heidegger and Being and Time* (London: Routledge, 1996), 165.

53. Heidegger, "On the Essence of Truth," 67.

54. Heidegger, "On the Essence of Truth," 71.

55. Martin Heidegger, *The Essence of Truth: On Plato's Cave Allegory and Theaetetus*, trans. Ted Sadler (Bloomington: Indiana University Press, 2002), 176.

56. Mulhall, *Heidegger and Being and Time*, 109.

57. Heidegger, "The End of Philosophy and the Task of Thinking," 321.

58. Charles Guignon, "Being as Appearing: Retrieving the Greek Experience of *Phusis*," in *A Companion to Heidegger's Introduction to Metaphysics*, eds. Gregory Fried and Richard Polt (New Haven: Yale University Press, 2001), 34–56.

59. Heidegger, *An Introduction to Metaphysics*, 91.

60. Heidegger, *An Introduction to Metaphysics*, 102.

61. Heidegger, *What is Called Thinking?* 237.

62. Heidegger, *The Essence of Truth*, 166 (ellipses in original).

63. Heidegger, *The Essence of Truth*, 221 and 228.

64. Heidegger, *An Introduction to Metaphysics*, 14.

65. Heidegger, *An Introduction to Metaphysics*, 61.

66. Heidegger, *An Introduction to Metaphysics*, 71–72.

67. Heidegger, *An Introduction to Metaphysics*, 72.

68. Heidegger, *What is Called Thinking?* 233 and 218.

69. Heidegger, *An Introduction to Metaphysics*, 35 and 74.

70. Cf. Friedrich Nietzsche, *Twilight of the Idols: Or, How to Philosophize with the Hammer*, trans. Richard Polt (Indianapolis and Cambridge: Hackett, 1997), 18–23.
71. Heidegger, *What is Called Thinking?* 152.

BIBLIOGRAPHY

Aho, Kevin. "Acceleration and Time Pathologies: The Critique of Psychology in Heidegger's *Beiträge*." *Time and Society* 16, no. 1 (2007): 25–42.

Aho, Kevin. "The Missing Dialogue between Heidegger and Merleau-Ponty: On the Importance of the Zollikon Seminars." *Body and Society* 11, no. 2 (2005): 1–23.

Bowie, Andrew. "Adorno, Heidegger and the Meaning of Music." *Thesis Eleven* 56 (February 1999): 1–23.

Egginton, William. "Staging the Event: The Theatrical Ground of Metaphysical Framing." In *Being Shaken: Ontology and the Event*, edited by Michael Marder and Santiago Zabala, 177–185. New York: Palgrave Macmillan, 2014.

Guignon, Charles. "Being as Appearing: Retrieving the Greek Experience of *Phusis*." In *A Companion to Heidegger's Introduction to Metaphysics*, edited by Gregory Fried and Richard Polt, 34–56. New Haven: Yale University Press, 2001.

Heidegger, Martin. *The Event*. Translated by Richard Rojcewicz. Bloomington: Indiana University Press, 2013.

Heidegger, Martin. "Introduction [to *Being and Time*]." Translated by Joan Stambaugh. In *Heidegger: Basic Writings*, edited by David Farrell Krell, 8–40. New York: Routledge, 1977 repr. 2011.

Heidegger, Martin. "What is Metaphysics?" In *Heidegger: Basic Writings*, edited by David Farrell Krell, 45–57. New York: Routledge, 1977 repr. 2011.

Heidegger, Martin. "On the Essence of Truth." In *Heidegger: Basic Writings*, edited by David Farrell Krell, 65–82. New York: Routledge, 1977 repr. 2011.

Heidegger, Martin. "On the Origin of the Work of Art." In *Heidegger: Basic Writings*, edited by David Farrell Krell, 89–139. New York: Routledge, 1977 repr. 2011.

Heidegger, Martin. "The Question concerning Technology." In *Heidegger: Basic Writings*, edited by David Farrell Krell, 217–238. New York: Routledge, 1977 repr. 2011.

Heidegger, Martin. "The End of Philosophy and the Task of Thinking." In *Heidegger: Basic Writings*, edited by David Farrell Krell, 311–325. New York: Routledge, 1977 repr. 2011.

Heidegger, Martin, *The Essence of Human Freedom: An Introduction to Philosophy*. Translated by Ted Sadler. London: Continuum, 2002.

Heidegger, Martin. *The Essence of Truth: On Plato's Cave Allegory and Theaetetus*. Translated by Ted Sadler. London: Continuum, 2002.

Heidegger, Martin. *Basic Questions of Philosophy: Selected 'Problems' of 'Logic.'* Translated by Richard Rojcewicz and André Schuwer. Bloomington: Indiana University Press, 1994.

Heidegger, Martin. *The Basic Problems of Phenomenology*. Translated by Albert Hofstadter. Bloomington: Indiana University Press, 1982.
Heidegger, Martin. *What is Called Thinking?*. Translated by J. Glenn Gray. New York: Harper and Row, 1968.
Heidegger, Martin. *Being and Time*. Translated by John Macquarrie and Edward Robinson. Oxford: Blackwell, 1962.
Heidegger, Martin. *An Introduction to Metaphysics*. Translated by Ralph Manheim. New Haven: Yale University Press, 1959.
Heuson, Jennifer. "Heidegger's Ears: Hearing, Attunement, and the Acoustic Shaping of *Being and Time*." *Contemporary Music Review* 31, nos. 5–6 (October–December 2012): 411–423.
Husserl, Edmund. *On the Phenomenology of the Consciousness of Internal Time (1983–1917)*. Translated by John Brough. Dordrecht: Kluwer Academic Publishers, 1991.
Krell, David Farrell. "Introduction to 'On the Essence of Truth.'" In *Heidegger: Basic Writings*, edited by David Farrell Krell, 61–63. New York: Routledge, 1977 repr. 2011.
McKenzie, Jon. Perform or Else: From Discipline to Performance. New York: Routledge, 2001.
Mulhall, Stephen. *Heidegger and Being and Time*. London: Routledge, 1996.
Nietzsche, Friedrich. *Twilight of the Idols: Or, How to Philosophize with the Hammer*. Translated by Richard Polt. Indianapolis and Cambridge: Hackett, 1997.
North, Paul. The Problem of Distraction. Stanford: Stanford University Press, 2012.
O'Callaghan, Casey. *Sounds: A Philosophical Theory*. New York: Oxford University Press, 2007.
Parker Dixon, Martin. "Dwelling and the Sacralisation of the Air: A note on Acousmatic Music." *Organised Sound* 16, no. 2 (2011): 115–119.
Scruton, Roger. *The Aesthetics of Music*. Oxford: Clarendon Press, 1997.
Wrathall, Mark. "Heidegger on Plato, Truth, and Unconcealment: The 1931–32 Lecture on *The Essence of Truth*." *Inquiry* 47 (2004): 443–463.

Chapter 4

Rilke and the "Tone of Death"

Music and Word in Heidegger

Babette Babich

*Ich bin die Ruhe zwischen zweien Tönen,
die sich nur schlecht aneinander gewöhnen:
denn der Ton Tod will sich erhöhn —*

*Aber im dunklen Intervall versöhnen
sich beide zitternd.
Und das Lied bleibt schön.*
—Rainer Maria Rilke, Das Stundenbuch[1]

Heidegger reads Rainer Maria Rilke with particular attention to the musical element that is poesy or song, as Heidegger cites Johan Gottfried Herder's "magic tone."[2] Quoting Rilke's "Song is existence" (*Sonnets to Orpheus*), observing that the "word for existence is Dasein," Heidegger tells us that "In the song, the world's inner space concedes space within itself."[3] This can be unpacked with a reading of Augustine on singing and time. Heidegger ranks Rilke below Friedrich Holderlin (the poet of poets) in a "needful time." The question of whether Rilke might be counted as such a poet constitutes the *Leitmotif*, it is the refrain, of "What Are Poets For?"[4] Elsewhere Heidegger is more explicit:

> Rilke stands, although more essentially and more poetically in his own proper course, as little as does Stefan George on the path of the vocation [*Berufung*] of the "poet," a vocation grounded by Hölderlin but nowhere taken up. Rilke has not—and even less has George—surmounted [*bewältig*] Western humanity and its "world" in a poetic-thoughtful way.[5]

Not all agree, some naming Rilke, quite in Heideggerian terms, the "ontological poet" *par excellence*.[6]

Here I foreground as Heidegger does, as Rilke does, as Herder does: the "music" of the words along with, here to add Hölderlin, the caesura and the the silences key to the "musical" parataxis that for Adorno characterizes Hölderlin's "transformation of language."[7] For his part, Heidegger speaks of *Aussage*, articulate expression. Thus the epigraph above drawn from Rilke's *Stundenbuch*, the *Book of Hours*, invokes the "rest" (*Rühe*)—a musical interval between the notes—"between two tones" (*zwischen zweien Tönen*), including dissonance and counterpoint with the "tone of death" (*Ton Tod*).

The poem dates from 1899 and was first published in 1905. It is the twentieth in *The Book of Monkish Life*, poems I elsewhere name "love songs to God":[8]

Mein Leben ist nicht diese steile Stunde,
darin du mich so eilen siehst.
Ich bin ein Baum vor meinem Hintergrunde,
ich bin nur einer meiner vielen Munde
und jener, welcher sich am frühsten schließt.[9]

Given the dates and not less given the reference to silence and death, one could make the case for a certain "anxiety of influence," as component of Heidegger's critique of Rilke. The reader can hear the "breath," as Herder says, as Rilke says, the "voice," the poetic tonality of harmony and tension with death as the poem closes with a dark "interval" and reconciliation, however fraught.

I have already noted what may surely be named the "Ur-phenomenology" of song, as Heidegger describes singing as "being present in what is present itself."[10] As we recall in Book 11 of Augustine's *Confessions*, singing the psalm, in collected memory of the song sung, carries the song as one sings it, and, present in full, unfolds to end with a resonance in silence, complete in mind in anticipation and memory.[11] That is Augustine. For Rilke, the reference is one of rhythm and meter, the beauty that remains—*Und das Lied bleibt schön.*

Phenomenologically, Rilke's line as spoken out, Heidegger's *Aussage* in *Being and Time*, is *music* as the poet writes musical allusions in his lines, in the poetic word. This is also what Nietzsche meant when he wrote of *The Birth of Tragedy Out of the Spirit of Music*, as this comes to voice and can be heard, literally, as music in Aeschylus, Sophocles, etc.[12]

In a chapter titled "*Mousike techne* in *The Hallelujah Effect*," I explain the phonetic word—the rhythmic unit of tragedy—as Nietzsche does, as music.[13]

But to just this end, I read Wallace Stevens echoing Robert Herrick's *Julia*. And yet, I do not cite Herrick's earlier poem because being-in the English language, it is already to be heard in Stevens. Herrick builds the image and the rhythm into English rhyme:

Whenas in silks my Julia goes,
Then, then (methinks) how sweetly flows
That liquefaction of her clothes.

Stevens' *Peter Quince at the Clavier* echoes to the extent that Stevens is as "absolutely" *modern* as Rimbaud (and thus we understand what Heidegger means by modern poetry):

Just as my fingers on these keys
Make music, so the self-same sounds
On my spirit make a music too.[14]

Stevens tells us the color of her "silks" in his poem *Suzannah and the Elders* as I elsewhere reflect on color and sound,[15] retraining the line:

Thinking of your blue-shadowed silk,
Is music,
It is like the strain
Waked in the elders by Susanna.[16]

Rilke's "monkish" reflection on his life to be distinguished from this "slanting hour" gives us alliteration and assonance, *diese steile Stunde*, the long *ei* and short and round *u*, we need—these *are* notes, this is the *tone* of the poems—to hear the long *ō* in both *Ton* and in *Tod*, an *ō* slightly shortened with the voiced "d," an *alveolar plosive* or *stop*, as Rilke sets the two together, which works musically inasmuch as the same "d" follows the "n" lengthened *ō* in *Ton*.

THE ESSENCE OF MUSIC

When is there song that sings essentially?

—Heidegger[17]

There is no lack of writing on Heidegger and art—consider the scholar Karsten Harries and many others including the current author.[18] But when it comes to music, scholars complain that Heidegger writes little,[19] maintaining that the role of music appears to be "as good as nothing."[20]

Of course, there are explicit references and I draw on music to explore Heidegger's style as important as a hermeneutic phenomenology of reading is key to the extent that music in Heidegger exceeds metaphoric resonances. Hence when Heidegger refers to *Tonkunst* in "On the Origin of the Work of Art," he echoes Herder (with reference to Rilke) on the breath but also and inevitably recollecting Eduard Hanslick's explicitly musical reflections on "hearing beauty."[21] As the "language of tones" similarly resonates in Wittgenstein's reflections on music, Heidegger's reflections on language, poetizing, thinking recall Hanslick's formula: "The composer poetizes and thinks . . . in tones." [*Der Komponist dichtet und denkt . . . in Tönen.*][22]

Music and tone include the acoustic, crucial for Heidegger, crucial for Nietzsche. And for Plato, music is a metaphor not only in *The Republic*'s Myth of Er but also in the *Phaedo*, where we learn that Socrates invokes just this ambiguity, as his daemon tells him: "ὦ Σώκρατες,' ἔφη, 'μουσικὴν ποίει καὶ ἐργάζου" (O Socrates, make/create/poetize music and let that be your work).[23] Note that even in antiquity what Heidegger would call the ontic dimensionality of music persists: thus Socrates sets a verse of Aesop to music, a move that permits Plato to define philosophy as the highest "music" while simultaneously articulating a demotic reading of the mantic command to "practice" music.[24]

Heidegger engages this notion, albeit obliquely, in an early lecture on the strange thing it is to "philosophize," noting that while we do not "biologize" we do "musicize."[25] Here, Heidegger reminds his students that "between 'philosophizing' [*philosophieren*] and 'musicizing' [*musizieren*] there is, as one says, an analogy."[26] Sight-reading Heidegger's lecture course, the terms are delimited with the markings patently named (in German): "goose feet." Thus "to philosophize" is effectively alien. Making the same (very cliché classical) point in his university lecture courses on ancient philosophy, Nietzsche argued that philosophic concerns are "inhumane," that is, bootless from a *humanist* point of view and similarly speaking to his own students—Hans-Georg Gadamer liked to say "philosophy bakes no bread."[27] Hence, for Pierre Hadot, "Socrates was called *atopos,* that is, 'unclassifiable.' What makes him *atopos* is precisely the fact that he is a 'philo-sopher' in the etymological sense of the word; that is, he is in love with wisdom."[28] Given this "alien" dimensionality, Heidegger emphasizes qua Aristotelian distinction that Plato would never name philosophy a "τέχνη."[29] But for Jean-Luc Nancy, "music—was the *tekhnē mousikē*" (musical culture)[30] quite to the extent that in antiquity "music" included all the arts of human culture.[31]

When Heidegger invokes "musicizing," he speaks as Plato does when he calls philosophy the "highest" kind of music. The reference to Plato includes a reference to death via the study of philosophy as we are charged to "study nothing but dying and being dead."[32] Similarly, Plato emphasizes the highest music as the music of the spheres in *The Republic*: a music we famously do not hear.

Contra the claim that there is as good as "no music" in Heidegger, there are references to music in his writing, to song, and to singing, and to "musicizing," and he mentions composers by name. To be sure, most scholars invoke music in connection with Heidegger metaphorically, referring to Heidegger's "symphonies" or else his "fugues," the latter an idiom for obscurity.[33] Such reproofs are compounded by charges of Heidegger's philistinism. The self-appointed "art-police"[34] have denounced Heidegger's focus on "great art"—inauspicious for his choice of music and his poetic judgment.

As an exemplar, in just this sense, Heidegger includes Beethoven's quartets, that is, as several authors have pointed out, the *printed scores*, bundled, Heidegger writes, like so much old paper in the cellars of publishing houses. Later, Heidegger goes on—I already noted the relevance of τέχνη—to write about "standing reserve" in "The Question Concerning Technology." And earlier, in his essay on the "Origin of the Work of Art" he makes a related point, raising the material matter of matter, good Aristotelian that he was, along with the question of the artist/artisan/*technites*, including "architectural works and pictorial works, tone- and linguistic works."[35] Here we hear a reference to Friedrich Schiller's "musicality" of poetry/poesie [*Dichtkunst*] as Heidegger invokes "tonal" works (quite where for Hanslick, the tone is, in its being/nonbeing, the material or "stuff" of music).[36]

In this way, Heidegger's work foregrounds the sounding, resonant, musical tone.[37] As Heidegger writes in his published version: "When a work is created, brought forth out of this or that work-material—stone, wood, metal, color, language, tone—we say also that it is made, set forth out of it."[38] In this sense, "metals come to glitter and shimmer, colors to glow, tones to sing, the word to speak."[39] What thus comes to work, as already noted in his earlier draft, is at the same time a withdrawal.

Heidegger compares *techné* and *techné*, and had we more scope we might include reference to *Gebrauchsmusik* (a musicological term that may be argued to have a debt to Heidegger): "the sculptor uses stone just as the mason uses it, in his own way. But he does not use it up. That happens in a certain way only where the work miscarries."[40] Thus:

> To be sure, the painter also uses pigment, but in such a way that color is not used up but rather only now comes to shine forth. The same holds for the poet as poet who also 'uses' the word—not, however, like ordinary speakers and writers who have to use them up, but rather in such a way that the word only now becomes and remains truly a word.[41]

Here we may continue to say, with Hanslick, that a tone only becomes a musical tone for the composer composing for musical hearing, such that those same scores bundled still indicate, formally, the tone that can thus—given the complex dimensions required for what Heidegger's student Günther Anders calls the musical "situation"—come to be and to "remain" through to its sounding silence at the end of a performance.

With reference to the artist as to τέχνη more generally, it is something else again to add the reproductive element, a Benjaminian, Adornian, Andersian, or indeed Bourdieu-style musico-performative addendum. This, in its recorded/broadcast/streaming instauration, is what the musical sociologist H. Stith Bennett calls "the music."[42] And then we would still have to say, post Adorno, post Cage, post Leonard Cohen and Johnny Cash, post legions of later cover versions, that the tone itself is insufficiently descriptive hence again we need Anders' "musical situation."[43]

For Heidegger, "the world is not simply the Open that corresponds to clearing, and the earth is not simply the Closed that corresponds to concealment."[44] Thus "truth" is at work in the musical work and I argue that Adorno sought to express something of this in his unfinished *Beethoven*.[45] Daniel Chua, referring with some ambivalence to Adorno, invokes Heidegger to insist on a point to be heard in Derrida (Chua cites Jay and Marion in addition to Lévinas in this constellation), using Heidegger to unpack Beethoven's "Prometheanism":

> Beethoven's music must therefore disclose an-Other human being whose very gaze questions the *"Da"* of my *"Dasein"* (there-being), to borrow Lévinas's play on Martin Heidegger's ontological concept of "being-in-the world"; it re-positions our right to be (there). . . . After all, the body particularizes; it constitutes the human being, defining each person as unique in relation to another in space and time; only then can its "this-ness" displace the "Da" of my "Dasein."[46]

Despite the significance of Beethoven's Prometheus for Nietzsche's *The Birth of Tragedy out of the Spirit of Music* and Goethe's Prometheus for Anders, Chua's *Prometheanism* refers to neither. If the strife between earth and world illuminates the musical work of art, the notion of harmony as we know this from Heraclitus' attuned reflex, sustained, or, as Nietzsche says, a "playing" dissonance become human, expresses what Heidegger characterizes as "the intimacy with which opponents belong to each other."[47] Thus Heidegger mentions Mozart's early presentiment of death to which Eugen Fink (in the wake of his own separate reading of Rilke and the play of the world)[48] replied that the composer was similarly "collected," as the reality of death "also commissioned his *Requiem*."[49]

SITUATION AND TONE

Alle Auslegung gründet im Verstehen

—Heidegger

Not only Mozart, beautifully and dramatically cited in conversation with Fink on Heraclitus, matching the Pythagorean contrast made in Plato's *Phaedo* between *symphônein/diaphonein* and Beethoven or Bach, Heidegger also instances (in connection with Nietzsche) Wagner. And like Wagner, one may say of Heidegger *und kein Ende*. Thus it is hard to exaggerate his influence and, among others, Heidegger's thought is important for musicologists and music sociologists.[50] Further, when it comes to *musica practica*, Heidegger not only inspires musical hermeneutics but contemporary composers, like John Cage and Paul Hindemith,[51] along with, as already mentioned, Wallace Stevens.[52] And, just as Woody Allen once put the cover of Heidegger's *Introduction to Metaphysics* full frame in one of his films, there are popular musical references to boot, including musical revues in English along with, on the German scene, Pigor and Eichhorn's *"Was ist Sein, Was ist Sein,"* lending Heidegger a "viral sensationality," calling Heidegger a philosophical "Rastamann"[53] with the Swabian refrain, *"da hat der Heidegger wider ma' recht"* which (maybe) offsets the more ominous *"Ich Heidegger euch in Grund und Boden."*

Most influential, perhaps, is the relevance of Heidegger and music with respect to listening and musical education.[54] Authors have noted Heidegger's reference to *Stimmung* (in German unavoidably musical) or attunement (the term has also been translated as disposition or state of mind). Here what Heidegger says about listening, key to what Anders says about listening, draws on Husserlian acoustic phenomenology.

I began, despite Heidegger's reservations, by citing Rilke for the sake of the sound of his words, underscoring the stillness between notes. As a reference to musical death, this also matters as such stillness comes at the end of a song as of a musical performance, when one can say, as a question of consummate practice, that such a thing "stood" or "was" among us/or not. Thus Gadamer emphasizes achievement/failure of the beautiful with reference to an organ improvisation—the "organist himself hardly knows afterwards just how he played."[55]

With reference to totality (death) and the absolute, it is worth noting Christopher Barry on Heidegger.[56] Barry argues in Heidegger's *Spirit* (also as noted above, indebted to Augustine which is why Barry can call this a "truism"):

That the totality of the music/Dasein/subject/organism cannot be grasped until after it is incapable of recursively generating more of itself is a music-analytical truism, albeit an uncomfortable one. But as Heidegger notes, this totality still becomes something even though it does not "live" in the sense of self reflective, recursive generation.[57]

I will come back to Heidegger's reflection on death in *Being and Time* if I will first seek to hear this in connection with the death of the note.

In Heidegger's reflections on "Being in As Such," in *Being and Time*, on assertion or statement or "*Aussage*"[58] what is at issue is the spoken qua expressed in what is said (in talking, casually and otherwise) and heard or unheard, attended to or ignored. Heidegger thus emphasizes what is involved in order to listen or hear or heed/observe/obey (*hörchen*). It is in this context of speaking/listening that Heidegger invokes negative speech, including silence and misspeaking, in addition to "negative listening, unattending, overhearing, mishearing."[59] In every case we find ourselves *already* in a world with pre-given concerns, attunements, significations. Creatures of the word as we are, we are also born into, thrown into, language as we are thrown into the world.

Speaking of tone in *Being and Time*, the science-minded Heidegger invokes experimental psychology or physiology when he notes that "A very artificial and complicated comportment is already needed in order to 'hear' a 'pure noise' [*reines Geräusch*]."[60] To this same extent, "Listening to . . ." as Heidegger says (ellipsis included) "is the existential being-open of Dasein as being-with [*Mitsein*] for the another."[61] Thus, "Only one who already understands, can listen [*zuhören*]."[62]

Drawing on this for his phenomenological sociology of music, Günther Anders characterizes "the musical situation"[63] as this differs for performers as for listeners actively engaged with music. What is key is "being-in-music" which can, to this same extent, "be" the world for some. Similarly, under the rubric "Situation," Adorno's *Aesthetic Theory* explains a reference to "improvisation" quite as the precondition for discovery and surprise:

> It is well known that even composers with the best ears are usually astonished when they actually hear their orchestral works performed. This indeterminateness, however—including the indeterminateness that results from the inability of the ear, as Stockhausen has noted, to distinguish, much less imagine, each tone of a tone cluster—is built into determinateness as an element of it rather than that it encompasses the whole. In the jargon of musicians: You have to know exactly if something sounds, and only to a certain extent how it sounds. This leaves room for surprises ...what made its precocious appearance as *l'imprevu* in Berlioz is a surprise not only for the listener but objectively as well; and yet the ear can anticipate it.[64]

In this performative, hermeneutic context, we understand Christopher Small's assertion in his *Musicking*,[65] "There is no such thing as music."[66]

Small foregrounds an anthropological definition not unlike the phenomenological sociologist of music, H. Stith Bennett, in stating, at all but an activity, something that people do."[67]

Small's references include Dahlhaus and Benjamin and Kant under the aegis of Bateson. The language is loosely inherited in the spirit of what Nietzsche called the "gay science," and infectiously, it has been "transmuted," in David Borgo's "Transmusicking in Cyberspace."[68] Heidegger seems a given in cyberspace transmusicking, what with Gerry Stahl and computer music and its ontological discontents.[69] For his part, Borgo invokes Miller Puckette's notion of "screen being,"[70] citing Puckette's "Not Being There"[71] in terms of "telepresence."[72]

Heidegger's focus on attunement in *Being and Time* highlights the articulative element of language: "Being-in and its state-of-mind are made known in discourse and indicated in language by intonation, modulation, the tempo of talk, 'the way of speaking.'"[73] This is musical articulation: attunement, intonation, modulation, tempo. Thus Anders designates "active listening," invoking Heidegger who explains that hearing is "an existential possibility that belongs to talking itself,"[74] that is, that "hearing is constitutive for discourse. And just as linguistic utterance is based on discourse, so is acoustic perception on hearing."[75]

Heidegger specifically invokes being-with-others and being-in-the-world but I note only Heidegger's clarification of hearing by contrasting it with the kind of acoustic perception quantified by psychology.[76] This is "the hearing which understands. What we 'first' hear is never noises or complexes of sounds, but the creaking waggon, the motor-cycle. We hear the column on the march, the north wind, the woodpecker tapping, the fire crackling."[77] Key for Heidegger is that:

> It requires a very artificial and complicated frame of mind to "hear" a "pure noise." The fact that motor-cycles and waggons are what we proximally hear is the phenomenal evidence that in every case Dasein, as Being-in-the-world, already dwells alongside what is ready-to-hand within-the-world; it certainly does not dwell proximally alongside "sensations"; nor would it first have to give shape to the swirl of sensations to provide the springboard from which the subject leaps off and finally arrives at a "world" Dasein, as essentially understanding, is proximally alongside what is understood.[78]

Notice that what is at stake is not a matter of high and low, great art and not, nor does it concern what one likes or does not like, much less what one takes music to be.

Being-in-the-music is requisite, as Anders says, in order to understand "the fourth [subdominant], the fifth [dominant]" as Leonard Cohen sings in his

Hallelujah, reflexively thematizing his song, "the minor fall, the major lift," in the singing of what he tells us has a tradition as David's "secret chord."[79] What does it take to know what this means? In Leonard Cohen's song, these are the words of his first verse, his *incipit*, composed in the key of C major and its chord progression: C, F, G, A minor, F. One can also hear instrumental variations, depending on the arrangement, piano as in the case of John Cale's setting, or, more typically, guitar or even a tiny orchestra of cellos with piano and bass as in k.d.lang's 2005 Juno performance. These articulate the song. For Heidegger as for Nietzsche, there is music in language, presupposing preunderstanding: "Both talking and hearing are based upon understanding. And understanding arises neither through talking at length [*vieles Reden*] nor through busily hearing something 'all around.' Only he who already understands can listen [*zuhoren*]."[80]

ON THE DEATH OF THE TONE OR MUSIC AS *TONKUNST*

bald sind wir aber Gesang

—Hölderlin

Recall, here to conclude, Heidegger's *Stimmung*, mood, disposition, noting the repetitive parallel with Rilke's *Duino Elegies*:

Stimme, stimme: Höre mein Herz, wie sonst nur Heilige hörten [81]

Nietzsche speaks of the "spirit of music" and Derrida reminds us that Heidegger thinks the ear which the neglected musicological phenomenologist, F. Joseph Smith, advances quite against the Husserlian phenomenological tradition, of the φαινόμενον (*phenomenon*), the *akoumenon*,[82] drawing on Pythagorean esotericism to do so. The esotericism is key as one needs a musicological legacy, Pythagorean and esoteric, the unwritten teaching, already mentioned with reference to Plato (*Phaedrus*).

As cited above with Heidegger's allusion to Mozart, the temporality of the song is eternity as Heidegger sought to show, as the early Nietzsche explored Pindar's *paian de lampei*, shining song, an at once: whole, entire.[83] Thus Heidegger glosses "Hearing is a viewing" (*das Hören ist ein Blicken*). For Heidegger, this "looking over 'the whole, with a glance,' and listening to everything all at once is indeed the best."[84] Here Heidegger cites Angelus Silesius' *Cherubinic Wanderer*: *Das Lautenspiel Gottes*: "A heart that is God-still at its foundations, as he will would, / gladly by him be touched; it is his lute play. (*Ein Herze, das zu Grund Gott still ist, wie er will Wird / gern von ihm beruhrt: es ist sein Lautenspiel*)."[85] In *What is Called Thinking?*[86] Heidegger sets his words together in such a way that only one to whom his saying is attuned *can* hear him: *whoever has ears, let him hear.*

We hear the word's "melodic mode, the song which says something in the singing"[87] and Heidegger uses similar language in his *Introduction to Metaphysics* as he reads a choral ode for the sake of approximating the strange essence of the human as *to deinotaton*, as Sophocles, writes, "musically" as Nietzsche tells us all Greek tragedians do.

If one may make the case for Heidegger's musical style of writing/thinking, this style as I characterize it as "concinnity" brings the reader along with him,[88] Adorno likewise calls attention to the paratactic in Hölderlin as Heidegger reads Hölderlin musico-poetically. I have argued that one can also hear Rilke's *Ton Tod*, two vowel notes tuned by consonants as presaging Heidegger's reflection on death in *Being and Time*. Thus throughout the complex turns of "What are Poets For?" Heidegger seems to allude to *Being and Time*, as he reflects that "the word for existence, Dasein, is used here in the traditional sense of presence," and not less as "a synonym of being."[89] To this extent, Heidegger argues less for rank orderings than with respect to "the poet's question," musically expressed: "when is there song that sings essentially?"[90] The focus on time, compelling our attention to Augustine (metric, retention, protention) is crucial.

For Heidegger, Hölderlin is the "precursor of poets in a destitute time." Thus neither Rilke nor any other contemporary poet can be imagined as being able, as it were, to "overtake him."[91] To the same extent, the beautiful "remains" quite in the way that Heidegger can say of Rilke that only Rilke's "poetry answers" and can answer "the question to what end he is a poet, whither his song is bound."[92]

Here as noted above, Heidegger traces Rilke's "song is existence" and elsewhere Heidegger draws on Hölderlin's " . . . but soon we shall be song" (. . . *bald sind wir aber Gesang*).[93] To this extent, Heidegger tunes ontology to the essence of music and not less to Dasein:

Our being is song, and indeed a song whose singing does not resound just anywhere but is truly a singing, a song who sound does not cling to something that is eventually attained, but which has already shattered itself even in the sounding, so that there may occur only that which was sung itself.[94]

This "already shattered" shattering "even in the sounding" includes an Augustinian protentionality, a being-unto-the-end which inevitably includes the tone of death, heard at the end of every musical work. Protention is not everything. But retention or memory, after the death of the final note, the sounding of what was sung remains as silence: the aura of music.

NOTES

1. Rainer Maria Rilke in *Das Buch vom mönchischen Leben, Das Stundenbuch* (Leipzig: Insel Verlag, 1905), 17. [I am the rest between two tones/that only badly accord with one another:/because the tone of death will elevate itself—/But in the dark interval reconciled/ trembling, both to themselves /And, beautiful, the song remains.]

2. Martin Heidegger, "What are Poets For?," in *Poetry, Language, Thought*, trans. Albert Hofstadter (New York: Harper & Row, 1971), 139.

3. Heidegger, "What are Poets For?," 138.

4. Heidegger, "What are Poets For?," 96ff.

5. Martin Heidegger, *Ponderings VII–XI: Black Notebooks 1938–1939*, trans. Richard Rojcewicz (Bloomington: Indiana University Press, 2017), 438.

6. Steven Cassedy, *Flight from Eden: The Origins of Modern Literary Criticism and Theory* (Berkeley: University of California Press, 1990), 217. In addition, Hans-Georg Gadamer reads his Rilke significantly, if this is not always noted, via Eugen Fink, as well as Günther Anders and Hannah Arendt. Many scholars write on Heidegger and Rilke, including Albert Cook's (typically unnoted) "Heidegger and the Wisdom of Poetry," *The Centennial Review* 34, no. 3 (Summer 1990): 349–380; in addition to more recent readings by Anthony Stephens, Krzysztof Ziarek, and Jennifer Gosseti-Ferencei among others. I discuss Anders' and Arendt's analysis of Rilke's *Duino Elegies* in *Günther Anders' Philosophy of Technology* (London: Bloomsbury, 2021).

7. Cited with specific engagement with Heidegger in Babette Babich, *Words in Blood, Like Flowers: Philosophy and Poetry, Music and Eros in Hölderlin, Nietzsche, and Heidegger* (Albany: State University of New York Press, 2006), 116.

8. See my chapter on Rilke's *Duino Elegies*, cited above.

9. Rilke in *Das Buch vom mönchischen Leben*, 16–17. [My life is not this precipitate hour/within which you see me harried./I am a tree before everything behind me /I am just one of my many mouths/and that one that closes the soonest.]

10. Heidegger, "What are Poets For?," 138.

11. Saint Augustine, *Confessions*, trans. Henry Chadwick (Oxford: Oxford University Press, 2008), 221–245.

12. See the last chapter of Babette Babich, *Nietzsches Antike* (Berlin: Nomos/Academia, 2020).

13. Babette Babich, *The Hallelujah Effect: Performance Practice, Music, and Technology* (London: Routledge, 2016 [2013]).

14. Cited in Babich, *The Hallelujah Effect*, 167.

15. Babette Babich, "Wallace Stevens, Heidegger, and the 'Virile Hölderlin,'" *Borderless Philosophy* 3 (2020): 1–31.

16. Cited in Babich, "Wallace Stevens, Heidegger, and the 'Virile Hölderlin,'" 20.

17. Heidegger, "What Are Poets For?," 141.

18. Karsten Harries, *A Critical Commentary on Heidegger's 'The Origin of the Work of Art'* (Frankfurt am Main: Springer, 2009).

19. See, e.g., Eduardo Marx, *Heidegger und der Ort der Musik* (Würzburg: Königshausen & Neumann, 1998).

20. Günther Pöltner, "Mozart und Heidegger: Die Musik und der Ursprung des Kunstwerkes," *Heidegger Studies* 8 (1992): 123. See too, very insightfully, Christophe Perrin, "De la musique avant toute chose ? Heidegger compositeur," *Hermeneia* 14 (2014): 10; and Charles Ford who also reads Heidegger for his own aesthetic and thus theoretical purposes, "Musical Presence: Towards a New Philosophy of Music," *Contemporary Aesthetics*. Online. https://www.contempaesthetics.org/newvolume /pages/article.php?articleID=582. See also more generally on the "art of hearing," Holger Schmid, *Kunst des Hörens. Orte und Grenzen der hermeneutischen Erfahrung* (Cologne: Bolnow, 1999).

21. Warren A. Shibles cites "the world worlds" and "the thing things" as well as "language speaks." In this vein, Hanslick would say, "Music musics," according to Shibles, "Hanslick on Hearing Beauty," *Iyyun: The Jerusalem Philosophical Quarterly* 44 (January 1995): 75. Cf., too, John Lysaker, "Heidegger's Absolute Music, or What Are Poets for When the End of Metaphysics Is At Hand?," *Research in Phenomenology* 30 (2000): 180–210, here especially 202f.

22. Eduard Hanslick, *On the Musically Beautiful*, trans. G. Payzant (Indianapolis: Bobbs-Merrill, 1986 [1891]), 144 (translation altered). Cf. here the first chapter of David B. Allison's *Reading the New Nietzsche* (Lanham, MD: Rowman and Littlefield, 2001) and Christoph Landerer und Marc-Oliver Schuster, "Nietzsches Vorstudien zur *Geburt der Tragödie* in ihrer Beziehung zur Musikästhetik Eduard Hanslicks," *Nietzsche-Studien* 31 (2002): 114–133.

23. Plato, *Phaedo*, 60e 6–7. Elsewhere I write on μουσική τέχνη [musical culture] in Babich, "*Mousike techne*: The Philosophical Praxis of Music in Plato, Nietzsche, Heidegger," in *Gesture and Word: Thinking Between Philosophy and Poetry*, eds. Robert Burch and Massimo Verdicchio (London: Continuum, 2002), 171–180; and see, more broadly, Deltef Otto, *Wendungen der Metapher: Zur Übertragung in poetologischer, rhetorischer, und Erkenntnistheoretischer Hinsicht bei Aristoteles und Nietzsche* (Munich: Fink, 1998).

24. Goetz Richter, offering a differently emphatic reading of Plato's *Phaedo*, picks up on this notion of a demotic *mousikê*. See Richter, "Silence as the greatest music: The harmony of philosophy and *Mousikê* in Plato's *Phaedo*," *Literature & Aesthetics* 19, no. 1 (2009): 88–113.

25. Martin Heidegger, *Phanomenologische Interpretationen zu Aristoteles: Einfuhrung in die Phanomenologische Forschung. II.Abteilung: Vorlesungen* (Frankfurt am Main: Klostermann, 1994), 60.

26. Heidegger, *Phanomenologische Interpretationen zu Aristoteles*, 60.

27. Cf. Babette Babich, "Philosophy Bakes No Bread," *Philosophy of the Social Sciences* 48, no. 1 (2018): 47–55.

28. Pierre Hadot, *Philosophy as a Way of Life* (Oxford: Blackwell, 1995), 57.

29. Heidegger, *Phanomenologische Interpretationen zu Aristoteles*, 63.

30. Jean-Luc Nancy, *The Muses*, trans. Peggy Kamuf (Stanford: Stanford University Press, 1996), 5.

31. For further discussion, see Babich, "*Mousike techne*" or *The Hallelujah Effect* more broadly.
32. Plato, *Phaedo*, 64a.
33. William J. Richardson uses musical language to write his "Dasein and the Ground of Negativity: A Note on the Fourth Movement in the Beiträge-Symphony," *Heidegger Studies* 9 (1993): 35–52. The language of "fugue" is Heidegger's own though he himself also notes other forms. See, among others, Iain Thomson, "The Philosophical Fugue: Understanding the Structure and Goal of Heidegger's Beiträge," *Journal of the British Society for Phenomenology* 34, no. 1 (2003): 57–73.
34. Jacques Derrida, *Truth in Painting*, trans. Geoff Bennington and Ian McLeod (Chicago: University of Chicago Press, 1987 [1978]), 325 (translation slightly amended).
35. Martin Heidegger, "Vom Ursprung des Kunstwerks. Erste Ausarbeitung," *Heidegger Studies* 5 (1989): 5.
36. Heidegger, "Vom Ursprung des Kunstwerks," 10.
37. Heidegger, "Vom Ursprung des Kunstwerks," 11.
38. Karsten Heidegger, "The Origin of the Work of Art," in *Poetry, Language, Thought*, trans. Albert Hofstadter (New York: Harper & Row, 1971), 44.
39. Heidegger, "The Origin of the Work of Art," 45.
40. Heidegger, "The Origin of the Work of Art," 47.
41. Heidegger, "The Origin of the Work of Art," 48.
42. I discuss H. Stith Bennett's sociological phenomenology of music in *The Hallelujah Effect*.
43. I discuss Anders together with Adorno on the aesthetic/musical situation in *Günther Anders' Philosophy of Technology*.
44. Heidegger, "The Origin of the Work of Art," 53.
45. Theodor W. Adorno, *Beethoven: The Philosophy of Music*, trans. Edmund Jephcott (Cambridge: Polity Press, 1998).
46. Daniel Chua, "Beethoven's Other Humanism," *Journal of the American Musicological Society* 62, no. 3 (Fall 2009): 604–605.
47. Heidegger, "The Origin of the Work of Art," 63.
48. Eugen Fink, *Play as Symbol of the World and Other Writings* (Bloomington: Indiana University Press, 2016).
49. Martin Heidegger and Eugen Fink, *Heraclitus Seminar (1966/1967)*, trans. Charles H. Seibert (University of Alabama Press, 1979), 152.
50. Andrew Bowie, "Adorno, Heidegger and the Meaning of Music," *Thesis Eleven* 56 (1999): 1–23.
51. See Daniel Charles on Heidegger and Cage in his "De-Linearizing Musical Continuity: John Cage's Aesthetics of 'Interpenetration without Obstruction,'" *Discourse* 12, no. 1 (Fall–Winter 1989–90): 28–38. For a helpful reading of Heidegger and Hindemith, for example, insightfully clarifying some of the limitations of mainstream musicologists' sometimes light dismissals, see Martin Scherzinger, "Heideggerian Thought in the Early Music of Paul Hindemith (With a Foreword to Benjamin Boretz)," *Perspectives of New Music* 43/44 (Summer 2005–Winter 2006): 80–125.

52. See not only my essay on Stevens cited above but also *Words in Blood, Like Flowers*.

53. Thomas Pigor and Benedikt Eichhorn, *Heidegger*, https://www.youtube.com/watch?v=7dtawhoZv1w. Declaring as part of the performer's patter, *"Philosophie ist tanzbar!"* [philosophy is danceable], Pigor's claim channels Nietzsche's imperative.

54. One such is the insightful opening claim of Erik Wallrup's "Music, Truth and Belonging: Listening with Heidegger," in *Philosophy of Music Education Challenged: Heideggerian Inspirations*, eds. Frederik Pio and Øivind Varkøy (Dordrecht: Springer, 2015), 131–146 in foregrounding the relation between belonging, attending, or attunedness, and listening.

F. Joseph Smith (ed.), *Understanding the Musical Experience* (New York: Gordon & Breach, 1989). See too David Lines, "'Working With' Music: A Heideggerian Perspective of Music Education," *Educational Philosophy and Theory* 37, no. 1 (2013): 65–75.

55. Hans-Georg Gadamer, *The Relevance of the Beautiful*, trans. Nicholas Walker (Cambridge: Cambridge University Press, 1986 [1974/1975]), 25.

56. Christopher M. Barry, "Being, Becoming, and Death in Twelve-Tone Music: 'Wie bin ich froh!' as Epitaph," *Intégral, Special Double Issue: Music with Text* 28/29 (2014–2015): 81–123.

57. Barry, "Being, Becoming, and Death in Twelve-Tone Music," 111.

58. Martin Heidegger, *Sein und Zeit*, 7th Ed. (Tübingen, Neomarius Verlag, 1946), 153.

59. Cf. Heidegger, *Sein und Zeit*, 163.

60. Heidegger, *Sein und Zeit*, 164.

61. Heidegger, *Sein und Zeit*, 163.

62. Heidegger, *Sein und Zeit*, 164.

63. Günther Anders, *"Philosophische Untersuchungen über musikalische Situationen."* Unpublished in his lifetime but included in Richard Ellesohn's edition of Anders, *Musikphilosophische Schriften. Texte und Dokumente* (Munich: Beck, 2017). This would have been Anders' *Habilitationschrift*.

64. Adorno, *Aesthetic Theory*, trans. Robert Hullot-Kentor (Minneapolis, MN: University of Minnesota Press, 1997), 38.

65. Christopher Small, *Musicking: The Meanings of Performing and Listening* (Middletown: Wesleyan University Press, 1998), 9. Note that Small does not claim to have invented the term. Eve Ruddock discusses "musicking" at length in her chapter of this volume.

66. Small, *Musicking*, 2.

67. Small, *Musicking*, 2. See H. Stith Bennett, *Becoming a Rock Musician* (New York: Columbia University Press, 2017 [1980]).

68. David Borgo, "Beyond Performance: Transmusicking in Cyberspace," in *Taking it to the Bridge: Music as Performance*, eds. Nicholas Cook and Richard Pettengill (Ann Arbor: University of Michigan Press, 2013), 319–348.

69. See Gerry Stahl, "Attuned to Being: Heideggerian Music in Technological Society." Online. Last updated. 5 January 2004. http://gerrystahl.net/publications/interpretations/attuned.htm. See also Stahl's chapter in this volume.

70. See Babette Babich, "Screen Autism, Cellphone Zombies, and GPS Mutes," in *How Technology is Changing Human Behaviour*, ed. C. Prado (Santa Barbara: Praeger, 2019), 65–71.

71. Miller Puckette, "Not Being There," *Contemporary Music Review* 28, nos. 4–5 (2009): 409–412. Cited in David Borgo, "Beyond Performance," 325.

72. The "ecological" approach, Bateson et al., can seem more relevant than Heidegger. See Eric Clarke, *Ways of Listening: An Ecological Approach to the Perception of Musical Meaning* (Oxford: Oxford University Press, 2005). Nevertheless Thomas B. Sheridan argues for the "cybernetic," hence his definition of music as "a supervisory control hierarchy: the composer and conductor setting commands for the musician's conscious mental activity of rendering the music..." in his "Musings on "Music Making and Listening: Supervisory Control and Virtual Reality," *Proceedings of the IEEE* 92, no. 4 (April 2004): 604; as well as his "Descartes, Heidegger, Gibson and God: Toward an Eclectic Ontology of Presence," *Presence: Teleoperators and Virtual Environments* 8, no. 5 (1999): 549–557.

73. Heidegger, *Sein und Zeit*, 162.

74. Heidegger, *Sein und Zeit*, 163.

75. Heidegger, *Sein und Zeit*, 163.

76. Here it is relevant to note that it was Anders' father, William Stern, who invented the tone-variator used to measure hearing.

77. Heidegger, *Sein und Zeit*, 163.

78. Heidegger, *Sein und Zeit*, 164.

79. See for discussion, the first chapters of Babich, *The Hallelujah Effect*.

80. Heidegger, *Sein und Zeit*, 164.

81. [Voices, voices: listen my heart, as once only saints listened].

82. See Smith's *The Experiencing of Musical Sound: Prelude to a Phenomenology of Music* (New York/Montreux: Gordon and Breach, 1979).

83. See further, Babette Babich, "Between Hölderlin and Heidegger: Nietzsche's Transfiguration of Philosophy," *Nietzsche-Studien* 29 (2000): 267–301.

84. Heidegger, *The Principle of Reason*, trans. Reginald Lilly (Bloomington: Indiana University Press, 1991), 67.

85. Heidegger, *The Principle of Reason*, 68 (translation altered).

86. Martin Heidegger, *What Is Called Thinking?*, trans. F. D. Wieck and J. Glenn Gray (New York: Harper & Row, 1968).

87. Heidegger, *What is Called Thinking?*, 266.

88. See Babette Babich, "A Musical Retrieve of Heidegger, Nietzsche, and Technology: Cadence, Concinnity, and Playing Brass," *Man and World* 26 (1993): 239–269.

89. Heidegger, "What are Poets For?," 138.

90. Heidegger, "What are Poets For?," 141.

91. Heidegger, "What are Poets For?," 142.

92. Heidegger, "What are Poets For?," 142.

93. Holger Schmid goes even further, taking Heidegger's account of "showing: (*Zeigen*) as the propriative, ownmost mode of appropriation and we quote again: "als eigenster Weise des Ereigens. Diese Weise nun, in der das Ereignis spricht soll

nicht *Modus*, sondern *Melos* bedeuten: 'das Lied das singend sagt.'" But as Schmid continues to observe that with this invocation of song in reference to Holderlin a good deal to be thought: "Das zuletzt zu Denkende ist also das zu Erfahrende, 'das Lied'." See Schmid, *Kunst des Hörens. Orte und Grenzen der hermeneutischen Erfahrung* (Cologne: Bolnow, 1999), 124.

94. Heidegger, "What are Poets For?," 139.

BIBLIOGRAPHY

Adorno, Theodor W. *Aesthetic Theory*. Translated by Robert Hullot-Kentor. Minneapolis, MN: University of Minnesota Press, 1997.

Adorno, Theodor W. *Beethoven: The Philosophy of Music*. Translated by Edmund Jephcott. Cambridge: Polity Press, 1998.

Allison, David B. *Reading the New Nietzsche*. Lanham, MD: Rowman and Littlefield, 2001.

Augustine, Saint. *Confessions*. Translated by Henry Chadwick. Oxford: Oxford University Press, 2008.

Babich, Babette. "Between Hölderlin and Heidegger: Nietzsche's Transfiguration of Philosophy." *Nietzsche-Studien* 29 (2000): 267–301.

Babich, Babette. *Günther Anders' Philosophy of Technology*. London: Bloomsbury, 2021.

Babich, Babette. *The Hallelujah Effect: Performance Practice, Music, and Technology*. London: Routledge, 2016 [2013].

Babich, Babette. "A Musical Retrieve of Heidegger, Nietzsche, and Technology: Cadence, Concinnity, and Playing Brass." *Man and World* 26 (1993): 239–269.

Babich, Babette. "*Mousike techne*: The Philosophical Praxis of Music in Plato, Nietzsche, Heidegger." In *Gesture and Word: Thinking Between Philosophy and Poetry*, edited by Robert Burch and Massimo Verdicchio, 171–180. London: Continuum, 2002.

Babich, Babette. *Nietzsches Antike*. Berlin: Nomos/Academia, 2020.

Babich, Babette. "Philosophy Bakes No Bread." *Philosophy of the Social Sciences* 48, no. 1 (2018): 47–55.

Babich, Babette. "Screen Autism, Cellphone Zombies, and GPS Mutes." In *How Technology is Changing Human Behaviour*, edited by C. Prado, 65–71. Santa Barbara: Praeger, 2019.

Babich, Babette. "Wallace Stevens, Heidegger, and the 'Virile Hölderlin'." *Borderless Philosophy* 3 (2020): 1–31.

Babich, Babette. *Words in Blood, Like Flowers: Philosophy and Poetry, Music and Eros in Hölderlin, Nietzsche, and Heidegger*. Albany: State University of New York Press, 2006.

Barry, Christopher M. "Being, Becoming, and Death in Twelve-Tone Music: 'Wie bin ich froh!' as Epitaph." *Intégral, Special Double Issue: Music with Text* 28/29 (2014–2015): 81–123.

Bennett, H. Stith. *Becoming a Rock Musician.* New York: Columbia University Press, 2017 [1980].
Borgo, David. "Beyond Performance: Transmusicking in Cyberspace." In *Taking it to the Bridge: Music as Performance*, edited by Nicholas Cook and Richard Pettengill, 319–348. Ann Arbor: University of Michigan Press, 2013.
Bowie, Andrew. "Adorno, Heidegger and the Meaning of Music." *Thesis Eleven* 56 (1999): 1–23.
Cassedy, Steven. *Flight from Eden: The Origins of Modern Literary Criticism and Theory.* Berkeley: University of California Press, 1990.
Charles, Daniel. "De-Linearizing Musical Continuity: John Cage's Aesthetics of 'Interpenetration without Obstruction.'" *Discourse* 12, no. 1 (Fall–Winter 1989–90): 28–38.
Chua, Daniel. "Beethoven's Other Humanism." *Journal of the American Musicological Society* 62, no. 3 (Fall 2009): 571–645.
Clarke, Eric. *Ways of Listening: An Ecological Approach to the Perception of Musical Meaning.* Oxford: Oxford University Press, 2005.
Cook, Albert. "Heidegger and the Wisdom of Poetry." *The Centennial Review* 34, no. 3 (Summer 1990): 349–380.
Derrida, Jacques. *Truth in Painting.* Translated by Geoff Bennington and Ian McLeod. Chicago: University of Chicago Press, 1987 [1978].
Ellesohn, Richard. *Musikphilosophische Schriften. Texte und Dokumente.* Munich: Beck, 2017.
Fink, Eugen. *Play as Symbol of the World and Other Writings.* Bloomington: Indiana University Press, 2016.
Ford, Charles. "Musical Presence: Towards a New Philosophy of Music." *Contemporary Aesthetics.* https://www.contempaesthetics.org/newvolume/pages/article.php?articleID=582
Gadamer, Hans-Georg. *The Relevance of the Beautiful.* Translated by Nicholas Walker. Cambridge: Cambridge University Press, 1986 [1974/1975].
Hadot, Pierre. *Philosophy as a Way of Life.* Oxford: Blackwell, 1995.
Harries, Karsten. *A Critical Commentary on Heidegger's 'The Origin of the Work of Art.'* Frankfurt am Main: Springer, 2009.
Hanslick, Eduard. *On the Musically Beautiful.* Translated by G. Payzant. Indianapolis: Bobbs-Merrill, 1986 [1891].
Heidegger, Martin. *Phanomenologische Interpretationen zu Aristoteles.: Einfuhrung in die Phanomenologische Forschung. II.Abteilung:Vorlesungen.* Frankfurt am Main: Klostermann, 1994.
Heidegger, Martin. *Ponderings VII–XI: Black Notebooks 1938–1939.* Translated by Richard Rojcewicz. Bloomington: Indiana University Press, 2017.
Heidegger, Martin. *The Principle of Reason.* Translated by Reginald Lilly. Bloomington: Indiana University Press, 1991.
Heidegger, Martin. *Sein und Zeit*, 7th Ed. Tübingen, Neomarius Verlag, 1946.
Heidegger, Martin. "Vom Ursprung des Kunstwerks. Erste Ausarbeitung." *Heidegger Studies* 5 (1989): 5–22.

Heidegger, Martin. *What Is Called Thinking?* Translated by F. D. Wieck and J. Glenn Gray. New York: Harper & Row, 1968.
Heidegger, Martin. "What are Poets For?" In *Poetry, Language, Thought*, translated by Albert Hofstadter, 89–142. New York: Harper & Row, 1971.
Heidegger, Martin and Eugen Fink. *Heraclitus Seminar (1966/1967)*. Translated by Charles H. Seibert. University of Alabama Press, 1979.
Landerer, Christoph and Marc-Oliver Schuster. "Nietzsches Vorstudien zur *Geburt der Tragödie* in ihrer Beziehung zur Musikästhetik Eduard Hanslicks." *Nietzsche-Studien* 31 (2002): 114–133.
Lines, David. "'Working With' Music: A Heideggerian Perspective of Music Education." *Educational Philosophy and Theory* 37, no. 1 (2013): 65–75.
Lysaker, John. "Heidegger's Absolute Music, or What Are Poets for When the End of Metaphysics Is At Hand?" *Research in Phenomenology* 30 (2000): 180–210.
Marx, Eduardo. *Heidegger und der Ort der Musik*. Würzburg: Königshausen & Neumann, 1998.
Nancy, Jean-Luc. *The Muses*. Translated by Peggy Kamuf. Stanford: Stanford University Press, 1996.
Otto, Deltef. *Wendungen der Metapher: Zur Übertragung in poetologischer, rhetorischer, und Erkenntnistheoretischer Hinsicht bei Aristoteles und Nietzsche*. Munich: Fink, 1998.
Perrin, Christophe. "De la musique avant toute chose? Heidegger compositeur." *Hermeneia* 14 (2014): 10–24.
Pöltner, Günther. "Mozart und Heidegger: Die Musik und der Ursprung des Kunstwerkes." *Heidegger Studien* 8 (1992): 123–144.
Puckette, Miller. "Not Being There." *Contemporary Music Review* 28/4–5 (2009): 409–412.
Richardson, William J. "Dasein and the Ground of Negativity: A Note on the Fourth Movement in the Beiträge-Symphony." *Heidegger Studies* 9 (1993): 35–52.
Richter, Goetz. "Silence as the Greatest Music: The Harmony of Philosophy and *Mousikê* in Plato's *Phaedo*." *Literature & Aesthetics* 19, no. 1 (2009): 88–113.
Rilke, Rainer Maria. *Das Buch vom mönchischen Leben, Das Stundenbuch*. Leipzig: Insel Verlag, 1905.
Scherzinger, Martin. "Heideggerian Thought in the Early Music of Paul Hindemith (With a Foreword to Benjamin Boretz)." *Perspectives of New Music* 43/44 (Summer 2005–Winter 2006): 80–125.
Schmid, Holger. *Kunst des Hörens. Orte und Grenzen der hermeneutischen Erfahrung*. Cologne: Bolnow, 1999.
Sheridan, Thomas B. "Descartes, Heidegger, Gibson and God: Toward an Eclectic Ontology of Presence." *Presence: Teleoperators and Virtual Environments* 8, no. 5 (1999): 549–557.
Sheridan, Thomas B. "Musings on "Music Making and Listening: Supervisory Control and Virtual Reality." *Proceedings of the IEEE* 92, no. 4 (April 2004): 601–605.
Shibles, Warren A. "Hanslick on Hearing Beauty." *Iyyun: The Jerusalem Philosophical Quarterly* 44 (January 1995): 73–89.

Small, Christopher. *Musicking: The Meanings of Performing and Listening.* Middletown: Wesleyan University Press, 1998.
Smith, F. Joseph. *The Experiencing of Musical Sound: Prelude to a Phenomenology of Music.* New York/Montreux: Gordon and Breach, 1979.
Smith, F. Joseph. (ed.) *Understanding the Musical Experience.* New York: Gordon & Breach, 1989.
Stahl, Gerry. "Attuned to Being: Heideggerian Music in Technological Society." Online. Last updated. 5 January 2004. http://gerrystahl.net/publications/interpretations/attuned.htm.
Thomson, Iain. "'The Philosophical Fugue: Understanding the Structure and Goal of Heidegger's *Beiträge.*" *Journal of the British Society for Phenomenology* 34, no. 1 (2003): 57–73.
Wallrup, Erik. "Music, Truth and Belonging: Listening with Heidegger." In *Philosophy of Music Education Challenged: Heideggerian Inspirations*, edited by Frederik Pio and Øivind Varkøy, 131–146. Dordrecht: Springer, 2015.

Part II

MUSICAL TRADITIONS OF THE WORLD

Chapter 5

Grand Style, Heidegger, Nietzsche
Elaborations of a Concept
Erik Wallrup

Unlike "grand style," the career of the contrasting concept of "late style" has been quite impressive during the latest century. Theodor W. Adorno forged the latter concept in the 1930s while he struggled with Beethoven's late music. A member of a younger generation of critical thought, Edward W. Said expanded the field to not only include composers such as Richard Strauss (at odds with Adorno) but also other arts. It is a critical concept, indeed: a concept for an aging culture. It is useful when understanding a situation where artful language falls apart, syntax is put under pressure, and something is formulated in between styles, in between passages, in between constellations of words or notes or color fields.

Today, the much more forceful grand style seems to be a much less attractive concept.[1] Matthew Arnold had reserved the term for the elevated poetic style, but if there is anyone who has formulated it in a way that still has a bearing on our culture, it is Friedrich Nietzsche. His main example of the grand style is the Palazzo Pitti in Florence—vast, severe, and mighty in its references to Roman architecture. It is bound to the will to power: "The highest feeling of power and sureness finds expression in a grand style."[2] Interestingly, Nietzsche holds that all the arts with one exception have tried to achieve this impressive style. That exception is music. In one of the earlier instances of "grand style" in Nietzsche's writings, a letter from 1886, he suggests: "that which is farthest from decadent taste is the *grand style*: among which the Palazzo Pitti counts for instance, but *not* the Ninth Symphony."[3] Again, Nietzsche demonstrates a distancing from music, with a strong candidate among musical works discarded. But Nietzsche's train of thought does not stop there. In the next sentence, he says: "The grand style as the greatest heightening of the art of melody."[4] Nietzsche finds no music that can be ranked as being in the grand style—neither Bach nor Beethoven and of course not Wagner—whereas the greatest heightening of the art of melody is a building. However, that does not exclude the sheer *possibility* of a musical work in the grand style; it just had not been composed yet.

Heidegger absorbed Nietzsche's skepticism about music during the 1930s, a critical view heralded in the early lectures on the phenomenology of religious life, where we find remarks on Augustine's notion *voluptas aurium* (the pleasures of the ear) and the dubious character of chant.[5] He had, though, collaborated with musicologists such as Wilibald Gurlitt and Heinrich Besseler during the 1920s, and Medieval music is mentioned as one possible field of phenomenological investigation in the *Natorp-Bericht*, but these preliminary projects were never realized.[6] Music had therefore been almost absent in Heidegger's writings and lectures until the 1930s, and when it turned up, Heidegger treated it with hostility. Since the publication of the Black Notebooks, we can detect the dislocations in Heidegger's thought, where his negative assessment of Wagner follows Nietzsche.[7] Wagner's attempt to repeat the festivities around the Greek tragedy with his *Gesamtkunstwerk* in Bayreuth is regarded as a monstrous activity in the lectures on Nietzsche. There are earlier tremors in the notebooks, where the racial theories of Wagner's are foregrounded in his criticism.

Heidegger's verdict is made in terms of essence. Music's essence does not allow a world to arise. Music is understood as vehemently emotional and mathematically calculable (a judgment echoing the early lectures on Augustine), and this circumstance makes it into the most modern of the arts in the era of machination. However, what Heidegger describes is actually a specific state of the art, and after the war, his outlook was to change slightly. A sign is an Angelus Silesius quotation in the lecture series *The Principle of Reason* from 1955 to 1956, describing Mozart as "The Lute Piece of God."[8]

Friends and former students have given witnesses of how Heidegger appreciated listening to music, especially Mozart, but also Bach and Haydn.[9] There is, however, one example of a much more intense relation to a musical work. In the beginning of the 1950s, Martin Heidegger traveled to Munich to listen to Carl Orff's music drama *Antigonæ*, not only once but twice. The return is noteworthy. It is Heidegger's friend Heinrich Petzet who tells the story (partly relying on Clemens Podewils[10]), but he also recounts that Heidegger became enthusiastic about a radio broadcast of Orff's *Carmina Burana*, lauding the interpretation of the conductor, Eugen Jochum.[11] This testifies to Heidegger's preference for musical works that are settings of texts, at least when not only savoring music. But there is more to find here that is again related to his reading of Nietzsche that could be described as works in the grand style.

THE CONFRONTATION WITH NIETZSCHE

Heidegger's confrontation with Nietzsche took place in different lecture courses during the period 1936–1945, in shorter theses and at seminars. In the two volumes of *Nietzsche*, which collect three of these lecture series, Heidegger describes his approach as an *Aus-einander-setzung*, which we can understand as putting two ways of thinking apart through a confrontation. Even if the *Nietzsche* volumes are Heidegger's readings of Nietzsche, his own thinking is drawn into the confrontation.

Heidegger treats Nietzsche as the fulfiller of metaphysics, the Western tradition of philosophy which Heidegger himself attempts to leave. Aesthetics has its own history in this process to be written, and Heidegger does so in an overview consisting of six basic developments: (1) the rise of great Greek art, appearing without ensuing theoretical reflection; (2) the treatment of aesthetic questions in Plato and Aristotle; (3) the birth of aesthetics as a discipline; (4) Hegel's aesthetics with its declaration of the end of (great) art; (5) Wagner's *Gesamtkunstwerk* with its theoretical underpinning; and (6) Nietzsche's declaration of the physiology of art as a reaction to nihilism, which had been ever-growing during history. Being the last important exponent of metaphysics, Nietzsche does not only fulfill this nihilistic development but also hints at the overcoming of nihilism. Here Heidegger also says what great artworks are: "they make manifest, in the way appropriate to works, what beings as a whole are, preserving such manifestation in the work"; art is great because it is an "absolute need," and therefore it must be "great in rank."[12]

It is important to recognize the double import of being included among the six basic developments. The inclusion means both being a part of a history of decadence after the Greek inception and having achieved something of weight in this history. In the passages on Wagner, the verdict sentenced by Heidegger is extremely harsh. The conception of the *Gesamtkunstwerk* is not only mistakenly founded upon music, but "it is the conception and estimation of art in terms of the very state to the point where it becomes the sheer bubbling and boiling abandoned to itself."[13]

When Heidegger elaborates Nietzsche's contribution to the history of aesthetics, the section on "the great style" is a central one. The great style is described as an antithesis to Wagner with a quotation from Nietzsche: "Farthest removed from the grand style is Wagner: the dissipatory character and heroic swagger of his artistic means are altogether *opposed* to the grand style."[14] In a dense passage, Heidegger establishes the character of greatness:

[T]he fundamental condition is an equally original freedom with regard to the extreme opposites, chaos and law; not the mere subjection of chaos to a form, but that mastery which enables the primal wilderness of chaos and the primordiality of law to advance under the same yoke, invariably bound to one another with equal necessity. Such mastery is unconstrained disposition over that yoke, which is as equally removed from the paralysis of form in what is dogmatic and formalistic as from sheer rapturous tumult. Wherever unconstrained disposition over that yoke is an event's self-imposed law, there is the grand style; wherever the grand style prevails, there art in the purity of its essential plenitude is actual.[15]

Heidegger points out that Nietzsche contends that this is not possible in music. There are many passages in his late works and in the *Nachlass* that corroborate this. Nietzsche famously contrasts Bizet's *Carmen* with Wagner's works, but even if the philosopher here is overflowing, he does not count *Carmen* among the works in the grand style. There are musical works with the pretention of being written in that style, but they only pretend to be so—either being untrue to the listeners or untrue to themselves.[16] Under the title of "'Music'—and the grand style," Nietzsche discards music from the grand style: it stands for the "counter-Renaissance," which is fulfilled in Romanticism as a counter-movement to classicism. Mozart is a "delicate and amorous soul," Beethoven the first Romanticist and Wagner the last one, "both instinctive opponents of classical taste, of severe style—to say nothing of 'grand style.'"[17] Yet, we must not forget Nietzsche's own words: "The grand style as the greatest heightening of the art of melody."

WHAT IS GREATNESS?

"Greatness" has become an awkward word, and "great" does not only appear in American presidential campaigns of late but also in nostalgic end-of-art theories. In "The Origin of the Work of Art," Heidegger explains that he only deals with "great art."[18] It might be possible to ridicule Heidegger for being a philistine concerning some of his judgments on art, but less amusing are his usages of the word in the field of politics. Here are two infamous examples.

Turbulence encloses the ending of Heidegger's 1933 Rectoral Address, where he willingly translates Plato in a violent fashion: "All that is great stands in the storm . . ."[19] Thanks to Derrida, we have an exacting penetration of the word *Geist*, spirit, with the Rectoral Address as its locus,[20] but in the speech, a less flagrant usage of different forms of greatness appears. One with reference to the great beginning in Ancient Greece: "The beginning has invaded our future. There it awaits us, a distant command bidding us catch up with its greatness."[21] Another one concerning will: "the constant decision between the will to greatness and letting things happen that means decline, will be the law presiding over the march that our people has begun into its future history."[22]

The following passage from *Introduction to Metaphysics* has been heavily disputed:

> In particular, what is peddled about nowadays as the philosophy of National Socialism, but which has not the least to do with the inner truth and greatness of this movement (namely, the encounter between global technology and modern humanity), is fishing in these troubled waters of "values" and "totalities."[23]

Of course, such words caused outrage when published in 1953.

Heidegger's usage of "greatness" has much—but, as we shall see, not everything—to do with his routes taken during the 1930s. Again, the Black Notebooks are of vital interest. Already on the first pages of his notes (Autumn 1931; the first notebook, probably from 1930, is missing), the reader can perceive the first upheavals. The perspective is always grandiose. The first instance is a short note on daring to choose "the great lone path."[24] Soon, Heidegger accuses himself of not having achieved "a Great enemy" with his first book—in a very Nietzschean way.[25] This can be seen as dramatic rhetoric, but when he writes that a philosopher in errancy is characterized as being in a "deep, uncanny, and thus at the same time great attunement," then it becomes obvious that we have to do with a dramatic mode of thought. That is soon underscored:

> The great difficulty of the new beginning: to let the voice exhort and to awaken attunement; but at the same time for the creating ones—to think all this in advance with clarity and to bring it into a creating concept. The exhortation exhorts humanity to its higher affiliation and deeper rootedness.[26]

Then in two short notes, he points out the relation both to the past and to the contemporary situation. First, he writes: "This uncanny knowledge of the possibilities of the past great one and the tasks of liberating and configuring the possibilities—and yet the equally powerful necessity of newly retracing the way oneself."[27] Then: "A great faith is passing through the young land."[28] We are only in the beginning of this huge and often shrill mass of pages, but we find the germs to both the notion of a history of being and Heidegger's decisionist choice to leave the lone path and to engage himself in politics. They are intertwined.

Despite the blunt character of the word "great" (or "greatness"), Heidegger includes it in some of the lists of keywords that ends almost every notebook. In themselves, these lists are surprising since Heidegger would later forbid the use of indexes in the *Gesamtausgabe*. The keywords have only indications for the most important passages, not for every instance of the word. In the notebooks, the keywords give orientation together with Heidegger's own references to different sections not only within the specific notebook but also between them. One of these instances, indicating the web of references, says: "*We must place ourselves back into the great beginning.*"[29] That is parallel to the demand in the Rectoral Address to ground the scientific and academic work in Greek philosophy. The demand is hortative. In one of the sections indicated, Heidegger answers the question: why one has to put oneself back in the great beginning, namely in order to find oneself in the position where "this greatness must come again, so that things can go to the 'end'—an end— which indeed can become a new great beginning."[30]

But what is "greatness"? Heidegger tries to answer that question many times in the Black Notebooks. One of the answers is: "An institution of beyng [*Seyn*] rooted in a self-grounded ground, an institution from which what strives to be a being must originate and which must remain a scandal to nonbeings."[31] Many years later he has reformulated himself: "Great is that which initiates in the inexhaustible of its essence and stays relieved from the hardship of effect."[32] These two different ways of understanding "greatness" give us a new perspective on the also politically awkward formulations on greatness. That which is great is grounded in its essence and it is bound to a non-metaphysical understanding of being. The last formulation by Heidegger above also seems to give a counter-statement to the most well-known formulation of Nietzsche on the "grand style": "Grand style originates when the beautiful carries off victory over the monstrous."[33]

MUNICH

And so, in the early 1950s, Heidegger went to Munich and two performances of Carl Orff's *Antigonæ*. Heidegger himself does not mention Orff in his works, but in the correspondence between them (five short letters from Heidegger have been published) Heidegger says that the performance is present to him twenty-two years later (1972). The circumstances around the actual letter are that Orff had sent a copy of the score to Heidegger, and the philosopher expresses his thanks for "the great gift" saying that he and his wife now can "listen closely to the whole into its particulars in its beauty and might, and repeatedly study it as well."[34] Heidegger's letters to Orff are not long, but he wants to be informed about performances of Orff's two other music dramas with texts related to Ancient Greece—*Oedipus* in Friedrich Hölderlin's translation and *Prometheus* in Aeschylus's Greek original. But even if the performance of *Antigonæ* goes without further mention, the sheer fact that Heidegger had went to Munich twice says something more. And the gift from Orff was "great." That is of course only a matter of speaking, a courteous phrase. Yet, Heidegger always chose his words with care, even in his most conventional letters.

The production of *Antigonæ* in Munich was something more than a standard one. The work had had its first performance in Salzburg in 1949 under awkward circumstances: there were only a few rehearsals, it was scheduled in the afternoon in order to allow the audience to be on time for the main attraction in the evening (Orff was even forced to cut the score since it was too long). The second production was in Dresden in 1950, with the comment from one of the leading critics that the work was asocial.[35] Only with the production in Munich in 1951 were circumstances good. The opera house was the Prinzregenten theater, which had been completed in 1901 as a theater especially for Wagner's operas, and built according to many of the composer's instructions for Bayreuth, such as the form of an amphitheater and a covered pit. These clearly Wagnerian traits did not disturb Heidegger.

There was an extraordinary resonance within the audience. Otto Pöggeler has pointed out that the production took place in a desolate Germany, now split into two different countries, after the years of devastating hubris: "Can someone, who like Antigone sacrifices herself, turn the times to something healing? About this turn or—as Heidegger said, *Kehre*—must a language speak that had gone through the most extreme disruptions and leave the familiar behind."[36] Petzet describes the import in historical terms:

> It had an effect not only primarily on the world of theatre; in its uniqueness, and even radicality, this performance also touched upon the issues pertaining to spiritual existence and matters of human insight, at a point in time when the openness of insecure humanity to essential claims had not yet been stifled by the approaching way of thinking that is devoted to prosperity.[37]

The only comment from Heidegger is delivered in second hand. After the first performance that he visited, he stepped up to the composer, grabbed his hands, and said: "Thank you for bringing ancient tragedy back to life. My name is Heidegger."[38] It is parallel to Heidegger's words on Stravinsky's *Symphony of Psalms* and *Perséphone*, describing both works as bringing back "age-old tradition to new presence," despite that they cannot "establish the place to which they belong."[39] The parallel depends on the movement back in history, to a beginning in the ancient Greek culture, which is brought forth again in modernity. It is not identical with (das Gleiche) but the same as (die Selbe) that which is past. It is not a coincidence that all works mentioned here are works where words are set to music, but also that they belong to works that in different ways have to do with the classical.

Is *Antigonæ* a great work of art according to Heidegger? The short answer is no. In "The Origin of the Work of Art," Heidegger had declared that it is no longer possible to bring about great works. They cannot, like the Greek temple or the cathedral in Bamberg, gather a world around themselves. They cannot make manifest what beings as a whole are. Yet, with his *Welttheater*, Orff had gathered an audience that was allowed to experience a world where brother stood against brother, where the tyrannical Creon forced the defiant Antigone to be buried alive, where the princess herself in vain tried to follow the rules of the gods but was crushed by the rules of man, whereas the king enforced his own rules and was crushed by the rules of the gods. He did not treat Hölderlin's translation as a libretto; instead, he put the poetic word at the center of his work, using the music as a way of underscoring, sharpening, and magnifying the words. Just as Heidegger himself, he had turned back to antiquity, to the beginning, with the help of Hölderlin, but not in order to follow the rules and forms of tragedy, but to allow tragedy to emerge once again. And yet, the performances did not mark a historical turning point. Germany went elsewhere, both Germanies.

If *Antigonæ* is not a great work, may it be a work in the grand style? There can be no doubt about Heidegger ranking Sophocles's play as a work written in the grand style. Orff turns to Sophocles, but he does not only repeat Sophocles' words. First of all, he uses Hölderlin's translation, bringing forth Greekness in the German language. Secondly, Orff presents a work in tones and words, or, to be more exact, in words and tones. *Prima le parole, dopo la musica*. It is clearly not the identical Antigone who speaks in these three works, but she is the same. The choir, which sings "The Ode on Man," sings in another way than the Greek choir, but it sings the same.

The Greek-German musicologist Thrasybulos Georgiades has pointed out that Hölderlin was not able to bring back the Greek world; when he translated ancient Greek into modern German he had turned "the sphinx-like stiffness" of ancient Greek into a "glowing stream" of a Western language.[40] What Orff does is not to repeat Hölderlin's words, but to reinterpret them: "The streaming force, the irresistible power of Orff's musical language—something that in itself contradicts the spirit of antiquity—is here used as a means for the creation of an Antigone valid today."[41] We must remember that Georgiades speaks from the perspective of his own notion of the ancient Greek language: that the words themselves had had an existence of their own, taking hold of the speaker. With the modern languages of the Western world, the subject speaks using the language as a tool. We can see the parallel to Heidegger's famous dictum: "*Die Sprache spricht* (language speaks)."[42] The main difference according to Georgiades is that this relation to language is something of the past, whereas Heidegger relates the true capability of language to his own thinking and to poets such as Stefan George and Georg Trakl.

How is language in *Antigonae*? The volume of words to be heard forces Orff to let it stream. He uses the whole of Hölderlin's translation, without deletions. But despite this stream of words, much of the music is rather static. Psalmodic recitation dominates, extending the notes on a higher pitch to underscore some of the keywords, or giving them flourishing ornamentation. The scoring is totally dominated by percussion, with 10–15 percussionists being asked for and the six grand pianos being treated as percussion instruments. The choice of percussion instruments has often been described in terms of the exotic: they include a lithophone, an African slit-drum, antique cymbals, Turkish cymbals, an anvil, and Javanese gongs. There are more defining instrumental groups in the soundscape: the only strings are nine basses, the wind instruments are grouped in flute, oboe and trumpet with six musicians in each section, and there are no less than four harps. The power is tremendous, you could even say over-powering. The impact on the listener is at least as powerful as that of Wagner, but to use Nietzsche's words, the music is not that of swimming, but of dancing—ecstatic dancing.

GRAND STYLE IN PAST AND PRESENT TENSE

There are some musical works or groups of works that aspire to the position of being in the grand style, some of them even to be great works of arts in Heidegger's sense. Wagner's *Gesamtkunstwerke* had the aspiration of being great artworks; that was Heidegger's trouble. With the Bayreuth festival, Wagner had been able to create a center for the cultural world of Germany, even of Europe; drawing on Norse and Germanic myth he had outlined a cultural-political rebirth. The National Socialistic appropriation of the festival was nothing but logical. But both Heidegger and Nietzsche were right: the transgressive aesthetics of Wagner excludes him from the grand style.

Wagner was not the first one with nation-building as an operatic aim. Already in the late eighteenth century, King Gustav III of Sweden accomplished a cultural revolution combined with his own political coup d'etat in 1772. He chose opera to be the means for the grounding of a Swedish nation, and since there were no prolific Swedish composers at that time, he called for Johann Gottlieb Naumann and Georg Joseph Vogler, while two other German composers went to Stockholm with the prospects of having a career in the northern kingdom, namely, Joseph Martin Kraus and Johann Christian Friedrich Haeffner. Noteworthy is that the king himself wrote the scenarios for the works, sometimes even with instructions for the character of the music. In that sense, Gustav III not only financed the projects, as King Ludwig II of Bavaria would do in his support to Wagner, but he gave also creative impulses to librettists, composers, set designers.

The reform opera of Gluck and Calzabigi served as a model, even if the Gustavian opera took its own path with its clearly nationalistic traits. In

Gustaf Wasa, the king's liberation of Sweden from Danish domination during the early 1520s was made into the nation-founding moment, with Naumann's music reaching heights he never came close to again. In Vogler's *Gustaf Adolf och Ebba Brahe*, the Swedish people, among them not only soldiers but also peasants, were allowed to be placed at the scene among king and noblemen—and folksong was introduced to Swedish serious opera. Preceding Hector Berlioz's *Les Troyens*, Kraus composed a six-hour work—*Aeneas i Cartago*—that combined his early *Sturm und Drang* with a powerful classicism, probing to master the yoke over chaos and law. Gluck's reform of opera started with works related to the royal sphere, but when it was placed in Paris in the 1780s, it heralded the revolution to come. A simplified notion of these works has labeled their classicism mild and relaxed, whereas the audiences at the time fell into tears by the operas' expressivity and Gluck's critics complained about the harshness and the force of his treatment of the orchestra.[43]

Georgiades has written a splendid book on the emergence of Western art music from the angle of musical settings of the mass.[44] Concerning older musical history, the choice of the mass has great merits, but when we turn to the period after 1600, then opera should be put in its place. The great watersheds in musical history have originated in operatic works when the relation between music and language has been renegotiated in recurring turns back to ancient Greek tragedy, beginning with the birth of opera and the Florentine Camerata, followed by Gluck's reform opera, and then Wagner's *Gesamtkunstwerk*. The notable German philologist Wolfgang Schadewaldt placed Orff as the fourth station in this series of developments.[45] The problem with his suggestion is that Orff never had any successors. His own works after *Antigonæ* go in the same direction, with *Oedipus der Tyrann* (1958), the even more archaic and brutal *Prometheus* (1968) and then the final *De temporum fine comoedia* (1973). However, one could find parallels between Orff and minimalistic opera, for instance, John Adams's *Nixon in China* where the mythological traits of Nixon and Mao can seem to come close to that of Antigone and Creon, or Philip Glass' *Satyagraha*, with its combination of current history and an old epic, *Mahabharata*. Yet while these American works may have repetitiveness in common with Orff, they have broken with the European roots back in Greek antiquity.

Another commencement is found in the music dramas by Wolfgang Rihm, with their rootedness in the European tradition (until its latest developments) and their new treatment of texts. He has turned to Hölderlin's translations of Sophocles in *Oedipus* (1987), but other texts are intermingled with the fragmented lines from the drama: on the one hand Nietzsche's early comments on Sophocles's play under the title *"Oedipus: Ein Fragment aus der Geschichte der Nachwelt,"* on the other hand Heiner Müller's poem *"Ödipuskommentar."* When Rihm was established as a composer in the early 1970s, he was put in the category of "new simplicity," and by that time the expressionism of his and his references to the Mahler and Bruckner tradition were enough to make him "simple." In his Oedipus opera, we find an energetic foundation that is put in conflict with a form that reaches its heights due to the conflict. Rihm is on his way to fragmentizing the scenes, the processes, and the text, but the dramatic form still holds, becoming a dramatized form. With its 1987 premiere in West Berlin, at the Deutsche Oper, it still witnesses the austere and pressing conditions of a divided Germany. We are far from the far more relaxed, but even more fragmented music drama that is *Dionysos* (2010)— again written in the German musico-philosophical mold, but now in a flow of fragments. Whereas the Oedipus opera is a work answering to the concept of grand style proposed here, the fluidity of *Dionysos* makes that opera into a Dionysian play with masks, sometimes gruesome, sometimes ironic—corresponding to Karl Heinz Bohrer's understanding of the aestheticism of Nietzsche's later Dionysos, ironic and ambiguous. Another version of the grand style,[46] maybe—or, rather, late style.

THE END

Greatness and grand style do not have an obvious resonance today. There seems to be more to say about less pretentious projects, focusing on practices on a much lower scale, forming networks of greater intimacy, spreading as the seeds of dandelion or the roots and shoots from the rhizome. In line with Heidegger's notes on Paul Klee, we can listen for the silences in Luigi Nono, the secret messages of György Kurtág, the breathing of Salvatore Sciarrino. It is music for the lonely and the few.

Yet, we find ourselves at a stage in history when the maltreatment of the earth has reached dimensions that endangers life itself, not only human life. The need of gathering, of solidarity reaching outside not only nations to humankind, but also to the non-human, becomes absolute. The greatness of such a project should not be understood in terms of vastness or magnitude, but as that which shows its essence. In one of his most apocalyptic moments during World War II, Heidegger wrote a passage in his notebooks that led to much controversy after its publication in 2014:

> Therefore, all imperialism is conjointly, i.e., in reciprocal increase and subsidence, pursued to a highest consummation of technology. The final chapter of this consummation will consist in the earth itself blowing up and the current humanity disappearing. That will not be a misfortune but, instead, the first purification of being from its most profound deformation on account of the supremacy of beings.[47]

The world did not blow up then, but we see it now slowly turning into desert. Heidegger's perspective lessened, and no more than ten years later, he seems to have left the grand, the great, and greatness behind: "The greatest risk is the same for the great ones as for the small ones, only in a different way, which both seldom take notice of. How does that come? Since both do not know the mild, which neither softly nor harshly gives away the richness of enowning."[48] Heidegger writes these words around a year before his travel to Munich. He sees the danger in that which is great and suggests that mildness has that which is missing. One can see his reaction to Orff's work as a relapse into an older position, which he has worked his way out from, or as a remembrance of something that was a manifestation of the rise against nihilism.

What would be great today? It is much easier to refer to practices of *Gelassenheit*, of works that stem from silence, of tones of mildness.[49] It may even be a relief that no music aspires to greatness or to the grand style. Can really a work of art be of any help when the desert grows ("Woe to him who harbours deserts"[50])? Or, to put it in Heideggerian terms: Can a work of art let truth happen in a situation such as ours? That can be doubted. But we should remember that when art does not have that pretention anymore, something else will.[51]

NOTES

1. However, some discussions of interest can be found in Claudio Magris's *L'anello di Clarisse: Grande stile e nichilismo nella letteratura moderna* (Milan: Einaudi, 1984) and Karl Heinz Bohrer's *Großer Stil: Form und Formlosigkeit in der Moderne* (Munich: Hanser, 2007).

2. Friedrich Nietzsche, *Twilight of the Idols*, trans. Richard Polt (Indianapolis: Hackett, 1997), 57.

3. Friedrich Nietzsche, *Sämtliche Briefe*, in *Kritische Studienausgabe*, vol. 7 (Munich: dtv, 1986), 176. My trans. If no reference is made to a translator in the footnotes, the translation is mine. The original texts are in these cases rendered in the footnote: "wovon ein Decadenz-Geschmack am entferntesten ist, das ist der *große Stil*: zu dem zum Beispiel der Palazzo Pitti gehört, aber *nicht* die neunte Symphonie."

4. Friedrich Nietzsche, *Sämtliche Briefe*, 176. "Der große Stil als die höchste Steigerung der Kunst der Melodie."

5. Cf. Martin Heidegger, *Phenomenology of Religious Life*, trans. Matthias Fritsch & Jennifer Anna Gosetti-Ferencei (Bloomington and Indianapolis: Indiana University Press, 2004), 161.

6. Cf. Rainer Bayreuther, "Musikwissenschaft: 'Phänomenologische Grundlegung' einer Disziplin," in *Heidegger-Handbuch: Leben – Werk – Wirkung*, ed. Dieter Thomä, 2nd ed. (Stuttgart and Weimar: Metzler, 2013), 510.

7. I elaborate on this in Erik Wallrup, "Against the Grain: Heidegger and Musical Attunement," in *An Interdisciplinary Approach to the Study of Mood*, eds. Birgit Breidenbach and Thomas Docherty (London and New York: Routledge, 2019), 202–217.

8. Martin Heidegger, *The Principle of Reason*, trans. Reginald Lilly (Bloomington and Indianapolis: Indiana University Press, 1991), 68.

9. Cf. Heinrich Petzet, *Encounters and Dialogues with Martin Heidegger 1929–1976*, trans. Parvis Emad and Kenneth Maly (Chicago and London: The University of Chicago Press, 1993), 16, 79; Martin Heidegger, *Erinnerung an Martin Heidegger* (Pfullingen: Neske, 1977).

10. Clemens Podewils, "Begegnungen mit Carl Orff," *Jahresring*, nos 70/71 (1970): 234–251.

11. Petzet, *Encounters and Dialogues*, 80.

12. Martin Heidegger, *Nietzsche*, 4 vols, trans. David Farrell Krell (New York: HarperCollins, 1991), vol. 1, 84.

13. Heidegger, Nietzsche, vol. 1, 88.

14. Heidegger, Nietzsche, vol. 1, 124.

15. Heidegger, Nietzsche, vol. 1, 128–129.

16. Friedrich Nietzsche, "The Case of Wagner," in *The Birth of Tragedy and The Case of Wagner*, trans. Walter Kaufmann (New York: Vintage, 2010), 188.

17. Friedrich Nietzsche, *The Will to Power*, trans. Walter Kaufmann and R.J. Hollingdale (New York: Vintage, 1968), 444.

18. Martin Heidegger, "The Origin of the Work of Art," in *Off the Beaten Track*, trans. Julian Young & Kenneth Haynes (Cambridge: Cambridge University Press, 2002), 19.

19. Martin Heidegger, "The Self-Assertion of the German University," trans. Karsten Harris, *The Review of Metaphysics*, vol. 38, no. 3 (1985), 470–480, cit. 480.

20. Jacques Derrida, *Éperons: Les styles de Nietzsche / Spurs: Nietzsches Styles*, trans. Barbara Harlow (Chicago: Chicago University Press, 1979).

21. Heidegger, "Self-Assertion," 475.

22. Heidegger, "Self-Assertion," 473.

23. Martin Heidegger, *Introduction to Metaphysics*, trans. Gregory Fried & Richard Polt (New Haven & London: Yale University Press, 2000), 213.

24. Martin Heidegger, *Ponderings II-VI: Black Notebooks 1931–1938*, trans. Richard Rojcewicz (Bloomington and Indianapolis: Indiana University Press, 2016), 7.

25. Heidegger, *Ponderings II-VI*, 8.

26. Heidegger, *Ponderings II-VI*, 12.

27. Heidegger, *Ponderings II-VI*, 20.

28. Heidegger, *Ponderings II-VI*, 21.

29. Heidegger, *Ponderings II-VI*, 40. Italics in the original.

30. Heidegger, *Ponderings II-VI*, 60.

31. Heidegger, *Ponderings II-VI*, 278. Heidegger's spelling of the German word for "being" with *Seyn* instead of *Sein* marks the difference between a being-historical understanding of being (as *Seyn*) and metaphysical understanding (as *Sein*), where

the former allows a thinking where being is given (or refused) in different ways in history.

32. Martin Heidegger, *Anmerkungen VI–IX (Schwarze Hefte 1948/49–1951)*, GA 98, (Frankfurt am Main: Klostermann, 2018), 31: "Groß ist, was in das Unerschöpfliche seines Wesens einweiht und der Not des Wirkens enthoben bleibt."

33. Friedrich Nietzsche, *Human, All Too Human*, trans. R. J. Hollingdale (Cambridge: Cambridge University Press, 1996), 334.

34. Martin Heidegger, letter to Carl Orff 21.12.1972, in: Pietro Massa, *Carl Orffs Antikendramen und die Hölderlin-Rezeption im Deutschland der Nachkriegszeit* (Frankfurt et al.: Peter Lang, 2006), 226: "das große Geschenk"; "das Ganze bis ins einzelne seiner Schönheit und Macht nachhören und es wiederholend gleichsam studieren."

35. Cf. Hellmut Flashar, *Inszenierung der Antike: Das griechische Drama auf der Bühne: Von der frühen Neuzeit zur Gegenwart* (München: Beck, 2009), 190.

36. Otto Pöggeler, *Schicksal und Geschichte: Antigone im Spiegel der Deutungen und Gestaltungen seit Hegel und Hölderlin* (München: Fink, 2004), 11–12: "Kann dadurch, dass jemand sich so wie Antigone zum Opfer bringt, die Zeit sich wenden zum Heilsamen hin? Von dieser Wende oder – wie Heidegger sagte – »Kehre« musste eine Sprache sprechen, die durch äußerste Erschütterungen hindurchgegangen war und das Gewohnte hinter sich gelassen hatte."

37. Petzet, *Encounters and Dialogues*, 16.

38. Petzet, *Encounters and Dialogues*, 162.

39. Martin Heidegger, "Über Igor Strawinsky" (1962), in *Denkerfahrungen 1910–1976* (Frankfurt: Klostermann, 1983), 113: "uralte Überlieferung zu neuer Gegenwart"; "den Ort zu stiften, an den sie gehören."

40. Thrasybulos Georgiades, "Zur Antigone-Interpretation von Carl Orff," in *Kleine Schriften*, ed. Hans Schneider (Tutzing: Schneider, 1977), 228: "[d]ie Sphinxhafte Starrheit," "in glühenden Strom."

41. Georgiades, "Zur Antigone-Interpretation von Carl Orff," 230.

42. Martin Heidegger, "Language," in *Poetry, Language, Thought*, trans. Albert Hofstadter (New York: Harper and Row, 1971), 198.

43. Jean-François Marmontel, *Essai sur les révolutions de la musique, en France* (Paris: Le Noir, 1777), 24.

44. Thrasybulos Georgiades, *Musik und Sprache: Das Werden der abendländischen Musik dargestellt an der Vertonung der Messe* (Berlin, Göttingen and Heidelberg: Springer, 1954).

45. Wolfgang Schadewaldt, liner notes to Carl Orff, *Antigonæ* (Deutsche Grammophon, DGG 138 717/19), 17.

46. Cf. Bohrer, *Großer Stil*, 225–235.

47. Martin Heidegger, *Ponderings XII–XV: Black Notebooks 1939–1941*, trans. Richard Rojcewicz (Bloomington: Indiana University Press, 2017), 187.

48. Martin Heidegger, *Anmerkungen VI–IX*, 72–73. "Daß Größe die Gefahr ist für die Großen gleichweise für die Kleinen, nur auf andere Weise, dessen achten beide zu selten. Woran liegt dies? / Weil beide die Milde nicht kennen, die weder weich noch hart den Reichtum des Ereignens weggibt."

49. On Heidegger, silence, and music, see the chapter by Trawny and de Morais in this volume and the second half of Zhu's chapter.
50. Friedrich Nietzsche, *Dithyrambs of Dionysus*, trans. R.J. Hollingdale (London: Anvil, 1984), 29.
51. The article is written in the author's project "The Affective Shift of Music in the Gustavian Era," financed by the Riksbankens jubileumsfond.

BIBLIOGRAPHY

Bayreuther, Rainer. "Musikwissenschaft: 'Phänomenologische Grundlegung' einer Disziplin." In *Heidegger-Handbuch: Leben – Werk – Wirkung*, 2nd ed., edited by Dieter Thomä, 509–512. Stuttgart and Weimar: Metzler, 2013.

Bohrer, Karl Heinz. *Großer Stil: Form und Formlosigkeit in der Moderne*. Munich: Hanser, 2007.

Derrida, Jacques. *Éperons: Les styles de Nietzsche / Spurs: Nietzsches Styles*. Translated by Barbara Harlow. Chicago: Chicago University Press, 1979.

Flashar, Hellmut. *Inszenierung der Antike: Das griechische Drama auf der Bühne: Von der frühen Neuzeit zur Gegenwart*. München: Beck, 2009.

Georgiades, Thrasybulos. *Musik und Sprache: Das Werden der abendländischen Musik dargestellt an der Vertonung der Messe*. Berlin, Göttingen and Heidelberg: Springer, 1954.

Georgiades, Thrasybulos. "Zur Antigone-Interpretation von Carl Orff." In *Kleine Schriften*, edited by Hans Schneider, 227–233. Tutzing: Schneider, 1977.

Heidegger, Martin. *Anmerkungen VI–IX (Schwarze Hefte 1948/49–1951): Gesamtausgabe* 98. Frankfurt am Main: Klostermann, 2018.

Heidegger, Martin. *Erinnerung an Martin Heidegger*. Pfullingen: Neske, 1977.

Heidegger, Martin. *Introduction to Metaphysics*. Translated by Gregory Fried and Richard Polt. New Haven & London: Yale University Press, 2000.

Heidegger, Martin. "Language." In *Poetry, Language, Thought*, translated by Albert Hofstadter, 187–210. New York: Harper and Row, 1971.

Heidegger, Martin. "Letter to Carl Orff 21.12.1972." In *Carl Orffs Antikendramen und die Hölderlin-Rezeption im Deutschland der Nachkriegszeit*, edited by Pietro Massa, 225–226. Frankfurt et al.: Peter Lang, 2006.

Heidegger, Martin. *Nietzsche, vol. I*. Translated by David Farrell Krell. New York: HarperCollins, 1991.

Heidegger, Martin. "The Origin of the Work of Art." In *Off the Beaten Track*, translated by Julian Young and Kenneth Haynes, 1–56. Cambridge: Cambridge University Press, 2002.

Heidegger, Martin. *Phenomenology of Religious Life*. Translated by Matthias Fritsch and Jennifer Anna Gosetti-Ferencei. Bloomington and Indianapolis: Indiana University Press, 2004.

Heidegger, Martin. *Ponderings II–VI: Black Notebooks 1931–1938*. Translated by Richard Rojcewicz. Bloomington and Indianapolis: Indiana University Press, 2016.

Heidegger, Martin. *Ponderings XII–XV: Black Notebooks 1939–1941*. Translated by Richard Rojcewicz. Bloomington: Indiana University Press, 2017.
Heidegger, Martin. *The Principle of Reason*. Translated by Reginald Lilly. Bloomington and Indianapolis: Indiana University Press, 1991.
Heidegger, Martin. "The Self-Assertion of the German University." translated by Karsten Harris. *The Review of Metaphysics* 38, no. 3 (1985): 470–480.
Heidegger, Martin. "Über Igor Strawinsky" (1962). In *Denkerfahrungen 1910–1976*. Frankfurt: Klostermann, 1983.
Magris, Claudio. *L'anello di Clarisse: Grande stile e nichilismo nella letteratura moderna*. Milan: Einaudi, 1984.
Marmontel, Jean-François. *Essai sur les révolutions de la musique, en France*. Paris: Le Noir, 1777.
Nietzsche, Friedrich. "The Case of Wagner." In *The Birth of Tragedy and The Case of Wagner*, translated by Walter Kaufmann, 153–192. New York: Vintage, 2010.
Nietzsche, Friedrich. *Dithyrambs of Dionysus*. Translated by R. J. Hollingdale. London: Anvil, 1984.
Nietzsche, Friedrich. *Human, All Too Human*. Translated by R. J. Hollingdale. Cambridge: Cambridge University Press, 1996.
Nietzsche, Friedrich. *Twilight of the Idols*. Translated by Richard Polt. Indianapolis: Hackett, 1997.
Nietzsche, Friedrich. *Sämtliche Briefe*. In *Kritische Studienausgabe*, vol. 7. Munich: de Gruyter, 1986.
Nietzsche, Friedrich. *The Will to Power*. Translated by Walter Kaufmann and R.J. Hollingdale. New York: Vintage, 1968.
Petzet, Heinrich. *Encounters and Dialogues with Martin Heidegger 1929–1976*. Translated by Parvis Emad and Kenneth Maly. Chicago and London: The University of Chicago Press, 1993.
Podewils, Clemens. "Begegnungen mit Carl Orff." *Jahresring* 70/71 (1970): 234–251.
Pöggeler, Otto. *Schicksal und Geschichte: Antigone im Spiegel der Deutungen und Gestaltungen seit Hegel und Hölderlin*. München: Fink, 2004.
Schadewaldt, Wolfgang. "Liner notes to Carl Orff." In *Antigonæ*. Deutsche Grammophon, DGG 138 717/19.
Wallrup, Erik. "Against the Grain: Heidegger and Musical Attunement." In *An Interdisciplinary Approach to the Study of Mood*, edited by Birgit Breidenbach and Thomas Docherty, 202–217. London and New York: Routledge, 2019.

Chapter 6

Heidegger, *Iki*, and Musical Resistance to *Gestell*

J. P. E. Harper-Scott

It has long been known that Heidegger's philosophy, particularly after the "turn," owes some debt to Eastern ways of thinking, which comprise what Reinhard May calls Heidegger's "hidden sources."[1] Irrespective of whether there might be ethical or professional concerns arising from any unacknowledged borrowing in Heidegger's later thinking, one useful consequence of viewing his later theoretical project partly from the perspective of a non-Western philosophical other is that it can shine a light on the potential in late Heidegger for an ideological critique of Western thinking that goes beyond his familiar antagonistic relationship to what he called "metaphysics," and reaches into something surprisingly close to Marxian theories of false consciousness. Although this might seem on the face of it a bizarre claim to make of a politically conservative philosopher, whose personal and intellectual links to political extremes seem to point entirely to the right rather than to the left, a broad similarity between the critical framework of Heidegger's philosophy of being and the radically leftist Adorno's critical theory—in which, for instance, Heidegger's "forgetfulness of being" (*Seinsvergessenheit*), "enframing" (*Gestell*), and "disclosure" (*aletheia*) bear uncanny resemblances to Adorno's analysis of rationalization, ideology, and the non-identical, however differently the two thinkers use them—suggests at least the possibility that thinking through such a connection with a "hidden Marxism" could, if it does not lead to distortion, be a fruitful endeavor.

Rather than argue for a "leftist" Heideggerianism directly, I aim to examine some of the ways in which Heidegger's points of contact with Eastern thought can provide an unexpected foundation for such an inquiry, not by arguing anything like what one might call an Eastern-determinist case against Heidegger's later thinking (i.e., that its special qualities are determined to some extent by his intellectual contact with Eastern thinkers and ideas), but instead by focusing on the suggestive but often contradictory relations between modes of thought that, in their simultaneous recognition and misrecognition of each other, enable a truth to emerge through a dialectical process of "disclosure" or *aletheia*. It focuses specifically on the relation between the later Heidegger's aesthetics and the *iki* aesthetics of the Japanese philosopher Kuki Shūzō, most extensively articulated in Heidegger's "Dialogue on Language Between a Japanese and an Inquirer," which he wrote in 1959.[2] Using Benjamin Britten's Japan-influenced later music (circa 1956–1973) as a case study, the chapter shows how certain kinds of music and music-making, which partly share the aesthetic commitments of Kuki and Heidegger, can bear witness to achievable forms of resistance to a *Gestell* that, I argue, largely overlaps with the ideology of late capitalism, the regulative idea which enframes being, and which the truth processes of both Kuki's and Heidegger's aesthetics subject to pitiless illumination.

A MUSICAL ENCOUNTER BETWEEN EAST AND WEST: BENJAMIN BRITTEN'S *CURLEW RIVER*

Curlew River, one of several works Britten wrote after a month-long trip to the Far East in 1955–1956, is (in a way which is roughly analogous to Heidegger's philosophy) a work whose European identity takes Japanese aesthetics and the practices of Nō theater as its constitutive other. Based on the Nō play *Sumidagawa* (*Sumida River*), Britten's opera is moved to an East Anglian setting, and its music is given European specificity by opening and closing with a plainchant of the Western Christian Church, the Compline hymn *Te lucis ante terminum* ("To thee before the close of day [creator of the world we pray]"). Perhaps the feature of the music that will strike the audience as being its most distinctive quality is the exceptionally high status it accords to melody. First, this chant, which provides the basic melodic material for the entire work, is used to generate the music's harmony by a simple process: the notes of the melody, sung "forwards" through time, are stacked "upwards" to form chords to accompany the melody. Emergence from the melodic total is the main "vertical" way that harmony is generated in *Curlew River*. But harmony also emerges, so to speak, *diagonally* through a process of heterophony that became a strong marker of Britten's later style. In this distinctive model of heterophony, individual musical actors go their own way, paying scant heed to the melodies, rhythms, dynamics, instrumentation, timbre, counterpoint, or harmony of any other parts of the music, and the actors are from time to time brought together by waiting for the other parts to catch up. These points of ligature Britten indicated with a birdlike symbol he called the "Curlew sign." The structure that binds together the musical personalities of the individual participants—that is to say, their melodies—is therefore not imposed from above but is generated from the bottom up, or to put it otherwise, is an immanent process.

The radicalness of this musical process should not be underestimated. The individual personalities whose independent musical identities create rather than being bound by a larger totality are, in an embryonic form, a glimpse of a society without ideology, without meter, tonality, harmony, without "tension" and "release," and without "norm" and "deviation." Britten's process of musical genesis in this work is an almost perfect instantiation of what Adorno claims to be the process of "subjectification" in music. The forms of harmony, meter, and so on are no longer simply accepted in their handed-down forms. They are subjectively generated by an immanent process of the music.

At certain times, as in the Madwoman's recitative "Near the Black Mountains there I dwelt," the larger world, both musical and dramatic, collapses into the subjective perspective of the individual. Flute, viola, double bass, and (later) horn, the only other inhabitants of the scene, create a solid but translucent musical space from the merest of materials presented in her wretched melody. At certain other times, though, the resultant schema constructs a more multi-perspectival world out of a single, heterophonically employed melody. This can be seen in the tutti in which the Madwoman is joined by the Traveller, Ferryman, and chorus tenors, all singing "like [the] Madwoman," as well as the flute, which plays "like the voices." Here, an individual's predicament is comprehended and communally felt, and this gives rise to a moment of solidarity that emerges from a dialectical process of growth. The only musical part that is not directly generated by the Madwoman's melody is the harp, which plays metrically and harmonically disconnected arpeggios, and this provides a schematic pole in dialectical opposition to the subjectivity of the other parts. In the dialectic of the moment, the harp's separation from the on-stage community provides a static, intermittently fluctuating schematic background, a context which confers, by its negation of the multiplicity of the counterpoint, a sense of wholeness or completion to the musical space. In the dramatic background of this moment there are certainly socially given concepts—of madness, loss, and grief—but the totality is determined not so much by those background concepts as by the foregrounded, subjective drive of the Madwoman's melodic expression. Rather than having its ideas poured into a pre-given formal vessel, here subjective content generates objective form.

Curlew River is, in a quite unexpected sense, a form of post-serial music where "the idea" of the row or any other kind of schema is no longer clear so that the totally rationalizing instinct that Adorno locates in New Music is absent.[3] The plainchant, the closest the piece comes to a determining "row," is as I have said an indication of where some of the materials come from, but it by no means determines everything, nor does a harmonic center, not even does anything as elementary as a sense of consonance or dissonance. *Curlew River* is a music of shadows, of uncertainty, but also of a gradually clarifying, and always a *social*, sense. The more we listen, the more the shadows reveal shapes and colors, and a new social organization begins to emerge.

The relocation of events from a Japanese to an East Anglian context is only one of the most obvious of this work's acts of translation. Just as important is the translation, into Britten's musical style, of aspects of Japanese *Gagaku* music—whose vertical projection of harmony out of a melody finds a parallel in *Curlew River*. But these acts of translation transform the target language, the symbolic network that to the casual eye might seem to capture and domesticate the foreign original. In "The Task of the Translator," Walter Benjamin asks: "What can fidelity really do for the rendering of meaning? Fidelity in the translation of individual words can almost never fully reproduce the sense they have in the original."[4] What he means by "the sense they have in the original" is partly articulated by the difference he draws between the German and French words for *bread*, respectively *Brot* and *pain*. In both cases, he insists, "what is meant is the same, but the way of meaning it is not."[5] The historical and cultural reality that congeals around *Brot*, namely the everyday existence of the German-speaking peoples, does not communicate the same reality as that of the French *pain*. This seems intuitively accurate, particularly from a Heideggerian perspective of being-in-the-world, and if the possibility of communicating something so simple as the essence of *bread* exceeds the capacities of a translator, how much more difficult is it in the case of an artwork? Ultimately, Benjamin suggests that this question implies a search for a smoothness of translation that would paradoxically close off rather than opening up communication:

> Our translations, even the best ones, proceed from a mistaken premise. They want to turn Hindi, Greek, English into German instead of turning German into Hindi, Greek, English . . . . The basic error of the translator is that he preserves the state in which his own language happens to be instead of allowing his language to be powerfully affected by the foreign tongue.[6]

In order to communicate the poetic meaning of an original, the historical and cultural information that is carried by a language's "way of meaning," a translation must do violence to the translating language, must cut the target language off from its own "way of meaning" in order to admit—by means of its dissonant strangeness—a hint of the way of meaning of the original. A translation must fail to translate something (the mere communication) if it is to succeed in transmitting something of the meaning. Lawrence Venuti explains Benjamin's theory in terms of a distinction between a "domesticating" strategy, that is, one that "turns Hindi into German," as opposed to a "foreignizing" one.[7]

To bring across a "true" account of what sounds fluid in the original, a translator must therefore, on this view, produce something rough-edged that brings us up short, a text that we struggle to hear either as operating in our own linguistic world or in that of an Other. It must gently break the signifying structure of the target language in order to make "both the original and the translation recognizable as fragments of a greater language, just as fragments are part of a vessel."[8] In translation, "everything" is the most pointless thing to communicate; what is needed is to communicate *nothing*—the nothing that the periods of "no acting" in a skilled Nō performance, can bring a world into being more powerfully than anything else—any of the dancing, singing, or speaking—in the artform. To make a space for the "nothing" to appear as part of the process of translating an encounter with an Other into a new form, it is therefore necessary to separate the Self, at least minimally, from itself. If a first essential purpose of Britten's (and, as I shall subsequently argue, Heidegger's) encounter with Japan is, therefore, to proclaim a minimal distance between the Western Self that is embodied in Britten's existing style, on the one hand, and the new Self that is revealed by a return to a subjectivity in which a fissure has been forced open on the other hand, then the second purpose is to ask what that encounter, and that newly created (or rather newly *discovered*) minimal distance, might mean for the world that has been fractured by its singing.

THE UNREALISTIC IDEALIST AESTHETICS OF *IKI*

The Japanese philosopher Shūzō Kuki, who is acknowledged as one of the leading figures—perhaps the leading figure—in Japanese aesthetics in the twentieth century, was also very exercised by the problems of translation, and in a way that relates closely to what has just been said. Kuki studied with Heidegger in the 1920s, before the writing of *Being and Time*, and the two exerted an ongoing influence on each other.[9] On his return to Japan, Kuki wrote the book for which he is most acclaimed, *Iki no kōzō* (*The Structure of Iki*, 1930), an often intensely Heideggerian reflection on traditional Japanese aesthetics and the term *"iki,"* which he takes to be its lodestar.[10]

But what is *iki*? Kuki's argument develops from the early observation that since *iki* does not exist in other languages, the assumption may be made that it is ethnically specific.[11] But even writing about it in Japanese involves him in a kind of "internal translation," because the term cannot be approached directly. Instead, he must explore its "intensional structure," that is, its identity as a mental content (here he is following the tradition of phenomenologists such as Husserl and, to a degree, the early Heidegger), and to do this he differentiates it from related words that swirl around and so delimit it. Only then can he examine its "extensional structure," its manifestations in the external world. Kuki's analysis makes the concept "foreign" in order to grasp it, in a similar manner to the way Heidegger performs a foreignizing translation of the concept of *being*. The foreignizing effect is of course doubled when the encounter with his thought is achieved from the outside, from the purview of Western consciousness.

Iki has three "moments": "The first, *bitai* ('coquetry'), constitutes the basic tonality of *iki*, while the following two—*ikiji* ('pride and honor') and *akirame* ('resignation')—define a people's ethnic and historical coloring."[12] The first quality, which he loosely defines as coquetry, "is a dualistic attitude" that places a sexual other "in opposition to the monistic self" and in so doing "posits a possible relationship between that person and the self."[13] The second and third facets are important to protect the possibility of this relationship as a possibility only, that is, to prevent it from achieving the fulfillment of a goal.

Kuki calls this quality of *iki* its "unrealistic idealism," its openly stylized presentation of gestures whose meanings are paradoxical, both stirring up the desire for a fulfillment, and its commitment never to lose the thrill by achieving it. Perhaps surprisingly, the potential of *iki* to be resistant to the circuits of capital—which in any case predates (for it was established in Japan before the forced opening of Japanese society to American economic imperialism in the nineteenth century)—begins dimly to appear. The goal of *iki* is thus, properly understood, not what it purports to be: not goal-orientated but practice-orientated: it is what Kieran Setiya (in an attempt to find a philosophical way around the inevitability of midlife crises) calls an *atelic* as opposed to a *telic* activity.[14]

To pursue this course requires both *ikiji* ("pride and honour") and *akirame* ("resignation"), which accounts for the interaction of the three moments of *iki*. Later in the essay, when he reflects on some artistic expressions of *iki* (part of its "extensional structure"), he makes remarks about *iki* in Japanese melodies. Despite their differences in specifics relative to Britten's musical style, his words indicate a certain overlap in attitudes to duality, tension, and resolution in music that can be described as exhibiting *iki*, whether in Japan or in Britain. The principle of *Curlew River* by which the entire texture is generated heterophonically by a rhythmically dislocated melodic presentation is, for instance, also an *iki* characteristic:

> We recognize that the instruments accompanying a melody establish the rhythm, and the melody thus sustains the rhythm. In Japanese music, in many cases, melodic rhythm and rhythm of accompanying instruments are not in step with one [an]other, thus causing a certain amount of variation between them. In

nagauta [long narrative songs], where narration is accompanied by *shamisen* [a three-stringed traditional Japanese musical instrument], both rhythms do match. In other instances in which both parts match rhythms, the melody imparts a sense of monotony. In music considered to represent *iki*, melody and accompaniment often deviate by as much as a quarter beat.[15]

The fundamental emphasis of this view of music is on a tension that does not resolve into identity with itself, all dislocations and divagations having been wrested back into order; it is a kind of music in which tension presents itself in such a way as to create a desire for resolution, but that is carried out in such a way that that resolution is avoided. Kuki is open to the possibility that *iki* may be found, in some form, in Western art and culture (he entertains the thought that it may exist in "certain melodies in the works of Saint-Saëns, Massenet, Debussy, and Richard Strauss"),[16] as long as the corollary of its untranslatability is remembered:

> Let us say, for the sake of argument, that *iki* is found in certain hypothetical cases in Western culture, and that such cases represent actual personal experience in exceptional circumstances.[17] Even then, the meaning is entirely different. In this case, *iki* is not manifested in the domain of the public as [the] meaning of an ethnic group. For a word to have a consistent meaning and value to a people, a linguistic path must be always open there. The fact that the West has no word corresponding to *iki* is itself evidence that the phenomenon of consciousness that is *iki* has no place in Western culture as a certain meaning in its ethnic being.[18]

So, *iki* may be found in Western culture, and yet it does not express in any way the meaning of the ethnic Westerner. The meaning that it carries cannot be expressed fully in the terms of the Western discursive situation, because on top of its domesticated meanings it is draped in an untranslatable, unnameable, almost unthinkable otherness. This thing, *iki*, which can penetrate "in exceptional circumstances" into a situation that cannot accommodate it, is a paradox: both in and perpetually outside of a situation, a part that does not fit into the whole. And yet if an artist like Britten can make it establish itself so firmly in this unaccommodating situation that the force of its strangeness can grow into something that can sustain its own artistic weight, and will not simply be dismissed as an ephemeral bit of Japonism, then *iki* can become more than just a thorn in the side of Western art. It can become a means by which a radically new cultural possibility, one which can pose a genuine ideological critique, can flourish.

HEIDEGGER, *IKI*, AND DIALOGUE

The perpetually "other" aesthetics of *iki*, in the hands of a European artist or philosopher, offer the possibility of a critique of identity thinking (in the language of Adorno) and metaphysics (in the language of Heidegger), that is, a mode of conceptually grasping the world as a totality that does violence to the object through forgetfulness of its being, or through forcing an object into a concept that it cannot fit without leaving a remainder.[19] There is nothing specifically Adornian about this perspective, which is central to Kant's critique of pure reason, nor is there anything specifically European about it. These ideas resonate strongly with the thinking of generations of members of the Kyoto School, a twentieth-century Japanese tradition of Buddhist thinking that has its origins in Nishida Kitaro's concepts of *basho* (場所, "place"), and more specifically *zettai mu no basho*, (絶対無の場所, "place of absolute nothingness"). This *basho* is not an empirically locatable "place" but rather a mediating process of thought, the dialectical moment itself, rather than the Hegelian *absoluter Geist* (absolute spirit) that emerges as its result and has a quality of *something-ness*. Tanabe Hajime prefers for this reason to speak of it as "absolute mediation" or "absolute dialectic."[20]

For Abe Masao, absolute nothingness (*mu*, 無) is defined as being "beyond subject–predicate judgement as such":[21] it is not possible, not even for the most fervent dogmatist, to say: "Absolute Nothingness is such and such." The term is thus "the ultimate predicate," "the predicate that is never a grammatical subject, cannot be subsumed by any superordinate predicate, and hence can never been determined or defined in any way."[22]

Heidegger's most detailed and ingenuous encounter with Japanese thought emerged through discussions he had throughout the 1920s (around the time of *Being and Time*) with Kuki Shūzō, himself sometimes considered a member of the Kyoto School. They center on the aesthetics of the Nō. In the essay "A Discourse on Language between a Japanese and an Inquirer," written in 1953–1954, Heidegger (represented by the figure of "an Inquirer," *I*) and Kuki ("a Japanese," *J*) delineate the relation of its aesthetic to the presencing of truth. *J* makes a fundamental distinction between the truth-disclosing art of Nō and realistic genres such as cinema or photography. The Nō, in contrast to the realism of Western cinema, does not attempt to present as mere objects the "suprasensuous" intimations of its heavily stylized gestures. Quite the opposite: its stylization is meant to emphasize its unrealistic idealism. And this, as Julian Young argues, is perhaps the most important difference to grasp between the two artistic worlds of which cinema and Nō might be considered poles:

> In a word—Rilke's word—Kurosawa's film, film and photography in general, is "opaque." It blocks thematization of anything other than beings, prevents

objects becoming, as one might put it, windows on to the "Other." It is purely representational, metaphysical. The pictorial, in this case, is not merely a possible "impediment to the breakthrough to the Origin" but an actual and absolute one. The Nothing never happens in Hollywood. . . . In the right conjunction of circumstances, the play allows "the Nothing," "the empty," to presence because emptiness is literally present: the stage is empty. Film, on the other hand, because it cannot avoid providing a denseness of naturalistic detail, cannot allow anything but objects to presence.[23]

Like Britten, Heidegger's engagement with Japanese aesthetics did not come only through direct contact (in Heidegger's case, with Kuki).[24] It came also from his reading of Zeami's treatise on Nō, the same one that *Curlew River*'s librettist, William Plomer, quoted at length in a letter to Britten, on the subject of gestures that produce a suprasensuous, unreal "excess" to the text which is the most beautiful and striking part of Nō.[25] Heidegger's Inquirer clearly saw in this aesthetic the possibility of grasping the ontological difference between being and beings that had been at the core of *Being and Time* and which provides the essential link to the later philosophy.

The Curlew River in Britten's opera, too, strikes a balance at times between the river as both a being and a bearer of being, and the duality of its most distinctive musical process—heterophonous generation of the totality from the subjective expression of melody—and its visual marker, the Curlew sign, epitomize this ontological difference. The being of the river is bound up with a connection between planes, the earthly one in which the action occurs and the heavenly one from which the Madwoman receives a saving grace. The Curlew sign itself symbolizes this beautifully. The sign indicates part of what follows from a perspective based on difference rather than identity: the things and beings of the world are separate, on their own course, but can be brought together through *waiting* for being to present itself. So, one performer waits until the others have aligned their temporality with his, or he has aligned his with theirs: there is no singular temporal perspective to confer a definitive answer. The meaning of these beings resides in their existence in-the-world, not just in their monadic identity, and in their failure to resolve the question of their temporal location—"am I ahead of? behind? faster than? slower than? the others." Through their interaction and surrender of identity is born a social world that is founded on care (Heidegger's *Sorge*).

What Heidegger calls being equates to the nothing that is communicated by what Zeami, in Plomer's quotation to Britten, means by the "unwavering inner strength" of the actor who does not "permit this inner strength to become obvious to the audience," because were that to occur, the inner strength "becomes an act, and is no longer 'no action.'"[26] An act is a being; no action is a presencing of being. But a substantial question remains: If the aim of Britten's art is to communicate this nothing, but (as Benjamin's argument makes clear) the nothing is exactly what is untranslatable, how is the project going to be aided by an encounter with the other?

An answer lies in the distinction Heidegger draws in *Being and Time* between *Rede* and *Gerede*, the authentic and inauthentic forms of language.[27] Being inauthentic does not mean being stupid or even especially "wrong" about something. On the contrary, inauthentic language, that is, "idle talk" or "gossip," is a normal part of what we do when we speak—especially when we are speaking in accordance with ideology. It is *Rede*, authentic talk or conversation, that gives Dasein a full disclosedness: "in disclosedness, . . . a world is opened up for us in the sense that we have a coherent way of being ready to respond to whatever we encounter as we go about our business."[28] In *Gerede*, by contrast,

> something gets communicated but in such a way that the parties cannot successfully participate in a shared orientation toward things in the world. There are a number of ways in which the participation can break down—a number of ways in which what is communicated cannot be put to work.[29]

Gerede, in short, does not disclose a world, and so does not make either the speaker or the listener "conversant" with the meaning of what is being said. *Gerede* is something like a translation, which permits a great deal to be communicated, but not conversance with or acculturation to particular historicity. In fact, *Gerede* may allow for an extremely well-developed capacity to do something, but a worldly *understanding* will still be lacking.

Ideology's noose is tight, but while it cannot be taken off, it can at least be loosened. The first step is to realize when we are talking *Gerede*, to thematize the fact that the terms we are using do not fit the reality of the world, and do not equip us to act in it in the right way when we encounter the difficulties that it presents us with. Surrendering the monadic identity of the Self in order to view one's own ideology from the essentially different, and ultimately inaccessible, position of the Other is perhaps one of the best hopes there is for taking the leap into this acknowledgment. The *Gerede* that is the limit of Britten's engagement with Japanese aesthetics—which are untranslatable, must be "foreignized," which "define a people's ethnic and historical coloring,"[30] and so on—this *Gerede* about the Other can ultimately enable a *Rede* about the Self.

ART AND THINKING AS FOCAL PRACTICES

Because we live in a perfectly commodified world, in which everything appears to consciousness as already pre-digested in relation to the commodity form (a thing is either a commodity, a producer, or a consumer), *Gerede* is the normal way we talk about our world. The task of philosophers, Marx famously remarked, is not simply to interpret the world but to change it.[31] Today a better aim might be not to change it but to *disclose* it. Change is what capitalism does, in its constantly evolving motion; but since it depends on a *Gerede* that conceals its real motive forces, capitalism never discloses a world. Heidegger argues that it is in the "enframing" (*Gestell*) of the modern (i.e., the late capitalist) world that everything appears simply as a "resource" (*Bestand*), and is shorn of any individual meaning or being that is proper to it. Indeed, Heidegger might easily have written Marx's observation that

> Whatever the social form of wealth may be, use-values always have a substance of their own, independent of that form. One can not tell by the taste of wheat whether it has been raised by a Russian serf, a French peasant or an English capitalist. Although the object of social wants and, therefore, mutually connected in society, use-values do not bear any marks of the relations of social production.[32]

The resource, the commodity, does not make its world perspicuous; it conceals the relations between people in the world behind the form of appearance as an exchangeable resource. In such a world, things appear only as fulfilling immediate desires, or failing to do so.

It is for this reason that "only a god can save us"[33] from the destitution of our world, but it is difficult to let one back in because the draw of technology is so great. Yet there is hope: there are ways we can learn to focus on things in a way that discloses a world, so that we can create, through a resilient refusal to submit to *Gerede*, a new world in which humans can "dwell." For Albert Borgmann, a philosopher much influenced by Heidegger's thoughts on technology and the enframing, the way out of the quagmire is to learn to resist "the device paradigm," to locate "focal things," and to participate in "focal practices."[34] On Borgmann's analysis, technology makes the ends of enjoyment (the ends that a capitalist, un-disclosed world focuses on to the exclusion of the truth of being) available as efficiently as possible by guaranteeing four essential qualities: instantaneousness, ubiquity, safety, and ease. For instance, the basic human requirement for heat used to be satisfied by a fire, but a fire satisfies none of those requirements. Central heating, by contrast, does. Central heating provides heat at the flick of a switch (whereas a stove requires wood to be collected and chopped); it provides heat in every room (rather than just the one with the hearth); it is safe (and does not put people, or houses, in danger of burning); and is easy (requiring no skills in chopping, starting a fire, stoking, or cleaning afterward). The technological promise of efficient provision of social ends is "the device paradigm," and things in the world are judged by their fit with it. Standing over against devices, the objects that efficiently satisfy our ideologically created needs, are *things*, and as they do for Heidegger, they "thing":[35]

> In calling forth a manifold engagement, a thing necessarily provides more than one commodity. Thus a stove used to furnish more than mere warmth. It was a *focus*, a hearth, a place that gathered the work and leisure of a family and gave the house a center. Its coldness marked the morning, and the spreading of its warmth the beginning of the day. It assigned to the different family members tasks that defined their place in the household. The mother built the fire, the children kept the firebox filled, and the father cut the firewood. It provided for the entire family a regular and bodily engagement with the rhythm of the seasons that was woven together of the threat of cold and the solace of warmth, the smell of wood smoke, the exertion of sawing and of carrying, the teaching of skills, and the fidelity to daily tasks. These features of physical engagement and of family relations are only first indications of the full dimensions of a thing's world.[36]

A fire thus described is "deep," because "all or most of its physically discernible features are finally significant"; central heating is "shallow," like every device, because "technology takes a shallow view of things and so begins their conversion into resources or devices."[37] The question of whether a focal practice is merely something that allows someone to "enjoy a bit of the simple life for a change," but effects no real change to their situation, depends entirely on context, on whether it is *Rede* or *Gerede*. Whatever the focal practice may be, it is always going to be subjected to the tyranny of the techno-capitalist enframing; the way to prevent this enframing from winning, and to enable the focal practice to open a world for dwelling, is "through *the practice of engagement.*"[38] For a new world to emerge from the ashes of our godless age (in Heidegger's sense),[39] focal practices need to become a way of life: such practices must not only "momentarily light up our life," like the homemade sourdough bread that makes the bourgeois dinner party swankier, but must "order and orient it focally" throughout.[40] Only in this way can the focal practice be defended against the assault of the enframing and our own natural tendency to take the efficient route of the non-world-disclosure of *Gerede*. This "practice of engagement" in respect of a focal practice is what Heidegger calls "preservation" and "repetition," particularly in relation to artworks.[41] Preserving an artform that reveals the being of beings is what protects a focal thing, such as an opera, from being subverted by the reifying, commodifying pressures of technology and being entirely lost. As Adorno would remind us, everything, even *Moses und Aron*, is already commodified before we can encounter it, and cannot escape but can only resist this fate.[42] And as Slavoj Žižek would add, even our own DNA and biological existence are nowadays already commodified.[43] But preserving and repeating the elements in the focal practice—the art of critical listening, the close analytical attention to a score, the quiet contemplation as an audience member, even—yes!—the darkness of the auditorium and the reverential silence at Bayreuth—this preservation and repetition, like a holy rite, "here and now and in little things . . . foster the saving power in its increase."[44]

This, then, is my argument about Britten's later music, the music that followed his engagement with Japan, and the possibility it still holds out, if it is engaged with thoughtfully and with a determination to be critical about his and our Western ideology, in a spirit moved equally by a left–right spectrum of German philosophy (Adorno and Heidegger), Buddhist philosophy (the Kyoto School), and the *iki* aesthetics of Britten's later music of absolute nothingness. In his later music, Britten found a way of honing a focal practice by writing a ritual music that discloses a new kind of world by gazing at itself from the perspective of the other. *Curlew River*'s mode of attack on ideology is not frontal but askance; rather than envisaging a wholly new musical technique, it refuses to give up on what can be resurrected from pre-capitalist forms of musical community-building—a pre-capitalist world which the pre-capitalist traditional aesthetics of Japan showed up to Britten—in a parallax view—as possibilities from his own historicity in a powerful new way. The practice of the work, the style of its construction, and the quiet *iki* aesthetic of the whole are some of the ways that it attempts to countermand the *telic* desires of the capitalist present, to make musical performance and listening into an *atelic* activity of sorts. As we wait for a return of Heidegger's gods, it offers a gently smoldering hearth light by which we can see disclosed a subjective truth that is obscured by an enframing false consciousness.

NOTES

1. Reinhard May, *Heidegger's Hidden Sources: East Asian Influences on His Work* (London: Routledge, 1996).

2. Martin Heidegger, "A Dialogue on Language Between a Japanese and an Inquirer," in *On the Way to Language*, trans. Peter D. Hertz (New York: Harper & Row, 1971), 1–54.

3. Cf. Adorno's argument in "The Aging of the New Music," in *Essays on Music*, ed. Richard Leppert, trans. Susan H. Gillespie (Berkeley and London: University of California Press, 2002), 181–202.

4. Walter Benjamin, "The Task of the Translator," in *Selected Writings*, ed. Marcus Bullock and Michael W. Jennings (Cambridge, MA and London: Belknap Press of Harvard University Press, 1996), 259.

5. Walter Benjamin, *Selected Writings*, ed. Marcus Bullock and Michael W Jennings (Cambridge, MA and London: Belknap Press of Harvard University Press, 1996), 257.

6. Quoted in Benjamin, "The Task of the Translator," 261–2.

7. Lawrence Venuti, *The Translation Studies Reader* (London: Routledge, 2000), 12.

8. Benjamin, "The Task of the Translator," 260.

9. For a conspectus of views on their relationship, see Chinatsu Kobayashi, "Heidegger, Japanese Aesthetics and the Idea of a 'Dialogue' between East and West," in *Migrating Texts & Traditions*, ed. William Sweet (Ottawa: University of Ottawa Press, 2012), 121–53; Michael F. Marra, "On Japanese Things and Words: An Answer to Heidegger's Question," *Philosophy East and West*, 54/4 (2004), 555–68; Michael F. Marra, "A Dialogue on Language between a Japanese and an Inquirer: Kuki Shūzō's Version," in *Neglected Themes and Hidden Variations*, ed. Victor Sōgen Hori and Melissa Anne-Marie Curley (Nagoya: Nanzan Institute for Religion and Culture, 2008), 56–77; and Graham Parkes, afterword to Heidegger's Hidden Sources: East Asian Influences on His Work, by Reinhard May (London, Routledge, 1996), 79–117.

10. This is translated, with critical essays that attempt to separate Kuki somewhat from Heidegger, in Hiroshi Nara, *The Structure of Detachment: The Aesthetic Vision of Kuki Shūzō* (Honolulu: University of Hawai'i Press, 2004).

11. Shūzō Kuki, "The Structure of Iki," in *The Structure of Detachment: The Aesthetic Vision of Kuki Shūzō*, ed. and trans. Hiroshi Nara (Honolulu: University of Hawai'i Press, 2004), 13. By way of expanding this point he adds, and Benjamin would agree with him, that "the meanings of the Latin *caesar* and the German *Kaiser* are clearly different" and that "certain meaning and language may not exist for another ethnic group when it does not possess that same experience at its core" (Kuki, "The Structure of Iki," 15.).

12. Kuki, "The Structure of Iki," 22.

13. Kuki, "The Structure of Iki," 19.

14. Kieran Setiya, "The Midlife Crisis," *Philosophers' Imprint* 14/31 (2014): 12. Telic and atelic refer to the Greek word *telos*, meaning "end."

15. Kuki, "The Structure of Iki," 52–3.

16. Kuki, "The Structure of Iki," 58.

17. Such an exceptional circumstance might be, say, Britten's engagement with Japanese Nō theater.

18. Kuki, "The Structure of Iki," 59.

19. Theodor W. Adorno, *Negative Dialectics*, trans. E. B. Ashton (London: Routledge, 1973), 5.

20. Hajime Tanabe, *Philosophy as Metanoetics*, trans. James W. Heisig (Berkeley, Los Angeles, and London: University of California Press, 1986), 23.

21. Masao Abe, "The Logic of Absolute Nothingness, As Expounded by Nishida Kitarō," *The Eastern Buddhist*, New Series/2 (1995), 172.

22. Abe, "The Logic of Absolute Nothingness," 172.

23. Julian Young, *Heidegger's Philosophy of Art* (Cambridge: Cambridge University Press, 2001), 149–50.

24. Heidegger was in fact invited to take up a three–year position as visiting professor on Tokyo, beginning in 1924, but declined the opportunity. As Parkes notes, "The possibility that *Being and Time* might have been written in Tokyo surely boggles the mind" Parkes, afterword, 92.

25. *I* notes that he has read Oscar Benl's German edition of Zeami, which was published in 1953: Heidegger, "Dialogue on Language," 17. Plomer's letter to Britten, 25 July 1963, is held in Britten–Pears Foundation archive. Zeami Motokiyo (1363–1443) was the most important figure in the history of Nō aesthetics.

26. Plomer to Britten, op. cit.

27. Martin Heidegger, *Being and Time*, trans. John Macquarrie and Edward Robinson (New York, NY: Harper & Collins, 1962).

28. Mark A. Wrathall, *Heidegger and Unconcealment: Truth, Language, and History* (New York: Cambridge University Press, 2011), 107.

29. Wrathall, *Heidegger and Unconcealment*, 111.

30. Kuki, "The Structure of Iki," 21.

31. Karl Marx, "Theses on Feuerbach," in *Karl Marx: Selected Writings*, ed. David McLellan (Oxford: Oxford University Press, 1977), 158.

32. Karl Marx, *A Contribution to the Critique of Political Economy*, trans. by N. I. Stone (Chicago: Charles H. Kerr, 1904), 20.

33. Heidegger said this famously in Martin Heidegger, "'Only a God Can Save Us': The Spiegel Interview (1966)," in *Heidegger: The Man and the Thinker*, ed. Thomas Sheehan (Brunswick, NJ: Transaction Publishers, 1981), 45–67.

34. Albert Borgmann, *Technology and the Character of Contemporary Life: A Philosophical Inquiry* (Chicago: University of Chicago Press, 1984).

35. Martin Heidegger, "The Thing," in *Poetry, Language, Thought*, ed. Albert Hofstadter (New York: Perennial, 2001), 161–84.

36. Borgmann, *Technology and the Character of Contemporary Life*, 41–2.

37. Borgmann, *Technology and the Character of Contemporary Life*, 191–2.

38. Borgmann, *Technology and the Character of Contemporary Life*, 207.

39. Wallrup discusses Heidegger's notion of god, art, and the loss of the gods in his chapter of this volume.

40. Borgmann, *Technology and the Character of Contemporary Life*, 207.

41. See Martin Heidegger, "The Origin of the Work of Art," in *Off the Beaten Track*, ed. Julian Young and Kenneth Haynes (Cambridge: Cambridge University Press, 2002), 1–56.

42. Theodor W. Adorno, "On the Social Situation in Music," in *Essays on Music*, ed. Richard D. Leppert, trans. Susan H. Gillespie (Berkeley: University of California Press, 2002), 391–436.

43. Slavoj Žižek, *First as Tragedy, Then as Farce* (London: Verso, 2009), 91.

44. Heidegger, "Only a God Can Save Us," 33.

BIBLIOGRAPHY

Abe, Masao. "The Logic of Absolute Nothingness, As Expounded by Nishida Kitarō." *The Eastern Buddhist* 28, no. 2 (1995): 167–74.
Adorno, Theodor W. "The Aging of the New Music." In *Essays on Music*, edited by Richard Leppert and translated by Susan H. Gillespie, 181–202. Berkeley and London: University of California Press, 2002.
Adorno, Theodor W. *Negative Dialectics*. Translated by E. B. Ashton. London: Routledge, 1973.
Adorno, Theodor W. "On the Social Situation in Music." In *Essays on Music*, edited by Richard D. Leppert and translated by Susan H. Gillespie, 391–436. Berkeley: University of California Press, 2002.
Benjamin, Walter. "The Task of the Translator." In *Selected Writings, Volume I: 1913–1926*, edited by Marcus Bullock and Michael W. Jennings, 253–63. Cambridge, MA, and London: The Belknap Press of Harvard University Press, 1996.
Borgmann, Albert. *Technology and the Character of Contemporary Life: A Philosophical Inquiry*. Chicago: University of Chicago Press, 1984.
Correspondence from William Plomer to Benjamin Britten, 25 July 1963, Britten–Pears Foundation Archive, The Red House, Aldeburgh, Suffolk, England.
Heidegger, Martin. *Being and Time*. Translated by John Macquarrie and Edward Robinson. New York, NY: Harper & Collins, 1962.
Heidegger, Martin. "A Dialogue on Language Between a Japanese and an Inquirer." In *On the Way to Language*, translated by Peter D. Hertz, 1–54. New York: Harper & Row, 1971.
Heidegger, Martin. "'Only a God Can Save Us': The Spiegel Interview (1966)." In *Heidegger: The Man and the Thinker*, edited by Thomas Sheehan, 45–67. Brunswick, NJ: Transaction Publishers, 1981.
Heidegger, Martin. "The Origin of the Work of Art." In *Off the Beaten Track*, edited by Julian Young and Kenneth Haynes, 1–56. Cambridge: Cambridge University Press, 2002.
Heidegger, Martin. "The Thing." In *Poetry, Language, Thought*, edited by Albert Hofstadter, 161–84. New York: Perennial, 2001.
Kobayashi, Chinatsu. "Heidegger, Japanese Aesthetics and the Idea of a 'Dialogue' between East and West." In *Migrating Texts & Traditions*, edited by William Sweet, 121–53. Ottawa: University of Ottawa Press, 2012.
Kuki, Shūzō. "The Structure of Iki." In *The Structure of Detachment: The Aesthetic Vision of Kuki Shūzō*, translated and edited by Hiroshi Nara, 13–94. Honolulu: University of Hawai'i Press, 2004.
Marra, Michael F. "A Dialogue on Language between a Japanese and an Inquirer: Kuki Shūzō's Version." In *Neglected Themes and Hidden Variations*, edited by Victor Sōgen Hori and Melissa Anne-Marie Curley, 56–77. Nagoya: Nanzan Institute for Religion and Culture, 2008.
Marra, Michael F. "On Japanese Things and Words: An Answer to Heidegger's Question." *Philosophy East and West* 54, no. 4 (2004): 555–68.

Marx, Karl. *A Contribution to the Critique of Political Economy*. Translated by N. I. Stone. Chicago: Charles H. Kerr, 1904.

Marx, Karl. "Theses on Feuerbach." In *Karl Marx: Selected Writings*, edited by David McLellan, 156–8. Oxford: Oxford University Press, 1977.

May, Reinhard. *Heidegger's Hidden Sources: East Asian Influences on His Work*. London: Routledge, 1996.

Parkes, Graham. Afterword to Heidegger's Hidden Sources: East Asian Influences on His Work, by Reinhard May (London, Routledge, 1996), 79–117.

Setiya, Kieran. "The Midlife Crisis." *Philosophers' Imprint* 14, no. 31 (2014): 1–18.

The Structure of Detachment: The Aesthetic Vision of Kuki Shūzō. Translated and edited by Hiroshi Nara. Honolulu: University of Hawai'i Press, 2004.

Tanabe, Hajime. *Philosophy as Metanoetics*. Translated by James W. Heisig. Berkeley, Los Angeles, and London: University of California Press, 1986.

Venuti, Lawrence. *The Translation Studies Reader*. London: Routledge, 2000.

Wrathall, Mark A. *Heidegger and Unconcealment: Truth, Language, and History*. New York: Cambridge University Press, 2011.

Young, Julian. *Heidegger's Philosophy of Art*. Cambridge: Cambridge University Press, 2001.

Žižek, Slavoj. *First as Tragedy, Then as Farce*. London: Verso, 2009.

Chapter 7

The "Silent Music" in Ancient Chinese Thought and Heidegger's Sound of Stillness

Qinghua Zhu

In ancient Chinese thought, the highest and purest music is said to be "the Grand Music" (大乐) or the "music of Heaven" (天乐), which is, mysteriously enough, silent. This notion of music is recorded in the ancient Chinese classic *Liji* (*The Book of Rites*), a collection of texts describing the ceremonies of the Zhou Dynasty (1046 BC–256 BC), written during a period that started during the Warring States and continued up until the former Han period (fifth century BCE–8 CE). *Yueji* (Record of Music) is an important chapter of the *Liji* in that it is believed that the music theory elaborated in this chapter is "the inheritance of the Six Dynasties,"[1] that is, a theory that dates back to as early as the beginning of the history of China. This text survived the "Burning of the Books" of the Qin Dynasty in 213 BCE and became the origin and source of many Chinese musical theories. Indeed, *Yueji* showcases the main ideas that undergird ancient Chinese music theory, which established the foundation for the creation and appreciation of music in China for more than two thousand years. It represents both the basic understanding of music in the two great Chinese traditions of Confucianism and Taoism, as well as of several other main schools of Chinese thought.

In *Yueji*, it is said, "Music is (thus) the production of the modulations of the voice, and its source is in the affections of the mind as it is influenced by (external) things."[2] Music comes into being when the human spirit is stimulated and affected by the outside world through sounds. The human capacity for joy and sorrow can make the sounds come forth differently, as in ways that induce happiness or sadness. Although it seems that music is triggered by outside stimuli on the human spirit and "all the modulations of the voice arise from the mind,"[3] this does not mean that music is merely the expression of subjective feelings, nor is it derived from the subject's affections or made to be subsidiary to our human affections. In order to clarify this, *Yueji* distinguishes between three levels of concepts: sound, modulations of sound, and music: "Hence, even beasts know sound, but not its modulations; and the masses of the common people know the modulations, but they do not know music. It is only the *junzi* (the noble man) who can (really) know music."[4] Birds and animals can make sounds to express feelings when they are stimulated, but only human beings can change sounds and voices according to certain rules to make modulations, in which sounds respond to each other. At the highest level, though, the *junzi* can listen to and hear the trends or "airs" of the age manifested in music: "Hence, the airs of an age of good order indicate composure and enjoyment. The airs of an age of disorder indicate dissatisfaction and anger."[5] From the air released by the music, the *junzi* can judge if the governance is good or evil.

Music bears the trends or the airs of an age because the origin of music is "the harmony between Heaven and earth (天地之和)."[6] And the original music is referred to as the Grand Music or the Music of Heaven.[7] The original music echoes the natural harmony between Heaven and earth, which is expressed in natural generation and declination in four seasons:

> The breath (or influence) of earth ascends on high, and that of Heaven descends below. These in their repressive and expansive powers [*yin* and *yang*][8] come into mutual contact, and, Heaven and earth act on each other. [The susceptibilities of nature] are roused by the thunder, excited by the wind and rain, moved by the four seasons, and warmed by the sun and moon; and all the processes of change and growth vigorously proceed. Thus, it was that music was framed to indicate the harmonious action of Heaven and earth.[9]

Heaven and earth shake each other: the sound of thunder vibrates; the air and rain moisten; the sun shines; the four seasons flow; all things grow and decline. The Grand Music arises from the same harmony and is involved in the same order and timing.

> There is Heaven above and earth below, and between them are distributed all the (various) beings with their different (natures and qualities) . . . Heaven and earth flow forth and never cease, and by their united action (the phenomena of) production and change ensue in accordance with this music arose.[10]

We can understand the original music generally as the overarching harmony of the movements.

From a more detail-oriented perspective, though, the "harmony" (和) of music has several layers of meaning.[11] First, the Grand Music arises from the harmony in the conflicting and unifying of Heaven (embodying *yang*) and earth (embodying *yin*). This harmony is the source of generation and growth of all things in nature. Second, it has to do with emotional and spiritual harmony as indicated by happiness and pleasure. Music attunes the moods of the people and the harmony of music modulates to a gentle and moderate state of mind, which promotes the virtue of their character. From this understanding, music is related to benevolence and love, which leads us to the third point, namely, that equilibrium and harmony are the highest state of mind, that is, the most valuable virtue of character.[12] Thus, if we combine all three, we can see how the Grand Music is linked with harmony, which is a virtue, which is thereby linked with equilibrium. Moreover, this equilibrium or state of harmony can be understood on an individual level or on a communal level. Communally, music, together with ceremonies (*Li*, 礼),[13] prepares the ground for politics:

> In music of the grandest style there is the same harmony that prevails between Heaven and earth; in ceremonies of the grandest form there is the same graduation that exists between Heaven and earth. . . . These things being so, in all within the four seas, there must be mutual respect and love.[14]

With the highest level of music there will be no complaints and dissatisfaction; with the highest level of ceremonies, there will be no fighting and quarrel. In other words, the highest level of music brings about social equilibrium. When the highest level of music is present, there is no need for punishment and war, as the happiness for the state and for the people would be achieved with the education of music and ceremonies. This is why it is said that to know music is one of the most important aspects of government.[15]

The idea that music has an important role to play in government is not a uniquely Chinese one. In the *Republic*, Plato also has a lot of discussions about music education. For him,

> Education in music and poetry is most important . . . because rhythm and harmony permeate the inner part of the soul more than anything else, affecting it most strongly and brining it grace, so that if someone is properly educated in music and poetry, it makes him graceful, but if not, then the opposite.[16]

In his ideal state, music is used to improve the public spiritual and moral state and to change the vulgar characters of the people. At this point, the thought of music education in *Yueji* and the *Republic* is common, but there are also significant differences between the two, the most obvious of which has to do with pleasure. Plato does not seem to ascribe much importance to the pleasure that music might deliver. In the *Symposium*, for instance, when Socrates and his friends were about to begin the serious dialogue that makes up the majority of the text, they asked the flute players to leave the room.[17]

Indeed, for Plato, most of the pleasures disturb or even harm the capacity for philosophical contemplation. He is worried that that the emotions, pleasures, and pains that accompany our actions and feelings while listening to music have the potential to overtake us.[18] If Homeric poetry is allowed into the city, Plato is afraid, pleasure and pain, instead of *reason*, will be the lords of the city.[19] As Plato reserves only an extremely limited space for this sort of pleasure in a good life,[20] music and other arts are mostly rejected. Compared with Plato, *Yueji* is more positive toward human emotions and the function of music in promoting pleasures of the proper kind. Ancient Chinese music is often classified into elegant music (雅乐) and Zheng music (郑声)—a type of music that indulges too much in sensual pleasure. Confucius said, "I hate the Zheng music for it confounds the elegant music."[21] So he suggested, Zheng music be cast aside by the governers (放郑声).[22] But generally, the pleasure aroused by music is not excluded from its basic educational function as promoting orderly harmony inside a person and in the state.

Yueji mentions repeatedly the highest or grandest music, which is termed as "the highest style of music," "music of the grandest style" (大乐), or "a universal music" (乐达).[23] It is said that this Grand Music does not seek to "satisfy the desires of the appetite and of the ears and eyes,"[24] and thus does not necessarily entail extremely attractive sounds (极音). On the contrary, "the highest style of music is sure to be distinguished by its ease."[25] Therefore, the grandest music must be simple and not sophisticated. As it pertains to the essence of music, Grand Music does not necessarily depend on the specific instruments utilized such as bells, drums, and pipes, and so on. Rather, those who truly understand the essence of music can make music in theoretically any musical modality. On the other hand, those who insistently stick to fixed instruments and melodies and rely only on restrictive dance postures simply lose the essence of music.[26] Indeed, the *Yueji* states that the Grand Music is "silent."[27] The essential music, coming from the deep stillness of the nature, is itself still and evokes the stillness of the mind.[28] This is why only the *shengren* (the superior person) can comprehend the nature of this silent Grand Music and create musical pieces accordingly.[29] However, although the Grand Music is simple and silent, it is not stalled and inanimate. On the contrary, it is the sound of the origin of life and has a distinctive historical dimension. This is why the sages and ancient kings hearkening the Grand Music did not adopt the musical pieces of their predecessors, as the pieces belonged to their special ages. As the events and situations had changed with times, music also needed to be changed.[30] The first rulers of China, often called the ancient Three Sovereigns and Five Kings,[31] created music of their own time and used proper music in ceremonies (*Li*) to attune the dispositions of the people.

In addition to the Confucian classics, the Taoist classics, particularly the *Daodejing* and the *Zhuangzi*, also paid much attention to the "Grand Music."

In the *Zhuangzi*, it is mentioned as "the music of Heaven (天乐)," which, together with "the music of earth" and "the music of man," is regarded as the highest music in three fields: the music of earth comes from the sounds of the earth's crevices, the music of man is produced by human beings on musical instruments, and the music of Heaven comes directly from Tao or nature and thus embodies the movements and changes of Tao.[32] In this context, "Heaven," *Tian* (天), does not refer to the sky but rather nature and includes all beings in the world. As perfect music and perfect joy, it

> must start out by resonating with human affairs but also flowing along the guideline of the Heavenly. It must run its course through all the Five Virtues but still accord with what is unforced in things. Only then can it concordantly adjust the four seasons within it, bringing all things into its great harmony.[33]

Only sages, who comprehend the Tao, in conforming to nature, enjoy the music of Heaven. At the same time, the music of Heaven participates in the natural process, reconciles *yin* and *yang*, and thus helps to harmonize all beings.

The music of Heaven cannot be perceived with bodily sensory organs. Indeed, in the great Taoist classic, the *Daodejing*, Laozi claimed that "the Grand sound has no sound" (大音希声).[34] The Grand sound is the sound of Tao. Tao is empty and void as an abyss, but it is useful for all things, as it is the origin of all beings.[35] Tao is inaudible, invisible, and untouchable,[36] therefore the music of Heaven also has no vocal sound. But how can one hear it? Zhuangzi attempts to explain it in the following way:

> Maintain the unity of your will. Do not listen with ears, but with the mind. Do not listen with mind, but listen with the spirit. The function of the ear ends with hearing, that of the mind, with symbols or ideas. But the spirit is an emptiness ready to receive all things. Tao abides in the emptiness; the emptiness is the fast of mind.[37]

In order to hear the Grand sound, one should not listen to the vibration of sound waves with ears but turn to the sound of silence with an empty mind and spirit since "only in silence can the harmony be heard."[38]

RESONATING IN HISTORY OF BEING: THE SILENT SOUND OF HEIDEGGER

Ancient Chinese musical thought discloses an original relationship between human existence and music. But as an original musical understanding, it has not been revealed in its full significance in philosophy. As the description of it is often poetic, it is sometimes regarded as mere literary rhetoric instead of true philosophical insight. In modern times, its true meaning is increasingly obscured. In addition, as the thought of the original music is very different from a scientific theory, it is improbable to be verified by scientific methods or formal logic. In the age of science and technology, when all kinds of novel sounds made by new skills and technology attract our attention, the silent music with its profound significance is, more often than not, forgotten. However, this thought of silent music finds its resonation in Heidegger's thought of being. Heidegger's sound of stillness (*die Stimme der Stille*) shows similarities with the silent music in ancient Chinese thought.

For Heidegger, stillness (*die Stille*) is an important character of being. There are several conceptions related to stillness, for example, keeping silent or reticence (*Schweigen, Erschweigen, Verschweigen*), and hearing or hearkening (*Hören, Gehörschenken*).[39] In Heidegger's view, the appropriating or enowning of being is still and silent (*die Stille des Seinsgeschehniseses, das seine Zeit hat und sein Schweigen*).[40] The sound of stillness (*die Stimme der Stille*) is the sound of the essencing of being (*das Wesen des Seins*); therefore, the truth of being is reticence (*das Erschweigen der Wahrheit des Seyns*), although the so-called "world historical" (*weltgeschichtliche*) upheavals always appear gigantic and roaring (*Riesige und Laute*), which we can understand as gaudy and sensationalist. But the more one focuses on such noisy sounds, the more one misses the great stillness of being.[41] In *Being and Time*, Heidegger claims that keeping silent has the same foundation as discourse, and, furthermore, it is an essential mode of discourse:

> Keeping silent authentically is possible only in genuine discoursing . . .; as a mode of discoursing, reticence articulates the intelligibility of Dasein in so primordial a manner that it gives rise to a potentiality-for-hearing which is so genuine, and to a being-with-one-another which is transparent.[42]

Only human beings can keep silent, as reticence is an authentic mode of discourse. Stones or windows and animals, etc., cannot keep silent, as they do not talk. From this perspective, even those who are physically unable to speak may not be capable of authentically being silent. But after years of reflection, when Heidegger comprehended the phenomenon of authentic silence more profoundly, he revised his thinking. In 1933–1934, he suggests that, although what he said in *Being and Time* laid a groundwork for understanding the relationship between language and silence, he still did not reach the essential thing: "Keeping silent is not just an ultimate possibility of discourse, but discourse and language arise from keeping silent."[43] Here, Heidegger expresses explicitly that silence is the origin or source of language, instead of a special mode of discourse and language. In keeping silent and listening to the stillness, there is language. Vocal sounds should be explained from the stillness and silence, not vice versa, "For the phonetic-acoustic-physiological explanation of the sounds of language does not know the experience of their origin in ringing stillness, and knows even less how sound is given voice and defined by that stillness."[44]

What is Heidegger's sound of stillness? Does it mean soundlessness, or does it mean some particular sound? To be sure, stillness is not a complete denial of sound: "It is in no way merely the soundless" or "a lack of the motion of intoning, sounding."[45] Heidegger claims, instead, that the sound of stillness is the source of hearable sounds. It sets the basic tone for the vocal speeches and melodies. Despite the stillness in the meaning of soundlessness, there is still another mode of stillness, which, together with sounds, comprises musical pieces. The pauses, as silence in the process of music, play an important part, and sometimes even the essential role in a musical work. In fact, John Cage suggests that sounds and silences are both materials of composition.[46] Silences used in musical discourses are intentional and have special aims. The pause or punctuation made by silence "might give definition either to a predetermined structure or to an organically developing one" in the structure or architecture of the musical discourse.[47] This mode of silence is meaningful. But is it the silence that Heidegger refers to? Iso Kern explains this kind of silence phenomenologically. In his view, this kind of silence is the halo (*Hof*) of the sounds before and after it. The hearing of it includes a retention and a protentional expectation for the sounds that have just vanished and the sounds that are coming.[48] That means the silence at this level is defined by the sounds that form the horizon of it, and it defines the sounds at the same time. This silence is the same kind of sound as the other sounds around it, except that it is silent. The essential stillness or silence is different from this kind of silence in that it has a deeper source in the appropriation of being.

Heidegger suggests that ready-to-hand sound is not original sound. The sound of being, that is, of appropriation, sets the tone for all sounds. The sound (*der Laut*) "is not first of all relative to the ear, but to the stillness, and it's a way of stillness. It's the tear of silence—'The rift (*Riß*).'"[49] For Heidegger, the essential sound of stillness comes from being, which is not a being, but rather nothing.[50] "Be-ing (and that means the nothing) is the in-between [*Inzwischen*] for beings and for godding."[51] Thus, what "nothing"/ be-ing means here is the open field between beings, which Heidegger also characterizes as an abyss (*Abgrund*).[52] *Abgrund* has no entities or substances as its ground, but is "in-between" (*Inzwischen*) in the sense of "the stretches of the free play of time-space" (*die Erstrekkungen des Zeit-Spiel-Raumes*).[53] This in-between differentiates being (*Sein*) from beings (*Seiende*). But it is not a boundary between them or an abyss in the sense of separating two sides.

Rather, it is the free time-space for the beings/things and being itself to stride across and unite with each other in this middle (*Sie durchgehen einander. Hierbei durchmessen die Zwei eine Mitte. In dieser sind sie einig*).[54] In this open space, the world becomes world by bestowing proper meaning to things, and things become things by bearing a world. The middle or the in-between, the dif-ference "disclosingly appropriates world into the granting of things."[55] In this abyss-like middle, the fourfold of the world—gods, sky, earth, and the mortal human beings—enowns the thing, and each has its essence.[56] From here the human being is also grounded as Da-sein.[57] The gods are also godding in this time-space; this is the "space" where meaning unfolds. The appropriation of being (*Ereignis*) happens in this openness of in-between. So, Heidegger claims that it is "always more in motion than all motion and always more restlessly active than any agitation."[58] With all the motions, this clearing open space is still. Heidegger states that there is a twofold stillness in the appropriating: by "letting things rest in the world's favor" the things rest in stillness, and by "letting the world suffice itself in the thing," the world gets still.[59] With its silent language being commands, the world and the things to gather into "the simple onefold of intimacy."[60] The saying of being prevailed by appropriation, which is the source of human language and speaking, "corresponds to the soundless tolling of the stillness of appropriating-showing saying."[61] In hearkening to the sound of stillness, Dasein brings itself to words: "Language speaks as the peal of stillness."[62] Only by corresponding to the silence of appropriating saying can Dasein essentially be silent. "Keeping silent thus turns out to be the happening of the original reticence of human Dasein."[63] This essential silence keeps the nature of abyss, gathering beings to their being, and exposing Dasein to beings as a whole.

An important way that the original silence speaks is through artworks. As Heidegger claims, "The statue and temple stand in silent dialogue with man in the unconcealed. If there were not the silent word, then . . . a temple could never, without standing in the disclosive domain of the word, present itself as the house of a god."[64] In silence, a world is opened to us through what we can refer to as a "soundless dialogue" with the artworks. For Heidegger, the mode of saying of appropriation is "the melodic mode, the song which says something in its singing. For appropriating saying brings to light all present beings in terms of their properties—it lauds, that is, allows them into their own, their nature."[65] The saying of appropriation always already consists in melody and rhythm, in that it is singing its specific song (μέλος).[66] Therefore, we can say that "Hölderlin sings" his poetries. Poetry as the most originary mode of art, with rhythm in its hidden essence,[67] brings the beings into creative conception,[68] so that beings have their names and emerge into presence.

In my view, Heidegger's sound of stillness indicates the same phenomenon as the music of silence in ancient Chinese thought, although ancient Chinese thinkers describe it pre-phenomenologically, while Heidegger discloses it phenomenologically and from his understanding of the history of being. This connection may be due to Heidegger's interest in ancient Chinese classics, especially in the *Daodejing*.[69] Heidegger is fully aware of the multiple meanings of Tao when he refers to this concept in his "The Nature of the Language" as being, as the Way, and as the Saying.[70] He interprets the language of being as the way-making for the disclosure of the fourfold world, as the saying that gathers all regions in the nearness. He calls it the ringing of stillness.[71] For Heidegger, his *Ereignis* as the essencing of being is just as profound as the Greek *logos* and the Chinese Tao.[72] In "The Uniqueness of the Poet," he quotes the full text of Chapter 11 of *Daodejing* and directly interprets Tao as being.[73] In this passage, Laozi indicates that the use or being of wheels, vessels, and houses depends on the emptiness or void contained in them. If there is no void inside a pot, it is not a pot, for it cannot be used as a pot. The void or nothingness bestows upon the things their usage or very being. The Tao is precisely the emptiness or nothing. Nothing is not the opposite of being; rather, it is more fundamental than what is. Heidegger indicates that the emptiness or nothing in this passage refers to being. Being as nothing operates as an "in-between" in which the beings as a whole are gathered to their being in time and space (*Augenblick und Zeit, Ort und Raum*), and which is also the home of the human being.[74] Heidegger's apparent translation of the *Daodejing* in his texts is a hermeneutical one, as it seems that he reads his own thought into the texts. But as Heidegger claims, every translation is an interpretation.[75] The reading-in is precisely necessary for the revealing of the meaning of the text in his thinking.

In ancient Chinese thought, music comes from "the harmony of the Heaven and the earth" (天地之和). From a Heideggerian perspective, this means that the origin of the Grand Music is the harmony and intimacy formulated in reaching each other and preserving and guarding each other of the fourfold of the world. The silent sound of the Grand Music is the simplest one, but it gathers the original sounds of sky, earth, gods, and mortals, that is, the sound of the beings as a whole. At the same time, it "arises in the human heart-mind" (生于人心), which signifies that only the one who listens to the silent sound can speak or make music according to the attunement of being. Only the person who is able to withdraw from the idle talk and noisy sounds is able to experience the silent sound of Grand Music.

KEEPING THE ESSENCE OF MUSIC

Now, when technology has developed to an extent that machines are able to compose music by themselves, and when computer programs, such as

Electric and Musical Industries (EMI) or other composition software, can effortlessly bring out one piece after another of "Bach," "Beethoven," or *High Mountain and Flowing Stream* (高山流水) styles of music from silicon crystal circuits, and the works composed by artificial intelligence (AI) are even "more perfect" than perhaps the music that flows from human beings, is it still necessary for human beings to listen to the "silent music" or the "sound of stillness"? Can music still be regarded as a sign of the uniqueness and the profoundness of human beings and human intelligence? In an attempt to think through these questions, I'm reminded that Douglas Hofstadter was upset when he heard the well-calculated and intelligence-filled music pieces composed by the circuit board and the computer chips.[76] These pieces are not emotionally empty for him; they even evoke the same feelings as when we are listening to Bach and Chopin, although the machine has never lived and loved, struggled, and been heartbroken, and thus there is something "off" about such a musical experience. Yet these feelings are traditionally regarded as the source of music creation. Hofstadter's frustration is reasonable if music is judged solely from the aesthetic experience of music. Actually, the traditional way of artistic creation is increasingly influenced by the development of technology. The products made by AI are more and more refined and acceptable, so much so that people are worried that the artists might be in danger of being replaced by AI completely or mostly one day.[77]

But if we go deeper into the origin of music, we will see that technology cannot replace human beings as the creator. Heidegger has already anticipated the danger music facing today, the essence of which is "the danger of understanding melody and rhythm also from the perspective of physiology and physics, that is, technologically, calculatingly in the widest sense."[78] He claims that the attempt to understand melody and rhythm technologically has lost "what is essential."[79] In the age of technology, the machination (*Machenschaft*) or producibility dominates the being of beings. But its mathematical essence has already been abandoned by being and leads to annihilation.[80] EMI sets out from a technological understanding of music and produces musical works by calculating and collecting information from the original musical pieces of Bach or Chopin and then reassembles the fragments through texture-matching. The new product is derived from the original music pieces, the sounds, and melodies of which are used as ready-to-hand parts. But it no longer rings "like the earth"[81] from the saying of being and is not able to create a world on the earth.[82] This kind of production is not a free creation of artwork but a kind of domination of the earth with calculative representation, which blocks our way from encountering face to face the four regions of the world.[83] The sound of such kind of product is not the resonation of the stillness of the appropriation, but leads astray from the sound of stillness. The musical products made by AI may arouse similar emotions as the original artworks do at first hearing, or even make a strong sensual impact on us for a long time. But, according to Heidegger, aesthetic experience is not the standard of judging a work. Sounds of the artwork are supposed to come from the earth where we live and die, that is, the earth of the fourfold of the world. The sound would lose its meaning without the earth as its roots, which also serves as the roots of mortals.[84] Although it may prove useful for musicians to arrange rhythms or melodies to achieve specific effects with the help of an AI composer, the real creation comes from hearkening the silent sounds from the appropriation. As Hubert Dreyfus suggests, the successful use of AI should be to augment rather than replace human beings.[85]

John Cage, arguably the most influential composer of the twentieth century, pays much attention to the phenomenon of silence. His most famous work, "4'33," which consists of four minutes and thirty-three seconds of silence, is considered by some music theorists as the practice of the "silent music" of Chinese ancient musical thought.[86] This "silent song" is controversial and also provokes reflection. For him, despite the intentional silence in musical pieces, as he described, there is still a kind of silence that does not have any overt external purpose. This silence actually invites people to listen to the sound usually ignored by us, that is, the sound of the surrounding environment and human body. These changing and unpredictable sounds are precisely what life depends on for existence.[87] Listening to the silence means to retreat from noisy sounds, and to listen to the fundamental sounds of the world that we are living in. This withdrawal involves the possibility of hearing the sound of stillness and the silent sound of the Grand Music. Although Cage did not necessarily approach the problem directly in an explicitly philosophical way, he reminds us of the significance of hearkening to the silence, as the phenomenon of silence is essential for music. We have seen it in ancient Chinese music thought, and we got a glimpse of its origin in Heidegger's sound of stillness.

NOTES

1. Wang, Fuzhi, *Chuanshan Quan Shu, Part IV: Liji Zhang Ju* (Changsha: Yue Lu Shu She, 2011), 887. The Six Dynasties, from Yellow Emperor Dynasty to early Zhou Dynasty, are traditionally regarded as the oldest Era of Chinese culture.

2. *Sacred Books of China: The Texts of Confucianism, Part IV: The Li Ki*, trans. James Legge (Oxford: Clarendon Press, 1885), 92. The "mind" here is "xin 心" in Chinese, which is often translated as "mind-heart" and includes volition, sentiments, and intellect.

3. *Sacred Books of China*, 92.
4. *Sacred Books of China*, 95.
5. *Sacred Books of China*, 93.

6. *Sacred Books of China*, 100. Translation slightly modified.

7. In ancient Chinese philosophy, Heaven or *Tian* (天) is a very important concept. It literally means the sky, but it has much wider significance. When transposed with earth (*Di*), it means nature. *Tian*, *Di*, and human being (*Ren*) make up the world. *Tian* is also sometimes regarded as the master of the world with divine power.

8. In ancient Chinese philosophy, *yin* and *yang* are the basic forces of the world. They are inseparable and contradictory power, as *yin* is more passive, dark, and feminine, while yang is related more to activity, lightness, and masculinity. The complementary yet contradictory natures of these forces control the emergence and decline of all things in the world. For our purposes, it is important to note that heaven (*Tian*) is linked with *yang*, while earth (*Di*) is linked with *yin*.

9. *Sacred Books of China*, 104.

10. *Sacred Books of China*, 102.

11. Chenyang Li analyzes the concept of harmony from the perspective of Confucian tradition in "The Confucian Ideal of Harmony," *Philosophy East and West* 56, no. 4 (2006): 583–603.

12. *Sacred Books of China*, 300: This equilibrium is the great root (from which all human actions are grown) in the world; and this harmony is the universal path (in which they should all proceed).

13. *Li*, which is sometimes translated as "rites" or "ritual," is a core concept of early Confucian philosophy. *Li* is not only the rituals in sacrifice or other important celebrations, but also in etiquette and comportment in daily life. It is commonly understood as the expression of benevolence in behavior. On *Li* and music, cf. James Garrison, "The Social Value of Ritual and Music in Classical Chinese Thought," *Teorema* 31, no. 3 (2012): 209–222.

14. *Sacred Books of China*, 99.

15. *Sacred Books of China*, 95.

16. Plato, *Republic*, trans. G. M. A. Grube (Indianapolis and Cambridge: Hackett, 1992), 401D-E. All references to Plato are in Stephanus numbers to accommodate those using alternate translations. Rentmeester also provides an analysis of Plato and music in his contribution to this volume.

17. Plato, *Symposium*, trans. Alexander Nehamas and Paul Woodruff (Indianapolis and Cambridge: Hackett, 1989, 176E.

18. *Republic*, 606D.

19. *Republic*, 607A.

20. See Plato, *Philebus*, trans. Dorothea Frede (Indianapolis: Hackett, 1993), 65A, 66C.

21. Confucius, *The Analects*, trans. James Legge (New York: Dover, 1971), chapter 3.

22. Confucius, *The Analects*, chapter 3.

23. *Sacred Books of China*, 98, 99.

24. *Sacred Books of China*, 96.

25. *Sacred Books of China*, 98.

26. Wang Meng-ou 王梦鸥, *Liji Jin Zhu Jin Yi*礼记今注今译 (Taibei: Taiwan Shang Wu Yin Shu Guan, 1970), 497.

27. This comes from the chapter "Kongzi Xianju" of *Liji*, *Sacred Books of China*, 279. Here, Confucius explains three "wu"(无) (three nothingness) as an important concept for an ideal ruler (junzi) to understand. Three *wu* is described as "the music that has no sound; the ceremonial usages that have no embodiment; the mourning that has no garb."

28. *Sacred Books of China*, 98.
29. *Sacred Books of China*, 100.
30. *Sacred Books of China*, 100.
31. The "Three Sovereigns and Five Kings" are said to be the emperors of ancient China. The Five Kings are the Yellow Emperor, Zhuanyu, Ku, Yao, and Shun, who ruled roughly around the period of 2600–2200 BCE. The Three Sovereigns' dates are much earlier than Five Kings but their dates are less clear. Traditionally, they are regarded as great sages wisdom and virtue.
32. Zhuangzi, *Chuang-Tzu: A new Selected Translation with an Exposition of the Philosophy of Kuo Hsiang*, trans. Yu-Lan Fung (New York: Paragon, 1964), 10.
33. Zhuangzi, *Zhuangzi: The Essential Writings: With Selections from Traditional Commentaries* (Indianapolis: Hackett, 2009), 235. The five virtues, which are the core virtues in traditional Chinese culture, are benevolence (*Ren*), righteousness (*Yi*), propriety (*Li*), wisdom (*Zhi*), and fidelity (*Xin*).
34. *Daodejing*, Chapter 41. All translations of the *Daodejing* are my own. While there are literally hundreds of English translations of the *Daodejing*, commonly cited versions include Lao Tsu, *Tao Te Ching*, trans. Gia-Fu Feng, and Jane English (New York: Vintage, 1972) and Laozi, *Daodejing: "Making This Life Significant": A Philosophical Translation,* trans. Roger T. Ames and David L. Hall (New York: Ballantine, 2003).
35. *Daodejing*, Chapter 4: "道冲，而用之或不盈。渊兮，似万物之宗."
36. *Daodejing*, Chapter 14: "视之不见" , "听之不闻," "搏之不得."
37. Zhuangzi, *Chuang-Tzu* 79–80.
38. Zhuangzi, *Chuang-Tzu*, 103.
39. In my view, these conceptions are closely related. The being or the essencing of being itself is still. But as the original saying (*Sagen*), it is silent. Dasein hearkens the silent word of Being in its stillness.
40. Martin Heidegger, *Überlegungen II–VI (Schwarze Hefte 1931/38): Gesamtausgabe* 94 (Frankfurt am Main: Vittorio Klostermann, 2014), 6.
41. Martin Heidegger, *Beiträge zur Philosophie (Vom Ereignis): Gesamtausgabe* 65 (Frankfurt am Main: Vittorio Klostermann, 1989), 19, 97, 98.
42. Martin Heidegger, *Being and Time*, trans. John Macquarrie and Edward Robinson (New York: Harper & Row, 1962), 208.
43. Martin Heidegger, *Being and Truth*, trans. Gregory Fried and Richard Polt (Bloomington: Indiana University Press, 2010), 87.
44. Martin Heidegger, *On the Way to Language*, trans. Peter D. Hertz (New York, Harper & Row, 1971): 121–122.
45. Martin Heidegger, *Poetry, Language, Thought*, trans. Albert Hofstadter (New York: HarperCollins, 1971), 204.

46. John Cage, *Silence: Lectures and Writings by John Cage* (Middletown, CT: Wesleyan University Press, 1961), 36. Trawny and de Morais also touch upon this in their chapter of this volume.

47. Cage, *Silence*, 22.

48. Iso Kern, *Das Wichtigste im Leben: Wang Yangming (1472–1529) und Seine Nachfolger Über Die Verwirklichung des Ursprünglichen Wissens*, (Basel: Schwabe, 2010) 1079.

49. Martin Heidegger, *Vom Wesen der Sprache: Gesamtausgabe* 65 (Frankfurt am Main: Klostermann, 1999), 118.

50. Polt excellently summarized the uses of "nothing" in history as meaning insubstantiality, negation, otherness, and meaninglessness. Polt argues that Heidegger mainly refers to the finitude of Dasein and the finitude of being in his concept of nothing. Cf. Richard Polt, "The Question of Nothing," in *A Companion to Heidegger's Introduction to Metaphysics*, ed. Richard Polt and Gregory Fried (New Haven and London, 2001), 60.

51. Heidegger, *Beiträge*, 267. "Godding" (*Götterung*) indicates that the divinity—the last god or the gods—is not a kind of entity, but rather a (divine) unfolding. See also, Heidegger, *Beiträge*, 508.

52. Martin Heidegger, *Besinnung: Gesamtausgabe* 65 (Frankfurt am Main: Vittorio Klostermann, 1997), 321.

53. Heidegger, *Besinnung*, 17.

54. Martin Heidegger, *Unterwegs zur Sprache: Gesamtausgabe* 12 (Frankfurt am Main: Vittorio Klostermann, 1985), 22.

55. Heidegger, *Unterwegs zur Sprache*, 23.

56. Heidegger, *Unterwegs zur Sprache*, 26.

57. Heidegger, *Besinnung*, 22.

58. Heidegger, *Unterwegs zur Sprache*, 26.

59. Heidegger, *Unterwegs zur Sprache*, 26.

60. Heidegger, *Unterwegs zur Sprache*, 27.

61. Heidegger, *Unterwegs zur Sprache*, 251.

62. Heidegger, *Unterwegs zur Sprache*, 27.

63. Heidegger, *Being and Truth*, 87, 88.

64. Martin Heidegger, *Parmenides: Gesamtausgabe* 54 (Frankfurt am Main: Vittorio Klostermann, 1982), 172–173.

65. Heidegger, *Unterwegs zur Sprache*, 254.

66. Heidegger, *Unterwegs zur Sprache*, 255.

67. Heidegger, *Unterwegs zur Sprache*, 33.

68. Martin Heidegger, *Überlegungen II–VI*, 14.

69. Cf. Reinhard May, *Heidegger's Hidden Sources: East-Asian Influences on his Work*, trans. Graham Parkes (New York and Oxon: Routledge, 1996).

70. In fact, Chang Chung-Yuan claimed that Heidegger "is the only Western philosopher who not only thoroughly intellectually understands but has intuitively grasped Taoist thought" in "Tao-A New Way of Thinking," *Journal of Chinese Philosophy* 1, no. 2 (1974), 138.

71. Heidegger, *Unterwegs zur Sprache*, 204.

72. Martin Heidegger, *Identity and Difference*, trans. Joan Stambaugh (Chicago: University of Chicago Press, 2002), 36.
73. Martin Heidegger, "Die Einzigkeit des Dichters," in *Zu Hölderlin: Griechenlandreisen: Gesamtausgabe* 75 (Frankfurt am Main: V. Klostermann, 2000).
74. Heidegger, "Die Einzigkeit des Dichters," 43.
75. Heidegger, *Being and Truth*: 102.
76. Douglas Hofstadter, "Staring Emmy Straight in the Eye," in *Virtual Music: Computer Synthesis of Musical Style,* ed. David Cope (Cambridge, MA and London: The MIT Press, 2001), 33–82.
77. Luca Casina and Marco Roccetti discuss this sentiment in "The Impact of AI on the Musical World: Will Musicians be Obsolete?" *Italian Journal of Aesthetics* 46, no. 4 (2018): 119–134.
78. Heidegger, *Unterwegs zur Sprache*, 193.
79. Heidegger, *Unterwegs zur Sprache*, 193.
80. Heidegger, *Besinnung*, 16.
81. Heidegger, *Unterwegs zur Sprache*, 196.
82. Rentmeester discusses the world-building capacity of music in the digital age in his chapter of this volume as well.
83. Heidegger, *Unterwegs zur Sprache*, 199.
84. Heidegger, *Unterwegs zur Sprache*, 194.
85. Hubert Dreyfus, *What Computers Can't Do: The Limits of Artificial Intelligence* (New York: Harper & Row, 1972), 213.
86. Cf. Feng Changchun, "From 'the Grand Sound is Soundless to 4'33'',''' *Huang Zhong* 1 (1999): 91–96.
87. Cage, *Silence*, 22.

BIBLIOGRAPHY

Cage, John. *Silence: Lectures and Writings by John Cage.* Middletown, CT: Wesleyan University Press, 1961.
Casina, Luca and Marco Roccetti. "The Impact of AI on the Musical World: Will Musicians be Obsolete?" *Italian Journal of Aesthetics* 46, no. 4 (2018): 119–134.
Changchun, Feng. "From 'the Grand Sound is Soundless to 4'33'.''' *Huang Zhong* 1 (1999): 91–96.
Chung-Yuan, Chang. "Tao-A New Way of Thinking." *Journal of Chinese Philosophy* 1, no. 2 (1974): 137–152.
Confucius. *The Analects.* Translated by James Legge. New York: Dover, 1971.
Dreyfus, Hubert. *What Computers Can't Do: The Limits of Artificial Intelligence.* New York: Harper & Row, 1972.
Garrison, James. "The Social Value of Ritual and Music in Classical Chinese Thought." *Teorema* 31, no. 3 (2012): 209–222.
Heidegger, Martin. *Being and Time.* Translated by John Macquarrie and Edward Robinson. New York: Harper & Row, 1962.

Heidegger, Martin. *Being and Truth*. Translated by Gregory Fried and Richard Polt. Bloomington: Indiana University Press, 2010.
Heidegger, Martin. *Beiträge zur Philosophie (Vom Ereignis): Gesamtausgabe 65*. Frankfurt am Main: Vittorio Klostermann, 1989.
Heidegger, Martin. *Besinnung: Gesamtausgabe 65*. Frankfurt am Main: Vittorio Klostermann, 1997.
Heidegger, Martin. "Die Einzigkeit des Dichters." In *Zu Hölderlin: Griechenlandreisen: Gesamtausgabe*, Edited by Curt Ochwadt, 33–44. Frankfurt am Main: V. Klostermann, 2000.
Heidegger, Martin. *Identity and Difference*. Translated by Joan Stambaugh. Chicago: University of Chicago Press, 2002.
Heidegger, Martin. *On the Way to Language*. Translated by Peter D. Hertz. New York: Harper & Row, 1971.
Heidegger, Martin. *Parmenides: Gesamtausgabe 54*. Frankfurt am Main: Vittorio Klostermann, 1982.
Heidegger, Martin. *Poetry, Language, Thought*. Translated by Albert Hofstadter. New York: HarperCollins, 1971.
Heidegger, Martin. *Überlegungen II–VI (Schwarze Hefte 1931/38): Gesamtausgabe 94*. Frankfurt am Main: Vittorio Klostermann, 2014.
Heidegger, Martin. *Unterwegs zur Sprache: Gesamtausgabe 12*. Frankfurt am Main: Vittorio Klostermann, 1985.
Heidegger, Martin. *Vom Wesen der Sprache: Gesamtausgabe 65*. Frankfurt am Main: Vittorio Klostermann, 1999.
Hofstadter, Douglas. "Staring Emmy Straight in the Eye." In *Virtual Music: Computer Synthesis of Musical Style,* edited by David Cope, 33–82. Cambridge, MA and London: The MIT Press, 2001.
Lao Tsu. *Tao Te Ching*. Translated by Gia-Fu Feng and Jane English. New York: Vintage, 1972.
Laozi. *Daodejing: "Making This Life Significant": A Philosophical Translation.* Translated by Roger T. Ames and David L. Hall. New York: Ballantine, 2003.
Li, Chenyang. "The Confucian Ideal of Harmony." *Philosophy East and West* 56, no. 4 (2006): 583–603.
Kern, Iso. *Das Wichtigste im Leben: Wang Yangming (1472–1529) und Seine Nachfolger Über Die Verwirklichung des Ursprünglichen Wissens*. Basel: Schwabe, 2010.
May, Reinhard. *Heidegger's Hidden Sources: East-Asian Influences on his Work*. Translated by Graham Parkes. New York and Oxon: Routledge, 1996.
Plato. *Philebus*. Translated by Dorothea Frede. Indianapolis: Hackett, 1993.
Plato. *Republic*. Translated by G. M. A. Grube. Indianapolis and Cambridge: Hackett, 1992.
Plato. *Symposium*. Translated by Alexander Nehamas and Paul Woodruff. Indianapolis and Cambridge: Hackett, 1989.
Polt, Richard. "The Question of Nothing." In *A Companion to Heidegger's Introduction to Metaphysics*, edited by Richard Polt and Gregory Fried, 57–82. New Haven and London, 2001.

Sacred Books of China: The Texts of Confucianism, Part IV: The Li Ki. Translated by James Legge. Oxford: Clarendon Press, 1885.

Wang, Fuzhi. *Chuanshan Quan Shu, Part IV: Liji Zhang Ju*. Changsha: Yue Lu Shu She, 2011.

Wang, Meng-ou 王梦鸥, *Liji Jin Zhu Jin Yi*礼记今注今译. Taibei: Taiwan Shang Wu Yin Shu Guan, 1970.

Zhuangzi. *Chuang-Tzu: A new Selected Translation with an Exposition of the Philosophy of Kuo Hsiang*. Translated by Yu-Lan Fung. New York: Paragon, 1964.

Zhuangzi. *Zhuangzi: The Essential Writings: With Selections from Traditional Commentaries*. Indianapolis: Hackett, 2009.

Chapter 8

Heidegger's *Musik-Sprache* or Silence and Bells in the Music of Arvo Pärt

Peter Trawny and Agamenon de Morais

Heidegger and music—there is significant difficulty in all well-intentioned attempts to formulate a topic out of it. Indeed, one could argue that all formulations are doomed to fail, especially if one wants to occupy oneself with the subject of music as such in Heidegger's thinking. Heidegger said nothing about the history of music—even if, as is usual with "masters," every little statement is worth its weight in gold. In any case, it makes no sense to compare his references to music, works, compositions, and so on with those of Friedrich Nietzsche or Theodor Adorno, both of whom wrote extensively on music.[1] Unlike his clear interest in poetry, Heidegger was apparently not interested in music. He thus seems to belong to a large group of German philosophers and writers who have almost no knowledge of music.

Nevertheless, Heidegger's language often used words and terms from the fields of music. For example, in his lecture "The Principle of Reason," he speaks of the "tonality (*Tonart*) of the sentence"[2] or of the "change of tonality."[3] In the "Black Notebooks," the occurrence of musically relevant words becomes saturated. For instance, in *Remarks V* [*Anmerkungen V*], which is entirely based on the motto "Play of silence / and / sound of bowl," he states, "Thinking is hearing; it hears the silence of the world. In hearing there is the broadest belonging and the purest retention of the world's suspension [*Vorhalt*]."[4] In *Remarks III* it reads:

> Here shows a hidden side of the writing—to be the silent saying [*Sage*] and yet salvaging the tone: the sound of the difference [*Schied*] from the tuning [*Stimmen*] of the event of disappropriation [*Enteignis*] in conserving [*Schonen*] and serenity. The sounding [*Lauten*] that is bound in the writing (in the written) can only be heard from the primordial sound of the silent saying of Brauch. But how does the written saying bind the primordial sound into language?[5]

In *Remarks VI*, "language" is referred to as "music of difference [*Unter-Schied*]."[6] Also, it says, "In worlding [*Welten*] meaning is based not on conceiving meaning. This tuning is the actual music."[7] In *Remarks IX*, the "counterpoint tensions of his [work] composition"[8] are mentioned. In *Four Books I*, Heidegger speaks of the "music of the same";[9] in *Four Books II*, of the "tonefall [*Tonfall*] of silence."[10] In *Vigiliae II*, it is mentioned once: "The unthought and that what is said of it is like the unplayed musical notation that calls for playing [*Spiel*]."[11] And in *Hints I* [*Winke I*], Heidegger even writes: "The event is that bell of silence [. . .],"[12] as well speaking of the "dance of the bell-rest [*Glockenruhe*]."[13]

That small selection of a *language of music* is only intended to give an impression of the certainly conscious use of expressions from the field of music in Heidegger's writings. The question, of course, is how to understand it. It is obvious that Heidegger is not philosophizing about specific musical phenomena. The "suspension of the world" is not suspension as in the step down of the second in a chord progression, from the theory of harmony, for instance.

Now it would be possible to think of a metaphor of music beyond Heidegger's thinking. The philosopher had transferred terms from music into his thinking in order to represent certain ideas of his in a specific mode. But within this thinking, which banishes the metaphor into the metaphysics to be overcome,[14] this cannot be the case. Of course, it is possible that a philosopher contradicts himself. But the measure would lack hermeneutic sensitivity and lead to rough conclusions. In addition, the basic question would be what a *metaphor of music* should be anyway. You would have to inscribe the procedure into the musical language to use pictures—for example, in relation to the harmonic movement in scores and the fingering when playing the piano—which appeared to be strange in the non-pictorial sound of the music. What is a "suspension" in listening to music?

Apart from the fact that this would probably be possible, Heidegger's allergy to metaphors remains. So, what should be done? We would like to try three things in this sketch of a somewhat larger project on the language of Heidegger's later philosophy. First, we would like to point out Heidegger's idea of the "abysmally sensual" [*abgründig Sinnlichen*], that is, a moment of his access to language that could shed light on Heidegger's incursion into the language of music, because it is clear that Heidegger's references to music are of linguistic importance. Second, we would like to refer to the importance of the semantic field of "voice," "mood," and so on, which Heidegger emphasizes repeatedly because it seems to be particularly close to music and musicality. Third, based on the interpretation of the sentence: "The event is the bell of silence [. . .]," as cited earlier, we would like to draw attention to a composer whose pieces could in turn enable a special look at Heidegger's later thinking in its musicality to be explained in more detail, that is, the work of the Estonian composer, Arvo Pärt, and his minimalist compositional technique called "tintinnabuli."

MUSIC, LANGUAGE, AND THE ABYSMALLY SENSUAL

Heidegger already pointed out in his Hölderlin lectures that the "distinction of the sensual [*aistheton*] and non-sensible [*noeton*]" was the "basic structure" of "what is called from ancient times metaphysics."[15] This difference, everywhere presupposed in thinking, determines the aesthetics into the rhetoric of the tropes, essential for our understanding of poetry. Because allegory, symbol, example, metaphor, and sign assume "the role of sensible phenomena," they offer "a sight" and give "such a picture." Heidegger adds, "Such pictures in poetry [. . .] represent not only themselves, but a non-sensible meaning. [. . .] The sensual picture indicates a 'spiritual' content, a meaning. The stream mentioned and appearing in the picture is a 'symbol.'"[16] Heidegger thinks that the "Rhine," if Hölderlin poetizes it in his hymn as "stream," is not a symbol, not a sign of something else, but merely and solely the "Rhine" itself.

In one of the written conversations, which applies to Hölderlin's poetry, Heidegger states that "the scheme that has been invalid since the Greeks, according to which, in linguistic structures we differentiate between the sensory body of the word (sound and typeface) and the sense of the word, is only superficial."[17] In language, it is about separating words from their meanings. Thinking does not understand the words as a unity of sense (meaning) and sensuality; that has to do with "metaphysics," because only therein lies "the physical and the sensual in contrast to the non-physical and non-sensual."[18]

Heidegger destroys these differences by—and this is important in understanding music language—first tearing down the difference between seeing and hearing of the word. The "glowing [*Leuchten*] and the sound" are "basically the same": they "concern neither the eye nor the ear only."[19] The word is therefore not just a visual object, but also an acoustic one. It sounds and is possibly even forming keys. Heidegger says that is the case even if we do not read out loud because making a difference between the sound in thinking or speaking out loud would confirm the difference between seeing and hearing.

But Heidegger goes a step beyond this thought. In the coincidence of seeing and hearing both non-sensual and sensual, everything *increases* that is at stake in the interpretation of meaning. Heidegger formulates this in a floating way: "More sensual [*sinnlicher*] is what is richer in meaning [*Sinn*], since it belongs more purely to the person who thinks it [*Sinnende*]."[20] Sensuality, meaning, and the activity of meaning, that is, of thinking, become more intense when the metaphysical differences and orders disappear. The comparatives "more sensual," "richer," and "more purely" form no hierarchy, no context. They become "abysmally sensual,"[21] that is, inexhaustible in sensuality [*Sinnlichkeit*], meaning [*Sinn*], and thinking [*Sinnen*].

With this consideration, the association of music with the sensual and language with the non-sensual also disappears. Language itself becomes sensual. It sounds and forms tones like music. But for Heidegger, this analogy should also remain halfway there. If music is what appears as sound and tone, then the language that appears as sound and tone is music.

Since *Being and Time*, Heidegger has referred to the phenomenon of "mood" or "attunement" of "being-in-the-world." Meanings do not reach *Dasein* in the neutral way of information. The relationship of *Dasein* to oneself and thus to the world is "always" not only imposed by "moods," but initially made possible by them. In interpreting Hölderlin's poetry, in particular, Heidegger emphasizes that a "grounding mood" [*Grundstimmung*] virtually "opens up" [*eröffnet*] the world.[22]

Heidegger spent a tremendous amount of time describing and interpreting "moods" and "grounding moods." Hardly any topic in his thinking is played through as often as this one. There is no doubt that some of these analyses give the impression that Heidegger is a "phenomenologist" who views the "moods" and "grounding moods" (e.g., "boredom")[23] as collective states of mind in the historically changing context of the considered "world." However, it cannot be overlooked that such an attempt only makes very limited sense. In fact, Heidegger later conceded this.[24]

Another way is to have the "mood" as linguistic experiences, that is, to be explained from the words and verses of poetry—but not exclusively. Then the "grounding mood of mourning"[25] goes into the interpretation of Hölderlin's poetry by receiving it and writing it into it. Heidegger's interpretation of this poetry then "swings" [*schwingt*][26] even in this "grounding mood."

If Heidegger now notes in one of the *Black Notebooks* that "in worlding [*Welten*], the meaning is based, not in the conceiving meaning [*vorstellenden Meinen*], [rather,] this tuning [*Stimmende*] is the actual music,"[27] then the error of "phenomenology" must not lead to misunderstandings. The word "worlding" does not mean an objective state of the world. Rather, it pertains to thinking that recognizes the "abysmally sensual" form of thinking that is specific in the sentence "The world worlds" [*Die Welt weltet*].[28] The "worlding" therefore stands for a "world" understood in a language that is experienced through an "abysmally sensual" language.

In this way, Heidegger can discover "meaning" in the "worlding"—and not in the metaphysical understanding of conceiving and meaning. This is the "actual music" as the "tuning." What Heidegger says about Hölderlin's "abysmally sensual" poetry returns here, in that he wants to note in the "meaning" [*Bedeuten*] an "actual music" that has passed through "tuning." It is obvious that there is now a connection between language and music, because the "tuning" and the "mood" can be described very generally and ambiguously, but aptly as a moment of music. Incidentally, Hölderlin characterized this situation as a *"change of tones."*[29]

Finally, we would like to attempt to draw the attention to a composer whose music, based on these preliminary considerations, should by no means merely provide a musical representation of Heidegger's language of music or thinking. That would only amount to a comparison, which is particularly cultivated in literary studies, if Heidegger's influence on certain writers and poets is to be examined. Even if it can be assumed that this composer knew about Heidegger, even if he had read him, we would like to refrain from drawing a comparison.

Heidegger says: "The event is the bell of silence [. . .]." The words "event," "bell," and "silence" are extremely present in Heidegger's late thinking. What they designate is "abysmally sensual." It is not a question of the fact that a precise knowledge of the work could bring together the various points where it may become clear what is meant by the words. Rather, it is about the fact that the extremely varied use and combination of these words testify to an inexhaustibility of meaning that a researcher of Heidegger's thinking could only corrupt. To explain "in other words" what this sentence means is ignoring its "actual music." This usual hermeneutics also does not want to consider what Heidegger is trying to think as "abysmally sensual" beyond the metaphysical distinction between word and meaning. Repeating it in Heidegger's own words (as much of Heidegger research still does today) is just futile.

It could be that Heidegger's thinking no longer strived for a hermeneutic that suspected of a meaning behind or in his thoughts that could not already be found in the precise form of the words and their immediate meaning. "Event," "bell," and "silence" are not symbols that ultimately represented something objective. Heidegger's thinking attempted to leave this view of language relatively early. In this way, Heidegger's thinking could also be easily ideologized. (In his "metapolitical" statements, however, he promoted this.) These approaches to Heidegger's thinking are ultimately absurd.

From this perspective, it can be said that in Heidegger's late thinking a hermeneutics that understands the writings of philosophers as representations of certain problems that are "given" outside of the texts is led to the absurd. Heidegger says what he says. One can think that there are still some insights to be found. But it is better to observe the configuration of meaning staged in this thinking and to draw conclusions from it for the thinking itself—if this alternative is not already to be clearly stated.

But listening to music or certain music could indeed be helpful. This music, of which so much can be said, is somehow connected to the sentence:

"The event is the bell of silence [. . .]." However, listening to these compositions could convey what he says more accurately than all interpretations of secondary literature. Perhaps it could also indicate what Heidegger means by "music of the same." We are talking about the music of the Estonian composer Arvo Pärt.

SILENCE AND BELLS IN THE MUSIC OF ARVO PÄRT

For Arvo Pärt, silence is the primary space in which compositional action takes place. Going beyond the traditional conception of music, the Estonian composer redefines silence and elevates it to the status of a musical element in its own right. In that same space of redefinition, bells also take on a distinctive character, representing the creative and solitary gesture of the author against the yielding word. From this perspective, the bells appear as the basic material that enacts the entanglement between text, melody, and chord. In his compositions, the constituent notes of the triadic chord are not characterized as representatives of silence itself, but as an attempt to fill in the time, which is occupied by silence.[30] In this sense, for Pärt, silence happens in a sort of a fore-realm: it is not something one may produce, but rather it already exists at the beginning of the compositional action. In fact, he affirms, "silence for a composer is like a clean canvas for a painter."[31] In silence, the event happens, one can read the text, sing the melody, play the chord. The perception of those events implies listening, since one cannot experience events by reading the score. In this sense, one should realize oneself within the silence, and in doing so, one can perceive it as sensory.

We present below a brief exposition of silence understood as a core trace of Arvo Pärt's work, from observing the role of silence in tintinnabuli, his original compositional practice and musical language, in which the bells play an important musical role in a structural relation between text, melody, and triadic chord, and in which silence is presented in a privileged manner.[32] A point to consider is that the suggested role of silence in Pärt exists in a relationship with the perception of musical elements. Silence in itself is already given before the composition or the performing of music.

Moreover, this attempt to characterize silence and the bells in the work of Arvo Pärt shall be presented in relation to the concept of silence and also of the meaning of the bells for Heidegger, thus prompting us to think through how to better understand Heidegger through a musical lens. This attempt to construct a relation to Heidegger is primarily based on the known existence of two of Heidegger's works at the Arvo Pärt Centre Library, a small library housing roughly 2,000 books consisting largely of texts related to music, art, and theology. At first glance, finding Heidegger's *Wegmarken* and *Being and Time* among these shelves may seem out of place,[33] but not, we think, if we are able to understand the use of the words "silence" and "bells" by the German philosopher himself, noted above. This relational approach to silence and bells ultimately intends to develop a relevant perspective regarding the philosophy of music, and thus a proposed research niche that exceeds the boundaries of musical theory, offering an alternative non-teleological comprehension of music. It is moreover important to note the presented relational approach does not consider the bells as material objects, but rather in terms of the abysmally sensual. The meaning and thinking that "happens" upon hearing lyrics, melody, and chords together prompt us to consider music as language.

According to the *Oxford Dictionary of Music*, silence basically means rest.[34] In the *New Grove Dictionary of Music and Musicians*, it indicates the moments when one or more performers are not performing with their voice and/or instruments.[35] From this perspective, in a traditional sense, silence is interpreted as equivalent to the musical pause, consisting of the temporary suspension of a notation element. In fact, the dictionary entries on pause do not describe, nor do they seem to refer to, a possible expected and intentional musical result silence may produce. Therefore, even if one considers pause as the notational resource for silence in music, it is still necessary to clarify the meaning of silence, both in the traditional and especially in the Pärtian sense. A definition of rest, pause, or silence, based on written musical reference, as a score, may not be useful to an interpretation of silence as an event of listening; to get closer to Pärt's musicality one should seek to understand silence in music as a hearing event.

Jennifer Judkins proposes a conceptualization also based on the conventional meaning of silence. She associates her interpretation to the fact that time has a direction. Considering that musical form builds itself or manifests itself in this directional temporal flow, the musical time interval in which a musical element or phenomenon is perceived can be shown as a space within the boundaries of a musical event in relation to any other events. That boundary implies the differentiation of an event in relation to the others. For Judkins, that differentiation takes place by using silence as a "time framing" factor.[36] Even if Judkins considers the silence in the heard music, she still conceives it as a perceived event, and thus, of certain materiality. That would imply the listener perceives the succession of frames between sound events, but in that case, if the frame could not be perceived, then silence would not exist.

Arvo Pärt does not seem to disagree with an interpretation of silence as a defining edge between temporal elements. However, the composer assumes, modifies, or even adds to that musical interpretation in his own understanding of silence, turning it into a musical element in its own right. In this sense, the meaning of silence for Pärt goes beyond the written (score) and the perceived (event in timeline) music.

The relationship Pärt establishes with silence is underpinned by an idea of isolation and solitude. He says, "Here [in *Tinntinnabulation*] I am alone with silence."[37] In those non-material bells, silence exists. In this point, therefore, lies the question of whether, for Pärt, silence gives rise to the possibility of the bells, whether the existence of the bells allows for the perception of silence, or whether the bells and silence are the same events. This punctuation is in a special way built up through the sound of the bells. Unlike other musical instruments, bells do not seem to refer to any recognizable element in nature, being therefore essentially different from other musical instruments (e.g., violin, saxophone, etc.) that clearly refer to sounds found in nature or in the human voice, or from compositional procedures that use or refer to sounds present in nature (e.g., the music of the Birds of Messiaen).[38]

By lacking an external natural reference object, being therefore "unnatural," the bells invite the listener to perceive the emptiness of the outer space and to perceive its presence in that empty place. Moreover, the use of bells by Pärt is connected to his clear intention to refer to the medieval liturgical chant.[39] The composer intends to perform melodic development by giving preference to direct and oblique movements between voices, an approach that is fundamentally the opposite of what has been taught since the times of the Palestrina style, where students were instructed to give preference to the contrasting movement of voices as a way of gaining certain independence between voices.[40] Instead, in Pärt, we find a perception of emptiness and silence related in the avoidance of contrasting movements, done so by sustaining the contrapuntal motion, which therefore implies the understanding of silence not as a pause, a rest, or a frame, but rather a constant that permeates the event of music, which refers to Heidegger's claim, previously mentioned, that "the event is the bell of silence[. . .]."[41]

There is another reference to the Gregorian musical practice related to the constant metric variation used to match the musical accent with the accent of the text. By privileging the direct movement and the metric match of the text and the music, Pärt interlaces the voices in a way in which they all have similar contours, resulting in the allegory of a unique musical discourse. It is also important to observe that Pärt's technique is characterized by minimalism and he uses this in relation to silence. According to Alexandra Belibou, his procedure consists of the repetition of undeveloped rhythm (which neither decrease nor increase over the course of the work), with durations of equal values.[42] Additionally, Pärt performs the arpeggio of the triadic chord on only one chord for either the entire work or a long excerpt.[43] This lack of development in the rhythm favors a narrative in the work of Pärt whereby the composer suggests an intention of adding a contemplation factor to silence. In that sense, one could say that, for the composer, the act of composing is an act of contemplating the music permeated by that constant, not developed, yet not still, as the essential mood of the compositional thinking.

It is noteworthy to characterize Pärt's technique as algorithmic: there is a formalized procedural pathway modeling his compositional action.[44] Thus, the composition of Pärt is essentially the musical representation of the composer's mystical convictions, through a "conversion" of the words of sacred texts into melody. The melodic component is in turn a set of relations with the triadic chord by conversion and relations that are ruled by algorithmic models constructed in a way in which silence then becomes an emanator of meaning. Pärt says: "The three notes of a triad are like bells. And that is why I called it tintinnabulation."[45] Notwithstanding the fact that the composer warns that his term tinntinnnabuli is not a transliteration of the bell properties for the compositional procedure,[46] the metaphorical allusion remains.

According to Percival Price, bells can be found in all human cultures and come in all sorts of varieties.[47] In this sense, they consist of a recurring result of the human practice of transforming nature, characterized as a constituent element of multifarious environments. Therefore, the bells appear as instruments that keep their "primitive manifestation."[48] The fact that Pärt uses the algorithmic technique, relating it to the intentional human transformation of nature, offers a rational gesture to the act of composing. The technique emerges as the medium so the composing thinking becomes a composing act.

The triadic chords originate and are used in a different musical context (e.g., regions, times in the history of music, genres), and if Pärt uses these chords as structural elements of his technique and language, he does so in a specific way, adding his own particular meaning or one developed from his musical or extra-musical reflections. By choosing the triadic chord as the musical material, which fills the silence, Pärt also considers an appropriate way to express his convictions and musical expectations. It emerges that this chord, as a material, must be used according to a certain pattern that constitutes the technique and language developed by the composer. This pattern has some elements of simplicity, such as his preference in using simple numbers to obtain maximum agreeability,[49] which showcases a direct relationship between text, melody, and harmony that the attentive listener is attuned to via the abysmally sensible. In the text-melody relationship used by the composer, there is a linear aspect of the melody as a layer of the relationship between musical and extra-musical elements. Additionally, Pärt develops a vertical relationship of the melody with the harmony of the triadic chord. In this sense, in Pärt's technique the triadic chord functions as a fundamental element, which combines those linear aspects and the instant of music as a single construct.[50]

Pärt frequently uses only the perfect—not diminished or augmented—triads. For him, dissonance is a nuisance, and it should not occur in a perfect consonance.[51] By developing his technique based on a perfect chord, the composer creates a statement toward "purity," exempt of dissonance, in structural terms. Hence, his procedural metaphor of using the bells related to his technique produces a reverberation of the melodic linearity with the temporal verticality of the chord and the sensory metaphor for the absence of dissonance. Furthermore, there is the intention of finding the element worthy of occupying the silence, one that can understand the silence of Pärt as an immanent environment of interaction, in which there is no discomfort, and understand that the bells represent the solitary action in the compositional space.

At this point, one could ask why Pärt not only uses but focuses on the perfect triadic chord. Pärt, in his words, "approaches silence with love."[52] The silence here, still according to Pärt, is "the 'nothing' from which God created the world"[53] and the love implies to "wait a long time for his music."[54] Considered not from a historical point of view, but rather in its musicality, the perfect chord appears as the origin for the melody. At this point, one can think of the thoroughbass method, in which one can obtain melodic notes from the chord or identify chords from the notes. But, for Pärt, approaching the silence from which the world emerged implies "waiting a long time"[55] in a state of "sublime anticipation,"[56] static at a single point, the chosen triad. Pärt focus on the representation of the man that waits for God and has chosen the triad as the point on an acoustic map where he sits waiting. In that sense, regarding Pärt's election of the triad results in the counterpoint losing its original character of *punctus contra punctus* and acquires a characteristic of unity.

For Pärt, one must address silence "with a feeling of awe"[57] and one must consider the external perceived silence in the environment in relation to the internal one, "that which is inside a person."[58] Such a perspective on silence could be placed in parallel to what Heidegger says in *On the Way to Language*, while commenting on the poetry of Georg Trakl and Hölderlin, when he speaks of "[entering into] the silence."[59] Furthermore, Heidegger makes a connection between looking, saying, and silence, in which silence is no longer the absence of sound nor lack of meaning: "Thus silence, too, which is often regarded as the source of speaking, is itself already a corresponding. Silence corresponds to the soundless tolling of the appropriating-showing saying."[60] As for Pärt, silence is not the opposite of sound, nor the absence of sound, but rather where music *happens*, and in that way it could be possible to benefit from Heideggerian philosophy in order to understand music, and especially the music of Arvo Pärt, but also to better understand Heidegger's notion of silence through Pärt's music.

NOTES

1. On the topic of Nietzsche and music, see Wallrup's chapter of this volume. Adorno and music is covered by various authors in this volume, most prominently by Harper-Scott.
2. Martin Heidegger, *Der Satz vom Grund: Gesamtausgabe 10*, ed. Petra Jaeger (Vittorio Klostermann: Frankfurt am Main, 1997), 65.
3. Heidegger, *Der Satz vom Grund*, 78.
4. Martin Heidegger, *Anmerkungen I–V: Gesamtausgabe 97*, ed. Peter Trawny (Vittorio Klostermann: Frankfurt am Main, 2015), 448.
5. Heidegger, *Anmerkungen I–V*, 317.
6. Martin Heidegger, *Anmerkungen VI–IX: Gesamtausgabe 98*, ed. Peter Trawny (Vittorio Klostermann: Frankfurt am Main, 2018), 8, 13.
7. Heidegger, *Anmerkungen VI–IX*, 8, 13.
8. Heidegger, *Anmerkungen VI–IX*, 341.
9. Martin Heidegger, *Vier Hefte I und II (Schwarze Hefte 1947–1950): Gesamtausgabe 99*, ed. Peter Trawny (Vittorio Kolstermann: Frankfurt am Main, 2019), 31.
10. Heidegger, *Vier Hefte I und II*, 149.
11. Martin Heidegger, *Vigiliae und Notturno (Schwarze Hefte 1952/53 bis 1957): Gesamtausgabe 100*, ed. Peter Trawny (Vittorio Kolstermann: Frankfurt am Main, 2020), 169.
12. Martin Heidegger, *Winke I, II (Schwarze Hefte 1957-1959): Gesamtausgabe 101*, ed. Peter Trawny (Vittorio Kolstermann: Frankfurt am Main, 2020), 76.
13. Heidegger, *Winke I, II*, 89.
14. Heidegger, *Der Satz vom Grund*, 72.
15. Martin Heidegger, *Hölderlins Hymne "Der Ister" (1942): Gesamtausgabe 53*, ed. Walter Biemel (Vittorio Kolstermann: Frankfurt am Main, 1984), 18.
16. Heidegger, *Hölderlins Hymne "Der Ister,"* 17.
17. Martin Heidegger, *Zu Hölderlin—Griechenlandreisen (1939–1970): Gesamtausgabe 75*, ed. Curd Ochwadt (Vittorio Kolstermann: Frankfurt am Main, 2000), 105.
18. Heidegger, *Zu Hölderlin*, 166.
19. Heidegger, *Zu Hölderlin*, 104.
20. Heidegger, *Zu Hölderlin*, 153.
21. Heidegger, *Zu Hölderlin*, 104.
22. Martin Heidegger, *Holderlins Hymnen "Germanien" und "Der Rhein" (1934–1935): Gesamtausgabe 39*, ed. Susanne Ziegler (Vittorio Kolstermann: Frankfurt am Main, 1989), 80.
23. Cf. Martin Heidegger, *Die Grundbegriffe der Metaphysik. Welt—Endlichkeit—Einsamkeit (1929-30): Gesamtausgabe 29/30*, ed. Friedrich-Wilhelm von Herrmann (Vittorio Kolstermann: Frankfurt am Main, 1983).
24. Martin Heidegger, *Identität und Differenz (1955-1963): Gesamtausgabe 11*, ed. Friedrich-Wilhelm von Herrmann (Vittorio Kolstermann: Frankfurt am Main, 2006), 24.

25. Heidegger, *Holderlins Hymnen "Germanien" und "Der Rhein,"* 81.
26. Heidegger, *Holderlins Hymnen "Germanien" und "Der Rhein,"* 81.
27. Heidegger, *Vier Hefte I und II*, 13.
28. Martin Heidegger, *Vorträge und Aufsätze (1936-1953): Gesamtausgabe 7*, ed. Friedrich-Wilhelm von Herrmann (Vittorio Kolstermann: Frankfurt am Main, 2000), 181, 183.
29. Friedrich Hölderlin, "Notizen zum Plan von Briefen über Homer," in *Sämtliche Werke und Briefe in drei Bänden*, Band II, ed. Michael Knaupp (Carl Hanswer Verlag: München, 1992), 64, 108.
30. Arvo Pärt, "An interview with Arvo Pärt," Interview with Martin Elste. Fanfarre, 1988. Laulasmaa: Arvo Pärt Centre. https://www.arvopart.ee/en/arvo-part/article/an-interview-with-arvo-part.
31. Arvo Pärt, "The Silence and Awe of Arvo Pärt," Interview with Thomas Huizenga, 2014. Laulasmaa: Arvo Pärt Centre. https://www.arvopart.ee/en/arvo-part/article/the-silence-and-awe-of-arvo-par.
32. Arvo Pärt Centre. "Biography," 2021. https://www.arvopart.ee/en/arvo-part/biography.
33. We should thank Toomas Schvak, librarian at the Arvo Pärt Centre, for making that information available.
34. Michael Kennedy and Gabriela Gomes Cruz, Dicionário Oxford de Música, ed. Michael Kennedy and Gabriela Gomes Cruz (Lisoboa: Publicações Dom Quixote, 1994), s.v. "Rest." Zhu also discusses the significance of silence in music in his chapter of this volume.
35. Stanley Sadie and John Tyrrell, The New Grove Dictionary of Music and Musicians, 2nd Ed., ed. Stanley Sadie and John Tyrrell (London: Macmillan, 2001), s.v. "Rest."
36. Jennifer Judkins, "The Aesthetics of Silence in Live Musical Performance," *Journal of Aesthetic Education* 31, no. 3 (1997), 44.
37. Andrew Shenton, "Arvo Part: In his Own Words," in *The Cambridge Companion to Arvo Pärt*, ed. Andrew Shenton (Cambridge: Cambridge University Press, 2012), 120.
38. The French composer Olivier Messiaen incorporated birdsong transcriptions into his music.
39. Alexandra Belibou, "Elements as the Minimalist Composition Technique in Arvo Pärt's Works Based on Psalmic Texts," *Bulletin of the Transilvania University of Braşov* 9, no. 2 (2016): 34–40.
40. Giovanni Pierluigi da Palestrina was an Italian Renaissance composer of sacred music.
41. Heidegger, *Winke I, II*, 76.
42. Belibou, "Elements as the Minimalist Composition Technique," 37.
43. Oranit Kongwattananon, *Arvo Pärt and Three Types of his Tintinnabuli Technique* (Master's thesis). University of North Texas. https://digital.library.unt.edu/ark:/67531/metadc271844/m2/1/high_res_d/thesis.pdf
44. Jelena Tokun, "Formal Algorithms of Tintinnabuli in Arbo Pärt's Musica—In memory of Yevgeny Vladimirovich Nazaikinsky," 2011. Laulasmaa: Arvo Pärt

Centre. https://www.arvopart.ee/en/arvo-part/article/formal-algorithms-of-tintinnabuli-in-arvo-parts-music.

45. Marguerite Bostonia, "Bells as Inspiration for Tintinnabulation," in *The Cambridge Companion to Arvo Pärt*, ed. Andrew Shenton (Cambridge: Cambridge University Press, 2012), 128.

46. Bostonia, "Bells as Inspiration for Tintinnabulation," 130.

47. Percival Price, *Bells and Man* (Oxford: Oxford University Press, 1983).

48. Bostonia, "Bells as Inspiration for Tintinnabulation," 128.

49. Arvo Pärt, "I Seek a Common Denominator," Interview with Enzon Restagno. 2012. Laulasmaa: Arvo Pärt Centre. https://www.arvopart.ee/en/arvo-part/article/i-seek-a-common-denominator.

50. Toomas Siitan, "Introduction to the book 'In Principio. The word in Arvo Pärt's Music'," 2014. Laulasmaa: Arvo Pärt Centre. https://www.arvopart.ee/en/arvo-part/article/introduction-to-the-book-in-principio-the-word-in-arvo-parts-music.

51. Arthur Lublow, "The Sound of Spirit," *The New York Times Magazine*. October 15, 2010. https://www.nytimes.com/2010/10/17/magazine/17part-t.html

52. Jeffers Engelhardt, "Perspectives of Pärt after 1980," in *The Cambridge Companion to Arvo Pärt*, ed. Andrew Shenton (Cambridge: Cambridge University Press, 2012), 35.

53. Engelhardt, "Perspectives of Pärt after 1980," 35.

54. Engelhardt, "Perspectives of Pärt after 1980," 35.

55. Engelhardt, "Perspectives of Pärt after 1980," 35.

56. Engelhardt, "Perspectives of Pärt after 1980," 35.

57. Pärt, "I Seek a Common Denominator."

58. Arvo Pärt, "Sources of Invention," Interview with Geoff Smith. 1999. Laulasmaa: Arvo Pärt Centre. https://www.arvopart.ee/en/arvo-part/article/sources-of-invention.

59. Martin Heidegger, *On the Way to Language*, trans. Peter D. Hertz (New York: Harper & Row, 1971), 166.

60. Heidegger, *On the Way to Language*, 131.

BIBLIOGRAPHY

Arvo Pärt Centre. "Biography." 2021. https://www.arvopart.ee/en/arvo-part/biography.

Belibou, Alexandra. "Elements as the Minimalist Composition Technique in Arvo Pärt's Works Based on Psalmic Texts." *Bulletin of the Transilvania University of Brașov* 9, no. 2 (2016): 34–40.

Bostonia, Marguerite. "Bells as Inspiration for Tintinnabulation." In *The Cambridge Companion to Arvo Pärt*, edited by Andrew Shenton, 128–39. Cambridge: Cambridge University Press, 2012.

Engelhardt, Jeffers. "Perspectives of Pärt after 1980." In *The Cambridge Companion to Arvo Pärt*, edited by Andrew Shenton, 29–48. Cambridge: Cambridge University Press, 2012.

Heidegger, Martin. *Anmerkungen I–V (Schwarze Hefte 1942–1948): Gesamtausgabe 97*. Edited by Peter Trawny. Vittorio Klostermann: Frankfurt am Main, 2015.
Heidegger, Martin. *Anmerkungen VI–IX (Schwarze Hefte 1948/49–1951): Gesamtausgabe 98*. Edited by Peter Trawny. Vittorio Klostermann: Frankfurt am Main, 2018.
Heidegger, Martin. *Der Satz vom Grund: Gesamtausgabe 10*. Edited by Petra Jaeger. Vittorio Klostermann: Frankfurt am Main, 1997.
Heidegger, Martin. *Die Grundbegriffe der Metaphysik. Welt—Endlichkeit—Einsamkeit (1929–30): Gesamtausgabe 29/30*. Edited by Friedrich-Wilhelm von Herrmann. Vittorio Kolstermann: Frankfurt am Main, 1983.
Heidegger, Martin. *Hölderlins Hymne "Der Ister" (1942): Gesamtausgabe 53*. Edited by Walter Biemel. Vittorio Kolstermann: Frankfurt am Main, 1984.
Heidegger, Martin. *Holderlins Hymnen "Germanien" und "Der Rehin" (1934–1935): Gesamtausgabe 39*. Edited by Susanne Ziegler. Vittorio Kolstermann: Frankfurt am Main, 1989.
Heidegger, Martin. *Identität und Differenz (1955–1963): Gesamtausgabe 11*. Edited by Friedrich-Wilhelm von Herrmann. Vittorio Kolstermann: Frankfurt am Main, 2006.
Heidegger, Martin. *On the Way to Language*. Translated by Peter D. Hertz. New York: Harper & Row, 1971.
Heidegger, Martin. *Vier Hefte I und II (Schwarze Hefte 1947–1950): Gesamtausgabe 99*. Edited by Peter Trawny. Vittorio Kolstermann: Frankfurt am Main, 2019.
Heidegger, Martin. *Vigiliae und Notturno (Schwarze Hefte 1952/53 bis 1957): Gesamtausgabe 100*. Edited by Peter Trawny. Vittorio Kolstermann: Frankfurt am Main, 2020.
Heidegger, Martin. *Vorträge und Aufsätze (1936–1953): Gesamtausgabe 7*. Edited by Friedrich-Wilhelm von Herrmann. Vittorio Kolstermann: Frankfurt am Main, 2000.
Heidegger, Martin. *Winke I, II (Schwarze Hefte 1957–1959): Gesamtausgabe 101*. Edited by Peter Trawny. Vittorio Kolstermann: Frankfurt am Main, 2020.
Heidegger, Martin. *Zu Hölderlin—Griechenlandreisen (1939–1970): Gesamtausgabe 75*. Edited by Curd Ochwadt. Vittorio Kolstermann: Frankfurt am Main, 2000.
Hölderlin, Friedrich. "Notizen zum Plan von Briefen über Homer." In *Sämtliche Werke und Briefe in drei Bänden, Band II*, edited by Michael Knaupp, 64–108. Carl Hanswer Verlag: München, 1992.
Judkins, Jennifer. "The Aesthetics of Silence in Live Musical Performance." *Journal of Aesthetic Education* 31, no. 3 (1997): 39–53.
Kennedy, Michael and Gabriela Gomes Cruz. In *Dicionário Oxford de Música*, ed. Michael Kennedy and Gabriela Gomes Cruz (Lisoboa: Publicações Dom Quixote, 1994), s.v. "Rest."
Kongwattananon, Oranit. Arvo Pärt and Three Types of his Tintinnabuli Technique. (Master's thesis). University of North Texas. https://digital.library.unt.edu/ark:/67531/metadc271844/m2/1/high_res_d/thesis.pdf

Lubow, Arthur. "The Sound of Spirit." *The New York Times Magazine*. October 15, 2010. https://www.nytimes.com/2010/10/17/magazine/17part-t.html
Pärt, Arvo. "An Interview with Arvo Pärt." Interview with Martin Elste. Fanfarre, 1988. Laulasmaa: Arvo Pärt Centre. https://www.arvopart.ee/en/arvo-part/article/an-interview-with-arvo-part.
Pärt, Arvo. "I Seek a Common Denominator." Interview with Enzon Restagno. 2012. Laulasmaa: Arvo Pärt Centre. https://www.arvopart.ee/en/arvo-part/article/i-seek-a-common-denominator.
Pärt, Arvo. "The Silence and Awe of Arvo Pärt." Interview with Thomas Huizenga. NPR Classical, 2014. Laulasmaa: Arvo Pärt Centre. https://www.arvopart.ee/en/arvo-part/article/the-silence-and-awe-of-arvo-par.
Pärt, Arvo. "Sources of Invention." Interview with Geoff Smith. 1999. Laulasmaa: Arvo Pärt Centre. https://www.arvopart.ee/en/arvo-part/article/sources-of-invention.
Price, Percival. *Bells and Man*. Oxford: Oxford University Press, 1983.
Sadie, Stanley and John Tyrrell. In *The New Grove Dictionary of Music and Musicians*, 2nd Ed., ed. Stanley Sadie and John Tyrrell (London: Macmillan, 2001), s.v. "Rest."
Shenton, Andrew. "Arvo Part in His Own Words." In *The Cambridge Companion to Arvo Pärt*, edited by Andrew Shenton, 111–27. Cambridge: Cambridge University Press, 2012.
Siitan, Toomas. "Introduction to the book 'In Principio. The word in Arvo Pärt's Music.'" 2014. Laulasmaa: Arvo Pärt Centre. https://www.arvopart.ee/en/arvo-part/article/introduction-to-the-book-in-principio-the-word-in-arvo-parts-music.
Tokun, Jelena. "Formal Algorithms of Tintinnabuli in Arbo Pärt's Musica—In Memory of Yevgeny Vladimirovich Nazaikinsky." 2011. Laulasmaa: Arvo Pärt Centre. https://www.arvopart.ee/en/arvo-part/article/formal-algorithms-of-tintinnabuli-in-arvo-parts-music.

Chapter 9

We Live Therefore We Are

African Musical Aesthetics Challenge Heidegger's Forgetfulness

Eve Ruddock

Contrary to common Western practice, this chapter is an exploration that has no beginning and no end; it begins with a coda (a tail; an ending). It is an *African* way. As philosopher John Murungi reflects in his *African Musical Aesthetics*, "a work does not necessarily have a beginning or an end."[1] In his case, he chooses to begin a deeply phenomenological play of *being* that is African, that is musical, that is aesthetics. Nigerian ethnomusicologist, composer, and scholar Meki Nzewi[2] also opens his detailed exposition of African traditional life with a coda. In his finely honed "culturally mediated philosophy of African musical life,"[3] the young hero *Okeke* brings alive traditional African musicking. To call Nzewi's mythical adventure, a *philosophy* could face challenges by those who, like Heidegger, "perpetuate the belief that philosophy is uniquely a Western phenomenon."[4] Yet this *African* philosophy is a practical philosophy that fascinates and informs.

HEIDEGGER'S FORGETFULNESS?

Heidegger questioned philosophy as he found it. In his concern that Western philosophy had lost an understanding of *being*, he embarked on a big journey. In his serious attempt to escape past misconceptions, *Being and Time*[5] creates an idiosyncratic vocabulary as one way to avoid inherited misunderstandings of what *is*. Yet, with a worldview colored by his beloved Black Forest and German traditions, it is worth questioning whether Heidegger could recognize those prejudices that would continue to blind him to the value of philosophies outside his Western European tradition. In this chapter,

I ask whether his *forgetfulness* applies not only to his inherited German philosophy but also to his failure to include the musical arts[6] in his philosophy. Despite recognizing his unique contribution to Western philosophy, I will question his one-sided view of human beings where he fails to see the central role played by our "humanning" musicality, that is, according to Nzewi, a connective living toward health and worth, which embraces participatory cultural inclusion.[7]

Heidegger was not alone in sensing that something was deeply amiss in the everyday reality of European culture. In his phenomenological exposé of a people where imposed non-musicality reduces vital humanity, Franz Kafka[8] provides an example of how Heidegger's exclusion of music reveals a gap in Western culture—one where many individuals feel distanced from their intrinsic musicality.[9] In his final story titled *Josefine*, written in the months preceding his death in 1924, Kafka points to the danger of reduced being—where a part of essential humanness is missing, where individuals are removed from their human capacity for expression, for connection. Referring to his people's "lack of musicality [Kafka laments that] we sigh and decline."[10] He presents a culture that leaves little space for musicking: a *Western* culture, including various European, Anglo-Saxon, and American traditions, that adopts a one-sided performative public sphere wherein communal connections lose potency. Swayed by objectivity, Heidegger reflects such a condition. Yet, in their paper drawing on disparate human and animal studies, Charles Snowdon and his colleagues report on how human emotional and musical beings communicate—even across species.[11] Their research supports understandings of Nzewi and Murungi who both demonstrate how musicality, a way of being whereby emotional connections are enhanced, plays a crucial role in communicative well-being. In his exploration of neurobiology and culture, Antonio Damasio[12] also brings a deeper understanding of the part emotion plays in everyday living, yet no trace of the essential place of musicality is to be found in Heidegger's *magnum opus*, *Being and Time*.

In contrast, Murungi captures the pathological effects of a world without an essential sense of musicality, where performativity dominates and individuals are distanced from an intrinsic part of being.[13] In his phenomenological exploration of *African Musical Aesthetics*, Murungi exposes a Western philosophy that separates, that fails to recognize connective humanning forces. Yet it is important to note that Heidegger also brings attention to a serious gap in European cultural reality as he redirects his focus to the essence of *being*, an aspect of Western consciousness eroded exponentially with technological development and consumerism. From a different culture, Murungi extends this understanding to project a world wherein embodied musical arts connect all; he states that: "[t]he body musics. The earth musics. Because we are embodied, and because the body is earthly we are music."[14]

Against widespread performative forces, *African Musical Aesthetics* invites us to become what *is*.

But how could such a world be taken seriously? It would be foreign to Heidegger where, steeped in European philosophy, his world would offer little opportunity for an African philosophy, which is an essentially "practical philosophy."[15] While the African *is* and lives *being* an integral part of *what is*, Heidegger constantly strives to reconcile a perceived void. He embarks upon his path toward an essential knowing of *being*. Acknowledging that while "we live in an understanding of being" we do not understand *being*, he commenced his big work toward the "meaning of being."[16] However, in seeking transparency toward knowing, Heidegger self-steers off a path to understanding when he is distracted by working out the "thatness and whatness" of *being*.[17] It is in his approach to the question about being where, quite properly, *as* a human being, he reflects that he already has some understanding—is already involved in being—that he attempts to objectify, to place himself apart from his quest. It is in his determination to work toward more structured knowing that he strives to find words to make explicit this knowing. The right words would offer control—would reveal.

From their perspectives, neither Murungi nor Nzewi would not be so deflected since they connect as part of the earth. An African does not need to work toward a knowing of being—for being simply *is*. Over our birth and death—intrinsically part of *being* human—we have no control. This remains so despite the "thatness and whatness" of how it is that one is alive for an indeterminate moment in time. Murungi considers that, in a way similar to the use of the term *Western*, it is his intent to use *African* to refer to "a mosaic of traditions"[18] that reveal a different philosophy, an *African* philosophy. The use of *African* in this chapter reflects Murungi's challenge to rethink much of what has been accepted as essential philosophical grounds within Western thinking. In his portrayal of the musical arts as central to living, to leadership, to life, Murungi offers insights into African philosophy.

Heidegger's *Being and Time* is intellectual and innovative, a welcome catalyst to break free from constricting philosophical traditions, and yet it disturbs. On a practical note, Heidegger's intent to go beyond traditional Western philosophy fails to include the musical arts, which, from an African perspective, leaves his principal work outside of essential human being. So, while his path is fruitful, Heidegger fails to find what *is*. For, as is now widely accepted, musicking is found in all human cultures,[19] yet an essential aspect of human being is left out of Heidegger's *magnum opus*. Even from the beginning of his exploration, when, early in his thinking, Heidegger seeks directions from within Greek philosophy, I posit that particular objectivity obscures his potential insight into the essence of being as he works "to let something be seen in its *togetherness* with something, to let something be seen *as* something."[20] It is revealing to consider Christopher Small's assertion that such a perception "is the trap of reification, and it has been a besetting fault of Western thinking ever since Plato, who was one of its earliest perpetrators."[21] Further, I suggest that this notion of "something" interferes with Heidegger's getting in touch with the essence of *being*.

Even before we are born, musicking is part of how and who we are; carers caress with rhythm and song, our heartbeat is central, we move with the rhythms of life. However, the central role of music did not appear to be of particular concern to Heidegger as he focused on *thinking* along his path to understanding. Throughout his life, he brilliantly pierced his world of European philosophy to cut through deeply entrenched philosophical traditions to find a way to ask a question that is vital to all: what is it to *be*? Even while he spent an immense effort to deliver a deeper understanding of *Man's* (*sic*) mortal journey, Heidegger's perception of *being* is far removed from the integrated understanding that *is* African musical aesthetics.

Heidegger continually emphasizes the importance of continual drawing upon and interaction with our understanding of the Greek "tradition of philosophy."[22] Yet, he notes the danger of Dasein becoming "entangled in a tradition"[23]—a tradition wherein strong beliefs direct possible action. In his determination to explore deeper answers to what *is* to uncover the nature of *being*, Heidegger reasons that this could be achieved by rethinking the very language of philosophy, which he realizes could lie within the work "of those early philosophers who he, persistently and indiscriminately, calls '*the Greeks.*'"[24] As an expert both in Greek studies and Heideggerian philosophy, Karalis is uniquely placed to comment on how Heidegger engaged with Greek texts. He points to both brilliance and serious flaws in Heidegger's efforts to take command of what Greek heritage could offer European philosophical understanding. For instance, through his use of *alētheia*, which he translates as "unconcealment,"[25] Heidegger works to *reveal*—to become open to what *is*.

Yet, we need to ask a question of Heidegger himself; could his own tradition be a problem? Could it be that his very own tradition obfuscates *being*? If humility were more integral to his being, then Heidegger may have been more perceptive, may have been able to offer a clearer way to engage with the "Greek notion of *alētheia*."[26] He could have led us toward a deeper understanding of how we could engage with insightful explorations of being. However, as Karalis recognizes, this was not to be. Rather, he asserts, Heidegger suffered from an inability to discern the place of history and culture in his understanding of how time and place influence how we (human beings) are, how we feel, think, and act. Nevertheless, Karalis notes the difficulties that both the *Greeks* and Heidegger experience in their attempts to capture the "is-ness"[27] of being in words and he applauds Heidegger's attempts to grasp elusive nuances. However, while he appreciates the genius of Heidegger, Karalis admits to disappointment in the German philosopher's idiosyncratic version of Greek texts,[28] which, in the end, "left behind an unfulfilled great promise."[29] Interestingly, he is not alone in noting Heidegger's "personal inability to confront history"[30] for Iain Thomson also argues that Heidegger's preconceived views may have gotten in the way of clear thinking.[31]

Further, Murungi's phenomenological exploration of African musical aesthetics delivers insights into *being* human that can tempt us to question Heidegger's thesis. As he challenges Western phenomenologists' mission to "return to the things themselves,"[32] Murungi reveals traditions that have not moved away from what *is*. Murungi's work provides a compelling study into a way of being that can lead us to question the veracity of Heidegger's Dasein. Like Karalis, Murungi questions Heidegger's meaning of *his* Greek words as his words echo Karalis' thoughts to wonder about Heidegger's association of *alethēia* with the act of revealing in a physical sense. Interestingly, Karalis' suggestion that Heidegger's "translation, . . . both inaccurate and original" can prepare us to be aware that Heidegger's notion of "forgetfulness"[33] could support an interpretation where, in the preeminence of *thinking* and the formulating of *the question*, human *being* is lost.[34]

Thus, while we might agree with Heidegger's challenge that we cannot locate the "essence of man"[35] within detailed scientific explanations, it defies credulity when he seeks to convince us that other animals are lesser because they cannot stand "outside their being as such and within the truth of being."[36] We might wonder at Heidegger's attempt to create an artifice, which he names "the ek-sistence of man,"[37] to solidify his claim to such a special aspect of *man*—who can stand "out into the truth of Being."[38] We may well read this as a demonstration of Heidegger's disorientated notion of forgetfulness, of the distancing from what *is*.

MUSIC IS LIFE

For the *African*, however, there is no claim to having privy to the essence of *being*. Rather, the community is what *is* and the individual is part of the community. *Music is life*, writes Nzewi.[39] And so, for the African, it is the chorus that "is a standard philosophical principle."[40] So, where global forces support a dominating sense of the prime place of performativity that leads to a loss of a sense of musicality for many individuals, it is the chorus who supports. It is the community that matters. Nzewi's work demonstrates how Western researchers fabricated reports of African musicking[41] to promote the idea of the *solo-chorus* such that it "misrepresent[s] the generic humanity principle of chorus-solo—community before individual."[42] Nzewi describes *musical arts*[43] as a "soft science" that offers societal and individual wellness. However, he argues, Western prejudices have misconstrued the life-affirming values within "indigenous African creative philosophy and theory,"[44] which has led to a misuse of African humanning musicking. When used in misinterpreted adaptations in the West, life-affirming attributes of African music are stripped of their function to enhance human existence. Nzewi asserts how aspects of African music, too often misused in "flippant attributions,"[45] have led to general misconceptions of what *African musical arts are* and what they can *do*. African musical aesthetics are threatened by the imported educational system where Africans are estranged from their intrinsic life force; they have learned that, in order to become experts in Western European music and philosophy, they feel a need to deny their African philosophy. Murungi reveals how difficult this can be. He describes how he feels complicit in the ending of his own tradition; how his Western education disrupted his sense of being such that it contributed to his own self-destruction.[46]

Rather than being a question of how we interpret texts (in Heidegger's case, those of the *Greeks*), and how we fine-tune our knowing to ask insightful questions, it is important to explore how everyday practical aesthetics work for the African musical aesthetic. As is the case for human cultures in general, we can recognize Damasio's understanding of "the powerful connection between . . . social . . . and biological phenomena."[47] Thus, when everyday practices are not destroyed by colonization, an *African's* culturally acquired use of the *musical arts* builds up from the time a baby begins its life journey. The unborn child senses the "mother's sonic, choreographic and emotional living,"[48] then develops musical capacities by means of everyday practice within the community.

Whereas, for Heidegger, "[l]anguage is the clearing-concealing advent of being itself,"[49] the African becomes an integral part of a *practical aesthetic* where cosmic awareness combines with creativity in the everyday. "Enriched spirituality [comes from a] creative theory and philosophy aspired to express or imbue utilitarian potency."[50] Philosophy for the African is not only for contemplation, for intellectual engagement, but is a functional aspect of everyday being.

Musical experiences for Western musickers contrast sharply with this reality of traditional African musical aesthetics. Rather than enjoying a supporting chorus, Hannah Arendt notes, "[p]erforming artists—dancers, playactors, musicians, and the like—need an audience to show their virtuosity . . . need a publicly organized space for their *work*."[51] We may agree with Heidegger that such *work* has the potential to reveal, to make present, as he argues in "The Origin of the Work of Art."[52] Yet, while this might be true for some, too often individuals feel a lack of meaningful musicking happening in their lives; they struggle to survive a void within everyday communal

Being. Importantly, we can recognize that instances of deeply integrated music-making also occur in Western practice—where there is a meaningful connection between people involved. One example of this is when a pianist senses "the collective awareness, the attentive mind of the audience";[53] he experiences a palpable link between himself and the listeners—a situation that takes away the "performer versus receiver" aspect as, together, the pianist and audience come together as a community of musickers. The pianist feels that he is "plugged into a meaningful circuit!"[54] This holistic experience, however, may not be common. Indeed, many individuals find themselves in a cultural abyss—distanced from their intrinsic musicality.[55] Such a plight is unexpectedly brought to light in Kafka's last story[56] written "only a dozen weeks before he died."[57] In *Josefine and the Mouse People*, Kafka brings a tangible resonance to reveal the damage to communicative cultural health that occurs with the separation of instinctive wholeness of the human being.

There is something about Josefine, her song, and the mouse people that challenge us to question our Western culture. Kafka's short story reveals a pathological lack of human connection, one that seems to be addressed by Josefine's *art*. Perhaps it is in the very ordinariness of her song that enables it to evoke memories of human communicative living, a way of being that is being endangered. Kafka captures the neurotic strangeness of humans living separated from their composite humanness—from their whole sensitized being. In capturing the estrangement from the wholeness of being, he brings an uneasy recognition of something, that essence of *being* human. He subtly draws a picture of a people where imposed non-musicality reduces vital humanity. In the story about *Josefine*, this singer did not exhibit amazing talent. Yet, Kafka reveals how, although her *work* is "detached from the fetters of everyday life, . . . it frees us . . . for a little while . . . [it] does get through to us . . . almost as a message from our people to the individual . . . [her] voice . . . makes its way to us."[58] When she disappears and there is no longer the *singer*, the *writer* suggests: "But we do not miss it very much."[59] The whole story deals with this missing!

Perhaps the singer could be a "mere memory"? In his perceptive comments on this story, Koelb notes that, although the singer disappears, the power of the *art* remains. He comments, "How unnecessary the singer is for the song to have its effect."[60] This understanding highlights the different ways of being to be found within Arendt's European aesthetic position of discerning judgment of taste noted above. It would, however, find resonance with *African Musical Aesthetics*. Indeed, Nzewi writes that "situational experiences [reveal how] functional aesthetics is the core of aesthetic conceptualization, expression, and valuation in indigenous African musical arts."[61]

Heidegger's experience, however, would not easily allow him to accept such practical aesthetics. In his *Letter on Humanism*, for instance, he fails to mention the musical arts, despite the fact that "[m]usic has depths that concern our existence as human beings. It has an artistic dimension, which belongs to the wordless area of our perception and recognition."[62] It is of interest, then, that Heidegger does recall how the arts (in Greece) reveal what *is*.[63] Between "our sheer aesthetic-mindedness"[64] and today's performativity as product, he warns, "we no longer guard and preserve the essential unfolding of art."[65] Yet, despite acknowledging the important place of the poet, he constantly stresses the need for a direct focus on *thinking*, on *language*. His lifework plays upon the use of words. His *ek-sistence*, for example, meaning "standing out into the truth of being"[66] stresses the important place of *thinking*.[67] For Heidegger, how he thinks, how his idiosyncratic Greek translations lead him to interpret a particular worldview, all become his necessarily correct way to work toward meaning through language, especially his German language. Where Kafka's writings suggest that the German language also affects his work,[68] it is relevant here to note how powerfully it is that Heidegger's language affects his sense of being in his world, a world with *thinking* at its center.

TOWARD AN UNDERSTANDING OF AFRICAN MUSICAL AESTHETICS

As readers, we feel in Kafka's anguish—his deep lament—something missing. As readers of his final story (*Josefine*), we sense the loss of a human *being*—of connection; a deep void—a sadness. We experience a longing for something; something to help us in our aloneness. What Kafka does not say, yet makes most clear, leads us to wonder: Might we have distant memories of human communicative living? Is our *way of being* mortally endangered in modern times? Are we separated by our misunderstanding of the world? Are our aesthetics, influenced by Western thought, distorted by notions of judgment and beauty? Have we forgotten that the earth, all life on earth, is not a mere "standing reserve" for profit? Can Heidegger's thoughts help? Could another view of being lead us toward different ways of knowing, of *being*? Could the philosophical entity, *African musical aesthetics* help?

In Murungi's view, exploring African musical aesthetics must be a cooperative task: "To be African . . . [it] cannot be a one man show. The engagement of others is indispensable. These others include not only the living but also the dead," whether African or non-African; those engaged with this are important to what "is a communal undertaking."[69] Here there is no singular guiding hand, no "shepherd of being" as Heidegger sought of *man*.[70] African musical aesthetics mean that we are part of the past, present, and future; part of the land, the oceans, the universe. With this view of integrated being,

Murungi argues that an "[an] inquiry into the nature of aesthetics cannot be divorced from the tradition in which the inquirer is situated."[71] This way does not ignore the Heideggerian notion of *care* but unlike Heidegger's perception of man as apart from, or even *alien* to other creatures, the *uncolonized* African *is* part of all that *is*. We see this way of being in Nzewi's mythical story, *Okeke*.[72] Okeke, a young adventurer, witnesses evils perpetuated upon unsuspecting populations. At great personal risk, the young man employs his finely honed musical skills to face devastated societies. With musicking as his only *tool*, Nzewi's tale demonstrates how the power of music, when a recognized part of a culture, can transform broken societies. It is important to explore ways toward understanding how it is that African musical aesthetics can work to affirm humanity.

In his phenomenological consideration of African musical aesthetics, Murungi demonstrates the importance of humility, how this quality can, most gently, allow what *is* to reveal its *being*.[73] As a phenomenologist, Murungi is necessarily aware of not knowing, of allowing understandings to come forth from what *is*. To assume an advanced knowing brings the danger of being locked away from understanding so that the searcher stays locked away from fresh insights.[74]

With his particular focus on thinking as a way of uncovering, of discerning what *is*, it is tempting to question to what extent Heidegger is caught within his cleverly uncovered philosophy such that he is unable to let what *is* inform him? His words lead the reader to wonder. We wonder when he writes, for instance, about the "essence of action . . . We view action only as causing an effect. The actuality of the effect is valued according to its utility. But the essence of action is accomplishment."[75] It would seem, however, that Heidegger understands this as he understands that "[t]hinking accomplishes the relation of being to the essence of man."[76] It is relevant to ask whether he would be able to put aside influences of his lived experiences as an intellectual in Germany to feel beyond his intellectual knowing, to wonder how it is that he claims "thinking is the thinking of being."[77] Indeed, Heidegger appears to be attempting to place thinking as a way of being apart from his embodied self—where thinking can somehow work toward a superior understanding of this "primal mystery for all thinking."[78] Further, when he concludes his *Letter on Humanism* with the claim that "language is the language of being, as clouds are the clouds of the sky,"[79] it is not unreasonable to suggest that he removes himself further from the totality of what *is*. It is Damasio who reminds us that "long before the dawn of humanity, beings were beings."[80]

From the beginning of his *Being and Time*, Heidegger's Dasein reveals the challenging notion of stepping away from the everyday world—making it clear just how difficult it is to recognize embedded influences of a tradition whose pervasive effects remain subtle—they stay hidden. Heidegger asks whether we can save ourselves through "the arts [via] . . . essential reflection upon technology [yet, he recognizes that] our sheer aesthetic-mindedness"[81] has rendered this impossible. Indeed, this might seem to be impossible when *thinking* is perceived as the overarching determining force for human being. However, recent research by van der Schyff and Schiavio shows that such a view underplays the complexity of human make-up.[82] Their wide-ranging exploration reveals recent *connectionist* views that effectively challenge a separatist notion of mind as a thinking tool. They carefully explore how flexible, interactive ways of how we experience and how we change mean that our whole body can directly connect with the environment to experience *what is*.[83]

Murungi remains aware of the care needed for effective research. Recognizing how important it is to maintain humility before the phenomenon in question, he warns that "[w]here man has construed himself as the lord of what he studies, what he studies withdraws and refuses to offer its meaning."[84] Heidegger, on the other hand, sometimes challenges us to "wrest . . . structures of being . . . from the objects of the phenomenon"[85] and to hold fast to the adopted method. While it is important to acknowledge that this understanding comes from his early work (*Being and Time*) and that his later thought offers a different emphasis with his notion of *Gelassenheit* (letting beings be), nevertheless, we can recognize clearly opposed views between the European and African.

For the African, the universe is created in sound,[86] and we are part of that sound. We are part of the cosmos. Murungi writes that "[t]he embodiment of the human blends the human with the body of the universe."[87] For the African, sound is more than this sound or that sound; it is life, it is death. For the African, music is not something we do, something we hear; we *are* the music, the music *is* us.[88] Far from being the elixir, the revealing method toward understanding, Murungi emphasizes the limits of language to capture what *is*. For the *African*, life *is*. Rather than a conglomerate of parts, *African musical aesthetics is*.[89] It is part of all that *is*.

Heidegger, on the other hand, governed by his European philosophically informed self, finds himself "forgetting being as a whole."[90] He loses direct access to his Dasein in his attempt to explain the unexplainable. Recognizing the futility of such an attempt, the African can accept the limitation of language and proceeds to *be* in rhythm with the universe.

To hear Murungi and Nzewi is to resist the temptation to name and explain; through this hearing, it becomes possible to imagine how African musical aesthetics simply *is*. To perceive Heidegger's notion of *thrownness* could help us to engage in the humanning processes of African musical aesthetics as we *become*, as we enter into what Heidegger might call authentic being. Tellingly, to be part of this process is to accept that all cannot be spoken in words; we can become aware that there is more to African musical aesthetics than can be said: "What remains unsaid completes what is said."[91]

CODA REPRISE: *WE LIVE THEREFORE WE ARE*

Rather than an "effort to think . . . primally," Nzewi's young hero, Okeke, is immediately aware of the ugliness, the dangers of man's enframing of nature[92]. He senses the devastation on both environment and humans themselves. We share his horror at the technological imposition on both place and person as the young traveler witnesses peoples distanced from their intrinsic humanity. Nzewi's imaginative drama demonstrates Heidegger's exposure of the power of technology as a means whereby human culture can be diminished and the environment damaged as both earth and man become "standing reserve" for use by those in power.

Where Heidegger constantly attempts to find a hidden truth through what he calls *alethēia*, Karalis explains that "[i]n the Greek understanding of the word there is nothing to be un-veiled or to be revealed; the presence of everything is the epiphany of truth."[93] This suggests how *African Musical Aesthetics* could be closer to *alethēia* than is Heidegger, and even more revealing when we consider that "*Alethēia* meant responsivity between the seer and the seen, a relation of mutual interpenetration."[94] Could Heidegger, himself, also be coming closer to *what is* in the final decade of his life when he writes *The End of Philosophy and the Task of Thinking?*[95] Here, he reconsiders an *aletheia* that could be mistaken for the *African* way; a way in which the ending is the beginning—the beginning is; the end is.

It is relevant to suggest that Heidegger's attempt to capture the essence of *being* in words leads him into his particular enclosed circle of questioning. I wonder whether his efforts to find a unique language to express what it is to *be* from the perspective of a *knowing* human, while, at times insightful, ultimately fails to see what *is*. I suggest that there is value in Murungi's question: "How is one to distinguish the life of thinking from other forms of life without alienating the life of thinking from itself?"[96] I wonder whether this question would lead toward a fruitful phenomenological path?

Yes, like Murungi and Nzewi, it is pertinent to begin again to reflect on possible ways to enlighten our *being* in the world. Could *African Musical Aesthetics* open a way for the sensual to become an essentially recognized part of our living? Murungi could be correct in his understanding that, while it might be generally understood that Descartes' notion of *cogito ergo sum* [I think, therefore, I am] has been properly explained away, Heidegger's words hold fast to a conviction that it *is thinking* that makes human *being* so special. Could Heidegger's thoughtful questioning be perceived as "an abstraction that is cut off from the life in which the truth of aesthetics is embedded"?[97] Like Heidegger, one might continue to question the essential wonder: *What is being?* I might also wonder whether Heidegger's perception, colored by his Western European tradition, remains caught in his own particular German interpretation of *what is*? Or, on the other hand, informed via *African Musical Aesthetics*, it might be wiser to refrain from placing a particular way of living to the fore, as opposed to any other. For, to separate is to do "an injustice to human life [since is it not the] essential unity" of life that counts.[98]

NOTES

1. John Murungi, *African Musical Aesthetics* (Newcastle Upon Tyne: Cambridge Scholars Publishing, 2011), 228.

2. Meki Nzewi, *Okeke: Music, Myth and Life: An African Story* (Unisa, 0003: University of South Africa, 2006). The *coda* here is used to pay tribute to Nzewi and his mythical story.

3. Kofi Agawu, "*Foreword*," in *Okeke: Music, Myth and Life: An African Story* (Unisa, 0003: University of South Africa, 2006), ix.

4. Murungi, *African Musical Aesthetics*, 83.

5. Martin Heidegger, *Being and Time*, ed. Dennis J. Schmidt and trans. Joan Stambaugh (Albany: State University of New York Press, 2010).

6. The term "the musical arts" embraces the arts in its varying forms comprising music, art, and dance.

7. Meki Nzewi, "Humanity Essence of African Musical Arts: The Soft Science of Repetition and Internal Variation Patterns," (Paper presented at the International Seminar) *Creating & Teaching Music Patterns*, Department of Instrumental Music, Rabindra Bharati University, 16–18 December 2013), 4.

8. Franz Kafka, "Josefine, the Singer, or the Mouse People," in *Metamorphosis and Other Stories*, trans. Michael Hofmann (London: Penguin Books, 2007), 264–283.

9. Eve E. Ruddock, "Misconceptions Underplay Western Ways of Musicking: A Hermeneutic Investigation," in *Action Criticism & Theory for Music Education*. doi:10:22176 16(2) (2017): 39–64.

10. Kafka, "Josefine, the Singer, or the Mouse People," 274.

11. Charles T. Snowdon, Elke Zimmermann, and Eckart Altenmüller, "Music Evolution and Neuroscience," in *Progress in Brain Research*, eds. E. Altenmüller, S. Finger, and F. Boller (Amsterdam: Elsevier, 2015), Vol. 217, 17–34.

12. Antonio Damasio, *Descartes' Error* (Revised ed.) (London: Vintage, 2006).

13. Eve Ruddock, "Sort of in Your Blood": Inherent Musicality Survives Cultural Judgement," *Research Studies in Music Education* 34, no. 2 (2012): 207–221.

14. Murungi, *African Musical Aesthetics*, 222.

15. Meki Nzewi, email to author, 27 August 2019.

16. Heidegger, *Being and Time*, 3.

17. Heidegger, *Being and Time*, 4.

18. Murungi, *African Musical Aesthetics*, 45.
19. Stephen Malloch and Colwyn Trevarthen, "Musicality: Communicating the Vitality and Interests of Life," in *Communicative Musicality: Exploring the Basis of Human Companionship*, eds. Stephen Malloch and Colwyn Trevarthen (Oxford: Oxford University Press, 2009), 1–11.
20. Heidegger, *Being and Time*, 31.
21. Christopher Small, *Musicking: The Meanings of Performing and Listening* (Hanover, NH: Wesleyan University Press, 1998). 2.
22. Heidegger, *Being and Time*, 71.
23. Heidegger, *Being and Time*, 20.
24. Vrasidas Karalis, "Martin Heidegger and the Aletheia of his Greeks," in *Heidegger and the Aesthetics of Living*, ed. Vrasidas Karalis (Newcastle Upon Tyne: Cambridge Scholars Publishing, 2008), 218.
25. Martin Heidegger, "Letter on Humanism," in *Basic Writings*, ed. David Farrell Krell (New York, NY: HarperCollins Publishers, 2008), 125.
26. Martin Heidegger, "Letter on Humanism," 225.
27. Karalis, "Martin Heidegger and the Aletheia of his Greeks," 216.
28. Karalis, "Martin Heidegger and the Aletheia of his Greeks," 216.
29. Karalis, "Martin Heidegger and the Aletheia of his Greeks," 226.
30. Karalis, "Martin Heidegger and the Aletheia of his Greeks," 225.
31. Iain Thomson, "Thinking Love: Heidegger and Arendt," *Continental Philosophy Review* 50 (2017): 453–78.
32. Murungi, *African Musical Aesthetics*, 75.
33. Karalis, "Martin Heidegger and the Aletheia of his Greeks," 221.
34. Heidegger, "Letter on Humanism," 232.
35. Martin Heidegger, "The End of Philosophy and the Task of Thinking," in *Basic Writings*, ed. David Farrell Krell (New York, NY: HarperCollins Publishers, 2008), 228.
36. Heidegger, "The End of Philosophy and the Task of Thinking," 229.
37. Heidegger, "The End of Philosophy and the Task of Thinking," 228.
38. Heidegger, "The End of Philosophy and the Task of Thinking," 230.
39. Nzewi, "Humanity Essence of African Musical Arts," 10.
40. Nzewi, "Humanity Essence of African Musical Arts," 9.
41. Christopher Small word "musicking" attempts to revive the vibrant place of music in human lives. To engage in musicking embraces all senses as we feel alive and respond musically to our lifeworld and includes listening, moving, singing, playing, observing, and responding to natural as well as humanly structured phenomena.
42. Nzewi, "Humanity Essence of African Musical Arts, 9.
43. Nzewi, "Humanity Essence of African Musical Arts," 2. Nzewi writes: "in indigenous Africa, the musical arts . . . is the sonic component of a conceptual synthesis of the sonic, the dramatic and . . . performative properties," 2.
44. Nzewi, "Humanity Essence of African Musical Arts," 4.
45. Nzewi, "Humanity Essence of African Musical Arts," 4.
46. Murungi, *African Musical Aesthetics*, 226–227.
47. Damasio, *Descartes' Error*, 124.

48. Nzewi, "Humanity Essence of African Musical Arts," 1.
49. Heidegger, "Letter on Humanism," 230.
50. Nzewi, "Humanity Essence of African Musical Arts," 4.
51. Hannah Arendt, *Between Past and Future: Eight Exercises in Political Thought* (New York: The Viking Press, 1968), 154.
52. Martin Heidegger, "The Origin of the Work of Art," in *Basic Writings*, ed. David Farrell Krell (New York: HarperCollins, 1993), 143–212.
53. William Westney, *The Perfect Wrong Note: Learning to Trust Your Musical Self* (Pompton Plains, NJ: Amadeus Press, 2003), 148.
54. Westney, *The Perfect Wrong Note*, 148.
55. Eve Ruddock, "Sort of in Your Blood: Inherent Musicality Survives Cultural Judgement," *Research Studies in Music Education* 34, no. 2 (2012): 207–221. doi:10.1177/1321103X12461747.
56. Franz Kafka, "Josefine, the Singer, or the Mouse People," 264–283.
57. Clayton Koelb, *Kafka: A Guide for the Perplexed* (London: Continuum International Publishing Group, 2010), 143.
58. Kafka, "Josefine, the Singer, or the Mouse People," 275–276.
59. Kafka, "Josefine, the Singer, or the Mouse People," 264.
60. Koelb, *Kafka: A Guide for the Perplexed*, 144.
61. Nzewi, email to author, 27 August 2019.
62. Hanne Rinholm & Øivind Varkøy, "Music Education for the Common Good? Between Hubris and Resignation: A Call for Temperance," in *Humane Music Education for the Common Good*, eds. Iris M. Yob and Estelle R. Jorgensen (Bloomington, Indiana 47405: Indiana University Press, 2020), 40–53.
63. Martin Heidegger, "The Question Concerning Technology," in *Basic Writings*, ed. David Farrell Krell (New York, NY: HarperCollins Publishers, 2008), 339.
64. Heidegger, "The Question Concerning Technology," 340.
65. Heidegger, "The Question Concerning Technology," 341.
66. Heidegger, "Letter on Humanism," 230.
67. Heidegger, "Letter on Humanism," 264.
68. Koelb, *Kafka: A Guide for the Perplexed*, 97.
69. Murungi, *African Musical Aesthetics*, 41.
70. Heidegger, "Letter on Humanism," 234.
71. Murungi, *African Musical Aesthetics*, 45.
72. Nzewi, *Okeke: Music, Myth and Life*.
73. Murungi, *African Musical Aesthetics*, 88–92.
74. Murungi, *African Musical Aesthetics*, 92.
75. Heidegger, "Letter on Humanism," 217.
76. Heidegger, "Letter on Humanism," 217.
77. Heidegger, "Letter on Humanism," 220.
78. Heidegger, "Letter on Humanism," 238.
79. Heidegger, "Letter on Humanism," 265.
80. Damasio, *Descartes' Error*, 248.
81. Martin Heidegger, "The Question Concerning Technology," in *Basic Writings*, ed. David Farrell Krell (New York, NY: HarperCollins Publishers, 2008), 340.

82. Dylan van der Schyff and Andrea Schiavio, "Evolutionary Musicology Meets Embodied Cognition: Biocultural Coevolution and the Enactive Origins of Human Musicality," *Frontiers in Neuroscience* 11 (2017): 4. doi:10.3389/fnins.2017.00519.
83. Van der Schyff and Schiavio, "Evolutionary Musicology Meets Embodied Cognition," 8.
84. Murungi, *African Musical Aesthetics*, 92.
85. Heidegger, *Being and Time*, 34.
86. Nzewi, "Assessing the Kernel and/or the Husk of Music Essence," 1–3.
87. Murungi, *African Musical Aesthetics*, 134.
88. Murungi, *African Musical Aesthetics*, 102–134.
89. Murungi, *African Musical Aesthetics*, 58.
90. Martin Heidegger, "On the Essence of Truth," in *Basic Writings: Martin Heidegger*, ed. David Farrell Krell (New York, NY: HarperCollins Publishers, 2008), 132.
91. Murungi, *African Musical Aesthetics*, 59. Zhu makes a similar argument about ancient Chinese music in his chapter of this volume, using the later Heidegger's thought as a complement to that tradition.
92. "Coda reprise" acknowledges Nzewi's finale to his Okeke revelatory myth and "We live therefore we are" refers directly to Murungi's African Musical Aesthetics, 48..
93. Karalis, "Martin Heidegger and the Aletheia of his Greeks," 224.
94. Karalis, "Martin Heidegger and the Aletheia of his Greeks," 224.
95. Heidegger, "The End of Philosophy and the Task of Thinking," 431–449.
96. Murungi, *African Musical Aesthetics*, 48.
97. Murungi, *African Musical Aesthetics*, 48.
98. Murungi, *African Musical Aesthetics*, 48.

BIBLIOGRAPHY

Agawu, Kofi. "Foreword." In *Okeke: Music, Myth and Life: An African Story*. Edited by Meki Nzewi, i–ix. Unisa: University of South Africa Press, 2006.
Arendt, Hannah. *Between Past and Future: Eight Exercises in Political Thought*. New York: The Viking Press, 1968.
Damasio, Antonio. *Descartes' Error*. Revised Ed. London: Vintage, 2006.
Gadamer, Hans-Georg. *Truth and Method*. Translated by Joel Weinsheimer and Donald G. Marshall. London: Continuum, 2004.
Heidegger, Martin. *Being and Time*. Translated by Joan Stambaugh. Albany: State University of New York, 2010.
Heidegger, Martin. "The End of Philosophy and the Task of Thinking." In *Basic Writings*. Edited by David Farrell Krell, 431–449. New York, NY: HarperCollins Publishers, 2008.
Heidegger, Martin. "Letter on Humanism." In *Basic Writings*. Edited by David Farrell Krell, 217–265. New York, NY: HarperCollins Publishers, 2008.

Heidegger, Martin. "On the Essence of Truth." In *Basic Writings*. Edited by David Farrell Krell, 115–138. New York, NY: HarperCollins Publishers, 2008.

Heidegger, Martin. "The Origin of the Work of Art." In *Basic Writings*. Edited by David Farrell Krell, 143–212. New York: HarperCollins Publishers, 1993.

Heidegger, Martin. "The Question Concerning Technology." In *Basic Writings*. Edited by David Farrell Krell, 311–341. New York, NY: HarperCollins Publishers, 1993.

Kafka, Franz. "Josefine, the Singer, or the Mouse People." In *Metamorphosis and Other Stories*. Translated by Michael Hofmann, 264–283. London: Penguin Books, 2007.

Karalis, Vrasidas. "Martin Heidegger and the Aletheia of his Greeks." In *Heidegger and the Aesthetics of Living*. Edited by Vrasidas Karalis, 208–227. Newcastle Upon Tyne: Cambridge Scholars Publishing, 2008.

Koelb, Clayton. *Kafka: A Guide for the Perplexed*. London: Continuum International Publishing Group, 2010.

Malloch, Stephen, and Colwyn Trevarthen. "Musicality: Communicating the vitality and interests of life." In *Communicative musicality: Exploring the basis of human companionship*. Edited by Stephen Malloch and Colwyn Trevarthen, 1–11. Oxford: Oxford University Press, 2009.

Murungi, John. *African Musical Aesthetics*. Newcastle Upon Tyne: Cambridge Scholars Publishing, 2011.

Nzewi, Meki. "Assessing the Kernel and/or the Husk of Music Essence? Positing Sustainable Humanity Directions/Actions." In *Music Assessment and Global Diversity: Practice, Measurement and Policy*. Edited by Timothy S. Brophy, Mei-Ling Lai, and Hsiao-Fen Chen. Chicago, IL: GIA Publications, Inc, 2014.

Nzewi, Meki. "Humanity Essence of African Musical Arts: The Soft Science of Repetition and Internal Variation Patterns." Paper presented at the International Seminar on "Creating & Teaching Music Patterns," Department of Instrumental Music, Rabindra Bharati University, 2013, 16–18 December 2013.

Nzewi, Meki. *Okeke: Music, Myth and Life: An African Story*. Unisa: University of South Africa Press, 2006.

Rinholm, Hanne, and Øivind Varkøy. "Music Education for the Common Good? Between Hubris and Resignation: A Call for Temperance." In *Humane Music Education for the Common Good*. Edited by Iris M. Yob, and Estelle R. Jorgensen, 40–53. Bloomington, Indiana: Indiana University Press, 2020.

Ruddock, Eve E. "Misconceptions Underplay Western Ways of Musicking: A Hermeneutic Investigation." *Action, Criticism & Theory for Music Education* 16, no. 2 (2017): 39–64. doi:10.22176.

Ruddock, Eve E. "Sort of in Your Blood: Inherent Musicality Survives Cultural Judgement." *Research Studies in Music Education* 34, no. 2 (2012): 207–221. doi:10.1177/1321103X12461747.

Small, Christopher. *Musicking: The Meanings of Performing and Listening*. Hanover, NH: Wesleyan University Press, 1998.

Snowdon, Charles T., Elke Zimmermann, and Eckart Altenmüller. "Music Evolution and Neuroscience." In *Progress in Brain Research*. Edited by Eckart Altenmüller, S. Finger, and F. Boller, Vol. 217, 17–34. Amsterdam: Elsevier, 2015.

Thomson, Iain. "Thinking Love: Heidegger and Arendt." *Continental Philosophy Review* 50, (2017): 453–478. doi:10.1007/s11007-017-9421-9.
Van der Schyff, Dylan, and Andrea Schiavio. "Evolutionary Musicology Meets Embodied Cognition: Biocultural Coevolution and the Enactive Origins of Human Musicality." *Frontiers in Neuroscience* 11, Article 519 (2017): doi:10.3389/fnins.2017.00519.
Westney, William. *The Perfect Wrong Note: Learning to Trust Your Musical Self.* Pompton Plains, NJ: Amadeus Press, 2003.

Part III

MUSICAL CREATION AND PERFORMANCE

Chapter 10

Improvising the Round Dance of Being

Reading Heidegger from a Musical Perspective

Sam McAuliffe and Jeff Malpas

The secondary literature concerned with the thought of German philosopher Martin Heidegger commonly attempts to elucidate key themes from Heidegger's thinking by appealing to simple examples. Hammers and jugs are particularly favored, being consistent with Heidegger's own examples. While discussions that draw upon such examples effectively convey, in broad terms, what is at issue in Heidegger's thought, the simplicity of these examples and the fact that the same examples appear time and time again often leave unsaid or underdeveloped certain progressions and consequences of Heidegger's philosophy.

In this chapter, three related themes from Heidegger's thought—"equipmentality" (*Zeugsein*), "dwelling" (*Wohnen*), and "Event" (*Ereignis*)—each of which relates to Heidegger's broader concept of "world"—are considered with respect to improvised musical performance. Such performance, and so "improvisation" more generally, is understood as a spontaneous attending and responding to the unexpected and unforeseen (*improviso*) that emerges from the temporospatial happening that is the "Event" (*extempore*), the *Ereignis*. As such, improvisation is not so much something subjects *do*, but something subjects *participate in*. At the same time as Heidegger's thinking can offer insight into the improvisational character of musical practice, the consideration of musical improvisation also illuminates aspects of Heidegger's thought that are commonly left unacknowledged or underdeveloped in standard readings, including Heidegger's own appeal to ideas of the improvisational and even the musical.

MUSICAL IMPROVISATION

Despite Heidegger's lack of direct engagement with music, there have been several attempts to draw on Heidegger's work to address questions pertaining to music.[1] In this chapter, we undertake our own exploration of the relevance of Heidegger's thinking to music, specifically with respect to improvised musical performance. We argue that Heidegger's thinking provides insight into the fundamental character of such performance, but equally, that its consideration also highlights certain aspects of key Heideggerian themes in ways typically not considered. A key point of focus in our discussion is Heidegger's idea of "world" as this relates to three central concepts: "equipmentality" (*Zeugsein*), "dwelling" (*Wohnen*), and "Event" (*Ereignis*), each of which is addressed in turn. With respect to improvised musical performance, "equipmentality" offers insight into the relationship between players and their instruments; "dwelling" highlights the way in which performing music always goes beyond a purely musical context; the "Event" draws out the dynamic and appropriative nature of improvisational engagement. What is offered is both a musical and improvisational understanding of what Heidegger refers to in *Being and Time* as being-in-the-world, and so of world itself, and a "world-oriented" ontological understanding of musical improvisation.

Improvisation is a commonplace term in musical discussion, as it is elsewhere, but as is the case with so many terms, such familiarity can be a barrier to thinking more essentially about what is at issue. One way of overcoming that barrier is, as Heidegger suggests, to "listen" to language,[2] that is, to attend to the larger context to which a word or phrase belongs and which is often initiated, in Heidegger's work, through a reflection on etymology. Such reflection is certainly instructive in the case of improvisation, which is originally connected to the Latin *improviso* and also *extempore*. *Improviso* means "unexpected" or "unforeseen." *Extempore* is literally "out of time"—*ex* (out of) *tempore*, ablative of *tempus* (time)—but in the sense of being that which is *of* time or "*of* the moment," and so stands out from time. *Improviso* and *extempore* convey the idea of a dynamic event that is without antecedent, and so is unprepared for and unanticipated, and, on reflection, one might say the same of improvisation. Understood thus, improvisation is not primarily the exercising of musical virtuosity, or the exhibiting of mastery of an instrument, musical genre, style, or structure, nor a demonstration of the collaborative possibilities of an ensemble. Rather, on the basis of a learned familiarity involving one's instrument, musical tradition and culture, and other performers—a "coming to be at home," or better, a "becoming oriented" in the *topos*[3] (the topological ordering) of the musical—one gives oneself over to the unexpected and unforeseen possibilities of the event, and so come to *belong* as well as contribute to a happening that is both singular and complex.

Although we may tend to think of improvisation, especially in music, as a particular kind of performance or performative skill, to understand it as an event in the way suggested allows it to be seen as something essential to human engagement in the world. Improvisation, in the broadest sense of the term, not only characterizes what it is to genuinely be in the world—to be genuinely *engaged*—it also characterizes the happening of world as such. Indeed, what Heidegger calls the Event is itself an improvisation, as will be made evident below. In the following sections we attempt to elucidate the details of what an improvisational account of being-in-the-world might mean and how, by drawing on improvised musical performance as an exemplar, such an improvisational account can be found in some of Heidegger's own key texts.

WORLD AND TRUTH

We begin where, in an important sense, Heidegger himself begins—with the world. It is Heidegger's overall understanding of world, a brief sketch of which is the aim of this section, that provides the immediate context for the ensuing discussion. Much of Heidegger's work can be understood as an attempt to elucidate *world* no less than *being*, and the idea of world is one that Heidegger claims has gone entirely unrecognized by previous thinkers.[4]

For the early Heidegger, "world is that which is already previously unveiled and from which we return to the being with which we have to do and among which we dwell."[5] World is prior to *Dasein*; it is that in which one always already finds oneself. It is that which there *is*, for *Dasein*. Importantly, world is that in which one is *situated* when one relates to other humans and things. To be "situated" is to be "set *in* place"—to find oneself *already placed* in a certain topological configuration with respect to other things and attend to the circumstances that arise from the way those things relate to one another.[6] The situation is the very structure that gives rise to thinking and acting—one *is* in response to the circumstances one encounters and attends to. The world in which one is situated is not something one can ever stand apart from and view objectively; one *is* in the world, in the midst of the world, always already there. According to Heidegger, the world is not for us, instead, the world is comprised of myriad things; we are but one of those things, albeit holding a certain privileged position insofar as we have a "world" and not merely an "environment." The "world" is an issue for us in a way that the animal's environment is not; for Heidegger, animals are "poor in world," and innate objects are "worldless."[7]

From the mid-1930s onward, the idea of world bears a more explicit relation to truth in Heidegger's thinking. For Heidegger, truth does not merely refer to "correctness" (Heidegger often uses the Greek term *orthotēs*), usually understood as a matter of correspondence between assertion (or thought) and world, but is rather that which itself makes such correctness possible. In simple terms, the possibility of making a claim about something that could be true or false (in the ordinary sense associated with correctness) already depends on things being made apparent such that claims can be made about them—the making apparent of things that occurs in the midst of world is thus necessary for making claims or having thoughts whether they are, in the ordinary sense, true or false. In the sense of that which first makes things apparent, and so makes correctness possible, Heidegger refers to truth as unconcealment or unhiddenness (*Unverborgenheit*), or disclosedness (*Erschlossenheit*), also using the Greek term *alétheia*.[8] Heidegger's developing account of truth, already presaged in *Being and Time*, but becoming more salient in the 1930s, is one in which truth is itself an event of the happening of world as that in the midst of which truth—as unconcealment or disclosedness—occurs. As fundamentally disclosive, truth is always a bringing of things to an appearance from out of concealment, and this means that truth, as *un*concealment or *dis*closedness, always stands against the background of concealment, closedness, or untruth.[9] This has the consequence that truth, as it is disclosive, is never apart from concealing, and so is never complete; truth is always tied to the situated and singular event of disclosedness, and yet is always open to the possibility of other disclosures.

Understood as the event of disclosedness or unconcealment that belongs to world, truth makes especially evident the character of world as relational, and so as always implicating a totality, and yet as also situationally articulated. The relationality of world is worked out in and through the singular happening of truth which is always the happening of a situation or place. For Heidegger, there is no genuine relation outside of the relationality of world and so outside of this sort of singular dynamic situatedness. The basic themes that appear here play out in various ways across Heidegger's thinking, and they bear closely on the other key concepts that are the focus for discussion: equipmentality, dwelling, and Event. In what follows, the concepts at issue are taken up in ways that draw on what has gone before but which also deploy those concepts in the more specific context of musical performance, and especially of improvisational musical performance, so as to illuminate both the nature of such performance, and the improvisation at work in it, and the concepts themselves. By considering the insights Heidegger's thinking offers for our understanding of musical performance and improvisation, a particular reading of Heidegger will emerge—a reading in which being-in-the-world is seen to be essentially improvisational in a way that mirrors the basic structure of improvisation in musical performance.

EQUIPMENTALITY IN MUSIC

"Equipmentality" is the first of the three ideas mentioned above that will be addressed—partly because it is the earliest of the three to which Heidegger gives detailed attention ("dwelling" has the same early provenance, but without the same development). What is at issue in equipmentality, simply put, is Dasein's active relation to things in the world. Some things are "ready-to-hand" (*Zuhanden*), such that one may use a thing without thinking about it directly, while others are "present-at-hand" (*Vorhanden*), such that one directs one's attention toward and actively considers a thing.[10] For Heidegger, equipment is "something in-order-to . . ."[11] We can thus infer from Heidegger that the proficient guitarist, for example, "uses" the guitar plectrum "in-order-to" strike the strings of the guitar without apprehending the plectrum theoretically. This is because the relationship between player and plectrum, Heidegger would say, "has in each case been outlined in advance in terms of the totality of such involvements."[12] When using a plectrum, the actions of the player are structured by the way in which plectrums are known to be functionally deployed. If the plectrum cracks and begins catching on the strings, however, the player may begin attending to the plectrum directly, as something "present-at-hand."

While examples such as these do some justice to what is at stake with respect to equipmentality, they pass over a wealth of information about the way in which equipmentality structures being-in-the-world. Considering equipment with respect to a more complex relationship, such as the broader relationship between musicians and their instruments, yields greater insight into what is at issue. It highlights, for instance, the way in which equipment not only serves a particular use but also the way in which equipment itself shapes and modifies modes of worldly activity and engagement (and so Heidegger's account of equipmentality, along with other aspects of his thought, can be seen to prefigure contemporary ideas of extended cognition[13]).

When an experienced player sits with an acoustic guitar, they do not consciously intend all of their actions toward the guitar. Largely, the guitar itself structures the bodily position and actions of the player. For instance, by virtue of the equipmental structuring of the guitar, the player's right hand (assuming they play right-handed) moves vertically between the highest and lowest strings, and horizontally, achieving brighter tones as they strike the strings closer to the bridge of the guitar, and warmer tones as they move up the body of the guitar toward the neck. The fingers on their left hand press strings to the fretboard to alter the pitch, and the hand stretches to execute certain large intervallic leaps. The right arm wraps around the guitar, gently holding it in position against the player's body as the left arm holds the player's hand in a position such that their thumb rests on the back of the guitar neck, stabilizing the fretting fingers to enable them to apply the appropriate pressure to the strings.

For the experienced guitarist, assuming they play in the traditional manner described above,[14] the instrument demands this basic configuration. The instrument configures the body and brain of the player.[15] Alva Noë observes,

> The expert's performance . . . deteriorates if he focuses on the mechanics of the task. . . . It has been shown, for example, that highly trained experts—musicians, athletes, etc.—show a decrease in overall level of brain activation when they are engaged in the performance of their skills compared to beginners.[16]

The player is not consciously acting toward the instrument. Rather, in their knowing how to play the guitar they allow the guitar to structure their acting.

To know how to play a guitar, then, is to know the *topos* the instrument brings with it—the player comports themselves, thinks, and acts in a manner consistent with that which is required of the instrument in the given situation. Playing one's instrument is the enactment of certain topological structures such that inasmuch as the player plays the instrument, the instrument plays the player. To spontaneously engage with one's instrument while one improvises music, then, is, in part, to allow oneself to be *played by* the instrument. There is a certain relationship between player and instrument that comes about only when player and instrument relate to one another in this way. If the relationship breaks down, as it were, perhaps the guitar breaks or malfunctions in some unexpected way during the performance, the topological structures that afford the decrease in brain activation mentioned above are interrupted, and new relationships emerge—perhaps the guitarist perseveres with a broken string and for the most part the original relationships are reconfigured, or perhaps the interruption is so severe the performance is forced to an early close.

At issue in "equipmentality" is the way in which certain material configurations of things we use structure our being-in-the-world. We are in the world, in part, through being amidst such configurations, and on this basis the way in which we each *are* in the world can be said to be structured by the world itself (although, since the world is not entirely given in terms of things for use, neither can the way we are in the world be entirely structured so either). Musicians develop certain skillsets because there exists in the world a reason to have such a skillset; musicians assume the *topos* of their instrument, in large part, because that is what the *instrument* demands. To engage in improvised musical performance, then, is to assume a certain topological relationality with the world. That situational responsiveness, and so the more specific relationship between player and instrument (a relationship captured in Heidegger's notion of the equipmental), obtains regardless of whether or not it is explicitly or consciously acknowledged by the player. Put in more general terms, the equipmental structure of the world—and so the way the world already configures possibilities for action—means that our being-in-the-world, as it is worked out in activity, is always shaped by the world itself. Our own being is thus inseparable from the being of the world.

FROM EQUIPMENTALITY TO DWELLING

The account of equipmentality in *Being and Time*, although more narrowly focused than any of his later discussions, is nevertheless a precursor to the account of "dwelling" Heidegger gives in essays from the 1950s such as "The Thing."[17] Indeed, the account of equipmentality is part of Heidegger's elaboration of the structure of being-in-the-world that, in *Being and Time*, he explicitly designates as having the character of "dwelling."[18] The problem, however, is that the focus on the equipmental can all too easily be read as implying that the world is in some sense produced by and in relation to the structure of "useful" or "practical" that arise from *Dasein's* own purposes and activities. The danger is thus that the world is seen as somehow a product of "subjectivity" (taking Dasein, as developed in *Being and Time*, to be a fundamental mode of subjectivity and so also of human being). The problem, which extends across the analysis of *Being and Time* more broadly, is one that Heidegger himself recognizes, even if he often treats it as a problem of the way his work is read rather than as intrinsic to that work.[19] Part of the shift that occurs between Heidegger's earlier and later works is in terms of a shift toward a clearer focus on the structure of the world as that in which dwelling is founded.

The idea of "dwelling" may thus be seen to develop or rearticulate the way in which the world is something of which mortals (the term that essentially replaces Dasein in the later work) are *a part*, as opposed to something produced by, or something that is *for*, Dasein. Heidegger's idea of the "fourfold," which is intimately tied to dwelling, presents the world as the co-responsiveness or happening of earth, sky, divinities, and mortals.[20] Earth, sky, and the divinities are not *for* or *produced by* mortals; the world only *is* insofar as there is this mutual *belonging* together of these four elements. While the basic ideas central to equipmentality are certainly present in Heidegger's account of dwelling and the fourfold, equipmentality alone does not capture, for instance, the way in which one's participation in an activity goes beyond the context of that individual activity. From the perspective of dwelling, playing music is a mode of being that encompasses more than just the music. To play music is to participate in the world, enacting the oneness of the fourfold—gathering earth, sky, divinities, and mortals. To play music is to set forth the world in a particular way, through the medium of music. In this section, we will outline what a consideration of dwelling offers our understanding of improvised musical performance.

What is at issue in dwelling is realizing that one is not separate from the world. To dwell is to find oneself intimately related to those other elements that belong to the fourfold, attending and responding to that which is given in the enactment of that relationality. Dwelling refers to a certain topological ordering where one finds oneself already placed as one of four essential elements in the fourfold. Indeed, what Heidegger addresses through the concept of dwelling, where the world is not merely some backdrop against which mortals conduct themselves or that is available to them, is exactly the sort of situatedness at issue in improvised musical performance. This situatedness is not particular to music alone; Heidegger argues that to *be* is to *dwell*—he writes, "I dwell, you dwell. The way in which you are and I am, the manner in which we humans *are* on the earth, is . . . dwelling."[21] Nonetheless, music and musical improvisation, like any and every human activity, can only be understood against the background of dwelling as that which characterizes the nature of human, or mortal, being. Moreover, as we argue below, by looking at the character of improvised musical performance we are also able to draw out the improvisational character of dwelling itself.

To improvise is to attend and respond to the unexpected and the unforeseen (exactly what is suggested by the etymology of *improviso* and *extempore*) in the temporospatidynamicity of the Event such that what the player encounters is neither reducible to the player alone nor to something only the player contributes. That which is encountered comes forth *in* and *from* the Event and is *there* with the player, calling for attention and response. When one improvises, one encounters the world as the world presents *itself* in *that* situation, and thus a certain aspect of the world is disclosed and made salient. In the openness of receptive engagement—an openness to the unexpected and unforeseen—the improviser does not offer responses on the basis of the world as it is already known. Rather improvisation allows the world to come to be in a way that is indeed unforeseen and new—*improviso* is also *innovare*—it is original and originary, as Heidegger would say. Through improvising one comes to "be at home" in the indeterminate happening of the musical—one comes to dwell in the musical, and therefore the world.

The improvisation of music is demonstrative of precisely what is at issue in Heidegger's account of dwelling, and improvisation more broadly points to what is at issue in a "dwelling life."[22] That improvised musical performance is a spontaneous attending and responding to the unexpected and unforeseen means improvisation cannot be reduced to a set of rules, principles, or precepts. Equally, as dwelling is a spontaneous happening, where one owns up (even if one does not recognize it as such) to being *a part* of the world and is therefore open to receiving the world, dwelling is equally not reducible to rules, principles, or precepts. That dwelling demands an improvisational comportment to a world largely concealed from mortals means there can be no overarching rules or principles that would allow us to shift our responsibility for engagement to those rules or principles. To dwell, one must simply attend and respond to the place in which one *is*. Rather than being an attempt to control or manipulate the world, dwelling is a participation in the improvisational happening of the world—improvised musical performance providing an especially salient exemplar of such engagement.

Thinking dwelling in terms of improvisation, we can make sense of what is sometimes thought to be a tension in Heidegger's thinking. On the one hand, says Heidegger, "to be a human being means to be on the earth as a mortal. It means to dwell,"[23] and on the other, he insists "that mortals . . . *must ever learn to dwell*."[24] There can be no method for attending and responding to that which is unexpected and unforeseen. To meaningfully engage with those aspects of the world one must be genuinely attentive and responsive. This improvisational engagement is never "over," as it were—one never "masters" improvisation, just as one never masters the world. Equally, no one ever masters dwelling. Although dwelling is indeed the fundamental way in which mortals *are* in the world, it is a constant task. Like improvisation, it is not something that can simply be set in motion and then forgotten, it is an activity always calling for engagement. We must, as Heidegger says, *"ever learn to dwell,"* in much the same way that we must "ever learn to improvise," since every encounter that calls for improvisational engagement is an encounter in which we learn to improvise anew.

THE "EVENT"

If Heidegger's analysis of equipmentality illuminates Dasein's engagement with things in the world, and the analysis of dwelling further acknowledges our topological embeddedness *in* the world, Heidegger's account of the Event or *Ereignis* draws out the appropriative nature of the fourfold. The idea of the Event is an improvisational happening in which mortals are "taken up by" the circumstances present in the situation in which they find themselves.[25] The Event is the co-responsive happening—the "mirror-play,"[26] as Heidegger says—of the fourfold. Players appropriate the broader structure of the situation while simultaneously being appropriated by the situation. To use Heidegger's language, it is an "event of appropriation."[27] Or as Heidegger's student and founder of philosophical hermeneutics, Hans-Georg Gadamer, says, not only do players "play" the game, "all playing is a being-played."[28] The Event, which emphasizes the experiential and transformative nature of the happening of the fourfold,[29] is thoroughly improvisational insofar as it is spontaneous and indeterminate.

In being appropriated by the Event, one finds oneself in the midst of the interplay of concealing and unconcealing. The musician who improvises, entering into the timespace opened up by the fourfold, also enters into a domain that encompasses the near and the far, the familiar and the strange, the authority of tradition, and the open possibility of futurity. As it can be compared to the Event itself, so the play of improvisation also mirrors the "turning," the *Kehre*,[30] that is at work in the Event; we are always turned back to the world and to our own being as given in and through the world. Improvisation is a constant responding to the improvisational situation, but a responding that is also shaped by that situation at the same time as it contributes to it.

For a player to be capable of orienting and reorienting themselves in the midst of the familiar and the strange, the expected and the unexpected, is not something achieved through a deliberate series of actions whose course is predictable in advance or that are arrived at through the application of a determinate technique or method. The very nature of *improviso* means players can never know in advance precisely what they will encounter. Yet insofar as they are improvising, as they are participating as one element in the happening of the fourfold, so they also allow themselves to be appropriated and *led* by possibilities disclosed in and through the situation.

Moreover, that one is genuinely improvising—that one is attending and responding to the unexpected and unforeseen that is disclosed in the situation, and not merely "going through the motions"—means that one necessarily engages with that which is given in the situational happening, no matter its strangeness or unexpectedness. In their "turning" and returning, in the oscillation or "vibration" of the Event, the anticipated and the unforeseen balance themselves through the responses of the players. From the perspective of the players themselves, this is experienced in terms of giving oneself over to the music and to the improvisational situation. Indeed, the player who endeavors to preempt the situation—which invariably means to focus on what can be predicted, on what is, in one sense or another, already known and familiar—has already lost touch with the very situation that calls for their response. Such a preemptive response is not only a problem for the player who is fixated on what is familiar or can be anticipated. The player who looks to engage purely with what is taken to be unfamiliar or the unexpected has also preempted the situational engagement that is called-for. Such a player risks losing any genuine sense of situatedness; they risk becoming overwhelmed, disoriented, or as jazz musicians say, "lost" (where to be "lost" may be understood as having been overwhelmed by the situation in a way that also entails alienation from it).[31] One should add too, that, to use the language of

Heidegger's fourfold, the fact that players are the recipients of possibilities granted to them by the divinities[32] does not necessarily mean that their improvisational appropriation of or responses to those possibilities will constitute a work that has worth or significance. The divinities grant, they make gifts, but they do not explain what is given just as they do not explain themselves or their giving (and one might even say that this is the very nature of the true grant or gift).[33] The divinities thus illuminate a way forward, they show a path, but they do not tell us how to move or to follow nor where the way is headed. The player is thus at the mercy of the divinities, is in thrall to the music, is, one might almost say (noting the qualification introduced below), "played" by the improvisational situation itself. The player's contribution is thus not in the conscious or insightful direction of what occurs, but in the preparedness that allows an appropriately rich and attentive participation in the improvisational event.

Neither in the musical case nor more generally, however, should the role of the human participant in the happening of the Event, which is also the happening of the fourfold, be taken to be merely "passive"—which might indeed be suggested by the idea of the player as the one who is "played." Thus, if we do emphasize the reversal of the primary focus of agency from player to situation or situational happening, then this cannot be construed to mean a complete loss of agency on the part of the player. The player, and mortals or human beings more generally, has a capacity for response that is not determined in advance, nor is it, in its own turn, merely a "product" of some situational context that stands apart from the player or from human being. The point is not that the human is entirely determined by its situation, by its place, but rather that the situation, the place—in which human being is already embedded—always exceeds any determination that human beings may attempt to impose. Insofar as one has a "world," one is active in and participates in that world, but one neither controls nor directs it. In the play of situational or improvisational engagement, the world is opened to us—as we are to the world—but the world also remains, as world, that which goes beyond us and is never subject to us. It is always we who are subject to the world and to the inexhaustible possibilities that it presents.

THE ROUND DANCE OF BEING

This chapter has positioned Heidegger's philosophy and the phenomenon of musical performance next to one another. On the one hand, Heidegger's concept of "world" has been employed to elucidate the way in which improvisation, as exemplified in musical performance, is no mere subjectively determined mode of engagement, but is rather a genuinely participatory engagement with the world. On the other hand, it has become clear that the idea of improvisation itself offers certain insight into the attentiveness, responsiveness, and engagement at issue in Heidegger's own thinking. Improvisation can be taken as a characteristic feature of what Heidegger refers to as the Event or the happening of world that is the fourfold. And more than this, one might even say that the musical is itself already at work in Heidegger's thinking—especially in his thinking of the fourfold.

In his meditation on the role of ordinary things in the bringing together of the elements of world, Heidegger writes, in "The Thing," that "the fouring, the unity of the four, presences as the appropriating mirror-play of the betrothed, each to the other in simple oneness. The fouring presences as the worlding of world. The mirror-play of world is the round dance [*Reigen*] of appropriating."[34] The mirror-play at issue here is the unified happening of each element of the fourfold—earth, sky, divinities, and mortals—as they are gathered into and reflected back within that unity. This happening or appropriating, which is the same happening or appropriating that is at issue in the Event, appears here as a round dance. Dance is "musical," both in the sense that it belongs to one of the muses and in the sense that it is bound up with music in the ordinary sense (Terpsichore is the muse to whom both dance and music belong together).[35] The Event, the happening of world or of the fourfold, is thus itself musical. Indeed, one may argue that the movements of the dance of the fourfold, the dance of the world, are themselves movements set to the music of the Event, in the sense of *extempore*. The tempo, rhythm, and dynamicity of the music emerge from the world and the Event *is* the round dance of the world—appropriating and being appropriated in and by music. The mirror-play of the world that is this joining in dance is "play" in the sense of improvisation, where one participates in and is taken up by the happening of the fourfold. The movements of the round dance—always responsive to the Event—cannot be pre-learned, due to the unexpected and unforeseen nature of its emergence. Rather the dance must be improvised—responding and attending to that which is given by the music of the world.

The music of the world, in the sense articulated here, has been present in philosophy almost from the very beginning, perhaps most evidently in Pythagoras' harmony of the spheres, where mathematics and philosophy are thought to derive from the structures of music. But Heidegger himself, in the Heraclitus Seminars of 1966/67 (with reference to Aeschylus' *Prometheus*), speaks of the way in which one is bound to the rhythm of language, such that one is "rhythmed."[36] Moreover, referencing the musicologist, Thrasybulos Georgiades, Heidegger asserts that humans do not make rhythm, rather, it is something that "approaches us."[37] We may say, then, that the rhythm to which

Prometheus says we are "bound" emerges from the music of the Event—from the "extemporary" music of the world. It is to this music that the round dance is responsive, so that the round dance is indeed "the ring that joins while it plays as mirroring."[38] The ring comprises the elements of the fourfold, dancing in unity; "the ring joins the four."[39]

Just like partners in a round dance, the four "nestle into their unifying presence, in which each one retains its own nature."[40] Mortals are immersed in the round dance of the fourfold, always retaining their own sense as mortals. But, as Heidegger tells us with respect to dwelling, mortals often do not live in the understanding of their dwelling, or of their round dance. Enraptured by the pace of modernity, of the leaps and bounds of science and technology, mortals typically forget to ponder and listen to the music of the world. Thus, Heidegger's call for mortals to "ever learn to dwell," may equally be a call for mortals to ever learn to improvise a round dance with earth, sky, and divinities to the music of world, and in their dancing, "so nestling, . . . join together, worlding, the world."[41]

NOTES

1. See, for instance, Günther Pöltner, "Heidegger," in *Music in German Philosophy: An Introduction*, eds. Stefan Lorenz Sorgner and Oliver Fürbeth and trans. Susan H. Gillespie, 187–210 (Chicago: The University of Chicago Press, 2010); Jeff R. Warren, *Music and Ethical Responsibility* (Cambridge: Cambridge University Press, 2014); Bruce Ellis Benson, *The Improvisation of Musical Dialogue: A Phenomenology of Music* (New York: Cambridge University Press, 2003); Eduardo Marx, *Heidegger und der Ort der Musik* (Würzburg: Königshausen & Neumann, 1998).

2. Martin Heidegger, "Art and Space," in *The Heidegger Reader*, ed. Günter Figal and trans. Jerome Veith (Bloomington, IN: Indiana University Press, 2009), 307.

3. The term '*topos*' is used here in a manner consistent with Malpas's account. See Jeff Malpas, *Place and Experience: A Philosophical Topography*, 2nd ed. (New York: Routledge, 2018), 26–28.

4. Martin Heidegger, *Basic Problems of Phenomenology*, trans. Albert Hofstadter (Bloomington: Indiana University Press, 1982), 165.

5. Heidegger, *Basic Problems of Phenomenology*, 165.

6. *Oxford English Dictionary*, 3rd ed., s.v. "situation," accessed July 24, 2020, https://www-oed-com.ezproxy.lib.monash.edu.au/view/Entry/180520?redirectedFrom=situation&. We employ the term "situation" in manner that is largely consistent with the topological associations Malpas evokes in his discussions of "place." See Jeff Malpas, *Heidegger's Topology: Being, Place, World* (Cambridge: The MIT Press, 2006).

7. Martin Heidegger, *The Fundamental Concepts of Metaphysics: World, Finitude, Solitude*, trans. William McNeill and Nicholas Walker (Bloomington, IN: Indiana University Press, 1995), 176.

8. Martin Heidegger, "The Origin of the Work of Art," in *Poetry, Language, Thought*, trans. Albert Hofstadter (New York: Harper Perennial, 2013), 15–86.

9. Heidegger, "The Origin of the Work of Art," 53.

10. Martin Heidegger, *Being and Time*, trans. John Macquarrie and Edward Robinson (New York: Harper & Row, 2008), 93–107.

11. Heidegger, *Being and Time*, 97.

12. Heidegger, *Being and Time*, 116.

13. See for instance, Andy Clark and David J. Chalmers, "The Extended Mind," *Analysis* 58, no. 1 (1998): 7–19; Shaun Gallagher, "Body Schema and Intentionality," in *The Body and the Self*, eds. José Luis Bermúdez, Anthony Marcel, and Naomi Eilan, 225–244 (Cambridge: The MIT Press, 2001); Alva Noë, *Out of Our Heads: Why You Are Not Your Brain, and Other Lessons from the Biology of Consciousness* (New York: Hill and Wang, 2009).

14. One's acting in the world is always historically mediated. While guitarists from other traditions and cultures may approach the instrument differently, and therefore the configuration will be altered, the basic relationship between player and instrument remains.

15. Heidegger's own discussion equally acknowledges the relationship between equipment use and experience. See *Being and Time*, 97–98.

16. Noë, *Out of Our Heads*, 100.

17. Martin Heidegger, "The Thing," in *Poetry, Language, Thought*, trans. Albert Hofstadter (New York: Harper Perennial, 2013), 161–184.

18. Heidegger, *Being and Time*, 80—the translation somewhat obscures what is at issue here, although Macquarie and Robinson do include an extensive note on the passage.

19. Heidegger's unhappiness with aspects of *Being and Time*, and especially with the way its treatment of equipmentality was taken up, emerges very soon after the publication of the work—see, for instance, Heidegger, *The Fundamental Concepts of Metaphysics*, 177.

20. Heidegger, "The Thing," 161–184.

21. Martin Heidegger, "Building Dwelling Thinking," in *Poetry, Language, Thought*, trans. Albert Hofstadter (New York: Harper Perennial, 2013), 145.

22. Martin Heidegger, ". . . Poetically Man Dwells . . .," in *Poetry, Language, Thought*, trans. Albert Hofstadter (New York: Harper Perennial, 2013), 209–227.

23. Heidegger, "Building Dwelling Thinking," 145.

24. Heidegger, "Building Dwelling Thinking," 159.

25. Although there is a commonplace tendency to think of the Event, the *Ereignis*, as *temporal*, the Event ought properly to be understood as encompassing both the temporal *and* the spatial—as, in fact, topological (place being both temporal and spatial). In the *Contributions*, for instance (in which the Event emerges as a central idea), time and space are dealt with as "time-space" (*Zeit-raum*)—see Martin Heidegger, *Contributions to Philosophy (Of the Event)*, trans. Richard

Rojcewicz and Daniela Vallega-Neu (Bloomington: Indiana University Press, 2012), 293–306.
26. Heidegger, "The Thing," 177–179.
27. Martin Heidegger, *Identity and Difference*, trans. Joan Stambaugh (New York: Harper & Row, 1969), 36–40.
28. Hans-Georg Gadamer, *Truth and Method*, trans. Joel Weinsheimer and Donald G. Marshall (London: Bloomsbury, 2013), 111.
29. See Malpas, *Heidegger's Topology*, 213–219.
30. Heidegger, *Contributions to Philosophy*, 246.
31. Thwaites writes on improvisation and jazz music in his chapter of this volume.
32. On the idea of the "divinities" (*die Göttlichen*) as they figure in Heidegger's fourfold, see Malpas, *Heidegger's Topology*, 274–276.
33. Julian Young, *Heidegger's Philosophy of Art* (Cambridge: Cambridge University Press, 2004), 96.
34. Heidegger, "The Thing," 178.
35. Terpsichore is one of the nine Muses in Greek mythology; her name literally means "delight in dancing."
36. Martin Heidegger and Eugen Fink, *Heraclitus Seminar*, trans. Charles H. Seibert (Alabama: The University of Alabama Press, 1979), 55.
37. Heidegger and Fink, *Heraclitus Seminar*, 55.
38. Heidegger, "The Thing," 178.
39. Heidegger, "The Thing," 178.
40. Heidegger, "The Thing," 178.
41. Heidegger, "The Thing," 178.

BIBLIOGRAPHY

Benson, Bruce Ellis. *The Improvisation of Musical Dialogue: A Phenomenology of Music*. New York: Cambridge University Press, 2003.
Clark, Andy, and David J. Chalmers. "The Extended Mind." *Analysis* 58, no. 1 (1998): 7–19.
Gadamer, Hans-Georg. *Truth and Method*. Translated by Joel Weinsheimer and Donald G. Marshall. London: Bloomsbury, 2013.
Gallagher, Shaun. "Body Schema and Intentionality." In *The Body and the Self*. Edited by José Luis Bermúdez, Anthony Marcel, and Naomi Eilan, 225–244. Cambridge: The MIT Press, 2001.
Heidegger, Martin. *Basic Problems of Phenomenology*. Translated by Albert Hofstadter. Bloomington: Indiana University Press, 1982.
Heidegger, Martin. *Being and Time*. Translated by John Macquarrie and Edward Robinson. New York: Harper & Row, 2008.
Heidegger, Martin. *Contributions to Philosophy (Of the Event)*. Translated by Richard Rojcewicz and Daniela Vallega-Neu. Bloomington: Indiana University Press, 2012.

Heidegger, Martin. *The Fundamental Concepts of Metaphysics: World, Finitude, Solitude*. Translated by William McNeill and Nicholas Walker. Bloomington: Indiana University Press, 1995.

Heidegger, Martin. *The Heidegger Reader*. Edited by Günter Figal. Translated by Jerome Veith. Bloomington: Indiana University Press, 2009.

Heidegger, Martin. *Identity and Difference*. Translated by Joan Stambaugh. New York: Harper & Row, 1969.

Heidegger, Martin. *Poetry, Language, Thought*. Translated by Albert Hofstadter. New York: Harper Perennial, 2013.

Heidegger, Martin, and Eugen Fink. *Heraclitus Seminar*. Translated by Charles H. Seibert. Alabama: The University of Alabama Press, 1979.

Malpas, Jeff. *Heidegger's Topology: Being, Place, World*. Cambridge: The MIT Press, 2006.

Malpas, Jeff. *Place and Experience: A Philosophical Topography*, 2nd Edition. New York: Routledge, 2018.

Marx, Eduardo. *Heidegger und der Ort der Musik*. Würzburg: Königshausen & Neumann, 1998.

Noë, Alva. *Out of Our Heads: Why You Are Not Your Brain, and Other Lessons from the Biology of Consciousness*. New York: Hill and Wang, 2009.

Oxford English Dictionary. 3rd Edition. s.v. "situation." Accessed July 24, 2020. https://www-oed-com.ezproxy.lib.monash.edu.au/view/Entry/180520?redirectedFrom=situation&.

Pöltner, Günther. "Heidegger." In *Music in German Philosophy: An Introduction*. Edited by Stefan Lorenz Sorgner and Oliver Fürbeth. Translated by Susan H. Gillespie, 187–210. Chicago: The University of Chicago Press, 2010.

Warren, Jeff R. *Music and Ethical Responsibility*. Cambridge: Cambridge University Press, 2014.

Young, Julian. *Heidegger's Philosophy of Art*. Cambridge: Cambridge University Press, 2004.

Chapter 11

Meditative Thinking in Jazz and the Challenge of the Technical

Trevor Thwaites

Heidegger delivered three lecture courses in Freiburg during the 1950s: *What Is Called Thinking?* (1951–1952); *The Principle of Reason* (1955–1956); and *Basic Principles of Thinking* (1957). In these lectures, Heidegger follows his earlier trajectory of relating back to Greek thinking and, in this case, to the Greek conception of the opening or clearing where things can be revealed or concealed. Heidegger promotes meditative thinking, thinking that begins with an awareness of the field and is open to its content and open to what is given (1951–1952). Throughout his writing, Heidegger expresses concern about scientific and technological calculative thinking which, he believes, ignores contemplative thought, and he reiterates that the essence of technology is nothing technological, which is as true in the current digital age as it was in Heidegger's atomic age. Technology enframes (*Gestell*), and the more we experience the intensity of digital technologies, the more our position in the world becomes tightly enframed. Our enframing makes us answerable to digital power and saturation, and we become positioned as technology's resource, on call as a standing reserve, which is the essence of technology.

In this chapter, I explore possibilities for using Heidegger's concepts of thinking to examine jazz in all its forms. I then take his notion of meditative thinking to probe more deeply into the sophisticated thought that goes on unannounced during the jazz performance. I conclude by questioning the challenge digital technologies place on jazz, not only in placing musicians in the role of the standing reserve but also in offering the wherewithal to eliminate the need for the collective, improvisatory jazz performance that, for this author, is the essence of jazz.

HEIDEGGER AND THINKING

For Heidegger, thinking is not so much an act as a way of living and dwelling.[1] We must ask questions of the world, for thinking defines the human being, and the more thought-*less* we are, the less human we are. The essence of an idea forming must be put into the language of thinking, something the jazz musician does as their ideas are shaped through music. The forming of ideas is also part of traditional thinking in which thought tells us what is. Memory gathers thought, but we might ask what happens when digital technologies erase our need for memory, for our digital recollections and replays are conveniently there, ready-to-hand (*Zuhandenheit*). Listening appears in Heidegger's understanding of thinking as he stresses that we must improve our ability to listen to our historical past, to our presence in the world, and to possibilities for the future.[2] This surely reflects a template for a successful jazz musician whose stored memories might reshape already existing ideas into new musical possibilities.

In his *Bremen and Freiburg Lectures* of 1957, Heidegger states that our historical ear is fine when it comes to world-guiding thinking, but our listening must be free, open, and within the breadth of our ear.[3] Poetic thinking does not make poetry. It is the primal telling in language, whether in words or music. It must stay close to poesy. Heidegger suggests that poesy is the mother tongue of the human race and thus that "poetically man dwells on this earth."[4] Further, "Thinking and being are grounded in language. It gives the relationship its hold."[5] Heidegger adds clarity, saying that "Even the speechless gesture" in its silence "resonates in saying"[6] because the essence of language lies in saying and this applies to the language of gestures, since "gestures are in themselves what they are through saying."[7] This leads Heidegger to claim that the essence of thinking is saying, whatever communicative language is used. Poetry and thinking can, therefore, meet each other as long as their nature remains distinct. Consider the possibilities in the poetic language of jazz in which the musician responds to such language by listening to its appeal—because "poetizing is singing. Every singing is saying, but not every saying is singing."[8] Singing speaks when the thoughtful musician is driven to join the play of poetic imagination.

Heidegger's notion of saying as *sagen* (to say), to let appear or to show, is related to *sehen* (to let be seen and heard). It is different from speaking, where a speaker may speak at length without saying anything. In jazz, musicians frequently refer to saying as praise—"I hear what you're sayin' man" or "Yeah, he's really saying something"—or derision—"he said nothing in that solo." *Saying Something* is also the title of a book of interviews with jazz musicians by ethnomusicologist Ingrid Monson. One musician interviewed is the American bassist Richard Davis, who gives clarity to the phrase:

"It happens a lot in jazz, it's like a conversation and one guy will create a melodic motif or a rhythmic motif and the band picks it up. It's like sayin' that you all are talking about the same thing."[9] Paul Berliner writes of the difficulties jazz musicians have in verbalizing the "essentially non-verbal aspects of improvisation." Two metaphors stand out: "a conversation that players carry on among themselves in the language of jazz," and "going on a demanding musical journey."[10]

Heidegger's (1957) proposal of a "leap into the abyss" might be understood as "saying," which has the basic characteristic of letting appear or bringing forth. Heidegger stresses that "saying" is not limited to words, but it communicates and is the interconnection of being, language, and thinking. Thinking leaps away from some thing and the abyss into which thinking leaps is, for example, the primal essence of the language of music, to a place of origin.

In 1957, Heidegger explained that we need to consider the original meaning of being as presence; it is the human being, open for being, that lets the latter arrive as presence.[11] In order to experience the belonging-together of human and being, a leap is necessary to where saying gathers and lets appear. This means we need an event or occurrence (*Ereignis*), such as a jazz performance, to which we can apply Heidegger's notion of present-at-hand (*Vorhanden*). Being appropriates the performer and makes them there (*Dasein*) at the site of being's revelation. It is clear that being belongs with thinking, and the essence of the identity is a property of *Ereignis*. A principle of identity, as the ground of being, requires a jump that leaps off from being, as the ground of beings, and therefore leaps into the abyss. This abyss is neither empty nothingness nor murky confusion, but rather *Ereignis*, and the essence of identity needs that leap if the belonging-together of the human and Being is to attain the essential light of *Ereignis*[12] as a self-resonating realm in which thinking provides the tools.[13] This suggests that the jazz musician, in their thoughtfull performance, should attempt to stay attuned to their authentic mode as a jazz being, ready to leap into the openness of the truth or meaningfulness of their being in jazz. Thus, their being is appropriated in its truth, experienced and thought of, in Heidegger's terms, as *Ereignis*, an appropriating event, thrown into the openness of possibilities and appropriated in its being. This brings about the emergence and luminous appearance of the meaningful jazz performance, and its element of stability and presence is the defining characteristic of the real where the musician has found their own sound and voice and where digital technologies do not act as a gatekeeper to what is possible.

In his rectorship address "The Production of Being in Science and Art," delivered at the University of Freiburg in May 1933, Heidegger hints that aesthetics, as agreeable experiences and appearances, pose a problem to grasping the essence of the arts. The arts attain their power from a willingness of the jazz musician (for example) to listen, hear, remember, and respond to the call that comes from being. Heidegger writes:

> The essence of art is not the expression of lived experience, and does not consist of the artist expressing his "soul life" . . . Neither does it consist in the artist depicting reality more accurately and more precisely than others, or producing (presenting) something that gives pleasure to others, that provides enjoyment of a higher or lower type. Rather, the artist possesses the essential insight for the possible. For bringing the hidden possibilities of beings into the work . . . What is essential in the discovery of reality happened, and happens, not through science but through originary philosophy as well as through great poetry and its projections . . . in order to understand what the work of art and poetry as such are, philosophy must first break the habit of grasping the problem of art as one of aesthetics.[14]

Here I see Heidegger cautioning against the vulgar baring of one's soul through the music, or catering for the eclectic tastes of some listeners. This suggests that jazz musicians are at their most original and authentic when they are open to possibilities, whether stylistic, harmonic, tonal, or atonal, expanding the scope of their instrument, to name but a few. While many jazz artists find it hard to resist the odd showstopper piece designed to have broad audience appeal, a deeper satisfaction comes from discovering new possibilities as they play live, and this contributes to their standing as an original player. Of course, one cannot always be original, but the openness to be continually exploring in a jazz context shows authenticity in the Heideggerian sense, digging deeper into the music rather than playing surface impressions, which would be regarded by Heidegger as inauthentic.

When a thing, such as jazz, emerges into a state of disclosedness it takes a stand; its being reflects its stability and staying power. The appearing thing of jazz creates space for itself and future jazz players emerge into this already prepared space; its intelligible appearance is experienced within the fixed dimensions of this space. We might regard the unexpected as essential to jazz, a whatness that is inherently disclosive of jazz, or else our interest would wane as the music settled in to becoming mundane. In the mid-1950s, Heidegger admitted that "truth" was an incorrect term and he began to use disclosedness instead—the disclosedness of things in showing themselves and being revealed. For Heidegger, disclosedness is not "truth" but *meaningfulness*—the meaningfulness of the meaningful.

Thinking, for Heidegger, is bound to life by an inner necessity suggesting that jazz musicians feel the need to be open-to-the-world. Heidegger tells us that meditative thinking is thinking that is "open to content and open to what is given";[15] it demands of the jazz performer that they engage themselves and other players with what at first hearing does not seem to go together at all. There is a need to primordially understand the possibilities of the music and this primal thinking is a constituted unity of determination, motivated by the experience of the factical jazz life. In factical life, the sense relations are "lived in the enactment of factical life, in personal existence and existence of the [jazz] community."[16] The being and consciousness of the music, both as the positing of being and as the positing of what is musically possible, are made available to the jazz musician as they demonstrate thinking in jazz.

When experienced jazz musicians improvise together, they also manifest a feel for their material and they make on-the-spot adjustments to the sounds they hear. Listening to one another and to themselves, they feel where the music is going and adjust their playing accordingly. They can do this, first of all, because their collective effort at musical invention makes use of a schema—a metric, melodic, and harmonic schema familiar to all participants—which gives a predictable order to the piece. In addition, each of the musicians has at the ready a repertoire of musical figures, that are part of their identity, which they can deliver at appropriate moments either when transitioning to a different section, or simply during an inspirational lull as a means of reinvigorating themselves. Creating the original work of jazz is a process of selection, the sifting through of possibilities, requiring constraints and processes of elimination. It requires decisions about something not mastered, something concealed, or else it would not be a decision. It requires the knowledge of how to discard in order to select and an awareness of the necessity of difference in order to unite. Sometimes an element of discontinuity is introduced that disrupts the flow and sets up a new pathway for the next generation of jazz musicians; the phenomenon of jazz becomes a phenomenon of speculation. The creative artist in their making the work of jazz calls us to think.[17]

MEDITATIVE THINKING IN JAZZ

Jazz is a mode of knowing, a recollecting, and a returning to origins as well as articulating the nature of the thingly-ness of the music. Jazz music is a reflexive response to the world and as such it transforms the world. The thinking jazz musician might play the same tune (usually referred to as the "head") every night, but each night it will be different, and the same applies for individual notes or improvised solos. Differences in mood might also vary from night to night. Mood is something directed at the world and not simply an emotional response directed at some thing or another. Fundamental mood, for Heidegger, is a form of attunement. Our sense of attunement is related to our situatedness (*Befindlichkeit*), which means, literally, "how I find myself," and is related to the past, to throwness, a fore-having, and the imposition of a structure of facticity. Creative jazz works are more than their presence. They are a projection into future possibilities for being. Thinking in a jazz performance requires creative, improvising jazz musicians to think expressively in, through, and with the music and to primordially understand the origins and possibilities of the music, synchronized and in collaboration with others. Thinking in jazz is bound to life by an inner necessity.

In "Conversations on a Country Path about Thinking," Heidegger discusses meditative thinking and contrasts it with calculative thinking, which is thinking characterized by human methods of approaching things. Meditative thinking is about something and begins with an awareness of the field within which it appears and an awareness of the horizon rather than merely an ordinary understanding. The horizon implies openness, rather than a boundary or limit. Meditative thinking is thinking that is open to its content and open to what is given. It is a higher activity of thinking in relation to the openness in it which Heidegger calls *releasement* (*Gelassenheit*). Releasement requires us to be open to an openness of that-which-regions, which both unveils and discloses. It is also all-too-easy for us to depend solely upon technologies (whether recordings, real instruments, or digital) and to "fall into bondage to them."[18] As such, a leap into the abyss is necessary where we must articulate our roots and this involves a beginning, and the nature of this kind of thinking, the nature of that-which-regions, is both grounded and open with its resolve for truth and the releasement of truth: "The region itself is at once an expanse and an abiding. It abides into the expanse of resting. It expands into the abiding of what has freely turned toward itself."[19]

Meditative thinking does not take the easiest way but seeks out that which is easily overlooked, because what appears as near is always the longest and hardest road to revealing fulfillment. Heidegger tells us that "meditative thinking demands of us not to cling one-sidedly to a single idea, nor to run down a one-track course of ideas. Meditative thinking demands of us that we engage ourselves with what at first sight does not go together at all."[20] For the jazz musician, thinking about how much or how little technology, or whether to use it or not, is *"releasement towards things."*[21] To merely include technology in an unthinking manner because it is there is to accept the calculative, because it promotes itself as merely a scientific and technological truth. Releasement is a "defining characteristic of man's true nature involving openness and, through it, direct and immediate reference beyond man to being."[22] For the jazz musician, to be open to what is given is both the retaining of our essential nature and of keeping meditative thinking alive. A leap into the abyss brings to a rest where all movement is first gathered so that we can begin from the source. To ignore the leap in favor of unthinkingly accepting some new technology to show one is trendy is to make the expressive jazz component simply a reserve waiting to be drawn upon by the technology for the purpose of being technological.

William Lovitt, in his introduction to Heidegger's *The Question Concerning Technology*, suggests that a leap into the abyss can be understood as "a leap to new ground, or to think in fresh ways."[23] The leap takes the jazz musician to the place of origin and then still further back, beyond the primordial conflict, to a crossroads where the jazz musician collaborates with other musicians as they talk through their music. Heidegger, in *The Principle of Reason*, clarifies that "in the leap off, the leap does not shove the leaping-off realm away from itself, rather in leaping the leap becomes a recollective appropriation of the *Geschick* of being."[24] A sending of meaning is related to the history of questioning: "For the leap itself, this means that it leaps neither away from the leaping-off realm, nor forward into a different, sequestered domain. The leap only remains the leap as a leap that recollectively thinks upon the *Geschick*"—validating or finding what is fitting[25]—in this case, that which is sent and is historically in place as the destiny of jazz.

To think is to recollectively fore-think and "thinking as a recollective fore-thinking is the leaping of the leap. This leap [*Sprung*] is a movement [*Satz*] to which thinking submits."[26] Thinking, as fore-thinking, must ever anew and more originally make the leap. There is no repetition and no recurrence, and leap is necessary until the "recollective fore-thinking to being *qua* being has been transformed by the truth of being into a different saying."[27] The *Geschick* of being is play, and play is without a "why" in its transmission and questioning of possibilities. The question is how jazz musicians accommodate to the play—that is, not playing in a mechanical, rule-governed way, but according to one's mood, where the rules are formed by the course the music takes and might be different the next time, say, a particular tune is performed, and further renditions can also be changing and varied, for play represents transformation or transcendence as in John Coltrane's performances of "A Love Supreme," for example.

JAZZ AND TECHNOLOGIES

In the Bremen lectures of 1949, Heidegger began to see *Gestell* as positionality and, further, that the essence of technology is positionality. Positionality orders what is present through conscription. It orders what is present into the standing reserve,[28] and it positions humans in positionality as part of the development or use of technology, for technology *uses us*. In music, one might become a programmer, a DJ, an arranger dependent on digital technologies, or assume the subjective role as a musician-user, keen to sound on trend, but technology generally sets the rules. The human is, in the age of technology's domination, essentially forced into the essence of technology, into *das Ge-Stell* (positionality), and is beset by it. In their own way, humans become inventory pieces in the strict sense of the words "inventory" and "piece." By this I mean that, through our intensifying engagement with digital technology, we each become a uniform piece in the inventory of algorithmic coding, parts of the whole in the service of technology. Heidegger stresses our need to understand and critically reflect on the sense and significance of the increased technologization of the world in modernity, a world characterized by a forgetfulness of being.

In the contemporary world of jazz music and beyond, musicians, with the aid of digital technologies (digital audio workstations, electronic instruments, access to web streaming, etc.), are now able to create, promote, and distribute their own work. The consumer or producer presents their own artistic work on platforms such as YouTube. For users, there are vast choices of music available through streaming. Consumption is often driven by the desire for abundance, and many online consumers seem to focus on the accumulation of thousands of tracks rather than assimilation of the music. Albums are raided for appealing tracks. It would be hard to imagine most older classic jazz albums reaching their status had they simply been raided for a single track. This positioning of some technologized contemporary musicians, fully dependent on technology, shows how technology has overtaken the human condition, and, in some cases, the desire to be noticed as a tech-savvy individual is greater than the desire to produce music in a dynamic, collective context. The human condition relies on our being empathetic toward one another; our independent thinking and doing help define our being without the approval of digital technologies. We might imagine technology has sentient qualities, and some musicians seek to be one with technology in the creation of trans-human technological musical spaces. Technology integrates itself into society and, being ready-to-hand, entices us to construct the kind of world the technology needs.

The early recording technologies had limitations in quality and length, and they left little space for the musician to engage with meditative thinking. The limited capacity of early recordings meant that previously lengthy works had to be trimmed or suffer being on either wax cylinder or several sides of the early 10-inch 78 rpm recordings at approximately three minutes per side. The later 12-inch 78s allowed for four-and-a-half minutes of music. This changed somewhat with the introduction of long-playing recordings (the LP), for this meant that longer works could be composed to a theme or concept; albums were written to fit into the usual forty minutes of available playtime. Early microphones were not efficient for recording jazz bands and sound was captured via a large horn and relayed to a needle moving across a wax cylinder. The needle was sensitive and loud sounds were therefore to be avoided (e.g., moving away from the mouth of the horn), and most drummers played on a suitcase or washboard to better control their sound. Recording qualities improved over the next three decades and by the 1960s the sonic quality of recordings changed from monaural (the sound coming unnaturally from a single perspective) to stereo (supposedly replicating the ears and adding a more spatial effect). Some jazz artists also began to record longer tracks, Miles Davis and John Coltrane for example, and some tracks spanned the whole side of an LP. The introduction of the Compact Disc (CD) offered more recorded time (storage space) and signaled the age of digital recording, although aficionados felt their digitally recorded sound lacked the warmth of vinyl.

In an earlier article on music and technology, I argued that "the rise of digital forms of sound manipulation and distribution have gradually eroded traditional methods of sound production and transmission, causing a disjuncture in the ontology of music."[29] Sound, the ambient phenomenon, is becoming disrupted and decentered by the struggles between long-established controls, beliefs, and desires as well as controls from within calculative technologized contexts. Modern technics are a world of codes and calculations that now come to define both how we hear and the *Gestell* of nature and humanity,[30] a world in which the community of musicians is in danger of being replaced by technicians. In jazz, while the artist-musician still prevails, technology has become a convenient portal through which musicians can exchange files and ideas. It also makes collaboration possible for musicians who have never actually performed jazz together in real time, in the same room, and sometimes even dwelling thousands of miles apart. In my conversations with both orchestral and big band musicians who had joined in a performance by their ensemble via Zoom, Skype, or similar digital communication platforms during the Covid-19 pandemic lockdowns of 2020–2021, the musicians found the idea of simply playing their part in their home quite unsatisfying. Playing live and at the moment within a big band or orchestra is a privileged aural experience, one where the player is responsible for such things as blending, intonation, accuracy, and consistency, and these require a heightened awareness during the performance. A dedicated performance space is also lacking in the Zoom context; a bedroom might be handy for practicing but the energy needed for an actual live performance with others is absent in this isolated context. The time lag commonly experienced with these platforms is also an issue. This runs counter to Heidegger's belief that the primary condition of the human *being* is to be immersed in and engaged with the world—interpreting "life from out of itself, primordially."[31] The performer loses the fulfillment experienced by a social being immersed in making music with adjacent others.

But what might new digital technologies mean for meditative thinking in these calculative technological environments that promote instantaneity over reflection and personal convenience over a living community of performing jazz musicians? Heidegger tells us that meditative thinking is thinking that is "open to content and open to what is given";[32] it demands of the jazz performer that they engage themselves and other players with what at first sight does not go together at all. The issue for jazz musicians engaged in contemporary digital jazz music production is how to retain their essential nature while at the same time keeping meditative thinking alive, seeking possibilities over what the technology already conveniently gives us.

Modern digital technologies impose their demands on everything and requisition it for use. Through this challenge of revealing, nothing is allowed to appear as itself. Digitized sounds sometimes replace the sound of the original instrument, silencing the actual instrument and using it simply as a trigger for the electronic replacement. Thomas Sheehan reinforces Heidegger's claim:

> In the modern world of calculative rationality, the instruments of technology and the mind-set of technik dominate the way we understand and relate to everything. Earth is now seen as a vast storehouse of resources, both human and natural; and the value and realness of those resources, their being, is measured exclusively by their availability for consumption.[33]

Availability for endless consumption is the hallmark of digital musical instrument technology.[34] Upgrades and new components can preoccupy the musician to such an extent that they have little time for meditative exploration. A digital keyboardist often finds it hard to be distinct, and many are simply trying to replicate the sound of an electric or an acoustic piano. In contrast, an alto saxophone player with a seventy-year-old Selmer Paris not only has a valued instrument, but they have time to explore its potential and add their own unique sound that separates them from other players.[35] Because of the length of time they have with their instrument, exploring its possibilities, it becomes their authenticity. We recognize Johnny Hodges and Charlie Parker through their personal sound on an alto saxophone just as we recognize the big bands of Duke Ellington and Count Basie through the distinctive sound of each. Despite a similar make-up of musicians in their bands, the band leaders' thoughtful arrangements result in the special character of their sound.

The technological understanding of being is that on which Greek metaphysics built its fundamental conceptual structure. As Heidegger searched for a different conceptual avenue for thinking the being of reality, he turned to the Greek word for things, *pragmata* (that with which we are concerned), in praxis (acting and reflecting on practical reason). The meaningfulness of things presupposes that they are not objectified but rather lived with in a pre-reflective referential context and their readiness-to-hand (*Zuhandenheit*) as their mode of being.

CONCLUSION

Not all technological developments in music have had a negative effect on jazz. I have already mentioned recordings being responsible for the distribution of jazz globally, and today YouTube plays a similar role, providing access to tuition videos, many of which are helpful to young musicians who live away from a live jazz scene of any sort.

In her introduction to Heidegger's 1957 lecture "Identity and Difference," Joan Stambaugh suggests, perceptively, that "technology isn't something man has acquired as an accessory. Right now it is what he *is*. . . . The manner in which man and being concern each other in the world of technology Heidegger calls a framework."[36] *Gestell*, as a framework, event, or positionality, might be a prelude to the event of appropriation (*Ereignis*) through which "they lose the determinations placed on them by metaphysics" and its regarding of identity as a "fundamental trait of being."[37] For Heidegger, "Our whole human existence everywhere sees itself challenged—now playfully and now urgently, now breathlessly and now ponderously—to devote itself to the planning and calculating of everything."[38] For the technologically embroiled jazz musician, this might mean, for example, pitching their streamed music to a more global taste or replacing skilled side musicians with digital substitutes. Here we enter the Greek world of *technê*—knowing how through a practical know-how. But on entering the digital world of the twenty-first century, we find the machine has absorbed centuries of *technai* to produce what it does, freeing up the musician creator from the time-consuming business of technique, musicianship, and facticity. Albums created by a synthesis of musical sounds digitally produced by one person are no longer the shared story-telling of the collaborating jazz musician working on the unexpected and maximizing their own limitations. The digital technology companies, it would seem, promote their digital products as knowing no limitations while appearing to know all, so that nothing appears impossible. Through my questioning, I posit that with the development of artificial intelligence there is the possibility that our devices and gadgets will be able to reproduce bebop or fusion, or any type of music from the past, through a simple verbal command. The only thing missing might be the commander's personal command of anything musical.

The creative meditative jazz artist acts upon the fixed-in-place of the work to "thrust into the Open of the 'that'," not to exhaust the possibilities of the work, but to take a "step toward which everything thus far said tends."[39] The "fixing in place" of the truth of the work does not run counter to the jazz artist "letting happen," not in a passive way, but as working to a "creative bringing forth,"[40] receiving and incorporating as it conceals.

Heidegger asks: "Could we think and poetize any other way than by contemplating thinking what it might be; contemplating poetizing and what it might be, and finally by contemplating the relationship of the two."[41] He adds, "Thinking and poetizing—each time a meditation, each time a saying, the reflective sound."[42] Thinkers speak reflectively and jazz musicians musically reflect; the jazz musician, through their spirit, has the ability to transform, and this spirit is the "determined resolve toward the essence of being,"[43] arousing and preserving the power of our existence.

Acoustic instruments have a permanence, which means that players can spend years refining their sound and technique; whereas, digital electronic instruments are constantly changing and imply impermanence, leaving the player little time to get to know their instrument. It is no exaggeration to suggest that the former allows for thoughtfulness, while the latter stimulates impatience to try the next new version. If the essence of jazz relates to collaborating improvising musicians, then the digitally committed jazz musician needs to think about how they can add *their own* voice in communal, collaborating jazz settings.

NOTES

1. J. Glenn Gray, introduction to *What Is Called Thinking?* by Martin Heidegger, trans. J. Glenn Gray (New York: Harper Perennial, 1976), xi.
2. Martin Heidegger, *What Is Called Thinking?* trans. J. Glenn Gray (New York: Harper Perennial, 1976), 55.
3. Martin Heidegger, *Bremen and Freiburg Lectures: Insight into That Which Is and Basic Principles of Thinking*, trans. Andrew J. Mitchell (Bloomington: Indiana University Press, 2012), 97.
4. Heidegger, *Bremen and Freiburg Lectures*, 162.
5. Heidegger, *Bremen and Freiburg Lectures*, 156.
6. Heidegger, *Bremen and Freiburg Lectures*, 159.
7. Heidegger, *Bremen and Freiburg Lectures*, 160.
8. Heidegger, *Bremen and Freiburg Lectures*, 161.
9. Ingrid Monson, *Saying Something: Jazz Improvisation and Interaction* (Chicago: University of Chicago Press, 1996), 32.
10. Paul F. Berliner, *Thinking in Jazz: The Infinite Art of Improvisation* (Chicago: University of Chicago Press, 1994), 348.
11. Martin Heidegger, "The Principle of Identity," in *The Heidegger Reader*, ed. Günter Figal (Bloomington: Indiana University Press, 2009), 289.
12. Heidegger, "Principle of Identity," 293.
13. McAullife and Malpas discuss *Ereignis* in music in their chapter of this volume.
14. Martin Heidegger, "The Projection of Being in Science and Art," in *The Heidegger Reader*, ed. Günter Figal and trans. Jerome Veith (Bloomington: Indiana University Press, 2009), 107.
15. Martin Heidegger, *Discourse on Thinking*, trans. John M. Anderson and E. Hans Freund (New York: Harper Perennial, 1966), 52.

16. Martin Heidegger, *Phenomenology of Intuition and Expression*, trans. Tracy Colony (London, England: Continuum, 2010), 151.
17. Trevor Thwaites, "Heidegger and Jazz: Musical Propositions of Truth and the Essence of Creativity," *Philosophy of Music Education Review* 21, no. 2 (2013): 121.
18. Heidegger, *Discourse on Thinking*, 54.
19. Heidegger, "Conversations on a Country Path," in *Discourse on Thinking*, trans. John M. Anderson and E. Hans Freund (New York: Harper Perennial, 1966), 66.
20. Heidegger, *Discourse on Thinking*, 53.
21. Heidegger, *Discourse on Thinking*, 53.
22. John Anderson, "Introduction" to *Discourse on Thinking* by Martin Heidegger, trans. John M. Anderson and E. Hans Freund (New York: Harper Perennial, 1966), 25.
23. William Lovitt, "Introduction" to *The Question Concerning Technology and Other Essays* by Martin Heidegger, trans. William Lovitt (New York: Harper & Row, 1977), xvi.
24. Martin Heidegger, *The Principle of Reason*, trans. Reginald Lilly (Bloomington: Indiana University Press, 1996), 94.
25. Heidegger, *The Principle of Reason*, 94.
26. Heidegger, *The Principle of Reason*, 94.
27. Heidegger, *The Principle of Reason*, 94.
28. Heidegger, *Bremen and Freiburg Lectures*, 38.
29. Trevor Thwaites, "Technology and Music Education in a Digitized, Disembodied, Posthuman World," *Action, Criticism and Theory for Music Education* 13, no. 2 (2014): 30.
30. Bernard Stiegler, *Technics and Time, 1: The Fault of Epimetheus*, trans. Richard Beardsworth and George Collins (Stanford, CA: Stanford University Press, 1998), 10.
31. Heidegger, *Phenomenology of Intuition and Expression*, 119.
32. Heidegger, *Discourse on Thinking*, 52.
33. Thomas Sheehan, "The Turn," in *Martin Heidegger: Key Concepts*, ed. Bret W. Davis, (Durham, England: Acumen, 2010), 258.
34. Rentmeester covers this terrain from the listener perspective at the end of his chapter in this volume.
35. Selmer Paris has been a leading manufacturer of professional-grade saxophones since the late 1800s.
36. Joan Stambaugh, "Introduction" to *Identity and Difference*, by Martin Heidegger, trans. Joan Stambaugh (New York: Harper & Row, 1969), 13–14.
37. Stambaugh, "Introduction," 14.
38. Martin Heidegger, *Identity and Difference*, trans. Joan Stambaugh (New York: Harper & Row, 1969), 34–35.
39. Martin Heidegger, "The Origin of the Work of Art," in *Poetry, Language, Thought*, trans. Albert Hofstadter (New York: Harper & Row, 1971), 64.
40. Heidegger, "The Origin of the Work of Art," 82–83.
41. Martin Heidegger, *Introduction to Philosophy—Thinking and Poetizing*, trans. Phillip Jacques Braunstein (Bloomington: Indiana University Press, 2011), 55.
42. Heidegger, *Introduction to Philosophy*, 59.

43. Martin Heidegger, "Rectorship Address," in *The Heidegger Reader*, ed. Günter Figal and trans. Jerome Veith (Bloomington: Indiana University Press, 2009), 112.

BIBLIOGRAPHY

Anderson, John. "Introduction" to *Discourse on Thinking*, by Martin Heidegger. Translated by John M. Anderson and E. Hans Freund, 11–39. New York: Harper Perennial, 1966.
Berliner, Paul F. *Thinking in Jazz: The Infinite Art of Improvisation*. Chicago: University of Chicago Press, 1994.
Figal, Günter, ed. *The Heidegger Reader*. Translated by Jerome Veith. Bloomington: Indiana University Press, 2009.
Heidegger, Martin. *Basic Concepts*. Translated by Gary E. Aylesworth. Bloomington: Indiana University Press, 1998.
Heidegger, Martin. *Being and Time*. Translated by John Macquarrie and Edward Robinson. San Francisco: Harper Collins, 1962.
Heidegger, Martin. *Bremen and Freiburg Lectures: Insight into That Which is and Basic Principles of Thinking*. Translated by Andrew J. Mitchell. Bloomington: Indiana University Press, 2012.
Heidegger, Martin. "Conversations on a Country Path about Thinking." In *Discourse on Thinking*. Translated by John M. Anderson and E. Hans Freund, 58–90. New York: Harper Perennial, 1966a.
Heidegger, Martin. *Discourse on Thinking*. Translated by John M. Anderson and E. Hans Freund. New York: Harper Perennial, 1966.
Heidegger, Martin. *Identity and Difference*. Translated by Joan Stambaugh. New York: Harper & Row, 1969.
Heidegger, Martin. *Introduction to Philosophy—Thinking and Poetizing*. Translated by Phillip Jacques Braunstein. Bloomington: Indiana University Press, 2011.
Heidegger, Martin. *On the Way to Language*. Translated by Peter D. Hertz. San Francisco: Harper Collins, 1982.
Heidegger, Martin. "The Origin of the Work of Art." In *Poetry, Language, Thought*. Translated by Albert Hofstadter, 15–86. New York: Harper & Row, 1971.
Heidegger, Martin. *Phenomenology of Intuition and Expression*. Translated by Tracy Colony. London, England: Continuum International, 2010.
Heidegger, Martin. "The Principle of Identity." In *The Heidegger Reader*. Edited by Günter Figal and translated by Jerome Veith, 283–94. Bloomington: Indiana University Press, 2009.
Heidegger, Martin. *The Principle of Reason*. Translated by Reginald Lilly. Bloomington: Indiana University Press, 1996.
Heidegger, Martin. "The Projection of Being in Science and Art." In *The Heidegger Reader*. Edited by Günter Figal and translated by Jerome Veith, 104–07. Bloomington: Indiana University Press, 2009.
Heidegger, Martin. *The Question Concerning Technology and Other Essays*. Translated by William Lovitt. New York: Harper & Row, 1977.

Heidegger, Martin. "Rectorship Address." In *The Heidegger Reader*. Edited by Günter Figal and translated by Jerome Veith, 108–16. Bloomington: Indiana University Press, 2009.

Heidegger, Martin. *What Is Called Thinking?* Translated by J. Glenn Gray. New York: Harper Perennial, 1976.

Inwood, Michael. *A Heidegger Dictionary*. Oxford, England: Blackwell, 1999.

Kisiel, Theodore. "Hermeneutics of Facticity." In *Martin Heidegger: Key Concepts*. Edited by Bret W. Davis, 17–32. Durham, England: Acumen, 2010.

Lovitt, William. Introduction to *The Question Concerning Technology and Other Essays*, by Martin Heidegger. Translated by William Lovitt, xiii–xxxix. New York: Harper & Row, 1977.

Monson, Ingrid. *Saying Something: Jazz Improvisation and Interaction*. Chicago: University of Chicago Press, 1996.

Sheehan, Thomas. "The Turn." In *Martin Heidegger: Key Concepts*. Edited by Bret W. Davis, 82–101. Durham, England: Acumen, 2010.

Stambaugh, Joan. Introduction to *Identity and Difference*, by Martin Heidegger. Translated by Joan Stambaugh, 7–18. New York: Harper & Row, 1969.

Stiegler, Bernard. *Technics and Time, 1: The Fault of Epimetheus*. Translated by Richard Beardsworth and George Collins. Stanford: Stanford University Press, 1998.

Thwaites, Trevor. "Heidegger and Jazz: Musical Propositions of Truth and the Essence of Creativity." *Philosophy of Music Education Review* 21 no. 2 (2013): 120–35.

Thwaites, Trevor. "Technology and Music Education in a Digitized, Disembodied, Posthuman World." *Action, Criticism and Theory for Music Education*, 13 no. 2 (2014): 30–47.

Chapter 12

Musical Performance as Poetic Thinking

Goetz Richter

When thinking about musical performance, musicians face a dilemma: their intuitive thinking is familiar to them in performance yet recedes as they seek an explicit account of it. It seems that seeking understanding of performative thinking in its original immediacy is not easily available as details withdraw from view upon objectifying reflection. This chapter will argue that Heidegger's conception of poetic thinking can help us understand musical thinking. I will initially follow selected accounts musicians give of their performative thinking. I suggest that these present us with significant questions, particularly where they are framed within dualistic metaphysical concepts. I suggest that we can obtain more satisfactory interpretations if instead we read such accounts in dialogue with Heidegger's fundamental characterization of poetic thinking. In the main, I will try to show musical performance is best understood as poetic thinking. As a consequence, interpretations of Heidegger that consider him peripheral to music and music as peripheral to his thinking may need to be revised.

MUSICAL PERFORMANCE

Performing musicians are often acutely aware of their conscious intentionality and seek to understand their thinking on a fundamental level. Their musical thinking connects embodied temporality with abstract form. Already from the outset, it seems problematic whether and in which sense we can speak of "thinking" here. How far can we expand the boundaries of thinking into the realm of the body or the imagination? Drawing them too tightly will clearly not do, as an expulsion of thinking from musical performance would obliterate the important and complex intellectual and abstract dimensions that we hear in music. Inversely, ignoring the affective and embodied dimension of their thinking dehydrates the musical experience.

In an attempt to capture this complexity, musicians speak of a "thinking through feeling" (*Empfindungsdenken*). According to the German composer and conductor Hans Zender, the musician

> thinks with his ears, yes, even with his entire body. The latter is "energised to vibrate" (*in Schwingung versetzt*) and this is not merely a metaphorical expression. Cezanne said that he thinks with the tip of his paint brush. In the same way the musician must say that he thinks directly with tones (*Klänge*) . . . music is a form of affective thinking (*Empfindungsdenken*).[1]

An immediate response may qualify such affective thinking as "subjective," imposing on musical performance and thinking limits of truthfulness and relevance. Yet, musicians claim autonomous intellectual, and indeed spiritual significance for their music making. If their thinking and practice were largely determined by subjective feeling, these claims lose their authority.

A way to address this might challenge reason itself. Nietzsche famously does so in his criticism of Socratism in the *Birth of Tragedy*. Some musicians, like the Austrian conductor Nikolaus Harnoncourt, similarly insist on the autonomy of musical thinking by affirming its unique validity. Invoking Pascal's distinction between *raison arithmétique* (rational thinking) and *raison du coeur* (affective thinking),[2] Harnoncourt affirms that affective thinking is

> irrational, full of fantasy, illogical, its thoughts evidently follow different paths, use other paths of our mind, they make us happy without knowing why, they allow us to feel beauty, love and hate . . . for us the logic-rational thinking is poised to devour everything. One thinks that the results of a logical chain of thought are much more important than the insights of art, which remain obscure to the rational vandal.[3]

Seeking value in irrational, affective thinking confronts us with questions, however. First, how does this qualify as thinking in the first instance? Second, how can it be meaningful, truthful, or compelling when it is subjective, irrational, fanciful, or illogical?

One possible answer affirms the absolute possibilities of attention found in ecstatic transcendence or mystical revelation. Thus, the Romanian conductor Sergiu Celibidache points to the autonomous affective power of tone. Invoking transcendent dimensions, Celibidache speaks of a "sacred possibility" (*heilige Möglichkeit*) to free consciousness from obstacles of conceptual thinking. Attending to the "so-and not otherwise of the musical tone"[4] creates a "pure consciousness." In this state, we are "free of all conscious conditioning through past or future. Only its open, spontaneously responsive behaviour guarantees its unbounded unfolding."[5] Focusing attention on such immediacy, the musician dwells in the space that is opened by the work of music. His playing takes the form of a rapture, divine utterance, and immediate articulation.

Questions remain in such an account especially in relation to our attention to music as a temporal form. To be sure, we make music with attendance to the sensuous immediacy of tone itself (*Klang*); however, we also hear it as a reflection of abstract form. The duality of tone and form in music might echo the contrast of feeling and reflection. This involves us in a multidimensional form of thinking, opening any holistic "pure consciousness" to dialogical challenge. Singular, reflexive thinking outlined by Celibidache lacks detail and does not account for form.

It might be necessary, then, to look at a balance between modalities of consciousness in a way articulated by the pianist and conductor Daniel Barenboim:

> In music ... intellect and emotion go hand in hand, both for the composer and for the performer. Rational and emotional perception are not only not in conflict with one another; rather, each guides the other in order to achieve an equilibrium of understanding in which the intellect determines the validity of the intuitive reaction and emotional element provides the rational with a dimension of feeling that renders the whole human ... rational understanding is not only possible but absolutely necessary in order for the imagination to have free rein.[6]

In balancing feeling and rational, conscious reflection, Barenboim points to the imagination. His contention is that intuitive experience and the imagination are advanced by rational understanding. In fact, when we speak of musical thinking, we should not so much refer to affective thinking but to creative imagination. Active in the process of listening, the imagination creates formal paths that are reflected, determined, and possibly restructured in the moment of performance. As Zender points out, musical listening gathers a sensuous, immediate sense (*sinnlicher Sinn*) and a reflected or formal meaning (*sinnhafter Sinn*).[7] Attention to reflected and formal meaning might then give rise to objectifying thinking. The objectifying thinking also advances an affective thinking that has an obvious temporal determination and is sensuous and immediate. It needs to be renewed through active temporal listening that requires us "to always scan (*abtasten*) the work temporally anew"[8] and is never complete.

A balance of feeling and thinking could be characterized as a permeation of thinking and listening through the work of the imagination. Rational, conscious reflection and affective, intuitive listening are sublated within a unifying poetic thinking: "Thinking conceives listening, listening follows thinking. Listening is an inner thinking."[9]

How is such a unifying thinking actually achieved, though?

In Barenboim's understanding, the musician aims to become part of the musical work. He writes that:

> The task of the performing musician, then, is not to express or interpret the music as such, but to aim to become part of it. It is almost as if the interpretation of a text creates a subtext for itself that develops, substantiates, varies and contrasts the actual text. This subtext is inherent in the score and is itself boundless. It results from a dialogue between the performer and the score, and its richness is determined by the curiosity of the performer.[10]

The metaphorical dialogue between the infinite textual possibilities of the score on the one hand and an imagined subtext conceived by the performer on the other permeates thinking and listening. However, a conception of infinite possibilities of a score[11] suggests challenges for the poetic thinking. Does the musician renew this dialogue with every performance? How does such a dialogue remain open and indeed a genuine dialogue given that subjective dimensions of affective thinking may overpower attention to text and form?

While performing musicians attempt to make sense of their thinking, playing, and listening; they tend to do so largely within dualistic metaphysical concepts. Interpreting their accounts raises questions. Emphasizing affective thinking as a unique search for sensuous meaning affirms the purely subjective act. A holistic "pure consciousness" leaves musical form unexplained. How does ecstatic rapture realize form?[12] Our musical experience requires that this be answered. Thinking of performance as balancing feeling and thinking dialogically and as an ongoing search[13] enables us to mediate subjectivity. It may proceed within a unity of listening and thinking. However, it leaves open how dialogical dimensions are maintained in the temporal process.

HEIDEGGER AND MUSIC

In the following, I turn to a discussion of Heidegger's thinking on music. We encounter in Heidegger initially only occasional thoughts about musical works themselves.[14] However, further inspection reveals a richness of musical thinking and a preoccupation with musical phenomena. Thinking and thoughts on music need to be distinguished here. This distinction reflects essential characteristics of Heidegger's philosophy itself, which emphasizes performance (*Vollzug*)[15] and culminates in the ontology of event (*Ereignis*).[16]

An interpretation of Heidegger that focuses only on thoughts about music risks to invert his essential philosophical concern. Heidegger does not say much about music directly and yet affirms music as fundamental to thinking and poetry.[17] Some commentators even attest to Heidegger "a certain musical deafness, a lack of musical education,"[18] ignoring that his own personal relationship to music was interested and differentiated.[19] There is no evidence for "deafness" nor is it philosophically helpful. In fact, Heidegger positions music in close proximity to poetic thinking. This seems obvious from the many musical references that are contained in writings from *Sein und Zeit* (e.g., *Stimmung*, commonly translated as "attunement") onward to the philosophy of the *Ereignis* (e.g., *Anklang* [resonating] and *Zu-Spiel* [playing forth]). Furthermore, a reading of Heidegger must remain attentive to the "unsaid." The fact that Heidegger does not explicitly discuss music as an aesthetic phenomenon does not mean that music was peripheral to Heidegger's thinking. Heidegger mentions music and musical phenomena in a number of contexts. First, there are brief comments about musicians, such as Schubert, Mozart, Stravinsky, or Orff.[20] Beyond their relevance as hints toward Heidegger's relationship with music, these comments do not interest me here as they are too isolated and singular. Second, there are discussions of art in the well-known essay "The Origin of the Work of Art" (1935) which have relevance to music.[21] These interest me in the first instance as they articulate indirectly how music is present in poetic thinking. In a brief discussion of the "Origin of the Work of Art" essay in the next section, I intend to indicate how this relationship might be conceived and how it might help us understand the main question of this essay: the musical thinking of performing musicians.

In a third order, there are Heidegger's interpretations of Nietzsche and the discussion of music in relation to Wagner. These seem to suggest ambivalent views.[22] We have on the one hand Heidegger's rejection of Wagner's demands that music is privileged among the arts and Heidegger's assertion that music is not itself an essential manifestation of truth, that is, that music cannot set forth a world. However, while this suggests a subordinate relevance of music, we cannot narrow Heidegger's consideration of music to the Nietzschean context and to his interpretation of Wagner.[23] The dialogue with Nietzsche also broadens the conception of music, hinting at the possibility that music (*lied, singen*) opens up a "new, higher and more original being of beings."[24] This gesturing toward the proximity of music to poetic thinking becomes increasingly important in Heidegger's later philosophy. While the details of Heidegger's discussion of Nietzsche and Wagner will only concern me briefly in this context, they have wider relevance for a more comprehensive study of Heidegger's conception of music.[25]

In a fourth order and following the Nietzsche lectures, music remains important to Heidegger's interpretation of Friedrich Hölderlin and Georg Trakl and to his discussion of language itself. These interpretations develop and are in turn sustained by the thinking of *Ereignis*. I will try to show how this philosophy brings music into closest proximity to thinking and develops a conception of poetic thinking beyond metaphysical dualities that is most insightful for any performing musician.

MUSIC AND "THE ORIGIN OF THE WORK OF ART"

Heidegger's 1935 essay "The Origin of the Work of Art" is a starting point in his contemplation about the relevance of art to the question of Being. Rather than containing thoughts about art, it advances a path of thinking leading to the thinking of *Ereignis*.[26] More specifically, the essay aims to show how art is an occurrence of truth. It opens a dynamic and performative perspective. The artwork is an event and a realm, not a thing. Heidegger commences with a critical destruction of our initial, always prevalent ontic perspectives of a work.[27] However, such perspectives miss the point as the artwork "works" against a reified metaphysical conception of being an aesthetic object. We begin to see this when we consider its origin. The simple fact that the artwork is created by the artist is insufficient in itself to enlighten us about its origin as art. It returns to a metaphysical view of a human subject creating an aesthetic object. Instead, the inquiry into the origin of the artwork needs to ask what occurs within the realm of the artwork.

At issue is the origin of the essence of the artwork rather than the essence of any particular work. This advances a developmental and genetic perspective. Heidegger sees the artwork as a realm of strife between world and earth. World (the horizon in which the human being encounters being) and earth (the natural shelter and familiar ground from which man sets out to encounter being) are set in tension. The strife of world and earth occurs between unconcealment (*Lichtung*) and dual concealment (*Verbergung*)—the concealment of being which is a necessary implication of unconcealment and the unconcealment of the earth as concealing. Its encounter with human beings, truth, or the unconcealment of being (*Aletheia*) shows its tendency to "enter into the work."[28] Art becomes the event (*Ereignis*) in which the meaning of being (*Sinn von Sein*) is determined.

Heidegger claims that the human creativity that achieves the realization of the work of art is *dichten* (poetic creation): "Truth as the lighting and concealment of being only occurs when it is poeticised (*gedichted wird*). All art is an acceptance of the arrival of the truth of being as such and always poetic creation (*Dichten*)."[29] The "Origin" essay culminates in the concept of poetic creation (*dichten*), which Heidegger develops on three levels. First, language itself is already poetic creation. Accordingly, the propositional truth structure that relates statements and facts is derivative and dependent on an original "saying" (*Sage*). Second, poetic creation refers to poetry itself in the narrow sense (poesy).[30] This is naturally a straightforward identification. It becomes problematic where Heidegger elevates poetry above other art forms (we will discuss this further). Finally, the origin of art itself is poetic creation:

> Truth as lighting and concealment of being occurs in so far as it is poetically created. All art is as an allowing of the arrival of truth as such in its essence poetic creation . . . From the poetic essence of art it occurs, that amongst being an opening is created where everything is different to the everyday.[31]

The identification of art as poetic creation suggests modalities of thinking: the artist creates realms or openings and allows for the arrival of truth. The essence of this creativity is a "founding of truth" (*Stiften der Wahrheit*). It takes place in a distance to the everyday. It suggests dynamic and temporal characteristic of artworks as occurrence (*Geschehen*) and movement (*Bewegung*).[32]

Given the emphasis on temporal and dynamic characteristics, Heidegger's neglect of music in the *Origin* essay seems surprising. This has been identified by Günther Pöltner, who argues that unacknowledged by Heidegger, music fulfills the central concern of art to "bring the truth of being into the work."[33] Pöltner's argument suggests that while poetry achieves this in an initial ontic relationship to the world, music is devoid of reference, has no such relationship, and thus opens an immediate ontological presence. Musicality and musical playing realize the musical work through presence and attention to the temporal dimension of music. The immediate power (*Macht*) of music needs no ontic reference and eludes human manipulative control. It rather seizes the musician and listener, reducing the musician to a medium. Music is "in an exceptional way the art of *Ereignis*."[34] Through music, human beings are addressed by being and directed to the attention of its silence. Quoting Heidegger, Pöltner writes:

> If "the essence of man consists in man being subject to the demand of being" then the art work realises the primordial act of the address of being (*Seinszuspruch*) and its answer, that is the provision of the "temporal opportunity for that which appear as it is." From this point of view music is the most human artform. Since through it the most common origin of all human communication finds its articulation in the work: the relation with that which allows him his essence and is no being, the "relation between Being and human being." Music is in an emphatic

way the art of man's belonging to world and with it to the temporal opportunity (*Zeit-Spiel-Raum*).[35]

It is the absence of ontic reference and the intimate relationship with a temporality that privileges music to do exactly what Heidegger asks of art: to allow for the arrival of truth into the work and to create the realm where "we are moved into this openness and removed from the ordinary."[36]

While Pöltner's suggestion, however, that poetry has a "decidedly ontic" way of setting forth truth in the work can be challenged,[37] his understanding of music is not dependent on such a challenge. Further, Heidegger's decision to remain largely silent about music in the context of the "Origin" essay says itself little about the significance of music to his thinking. In fact, the selection of artworks that are discussed seems to follow an instrumental purpose of developing Heidegger's philosophy of the disclosure of being more compellingly. The works discussed are used to illustrate particular directions on the path of thinking. If music is indeed as central as Pöltner suggests, then a concrete discussion of musical works might even distract us from such a fundamental centrality. It would undermine Heidegger's point about the immediacy in which art (in this case music) becomes the realm for the arrival of truth by situating the discussion in the context of a metaphysically determined discipline of aesthetics. Any discussion of works is mediated by metaphysical determinations that remove the work from this immediacy. This leads to a forgetting of the original disclosure of truth as *aletheia*[38] and carries a risk to move the dialogue with music into the metaphysical realms of meaning and essence. Pöltner's argument achieves its persuasion because it reminds us of the phenomenological characteristics of music in the fundamental way in which truth arrives in (the) musical work. In the following, I turn toward Heidegger's conception of poetic thinking as it is developed in the context of his dialogue with Hölderlin. We encounter at the basis of this thinking important musical commitments.

POETIC THINKING (*DICHTEN*) AND MUSIC

The major development of Heidegger's thinking following *Sein und Zeit* referred to as philosophy of the event (*Ereignis-Philosophie*) is progressed to a large extent through Heidegger's dialogue with Hölderlin. The thinking of *Ereignis* is a way of conceiving how the human being (*Dasein*) and the truth of being belong to each other. This is reflected through Hölderlin's conception of how poetry and the poet respond to the flight and absence of the gods that characterize modernity. The detail and order of this thinking are not derived from an argument referring subjectivity to reason as modernity would conceive it but articulates the attempt to conceive an immanent "jointure" (*Fuge*), a way in which being belongs to Dasein.[39] Heidegger finds in Hölderlin's poetry the opportunity to retrace his thinking of the truth of being. Heidegger's dialogue with Hölderlin is no ordinary interpretation that aims to convey a coherent or correct meaning, but an "original re-saying" (*wiedersagen*), a form of poetic thinking itself.

In his dialogue with Hölderlin, Heidegger finds the possibility of a poetic thinking that discloses truth and non-metaphysical essence (*Wesen*)—the truth of being. This thinking sets itself apart from a metaphysical distinction between reality and semblance underpinning modern calculative thinking particularly.[40] It reaches beyond the sayable and receives rather than constructs intentionally. Poetic creativity (*dichten*) emanates from a "realm of essence" (*Wesensbereich*) and with exposure to "the truth of poetry" (*Wahrheit des Dichtens*).[41] It is variously a "greeting,"[42] naming, gesturing-disclosure (*weisendes Offenbarmachen*),[43] and most importantly a "founding" (*stiften*).[44] It seems playful,[45] particularly where it occurs in the absence of the gods.[46]

The naming, gesturing, and founding of the poet are in itself essentially wordless. It occurs in song (*Lied, Gesang*) inspired by the spirit of the "holy" (*das Heilige*). The poet does not receive the song (*Gesang*) through a transcendent God. His essential stance is grounded in "a receptive embrace by the holy."[47] The location of the song at the heart of poetic creativity is most notable. It indicates that Heidegger's *Seinsdenken*, the thinking of Being, is fundamentally musical.

Heidegger indicates the congruence of thinking and singing that emerges from the poetico-contemplative dialogue with Hölderlin in one of his own poetic works:

> Singing and thinking are the neighbouring trunks of poetry (*Dichten*). They grow from Being (*Seyn*) and reach toward its truth. Their relationship inspires Hölderlin who sings of the trees in the forest: "And unknown remain to each other, as long as they stand, the neighbouring trunks."[48]

The Hölderlin quote in this stanza has possibly a twofold interpretation: the trunks of singing, thinking, and poetry remain unknown as long as they remain static and self-contained, notwithstanding that their sustaining ground (being) and the direction of their growth are identical (truth). If they cease to stand, however, and develop momentum and dynamic, that is, if they come to life in poetic thinking, they cease to remain "unknown to each other" and may start to recognize their sameness. As a result, we encounter a "singing thinking" (*singendes Denken*)[49] that is closely related to poetic creativity and thinking in the wider sense.

LISTENING AND LANGUAGE

Heidegger's conception of poetic thinking (*dichten*) would not be complete without a look at his approach to language and listening. Both phenomena are closely related as Heidegger conceives language as speaking to us in addition to being spoken by us. We speak in so far as we listen. Listening is here far more detailed than the mere perception of the audible. It always already reaches ahead of itself through "hearkening" (*horchen*) and through the obedience (*hörig, Gehorsam*) to that which is to be heard. Heidegger writes:

> Does man hearken because he can hear or can he hear because he can hearken? And what does it mean to be able to hearken? And what does man "hear"? That, to which he hearkens—what does he hearken to? . . . only through hearkening listening becomes possible and what is audible is perceived (*Hörbares vernehmlich*).[50]

These notes from Heidegger's 1939 seminar on Johan Gottfried Herder's *Über den Ursprung der Sprache* follow earlier observations of the importance of listening in *Sein und Zeit*.[51] Listening and hearkening reach beyond the audible toward the disclosure of being. They attend in the context of language to the "ringing of silence" (*Geläut der Stille*)[52] and enable the speaker to bring the *melos*, the "silent saying" (*lautlose Sage*), into the human speech. Listening and hearkening connect us to the musical foundations of language.

We find an interesting example of Heidegger's musical focus in the lectures from 1951 to 1952 *Was heisst Denken?* A discussion here of opinion and scientific knowing leads to an observation that it seems "most thoughtworthy that we are not yet thinking."[53] This assertion becomes a *leitmotif* in the first parts of this lecture. It leads Heidegger to draw attention to the tone of such a statement. Heidegger remarks that on the one hand the "tone, to which our statement is tuned, may not be readily determinable in the manner of our ordinary statements."[54] He concludes, somewhat perplexingly, that "we need to reflect on the statement not only according to its tone but also to its propositional character,"[55] suggesting a privilege, certainly immediacy, of the tonal elements initially.

We gain further clues when we follow Heidegger in the consideration that the propositional character (*Aussagecharakter*) is articulated in a "*Weise*," initially understood as "way" or mode, but intended as a musical designation, as "melody":

> The way (*Weise*), in which our statement speaks, can however only be indicated conclusively, when we are able to reflect what the statement actually says. We must already now draw attention to the question, which the assertion assigns to

us, when we reflect about the mode of this saying. Mode (*Weise*) we understand differently from way and mean (*Art und Weise*), from *modus*. Mode (*Weise*) is here melody, sound (*Klang*) and tone, which does not only relate to the articulation of the said (*Sagens*). Mode (*Weise*) of speech is the tone, from which and through which the spoken is tuned. With this we indicate that both questions, the question of the "tone" of the statement and its propositional character are related.[56]

This reflection suggests to me that Heidegger uses the metaphorical potential of "mode" (*Weise*) as a theoretical way (*methodos*) on the one hand and as music (*melos*) on the other, to draw attention to the grounding of meaning in the unity of path and focus (*melody*). In this example, language speaks through tone and through propositional reference, its disclosure converging to both. Attending to *melos* thinking becomes musical. We have here an example of the concealed musicality in Heidegger's thinking that listens to being (*das Lied des Seyns*) always already before any conscious thinking and speaking takes place.[57]

SINGING THINKING (*SINGENDES DENKEN*)

The discussion of Heidegger has exposed how poetic thinking (*Dichten*) is fundamentally musical. While the "Origin" essay shows art as a realm for the arrival of the truth of being, the ultimate significance of poetic thinking rests with its wider, wordless, and musical sense. The Hölderlin interpretations and the thinking about language transcend metaphysical determinations and disclose musical dimensions of poetic thinking on the path to an immediate thinking of being (*Seinsdenken*). Within this *Ereignis* thinking, attending to the truth of being is a musical undertaking—we listen to the "song of being" (*Lied des Seyns*). Being is initially disclosed in an *Anklang*—in the context of language as a "sounding of silence" (*Geläut der Stille*). No longer reflective of a metaphysical essence or meaning, thinking in closeness to poetic thinking (*dichten*) is a founding (*stiften*) of truth.

Transposing Heidegger's thinking of being into our original context now helps to resolve some of the questions we raised earlier. Musical performance itself is the realm of an arrival of the truth of being. The affective thinking of the musician is better conceived as a singing thinking beyond metaphysical conceptions of object (artwork) and subject (artist). This is why Heidegger's articulation of poetic thinking within the context of the philosophy of *Ereignis* gives us a coherent perspective for an account of performative thinking. It also makes clear why accounts from within a metaphysical perspective lead to perplexity. Music speaks directly to the musician who hearkens. The musician is part of the music just as the speaker is part of language. As "singing and playing become the means of music,"[58] singing thinking becomes the listening thinking (*denkendes Hoeren*) identified by Zender. Playing music is a form of poetic thinking: it originates from and through silence in which the musician collects their entire behavior and sensibility.[59] The musical thinking of the imagination creates freedom of realization (*nicht erzwingbares Gelingen*)[60] in which the music arrives. This arrival mirrors Heidegger's "greeting" and "foundation" of being in poetic thinking. The singing thinking of the performer seeks attention beyond the metaphysical duality of emotion and reason. The Polish harpsichordist Wanda Landowska identifies such hearkening attention as follows:

> To be aware, to be conscious at all times is what appears to be the worthiest in my thoughts and in my work. While interpreting, even at the most impetuous moments when a musical phrase overflows with passion, I want to remain conscious. I may forget a liberty I took at one place or another, but this does not change in any way my state of consciousness, which is always on the alert.[61]

Attention to singing thinking receives the presence of music within *Ereignis* through the "embrace of the holy" which we found in Heidegger's interpretation of Hölderlin. The "holy possibility" of a rapture indicated by Celibidache, akin to Wagnerian intoxication, is really an "embodied attunement" (*leibendes Gestimmtsein*) and "thorough becoming of form and lawful determination."[62] The importance of Heidegger's conception of poetic thinking for the performing musician lies in its possibility to conceive more clearly the balance between form and performance and to establish performance as autonomous beyond subjectivity. Heidegger's thinking dissolves core dilemmas for performing musicians whose intuitions of profound endurance are thwarted by metaphysical conceptions of subjectivity. Instead, it positions music at the center of artistic thinking and creation and opens powerful perspectives for performers who open a realm for truth in their music making.

NOTES

1. Hans Zender, *Waches Hören—Über Musik* (München: Hanser Verlag, 2014), 128.
2. Nikolaus Harnoncourt, *Töne sind höhere Worte* (Salzburg: Residenz Verlag, 2014), 26.
3. Nikolaus Harnoncourt, *Die Macht der Musik* (Salzburg: Residenz Verlag, 1993), 24–25.

4. Sergiu Celibidache, *Über musikalische Phänomenologie* (München: Triptychon, 2001), 49.
5. Celibidache, *Über musikalische Phänomenologie*, 47.
6. Daniel Barenboim, *Everything is Connected—The Power of Music* (London: Phoenix, 2009), 46/47.
7. Zender refers to Jean-Luc Nancy (Zender, *Waches Hören*, 142).
8. Zender, *Waches Hören*, 147.
9. Hans Zender, *Denken Hören—Hören Denken. Musik als eine Grunderfahrung des Lebens* (Freiburg: Alber, 2016), 59.
10. Barenboim, *Everything is Connected*, 52.
11. Kent Nagano and Inge Kloepfer, *Erwarten Sie Wunder—Expect the Unexpected* (Berlin: Berlin Verlag, 2014), 232.
12. See also Heidegger's discussion of Wagner in the 1936/37 lecture course on Nietzsche. Heidegger hints at a sober conception of rapture (*Rausch*) (Martin Heidegger, *Nietzsche: Der Wille zur Macht als Kunst* (Frankfurt: Klostermann, 1985), 139) against Wagner's conception of rapture as mere intoxication, loss of self and excitation (Heidegger, *Nietzsche: Der Wille zur Macht*, 104).
13. Erich Leinsdorf, *The Composer's Advocate—A Radical Orthodoxy for Musicians* (Binghamton: Vail-Ballou Press, 1981), 46 ("for the performer the search is what counts"). See also: Barenboim, *Everything is Connected*, 52 ("To be able to grasp the substance of the music itself is to be willing to begin a never ending search") and Zender about "inquisitive listening" (*fragendes Hören*) (Zender, *Denken Hören*, 53).
14. For commentary on this, see Erik Wallrup, *Being Musically Attuned—The Act of Listening to Music* (Farnam: Ashgate, 2015), 69.
15. "Heidegger regards *Dasein* as that which 'achieves/carries out' (*vollzieht*) its existence by relating to being" according to Andrew Bowie, *Music, Philosophy, and Modernity* (Cambridge: Cambridge University Press, 2007), 296.
16. On musical performance as the event, see the chapter by McAullife and Malpas in this volume.
17. Eduardo Marx, *Heidegger und der Ort der Musik* (Würzburg: Königshausen & Neumann, 1998), 33.
18. Julian Young, *Heidegger's Philosophy of Art* (Cambridge: Cambridge University Press, 2001), 169/170.
19. Marx, *Heidegger und der Ort der Musik*, 31.
20. Wallrup discusses Heidegger's interest in Orff at length in his chapter of this volume.
21. Rentmeester takes up this discussion in his chapter of this volume.
22. Marx, *Heidegger und der Ort der Musik*, 26.
23. Young, *Heidegger's Philosophy of Art*, 168.
24. Marx, *Heidegger und der Ort der Musik*, 25.
25. Wallrup comments more substantially the connection between Nietzsche and Heidegger on music in his chapter of this volume.
26. See: Friedrich Willhem von Herrmann, *Heideggers Philosophie der Kunst* (Frankfurt: Klostermann, 1994), 9, and Julian Young, *Heidegger's Philosophy of Art*, 5.

27. For Heidegger "ontic" refers to beings, while "ontological" refers to being.
28. Martin Heidegger, "Der Ursprung des Kunstwerkes," in *Holzwege* (Frankfurt: Klostermann, 1980), ed. Friedrich-Wilhelm von Herrmann 1–72, 21.
29. Heidegger, "Der Ursprung des Kunstwerkes," 58.
30. See also, Günther Pöltner, "Heidegger," in *Music in German Philosophy—An Introduction*, eds. Stefan Lorenz Sorgner and Oliver Fürbeth (Chicago: University of Chicago Press, 2010), 121–140, 201/2.
31. Heidegger, "Der Ursprung des Kunstwerkes," 58.
32. Heidegger, "Der Ursprung des Kunstwerkes," 34.
33. Günther Pöltner, "Mozart und Heidegger. Die Musik und der Ursprung des Kunstwerkes," *Heidegger Studies* 8 (1992): 124.
34. Pöltner, *Mozart und Heidegger*, 143.
35. Pöltner quotes Heidegger here from the "Origin" essay and from the lectures *Der Satz vom Grund* (Pöltner, *Mozart und Heidegger*, 143). The topic of music and silence from a Heideggerian perspective is covered by Trawny and de Morais and also by Zhu in their respective chapters.
36. Heidegger, "Der Ursprung des Kunstwerkes," 52.
37. See Marx, *Heidegger und der Ort der Musik*, 10.
38. For a discussion about concretizing Heidegger's thinking to support an aesthetic analysis of concrete works, see Marx, *Heidegger und der Ort der Musik*, 16.
39. Von Herrmann, *Heideggers Philosophie*, 13–17.
40. The distinction between calculative thinking (*rechnendes Denken*) and essential thinking (*besinnliches Denken*) is found in Heidegger's address to honor the one-hundredth birthday of the composer Conradin Kreutzer (Martin Heidegger, *Gelassenheit* (Pfullingen: Neske, 1992), 12–14). Thwaites discusses this distinction in his chapter of this volume.
41. Martin Heidegger, *Hölderlins Hymne "Andenken." Gesamtausgabe Band 52* (Frankfurt: Klostermann, 1982), 40.
42. "Im Gruss des Dichters denkt ihm das Gegrüsste zu.. das Grüssen des Dichters ist ein 'Denken', das grüssende Sagen ist aber ein Wort eines Gedichtes, ist ein Dichten." (Heidegger, *Hölderlins Hymnen*, 55).
43. Martin Heidegger, *Hölderlins Hymnen "Germanien" und "Der Rhein." Gesamtausgabe Band 39* (Frankfurt: Klostermann, 1980), 30/1 ("*Dasein* is nothing but the *exposure to overwhelming Being (Ausgesetztheit in die Übermacht des Seyns)*").
44. "*Was bleibet aber, stiften die Dichter.* Dichtung ist Stiftung, erwirkende Gründung des Bleibenden. Der Dichter ist der Begründer des Seyns . . . Dichtung—Aushalten der Winke der Götter—Stiftung des Seyns." (Heidegger, *Hölderlins Hymnen*, 33 and Martin Heidegger, *Erläuterungen zu Hölderlins Dichtung* (Frankfurt: Klostermann, 2012), 41).
45. Heidegger, *Erläuterungen*, 35.
46. Heidegger refers to the poet as a *Spielmann* who might achieve the most serious witness of the jointure of *Dasein* and Being at a time of an absence of the gods. See also Marx, *Heidegger und der Ort der Musik*, 44.

47. Heidegger, *Erläuterungen*, 69.

48. Martin Heidegger, *Aus der Erfahrung des Denkens* (Stuttgart: Klett-Cotta, 2005), 25. In his later thought, Heidegger spells *Sein* (being) as *Seyn* to stress that it is not to be understood metaphysically.

49. The term *"singendes Denken"* is found in Carl Phillip Emanuel Bach's keyboard treatise. Cf. Carl Phillip Emmanuel Bach, *Versuch über die wahre Art, das Clavier zu spielen* (Wiesbaden: Breitkopf & Härtel, 1986), 122.

50. Martin Heidegger, *Vom Wesen Der Sprache. Gesamtausgabe Band 85* (Frankfurt am Main: Klostermann, 1999), 110–111.

51. Martin Heidegger, *Sein und Zeit* (Tübingen: Niemeyer, 1986), 163/4. "Listening is constitutive for speaking. Listening constitutes the primary and authentic openness of *Dasein* for its own possibility of being (*Seinkönnen*)."

52. see Marx, *Heidegger und der Ort der Musik*, 61.

53. Martin Heidegger, *Was heisst Denken?* (Tübingen: Niemeyer, 1997), 2.

54. Heidegger, *Was heisst Denken?*, 60.

55. Heidegger, *Was heisst Denken?*, 60.

56. Heidegger, *Was heisst Denken?*, 13/4.

57. A musical emphasis of *Weise* (mode) suggests that Bowie's point that Heidegger neglects "the musical" in his later work is in this form not tenable. Bowie contends: "the problem with his later work is that it gestures towards something which inherently resists being specified, and yet makes nothing of the idea of the musical as a possible aspect of what it is that he is gesturing towards" (Bowie, *Music, Philosophy, and Modernity*, 305). However, Bowie suggests an objectification of being which is not what Heidegger has in mind. The musical is never a characteristic of this circumstance itself but a way in which human being attend and hearken to the question of being. In a post-metaphysical constellation of questions, thinking and poetic creativity (*dichten*) listen to the address of being and provide the clearing in which being discloses itself. Any "gesturing towards" suggests that Being is already always present, yet it is precisely man's mode of being musical that allows for the arrival and presence in the first instance.

58. Pöltner, *Mozart und Heidegger*, 138.

59. "I live the concert before even the first note sounds. Music must come from silence, from rest." (Andras Schiff, *Musik kommt aus der Stille* (Kassel: Bärenreiter, 2017), 23).

60. See also Peter Rohs, "Singend denken—Musikästhetische Überlegungen im Anschluss an einen Begriff von C. Ph. E. Bach," in *Vom Sinn des Hörens— Beiträge zur Philosophie der Musik*, ed. Georg Mohr, Johann Kreuzer (Würzburg: Königshausen & Neumann, 2012), 55–76, 59. Rohs' discussion of *Singend Denken* in the context of Kant's concept of beauty and Hanslick's "contemplation of fantasy" or pure, free intuition is relevant here.

61. Wanda Landowska, *Landowska on Music* (New York: Stein and Day, 1964), 367.

62. Heidegger, *Nietzsche: Der Wille zur Macht*, 124.

BIBLIOGRAPHY

Bach, Carl Phillip Emmanuel. *Versuch über die wahre Art, das Clavier zu spielen.* Wiesbaden: Breitkopf & Härtel, 1986.
Barenboim, Daniel. *Everything is Connected—The Power of Music.* London: Phoenix, 2009.
Benson, Bruce Ellis. *The Improvisation of Musical Dialogue—A Phenomenology of Music.* Cambridge: Cambridge University Press, 2003.
Bonds, Mark Evans. *Music as Thought—Listening to the Symphony in the Age of Beethoven.* Princeton: Princeton University Press, 2006.
Bowie. Andrew. *Music, Philosophy, and Modernity.* Cambridge: Cambridge University Press, 2007.
Celibidache, Sergiu. *Über musikalische Phänomenologie.* München: Triptychon, 2001.
Harnoncourt, Nikolaus. *Die Macht der Musik.* Salzburg: Residenz Verlag, 1993.
Harnoncourt, Nikolaus. *Töne sind höhere Worte.* Salzburg: Residenz Verlag, 2014.
Heidegger, Martin. *Hölderlins Hymnen "Germanien" und "Der Rhein." Gesamtausgabe Band 39.* Frankfurt: Klostermann, 1980.
Heidegger, Martin. "Der Ursprung des Kunstwerkes," in *Holzwege,* edited by Friedrich-Wilhelm von Herrmann, 1–72. Frankfurt: Klostermann, 1980.
Heidegger, Martin. *Hölderlins Hymne "Andenken." Gesamtausgabe Band 52.* Frankfurt: Klostermann, 1982.
Heidegger, Martin. *Hölderlins Hymne "Der Ister." Gesamtausgabe Band 53.* Frankfurt: Klostermann, 1984.
Heidegger, Martin. *Nietzsche: Der Wille zur Macht als Kunst.* Frankfurt: Klostermann, 1985.
Heidegger, Martin. *Sein und Zeit.* Tübingen: Niemeyer, 1986.
Heidegger, Martin. "Was heisst Denken." In *Vorträge und Aufsätze,* edited by Friedrich-Wilhelm von Herrmann, 125–138. Pfullingen: Neske, 1990.
Heidegger, Martin. "Wissenschaft und Besinnung." In *Vorträge und Aufsätze,* edited by Friedrich-Wilhelm von Herrmann, 41–66. Pfullingen: Neske, 1990.
Heidegger, Martin. *Gelassenheit.* Pfullingen: Neske, 1992.
Heidegger, Martin. *Was heisst Denken?.* Tübingen: Niemeyer, 1997.
Heidegger, Martin. *Logik als die Frage nach dem Wesen der Sprache. Gesamtausgabe Band 38.* Frankfurt: Klostermann, 1998.
Heidegger, Martin. *Vom Wesen Der Sprache. Gesamtausgabe Band 85.* Frankfurt am Main: Klostermann, 1999.
Heidegger, Martin. *Sein und Wahrheit. 1. Die Grundfrage der Philosophe. 2. Vom Wesen der Wahrheit. Gesamtausgabe Band 36/37.* Frankfurt: Klostermann, 2001.
Heidegger, Martin. *Aus der Erfahrung des Denkens.* Stuttgart: Klett-Cotta, 2005.
Heidegger, Martin. *Das Ereignis. Gesamtausgabe Band 71.* Frankfurt: Klostermann, 2009.
Heidegger, Martin. *Erläuterungen zu Hölderlins Dichtung.* Frankfurt: Klostermann, 2012.

Herrmann, Friedrich Wilhem von. *Heideggers Philosophie der Kunst.* Frankfurt: Klostermann, 1994.
Landowska, Wanda. *Landowska on Music.* New York: Stein and Day, 1964.
Leinsdorf, Erich. *The Composer's Advocate—A Radical Orthodoxy for Musicians.* Binghamton: Vail-Ballou Press, 1981.
Marx, Eduardo. *Heidegger und der Ort der Musik.* Würzburg: Königshausen & Neumann, 1998.
Nagano, Kent and Inge Kloepfer. *Erwarten Sie Wunder—Expect the Unexpected.* Berlin: Berlin Verlag, 2014.
Picht, Georg. *Kunst und Mythos. Vorlesungen und Schriften.* Stuttgart: Klett-Cotta.
Pöltner, Günther. "Mozart und Heidegger. Die Musik und der Ursprung des Kunstwerkes." *Heidegger Studies* 8 (1992): 123–144.
Pöltner, Günther. "Heidegger," In *Music in German Philosophy—An Introduction.* Edited by Stefan Lorenz Sorgner and Oliver Fürbeth, 121–140. Chicago: University of Chicago Press, 2010.
Rohs. Peter. 2012. "Singend denken – Musikästhetische Überlegungen im Anschluss an einen Begriff von C. Ph. E. Bach." In *Vom Sinn des Hörens—Beiträge zur Philosophie der Musik.* Edited by Georg Mohr, Johann Kreuzer, 55–76. Würzburg: Königshausen & Neumann, 2012.
Schiff. Andras. *Musik kommt aus der Stille.* Kassel: Bärenreiter, 2017.
Wallrup, Erik. *Being Musically Attuned—The Act of Listening to Music.* Farnam: Ashgate, 2015.
Young, Julian. *Heidegger's Philosophy of Art.* Cambridge: Cambridge University Press, 2001.
Zender, Hans. *Waches Hören—Über Musik.* München: Hanser Verlag, 2014.
Zender, Hans. *Denken Hören— Hören Denken. Musik als eine Grunderfahrung des Lebens.* Freiburg: Alber, 2016.
Zender, Hans. *Mehrstimmiges Denken—Versuche zu Musik und Sprache.* Freiburg: Alber, 2019.

Chapter 13

Being-with in Music

Justin Christensen and Janeen Loehr

Much of Martin Heidegger's writing on art discusses an active interaction between artworks and persons who experience them. In this chapter, we will explore how we engage with others while playing music together and how this can open up our being toward the world. To do so, we will first examine Heidegger's concepts of unconcealing and concealing, and how these concepts play a role in our everyday modes of encounter in the world. We will next focus on Heidegger's proposal that art works to unconceal new ways of being-in-the-world while simultaneously highlighting the play of unconcealing and concealing that is part of our everyday being-in-the-world. Heidegger believes that this dual-layered act of unconcealing gives art the ability to take us out of our mundane routines and allows us to recognize a fuller and more radiant appearance of the beings that we encounter. Also, he suggests that this partly occurs through us increasing our flexibility and freedom in adopting our modes of encountering the world, and that this and our opening up to the world may lead to us having a more authentic way of being-in-the-world.

Upon exploring this possibility, we then turn to the concept of being-with to better understand how our being-in-the-world impacts our making music together. Similar to unconcealing and concealing being described as opposing but complementary forces, Heidegger presents his concept of *being-with* as ranging between the opposing poles of being-alongside (*Sein bei*—the common mode of simply being in the presence of others) and being-among-one-another (*Untereinandersein*—where our openness of being and sense of self are lost through being "thrown into the publicness of the they").[1] For example, when we unconceal our communal experiences of the world, we necessarily also conceal our more individual experiences of the world and vice versa. Jean-Luc Nancy has since proposed that there is a *liminal* space between these endpoints of being-with that might better explain many of our

213

cooperative interactions in the world.[2] We will argue that this in-between of being-with is often seen in musical performance situations, where performers have to balance the degree to which they keep themselves distinct or integrate themselves with other performers in order to achieve the best performance possible. We will conclude this chapter by speculating that, as group music performance straddles a liminal space where our openness of being can act both on our being-singular and being-plural, the social bonding and mental health benefits of group music making may result from the balancing act of keeping ourselves distinct while simultaneously integrating our actions with those of others as we dwell in the unconcealing of the artwork.

In this chapter, we will sometimes draw on empirical findings from cognitive and biological studies to support our arguments. Although Heidegger considered Dasein to be separate from our biological being, a growing number of phenomenologists are turning to empirical findings and cognitive underpinnings to support their philosophical work on action and perception as a part of being.[3] We view our work as consistent with such efforts.

CONCEALED AND UNCONCEALED ASPECTS OF EXPERIENCE

In his writing on the nature of being, Heidegger demands us to unshackle ourselves from our preconceived notion of our world being presented to us as an object in front of us across a subject/object divide. When discussing the nature of an artwork, Heidegger's demands are the same. He wants us to free ourselves from thinking of an artwork merely in terms of what it is in front of us, that is, a work made by an artist. Instead, he wants us to think of what it does and how it can affect us through our interactions with it.[4] He argues that this interactivity occurs because we exist as thrown into a shared world, where we understand ourselves and others in terms of the shared public norms and practices of our world.[5] Due to our being fully part of the world through our being-in-the-world, things have meaning for us and we *care*, with care being a primordial and historical concept that structures our experience. From this care, our interactions with others, art, and things can never occur as disconnected from us across a subject/object divide, as they are interpreted in terms of what they mean to us.[6]

For Heidegger, perception is not a subjective experience that occurs in the mind of the observer, but rather is something that occurs in an in-between space that includes both the observer and the observed.[7] In this way, perceiving an object could be seen as a two-stage process whereby the perceived object reveals itself in a way that its material matter affords, and the perceiver interacts with this revelation of matter in a way that his or her biology, history, and expertise allow. Supporting this, childhood development studies have shown that perception is not a passively acquired skill, but that infants already develop a rich and inseparable coupling between their actions and their concurrent multimodal perceptions through their everyday interactions with their environment.[8] If we were to expect that the brain's role was to passively construct representations of our environment, we might also expect brain areas associated with visual processing in individuals born blind, or auditory processing in individuals born deaf, to atrophy from lack of use. This does not happen.[9] Instead, the visual cortex in blind individuals adapts, such as showing activation in response to the tactile sensations of reading braille[10] or in response to the returning clicking sounds of echolocation.[11] Additionally, the auditory cortex in deaf individuals shows activation in response to visual stimuli[12] and plays a role in "hearing" sign language.[13] These findings suggest that the brain organizes itself in a way that supports a skillful engagement in our environment, that is, our brain has a task-based division rather than a sensory modality division.[14]

In addition to our perception being heavily adapted to our tasks, it is also imbued with the copresence of other individuals in our environment. Heidegger considered being-with-others to be an a priori structure in our existence, in that our perspective is always already one of *being-with*.[15] Although Heidegger did not write extensively on perception in terms of being-with-others, Zahavi has suggested that there are links between his view and his teacher Husserl's on this topic,[16] with Husserl considering perception to be intersubjectively accessible: Everything

> that stands before me in experience and primarily in perception has an apperceptive horizon of possible experience, including my own and that of others. Ontologically speaking, my perception of the world is, from the very beginning, part of an open but not explicit totality of possible perceptions [that others may also have].[17]

Because our current perceptions are saturated with the previous interactions that we have had with similar objects, Husserl considers that we are afforded the ability to see beyond our current perspective to be able to share horizons of possible experience with others. Also, when we see and interact with other individuals, we see them in relation to ourselves as part of our shared space.[18] Basically, similar to our having expectations that a house has sides that we cannot see (i.e., we believe it to not be the facade of a movie set) based on our past experiences of walking around similar houses, we can have expectations of what another person in our shared space is potentially viewing based on past similar experiences that we have had. Supporting this, Baldwin has shown that infants are already able to follow the gestures and attentional cues of their parents, and that this ability for infants to latch onto their parent's attention plays an important role in them improving their social coordination and language learning skills.[19] Baldwin has also provided evidence that we have developed this skill to share perspectives with others since infancy, and that much of our experience of others' attentional cues is implicit; it forms part of the background of our experience. Heidegger considers the potential perceptual interactions that are unseen but inform our current experience to be the hidden or *concealed* aspects of our experience, while those that are currently present to our view to be the aspects that are revealed or *unconcealed*.[20] The degree to which these hidden aspects of our experiences reveal themselves to us depends on our modes of encounter, so we will discuss these in the following section.

MODES OF ENCOUNTER (*SEINWEISEN*)

As care is a primordial structure of our being, it demands that we interpret our being and our experiences in terms of what they mean to us. Generally when we enter into a room, we experience the room as a referential whole that is familiar to us, and we are ready to cope with the many familiar things in the room.[21] We have multiple modes of encounter that aid us in our interactions: two that are part of our everyday life for interacting with things (handiness and presence-to-hand), one for interacting with art, and others for interacting with people. Through having the ability to flexibly and freely match our modes of encounter to the beings that we encounter, we can adopt multiple modes of encounter toward them, allowing them to unconceal themselves as they are. Also, this flexibility of encountering beings allows us to encounter beings as a radiant self-showing of themselves rather than as a flattened-out worn-out familiarity, which leads us to having a more authentic understanding of our world.

Handiness (*Zuhandenheit*) is the way that we most often encounter things in our everyday life. Therefore, in our everyday activities, we are often caught up in seeing the possibilities for action in the things that we encounter, immediately and implicitly knowing how to grasp and use these entities.[22] Our current experience of an entity includes a horizon of expectations on how we might use it in the near future, as we are oriented toward the future and its realm of possibilities. Heidegger stated, "our dealings with useful things are subordinate to the manifold of references of the 'in-order-to' . . . What is peculiar to what is initially at hand is that it withdraws, so to speak, in its character of handiness in order to be really handy."[23] This sense of the equipment withdrawing into use especially occurs when we find the equipment to be useful and reliable.

Learning a musical instrument and coming to grips with the equipmental nature of the instrument could be considered an example of this handiness mode of encounter. This might help explain why expert pianists playing the piano show a greater efficiency of brain activity in comparison to novices as a result of practice.[24] The experts also no longer need to pay as much attention to their actions on a moment-by-moment level, and they have less need to consciously interfere in their motor planning and execution, as these aspects of playing have receded from consciousness.[25] Unsurprisingly, this greater efficiency in brain activity from increased skill does not result in a loss of recognition ability in their skill area. Drummers show enhanced precision in recognizing rhythms, conductors have greater spatial awareness, and cellists show an increased ability for pitch recognition.[26] This handiness mode of encountering the world also affects us outside of this mode, with our practices even making slow changes to the bone structure and anatomy of our bodies.[27] For example, Korean pansori singing can alter the physiology of their vocal cords.[28] These findings suggest that our practices can be written onto our bodies.

Presence-at-hand (*Vorhandenheit*) is stepping back from the everyday use of equipment. In the first case, it can result from the equipment malfunctioning or resisting our work, which brings us into a state of unhandiness. In this case, the material or equipment quickly becomes noticeable to us, showing us more of its salient physical properties. Presence-at-hand can also occur through the conscious move to step back from everyday practice into a mode of scientific inquiry or reflective contemplation. In this way, presence-at-hand is a way that we can unconceal the descriptive properties of things in our environment and gain knowledge about them. However, even though this mode is a stepping back from everyday practice, we still cannot separate ourselves from caring and thus still encounter things in a meaningful way.[29]

BEING-TOWARD ART

For Heidegger, the two above-mentioned modes of encounter (handiness and presence-at-hand) are part of our everyday being. Part of art's role is to present us with a clearing that can give us access to a moment of vision, which reveals to us some of the hidden aspects of our being.[30] This is important for Heidegger as the everyday can flatten out our being into the routine through our attempts to just manage day-to-day life. He stated, "The care of averageness reveals, in turn, an essential tendency of Dasein, which we call the leveling down of all possibilities of being."[31] Through this everyday leveling down of being, the mystery is lost to us and the range of experiences and being available to us become more and more limited and inflexible over time.

Heidegger considers that art can allow us to "transport ourselves out of the habitual and into what is opened up by the work so as to bring our essence itself to take a stand within the truth of beings."[32] Interacting with art can benefit us by exposing us to our preconceptions and habits, leading us to question these preconceptions. This then encourages us to have a more adaptable and flexible way of being-in-the-world and develops our cognitive complexity.[33]

Art achieves a dual-layered act of unconcealing, both unconcealing new ways of being-in-the-world and highlighting the existence of the play of unconcealing and concealing, by presenting itself as a "strife" between the "setting up of a world" and the "setting forth of earth."[34] First, our way of being and our preconceptions are challenged because we bring our world (the background realm of understandings and actions that we think are possible of ourselves as being-in-the-world) along with us when we enter into the clearing of the artwork. Since the world of the artwork that we encounter stands on its own, the self-subsistence of the artwork affords us access to a world that is not our own. Heidegger stated, "Only this clearing grants and guarantees to us humans a passage to those beings that we are not, and access to the being that we ourselves are."[35] From this passage to the free and tangible disclosures of the world of the artwork, we are encouraged to question the preconditions of our being-in-the-world by being afforded the ability to compare the being that we are with the freedom of the beings that we are not. Furthermore, we still have access to these disclosures of the artwork while being a performer of the artwork. Høffding has proposed that there is a "performative passivity" that can occur to performers during a performance situation when they are deeply absorbed in the music. In this passivity, there is a sense that the music has an inherent necessity to move in a certain way, and that the performer feels that he or she wants to be open to convey the music's wishes. To describe this, Høffding cites cellist Fredrik Sjölin, who states, "suddenly we find ourselves in a tempo we hadn't planned for at all, but we couldn't have done otherwise, because the preceding notes leading into it, they had laid the ground for it."[36] Supporting this, Heidegger stated that the artist acts "almost like a passageway that destroys itself in the creative process for the work to emerge"[37] (GA 5: 26.9-10 = 19.23-24). Through being a passageway for the artwork the artist has passage to the beings that they are not.

Second, art reveals to us the play of unconcealing and concealing by giving us access to the inexhaustible and mysterious darkness of the earth (a grounding for the unconcealed beings of the world with its inexhaustible possibilities for being) hidden behind and surrounding the world, even when the world is the only aspect that is illuminated for us.[38] We do not normally experience the aura of the decisions we could have taken or the modes of encounter we could have adopted in our everyday engagements in the world, but the strife in the artwork draws us in and affords us access to this hidden earth.[39]

Because one of the more important roles of the hidden earth is the revelation of the play of unconcealing and concealing, we inauthentically interact with the artwork when we ignore the hidden and cling to the illuminated aspects that already easily fit into our worldview. For us to authentically interact with the artwork, Heidegger argues that we need "to let beings be as the beings which they are—[this] means to engage oneself with the open region and its openness into which every being comes to stand, bringing that openness, as it were, along with itself."[40] Supporting the idea that we should be open when encountering an artwork, many musical artworks have qualities that afford us the ability to explore their bistable or even multistable perceptual organizations (i.e., musical qualities that can be perceived in two or more ways, that can shift the figure and ground of the stimulus). These bistable relations in music include polyrhythm, polymeter, polyphony, polytonality, polystylism, "phantasmagoric instruments," "chimeric percepts," and so on. For example, the French composer Pierre Boulez often orchestrated his music in order to hide the timbres of the individual instruments that contribute to the blended overall sonority of his music, accumulating his instruments together into a phantasmagoric instrumental fusion.[41] Given our familiarity with the timbres of individual instruments, it is expected that the individual contributions sometimes temporarily stick out and reveal themselves before becoming hidden again into the texture of the whole. For this reason, others have described this method of orchestration as creating chimeric percepts, having the ability to be both stable as a mixed whole and as blended individual contributions.[42]

BEING-WITH

Along with care, Heidegger proposed that being-with is an a priori concept that structures our being. He then suggested that there are three levels within this concept of being-with. First, there is being-alone, where feelings of loneliness and isolation can only occur due to our loss from the primordial concept of being-with. Second, there is being-alongside, which is the everyday experience of being in the same space at the same time as others but doing tasks on our own. Finally, there is a being-among-one-another, where we are engaged in the same task in common, often leading to a sense of one-ness and a loss of individuality.[43] In *Being and Time*, it appears that Heidegger mentions being-alone in order to explain the a priori nature of being-with, but then focuses on being-alongside and being-among-one-another to present an opposition between these two latter states of being-with. In being-alongside, others have an exteriority to us, while in being-among-one-another, others have an interiority with us, becoming one as a herd.[44] Heidegger argues that being-among-one-another has a negative aspect, namely that it leads us to not be able to separate ourselves and our actions from those of others. He argues that engaging oneself with the disclosedness of beings does not necessarily entail losing oneself in them.[45] Heidegger fears we will become lost in the community of being-among-one-another, which will inevitably lead to an imbalance in relations where we either subjugate others' being under our own or we become subjugated under the being of others. Instead, he wants for us to let beings be as a principle of being-with.[46]

In response to this, Nancy has proposed that there is a middle-ground between the extremes of being-alongside and being-among-one-another that fulfills this principle of letting beings be. In this liminal boundary space, Nancy suggests a type of being-with that is "neither in exteriority, nor in interiority. Neither a herd, nor a subject. Neither anonymous, nor 'mine.'"[47] Nancy also argues that when we overlook this boundary space between the extremes of being-with, we lose the ability to describe many of our interactions with one another. This is because being-alongside misses the intersecting of horizons or lines of sight between people, and it misses the potential for people to cooperate and/or interfere with one another when they interact, while being-among-one-another provides a sense of one-ness that is not a part of most basic interactions between people. Nancy proposes that:

> There must be a contact, therefore a contagion and encroachment, even if minimal, even if only as an infinitesimal drift of the tangent between the concerned openings. A relative indistinction of the edges of the openings must occur and their lines of sight or horizons must at least tend to intersect one another. I can only open myself *there* by opening at the same time onto other *theres*, as we say of a door that it opens onto a *garden*.[48]

Being-alongside does not include the possibilities for this contact, contagion, or encroachment between our being and the being of those that we are interacting with, and these are necessary for us to at least minimally accomplish tasks together. Lacking these fundamentals of interaction, being-alongside does not adequately describe our mode of encounter that we have toward others when we perform tasks with one another (which have been called "joint actions"[49]), whether it is handing money to a cashier, moving a couch together, or performing music together. Therefore, Nancy suggests the fourth category of being-with as *being-as-intersecting*.

Nancy's suggestion that our interactions with others at least demands a minimal contact or encroachment between our being and the being of those that we are interacting with, aligns well with the idea from the joint action literature that there is a degree of self-other integration in the actions that people make together. Additionally, while for Nancy this coming into contact is a making sense of one another, there is no interpenetration of being between the partners. This is because "there is contiguity but not continuity. There is proximity, but only to the extent that extreme closeness emphasizes the distancing it opens up. All of being is in touch with all being, but the law of touching is separation."[50] Similar to Nancy's belief that we always simultaneously exist as plural and singular beings (his interpretation of Heidegger's being-with as an a priori to being, where for Nancy being-plural is a necessary a priori to being-singular), self-other integration and self-other distinction form an inseparable pair of concepts. Subsequently, we can never be fully self-other integrated nor fully self-other distinct, as anything else would presuppose the collapsing of being into a singular level and an eradication of being-with. Therefore, similar to our being both singular and plural, we propose that there is a liminal in-between of self-other integration and distinction. This means that when we are in the mode of being-as-intersecting we have the ability to find a good balance between self-other integration and distinction where our individuality is preserved and we have some access to experience on our joint level. This balancing between self-other integration and self-other distinction has been experienced in dance as a flickering between I and we (Himberg et al. 2018), and is a balancing act that very often happens in group musical performances.

APPLICATIONS OF BEING-WITH OTHERS IN JOINT MUSIC PERFORMANCE

Having explored the concepts of modes of encounter, being-toward art, and being-with, we can now examine their application in group music making. As Heidegger considers that a goal of the presentation of an artwork is for the artwork to be able to unconceal itself as it is, a goal of a musical performance could be considered for the musical artwork to be able to unconceal itself as it is. This goal is the same for both solo and ensemble performances. However, the added complexity of the ensemble performance is that this musical goal is achieved by performers precisely coordinating with one another, anticipating and adjusting to each other's actions. One way that ensemble performers achieve this is by dividing their attention between the overall sound, their own part, and others' parts, and by being aware of how their part fits into the overall sound.[51] Ensemble musicians can also dynamically alter the degree to which others' actions are integrated with their own or kept distinct from their own, depending on how beneficial others' actions are for their ability to synchronize and to contribute to the overall sound at any given moment.[52]

Self-other integration can help in the coordination process when performers have shared goals, as it can help them anticipate each other's actions through their contact with one another.[53] Self-other integration is often developed during the rehearsal process through the negotiation of shared performance goals and through developing an understanding of the conductor's performance intentions. These negotiations both during the rehearsal process and during the performance are important as they play a role in forming an opening between each of the performers' worlds. For example, musicians' movement patterns can be seen as reflecting their training and their musical practice written onto their bodies as an exposure of their handiness. Also, individual musicians have a preferred performance speed that reflects their level of alertness and musical training.[54] Performers therefore synchronize better when performing with a recording of themselves than with recordings from other people,[55] and also synchronize better with other performers who more closely match their own preferred performance speed.[56] Through effortful correction against this variability between performers, musicians become more able to adapt to each other's natural movement frequencies than non-musicians as a result of their training.[57] Because of these many small differences between each of the performers' musical worlds that need to be aligned in an ensemble musical performance, self-other integration and finding contact with one another are seen as both quasi-automatic and effortful.[58]

For example, performers form a strong interdependent relation of actions and action plans with one another.[59] They also increase the size and regularity of their movements to enhance coordination,[60] and make ancillary movements, such as body sway, to facilitate the communication of expressive intentions.[61] In terms of making it easier for others to integrate with our actions, Heidegger asks that we should "leap ahead" rather than "leap in" for another as this "helps the other become transparent to himself *in* his care and to *become free* for it."[62] Musicians that make use of both steady and ancillary movements *leap ahead* of their fellow musicians, giving a clear framework for interaction while allowing their partners to integrate these movements on their own terms so as to still allow them their distinct identity. When interacting with other people, Heidegger asks us to not "leap in" to take over the care that others have toward their own actions. When leaping in we can dominate their way of interacting in the world, which can lead to them losing their sense of distinct identity and individual control over their actions.[63] This is the same in a musical performance, where self-other distinction is required because the performers need to be able to maintain a sense of autonomous action control and to hear and separate out their own part in order to perform it well.[64] The vocal control of choir singers suffers[65] and pianists make more errors when they are unable to maintain a degree of distinction between themselves and their fellow performers.[66] Self-other distinction especially occurs when a performer's intended actions are incompatible with the activity surrounding them[67] and when they have difficulty separating their sounds from co-performers' due to acoustic masking.[68]

THE BENEFITS OF GROUP MUSIC MAKING ON BEING-WITH-OTHERS

As a conclusion to this chapter, we explore how the interrelation of being-toward art and being-with others in a group musical performance might affect our being. Group music making offers considerable social bonding and mental health benefits.[69] It strengthens our social relationships and affords us the development of a positive sense of self.[70] A first simpler proposal is that group music making is a safe space that affords an authentic being-with, where leaping ahead of each other is the norm, which leads to our having a strong sense of connection with one another. In this case, it does not matter whether the performer has an authentic engagement with the artwork or not, as the benefits rest on their authentic engagement with their fellow performers. People achieving social bonding merely through tapping their fingers in unison with one another supports this viewpoint.[71] A second richer proposal is that the social benefits of music come from a synergistic interrelation of our authentically being-toward the artwork while also authentically being-with others. In this case, the benefits come from the balancing act between our integrating our actions with those of others and keeping ourselves distinct simultaneous with the artwork highlighting the play of unconcealing and concealing that is going on between our being-singular and being-plural. Let us examine this latter possibility in more detail next.

Heidegger argues that we become rigid over time from our everyday interacting in the world. As a result of our rigidness of engagement with the world, "the openedness of beings gets flattened out into the apparent nothingness of what is no longer even a matter of indifference, but rather is simply forgotten."[72] He then suggests that encountering works of art highlights the play of unconcealment and concealment through engaging us with its mystery, which thereby recovers some of the openedness of the beings that we encounter. In the case of group music making, we recover the openedness of the being of the artwork and the being of our fellow musicians that we are engaged with. Engaging with music in a solo situation already provides social benefits for people in a music therapy situation, with the people playing music as a way of "asserting and trying out values, stances, identities and ways of relating to others."[73] In this way, DeNora considers that a solo musical performance is a double performance in that we perform the music while simultaneously performing ourselves. In group music making, this exploration of ourselves through performing music is then enhanced through our having meaningful social engagement with others in addition to our engagement with the musical artwork,[74] synergistically bringing together our authentic being-toward the artwork and authentic being-with-others. Through group music making we are granted passage to the being of the artwork, our own being, and the being of those around us, allowing us to compare the freedom of our being-with the beings that we are not. In this way, group music making affords us the ability to open up to our own being, the being of others, and the being of the musical artwork through our interactions with others in music. We argue that it is this act of opening ourselves up to being that offers us the mental health benefits, as well as improvements in social bonding and to our sense of self. In describing a powerful musical experience, a concertgoer stated that:

> For me, the concert was an expression of what it means to be human. The difficulties, love, joy, drivel, playing, seriousness, guilt, hopelessness. All of this was incorporated in the concert in a way that moved me extremely strongly... It was both an experience that was said, sung, and expressed in the music [that] affects me especially and an experience of fellowship with the other 8,000 people who were in the hall.... The experience has lived on inside me since then, and is still there. It was a sort of paradigm change in my way of meeting life.[75]

This concert experience supports the viewpoint that the power of group music making can reach toward transcendent experience. It also describes an opening up toward music and others that goes well beyond the more minimal case of social bonding, such as is experienced through tapping in rhythmic unison with others, as was described above.

In sum, this chapter has explored how we engage with the artwork and with others as part of the process of making music together and how this can open up our being-in-the-world. Heidegger's opposing forces of the world and earth of the artwork have been presented as bringing about the opposing but complementary acts of unconcealing and concealing, resulting in an unconcealing of new ways of being-in-the-world while highlighting the play of unconcealing and concealing. This increases our freedom and flexibility in how we encounter the world. In group music performance, this partly occurs through our ability to leap ahead of others by flexibly varying the degree of self-other integration and self-other distinction with others that opens up our being-with toward our fellow performers and the musical artwork. As a result, the group music making interaction with the artwork and others takes us out of our mundane routine and opens us up to our own being and to the beings around us, leading us to have a more authentic way of being-in-the-world.

NOTES

1. Martin Heidegger, *Being and Time*, trans. Joan Stambaugh, Rev. Ed. (Albany, NY: SUNY Press, 2010), 169.

2. Jean-Luc Nancy, "The Being-with of Being-There," *Continental Philosophy Review* 41 (2008): 1–15.

3. Myrto Mylopoulos and Elisabeth Pacherie, "Intentions: the Dynamic Hierarchical Model Revisited," *Wiley Interdisciplinary Reviews: Cognitive Science* 10, no. 2 (2019): e1481.

4. Martin Heidegger, "The Origin of the Work of Art," in *Basic Writings*, ed. and trans. David F. Krell, Rev. (San Francisco: Harper & Row, 1993), 139–212.

5. Irene McMullin, *Time and the Shared World* (Evanston, IL: Northwestern University Press, 2013).

6. Heidegger, *Being and Time*, 53–72.

7. Heidegger, *Being and Time*, 53–62.

8. Esther Thelen, "Motor Development: A New Synthesis," *American Psychologist* 50, no. 2 (1995): 79–95.

9. Cf. Jiefeng Jiang, Wanlin Zhu, Feng Shi, Yong Liu, Jun Li, Wen Qin, Kuncheng Li, Chunshui Yu, and Tianzi Jiang, "Thick Visual Cortex in the Early Blind," *The Journal of Neuroscience* 29, no. 7 (2009): 2205–11; Patrice Voss, Bruce G. Pike, and Robert J. Zatorre, "Evidence for Both Compensatory Plastic and Disuse Atrophy-Related Neuroanatomical Changes in the Blind," *Brain* 137, no. 4 (2014): 1224–40.

10. Norihiro Sadato, Alvaro Pascual-Leone, Jordan Grafman, Vicente Ibañez, Marie-Pierre Deiber, George Dold, and Mark Hallett, "Activation of the Primary Visual Cortex by Braille Reading in Blind Subjects," *Nature* 380 (1996): 526–8.

11. Liam J. Norman and Lore Thaler, "Retinotopic-Like Maps of Spatial Sound in Primary 'Visual' Cortex of Blind Human Echolocators," *Proceedings of the Royal Society B* 286 (2019): 20191910.

12. Eva M. Finney, Ione Fine, and Karen R. Dobkins, "Visual Stimuli Activate Auditory Cortex in the Deaf," *Nature Neuroscience* 4, no. 12 (2001): 1171–3.

13. Hiroshi Nishimura, Kazuo Hashikawa, Katsumi Doi, Takako Iwaki, Yoshiyuki Watanabe, Hideo Kusuoka, Tsunehiko Nishimura, and Takeshi Kubo, "Sign Language 'Heard' in the Auditory Cortex," *Nature* 397 (1999): 116.

14. Norman Thaler, "Retinotopic-Like Maps of Spatial Sound," 20191910.

15. Heidegger, *Being and Time*, 114–21.

16. Dan Zahavi, "Second-Person Engagement, Self-Alienation, and Group-Identification," *Topoi* 38 (2016): 251–60.

17. Edmund Husserl, *Zur Phänomenologie Der Intersubjektivität*, edited by Iso Kern (The Hague: Martinus Nijhoff, 1973); Shaun Gallagher and Dan Zahavi, *The Phenomenological Mind* (London: Routledge, 2012).

18. Thomas Fuchs, *Ecology of the Brain* (Oxford: Oxford University Press, 2018).

19. Dare Baldwin, "Understanding the Link Between Joint Attention and Language," in *Joint Attention*, eds. C. Moore and P. J. Dunham (Hillsdale, NJ: Lawrence Erlbaum Associates, 1995), 131–59.

20. Heidegger, *Being and Time*, 204–20.

21. Martin Heidegger, *History of the Concept of Time*, trans. Theodore Kisiel (Bloomington, IN: Indiana University Press, 2009).

22. Heidegger, *Being and Time*, 66–71.

23. Heidegger, *Being and Time*, 69.

24. L. Jäncke, N. J. Shah, and M. Peters, "Cortical Activations in Primary and Secondary Motor Areas for Complex Bimanual Movements in Professional Pianists," *Cognitive Brain Research* 10, no. 1–2 (2000): 177–83.

25. Bradley D. Hatfield, Amy J. Haufler, Tsung-Min Hung, and Thomas W. Spalding, "Electroencephalographic Studies of Skilled Psychomotor Performance," *Journal of Clinical Neurophysiology* 21, no. 3 (2004): 144–56.

26. Jason Sherwin and Paul Sajda, "Musical Experts Recruit Action-Related Neural Structures in Harmonic Anomaly Detection: Evidence for Embodied Cognition in Expertise," *Brain and Cognition* 83, no. 2 (2013): 190–202.

27. Carrie Noland and Sally Ann Ness, *Migrations of Gesture* (Minneapolis: University of Minnesota Press, 2008); Ben Spatz, *What a Body Can Do* (London and New York: Routledge, 2015).

28. Tara McAllister-Viel, "Speaking with an International Voice?" *Contemporary Theatre Review* 17, no. (2007): 97–106.

29. Heidegger, *Being and Time*, 184–9.

30. Heidegger, "The Origin of the Work of Art."

31. Heidegger, *Being and Time*, 123.

32. Heidegger, "The Origin of the Work of Art," 199.

33. Beau Lotto, *Deviate* (New York: Hachette Books, 2017).

34. Heidegger, "The Origin of the Work of Art," 174.

35. Heidegger, "The Origin of the Work of Art," 178.

36. Simon Høffding, *A Phenomenology of Musical Absorption* (Cham: Springer International Publishing, 2018), 69.

37. Heidegger, "The Origin of the Work of Art," 166.

38. Heidegger, "The Origin of the Work of Art," 174.

39. Julian Young, *Heidegger's Philosophy of Art* (Cambridge: Cambridge University Press, 2001).

40. Martin Heidegger, "On the Essence of Truth," in *Basic Writings*, ed. and trans. David F. Krell, Rev. (San Francisco: Harper & Row, 1993), 125.

41. Pierre Boulez, "Timbre and Composition—Timbre and Language," *Contemporary Music Review* 2, no. 1 (1987): 161–71.

42. Albert S. Bregman, *Auditory Scene Analysis: the Perceptual Organization of Sound* (Cambridge, MA and London: MIT Press, 1990).

43. Heidegger, *Being and Time*, 113–30.

44. Nancy, "The Being-with of Being-There," 1–15.

45. Heidegger, "On the Essence of Truth."

46. Heidegger, "On the Essence of Truth," 125.

47. Nancy, "The Being-with of Being-There," 9.

48. Nancy, "The Being-with of Being-There," 10.

49. Günther Knoblich, Stephen Butterfill, and Natalie Sebanz, "Psychological Research on Joint Action: Theory and Data," in *Psychology of Learning and Motivation*, ed. B. H. Ross (San Diego: Academic Press, 2011), 59–101.

50. Jean-Luc Nancy, *Being Singular Plural*, eds. Werner Harnacher and David E. Wellbery and trans. Robert D. Richardson and Anne E. O'Byrne (Stanford: Stanford University Press, 2000), 5.

51. Peter E. Keller, "Joint Action in Music Performance," in *Enacting Intersubjectivity a Cognitive and Social Perspective on the Study of Interactions*, eds. F. Morganti, A. Carassa, and G. Riva (Amsterdam: IOS Press, 2008), 205–21; Janeen D. Loehr, Dimitrios Kourtis, Cordula Vesper, Natalie Sebanz, and Günther Knoblich, "Monitoring Individual and Joint Action Outcomes in Duet Music Performance," *Journal of Cognitive Neuroscience* 25, no. 7 (2013): 1049–61.

52. Giacomo Novembre, Daniela Sammler, and Peter E Keller, "Neural Alpha Oscillations Index the Balance Between Self-Other Integration and Segregation in Real-Time Joint Action," *Neuropsychologia* 89, no. 1 (2016): 414–25; Marie Uhlig, Merle T. Fairhurst, and Peter E. Keller, "The Importance of Integration and Top-Down Salience When Listening to Complex Multi-Part Musical Stimuli," *NeuroImage* 77, no. 8 (2013): 52–61.

53. Knoblich, Butterfill, and Sebanz, "Psychological Research," 59–101.

54. Shannon E. Wright and Caroline Palmer, "Physiological and Behavioral Factors in Musicians' Performance Tempo," *Frontiers in Human Neuroscience* 14 (2020): 2724.

55. Peter E. Keller, Günther Knoblich, and Bruno H. Repp, "Pianists Duet Better When They Play with Themselves: On the Possible Role of Action Simulation in Synchronization," *Consciousness and Cognition* 16, no. 1 (2007): 102–11.

56. Janeen D. Loehr and Caroline Palmer, "Temporal Coordination Between Performing Musicians," *The Quarterly Journal of Experimental Psychology* 64, no. 11 (2011): 2153–67.

57. Rebecca Scheurich, Anna Zamm, and Caroline Palmer, "Tapping Into Rate Flexibility: Musical Training Facilitates Synchronization Around Spontaneous Production Rates," *Frontiers in Psychology* 9 (2018): 66.

58. Peter E. Keller, Giacomo Novembre, and Janeen D. Loehr, "Musical Ensemble Performance: Representing Self, Other and Joint Action Outcomes," in *Shared Representations Sensorimotor Foundations of Social Life*, eds. Sukhvinder S. Obhi and Emily S. Cross (Cambridge: Cambridge University Press, 2016), 280–310.

59. Cristina Iani, Filomena Anelli, Roberto Nicoletti, Luciano Arcuri, and Sandro Rubichi, "The Role of Group Membership on the Modulation of Joint Action," *Experimental Brain Research* 211, no. 3–4 (2011): 439–45.

60. Werner Goebl and Caroline Palmer, "Synchronization of Timing and Motion Among Performing Musicians," *Music Perception: An Interdisciplinary Journal* 26, no. 5 (2009): 427–38; Cordula Vesper, Robrecht P. R. D. van der Wel, Günther Knoblich, and Natalie Sebanz, "Making Oneself Predictable: Reduced Temporal Variability Facilitates Joint Action Coordination," *Experimental Brain Research* 211 (2011): 517–30.

61. Andrew Chang, Haley E. Kragness, Steven R. Livingstone, Dan J. Bosnyak, and Laurel J. Trainor, "Body Sway Reflects Joint Emotional Expression in Music Ensemble Performance," *Scientific Reports* 9 (2019): 340.

62. Heidegger, *Being and Time*, 119.

63. Heidegger, *Being and Time*, 120.

64. Elisabeth Pacherie, "The Phenomenology of Joint Action," in *Joint Attention*, ed. Axel Seemann (Cambridge, MA and London: MIT Press, 2012), 343–89.

65. Sten Ternström, "Preferred Self-to-Other Ratios in Choir Singing," *The Journal of the Acoustical Society of America* 105, no. 6 (1999): 3563–74.

66. Ulrich C. Drost, Martina Rieger, Marcel Brass, Thomas C. Gunter, and Wolfgang Prinz, "When Hearing Turns Into Playing: Movement Induction by Auditory Stimuli in Pianists," *The Quarterly Journal of Experimental Psychology Section A* 58, no. 8 (2005): 1376–89.

67. Novembre, Sammler, and Keller, "Neural Alpha Oscillations Index," 414–25.

68. Jürgen Meyer, *Acoustics and the Performance of Music* (New York: Springer Science & Business Media, 2009).

69. Victoria J. Williamson and Michael Bonshor, "Wellbeing in Brass Bands: The Benefits and Challenges of Group Music Making," *Frontiers in Psychology* 10 (2019): 1176.

70. Jane W. Davidson and Benjamin Leske, "Effects of Singing on Social Support and Wellbeing Among Marginalized Communities," in *The Routledge Companion to Interdisciplinary Studies in Singing, Volume III: Wellbeing*, eds. Rachel Heydon, Daisy Fancourt, and Annabel J. Cohen (New York and Oxon: Routledge, 2020), 146–57.

71. Michael J. Hove and Jane L. Risen, "It's All in the Timing: Interpersonal Synchrony Increases Affiliation," *Social Cognition* 27, no. 6 (2009): 949–60.

72. Heidegger, "On the Essence of Truth," 129.

73. Tia DeNora, *Music Asylums: Wellbeing Through Music in Everyday Life* (London and New York: Routledge, 2016), 96.

74. Davidson and Leske, "Effects of Singing," 146–57.

75. This quote comes from subject 12.1A, as cited in Alf Gabrielsson and Rod Bradbury, *Strong Experiences with Music* (Oxford: Oxford University Press, 2011), 150. Rentmeester analyzes musical experience via the lens of cultural paradigms in his chapter of this volume.

BIBLIOGRAPHY

Baldwin, Dare. "Understanding the Link Between Joint Attention and Language." In *Joint Attention*, edited by C. Moore and P. J. Dunham, 131–59. Hillsdale, NJ: Lawrence Erlbaum Associates, 1995.

Boulez, Pierre. "Timbre and Composition - Timbre and Language." *Contemporary Music Review* 2, no. 1 (1987): 161–71. doi:10.1080/07494468708567057.

Bregman, Albert S. *Auditory Scene Analysis: the Perceptual Organization of Sound*. Cambridge, MA and London: MIT Press, 1990.

Chang, Andrew, Haley E. Kragness, Steven R. Livingstone, Dan J. Bosnyak, and Laurel J. Trainor. 2019. "Body Sway Reflects Joint Emotional Expression in Music Ensemble Performance." *Scientific Reports* 9 (2019): 340. doi:10.1038/s41598-018-36358-4.

Davidson, Jane W., and Benjamin Leske. "Effects of Singing on Social Support and Wellbeing Among Marginalized Communities." In *The Routledge Companion to Interdisciplinary Studies in Singing, Volume III: Wellbeing*, edited by Rachel

Heydon, Daisy Fancourt, and Annabel J. Cohen, 146–57. New York and Oxon: Routledge, 2020.
DeNora, Tia. *Music Asylums: Wellbeing Through Music in Everyday Life*. London and New York: Routledge, 2016.
Drost, Ulrich C., Martina Rieger, Marcel Brass, Thomas C. Gunter, and Wolfgang Prinz. "When Hearing Turns Into Playing: Movement Induction by Auditory Stimuli in Pianists." *The Quarterly Journal of Experimental Psychology Section A* 58, no. 8 (2005): 1376–89. doi:10.1080/02724980443000610.
Finney, Eva M, Ione Fine, and Karen R Dobkins. "Visual Stimuli Activate Auditory Cortex in the Deaf." *Nature Neuroscience* 4, no. 12 (2001): 1171–3. doi:10.1038/nn763.
Fuchs, Thomas. *Ecology of the Brain*. Oxford: Oxford University Press, 2018.
Gabrielsson, Alf, and Rod Bradbury. *Strong Experiences with Music*. Oxford: Oxford University Press, 2011.
Gallagher, Shaun, and Dan Zahavi. *The Phenomenological Mind*. London: Routledge, 2012.
Goebl, Werner, and Caroline Palmer. "Synchronization of Timing and Motion Among Performing Musicians." *Music Perception: An Interdisciplinary Journal* 26, no. 5 (2009): 427–38. doi:10.1525/mp.2009.26.5.427.
Hatfield, Bradley D., Amy J. Haufler, Tsung-Min Hung, and Thomas W. Spalding. "Electroencephalographic Studies of Skilled Psychomotor Performance." *Journal of Clinical Neurophysiology* 21, no. 3 (2004): 144–56.
Heidegger, Martin. *Being and Time*. Translated by Joan Stambaugh, Rev. Ed. Albany, NY: SUNY Press, 2010.
Heidegger, Martin. *History of the Concept of Time*. Translated by Theodore Kisiel. Bloomington, IN: Indiana University Press, 2009.
Heidegger, Martin. "On the Essence of Truth." In *Basic Writings*, edited and translated by David F. Krell, Rev. Ed., 111–38. San Francisco: Harper, 1993.
Heidegger, Martin. "The Origin of the Work of Art." In *Basic Writings*, edited and translated by David F. Krell, Rev. Ed., 139–212. San Francisco: Harper, 1993.
Himberg, Tommi, Julien Laroche, Romain Bigé, Megan Buchkowski, and Asaf Bachrach. "Coordinated Interpersonal Behaviour in Collective Dance Improvisation: the Aesthetics of Kinaesthetic Togetherness." *Behavioral Sciences* 8, no. 2 (2018): 23. doi:10.3390/bs8020023.
Høffding, Simon. *A Phenomenology of Musical Absorption*. Cham: Springer International Publishing, 2018.
Hove, Michael J., and Jane L. Risen. "It's All in the Timing: Interpersonal Synchrony Increases Affiliation." *Social Cognition* 27, no. 6 (2009): 949–60. doi:10.1521/soco.2009.27.6.949.
Husserl, Edmund. *Zur Phänomenologie Der Intersubjektivität*. Edited by Iso Kern. The Hague: Martinus Nijhoff, 1973.
Iani, Cristina, Filomena Anelli, Roberto Nicoletti, Luciano Arcuri, and Sandro Rubichi. "The Role of Group Membership on the Modulation of Joint Action." *Experimental Brain Research* 211, no. 3–4 (2011): 439–45. doi:10.1007/s00221-011-2651-x.

Jäncke, L., N. J. Shah, and M. Peters. "Cortical Activations in Primary and Secondary Motor Areas for Complex Bimanual Movements in Professional Pianists." *Cognitive Brain Research* 10, no. 1–2 (2000): 177–83.

Jiang, Jiefeng, Wanlin Zhu, Feng Shi, Yong Liu, Jun Li, Wen Qin, Kuncheng Li, Chunshui Yu, and Tianzi Jiang. "Thick Visual Cortex in the Early Blind." *The Journal of Neuroscience* 29, no. 7 (2009): 2205–11. doi:10.1523/JNEUROSCI.5451-08.2009.

Keller, Peter E. "Joint Action in Music Performance." In *Enacting Intersubjectivity a Cognitive and Social Perspective on the Study of Interactions*, edited by F. Morganti, A. Carassa, and G. Riva, 205–21. Amsterdam: IOS Press, 2008.

Keller, Peter E., Günther Knoblich, and Bruno H. Repp. "Pianists Duet Better When They Play with Themselves: On the Possible Role of Action Simulation in Synchronization." *Consciousness and Cognition* 16, no. 1 (2007): 102–11. doi:10.1016/j.concog.2005.12.004.

Keller, Peter E., Giacomo Novembre, and Janeen D. Loehr. "Musical Ensemble Performance: Representing Self, Other and Joint Action Outcomes." In *Shared Representations Sensorimotor Foundations of Social Life*, edited by Sukhvinder S. Obhi and Emily S. Cross, 280–310. Cambridge: Cambridge University Press, 2016.

Knoblich, Günther, Stephen Butterfill, and Natalie Sebanz. "Psychological Research on Joint Action: Theory and Data." In *Psychology of Learning and Motivation*, edited by B. H. Ross, 59–101. San Diego: Academic Press, 2011. doi:10.1016/B978-0-12-385527-5.00003-6.

Loehr, Janeen D., and Caroline Palmer. "Temporal Coordination Between Performing Musicians." *The Quarterly Journal of Experimental Psychology* 64, no. 11 (2011): 2153–67. doi:10.1080/17470218.2011.603427.

Loehr, Janeen D., Dimitrios Kourtis, Cordula Vesper, Natalie Sebanz, and Günther Knoblich. "Monitoring Individual and Joint Action Outcomes in Duet Music Performance." *Journal of Cognitive Neuroscience* 25, no. 7 (2013): 1049–61. doi:10.1162/jocn_a_00388.

Lotto, Beau. *Deviate*. New York: Hachette Books, 2017.

McAllister-Viel, Tara. "Speaking with an International Voice?" *Contemporary Theatre Review* 17, no. (2007): 97–106. doi:10.1080/10486800601096204.

McMullin, Irene. *Time and the Shared World*. Evanston, IL: Northwestern University Press, 2013.

Meyer, Jürgen. *Acoustics and the Performance of Music*. New York: Springer Science & Business Media, 2009.

Mylopoulos, Myrto, and Elisabeth Pacherie. "Intentions: The Dynamic Hierarchical Model Revisited." *Wiley Interdisciplinary Reviews: Cognitive Science* 10, no. 2 (2019): e1481. doi:10.1002/wcs.1481.

Nancy, Jean-Luc. *Being Singular Plural*. Edited by Werner Harnacher and David E. Wellbery and translated by Robert D. Richardson and Anne E. O'Byrne. Stanford: Stanford University Press, 2000.

Nancy, Jean-Luc. "The Being-with of Being-There." *Continental Philosophy Review* 41 (2008): 1–15. doi:10.1007/s11007-007-9071-4.

Nishimura, Hiroshi, Kazuo Hashikawa, Katsumi Doi, Takako Iwaki, Yoshiyuki Watanabe, Hideo Kusuoka, Tsunehiko Nishimura, and Takeshi Kubo. "Sign Language 'Heard' in the Auditory Cortex." *Nature* 397 (1999): 116. doi:10.1038/16376.

Noland, Carrie, and Sally Ann Ness. *Migrations of Gesture*. Minneapolis: University of Minnesota Press, 2008.

Norman, Liam J., and Lore Thaler. "Retinotopic-Like Maps of Spatial Sound in Primary 'Visual' Cortex of Blind Human Echolocators." *Proceedings of the Royal Society B* 286 (2019): 20191910. doi:10.1098/rspb.2019.1910.

Novembre, Giacomo, Daniela Sammler, and Peter E Keller. "Neural Alpha Oscillations Index the Balance Between Self-Other Integration and Segregation in Real-Time Joint Action." *Neuropsychologia* 89 (1): 414–25. doi:10.1016/j.neuropsychologia.2016.07.027.

Pacherie, Elisabeth. "The Phenomenology of Joint Action." In *Joint Attention*, edited by Axel Seemann, 343–89. Cambridge, MA and London: MIT Press, 2012.

Sadato, Norihiro, Alvaro Pascual-Leone, Jordan Grafman, Vicente Ibañez, Marie-Pierre Deiber, George Dold, and Mark Hallett. "Activation of the Primary Visual Cortex by Braille Reading in Blind Subjects." *Nature* 380 (1996): 526–8. doi:10.1038/380526a0.

Scheurich, Rebecca, Anna Zamm, and Caroline Palmer. "Tapping Into Rate Flexibility: Musical Training Facilitates Synchronization Around Spontaneous Production Rates." *Frontiers in Psychology* 9 (2018): 66. doi:10.3389/fpsyg.2018.00458.

Sherwin, Jason, and Paul Sajda. "Musical Experts Recruit Action-Related Neural Structures in Harmonic Anomaly Detection: Evidence for Embodied Cognition in Expertise." *Brain and Cognition* 83, no. 2 (2013): 190–202. doi:10.1016/j.bandc.2013.07.002.

Spatz, Ben. *What a Body Can Do*. London and New York: Routledge, 2015.

Ternström, Sten. "Preferred Self-to-Other Ratios in Choir Singing." *The Journal of the Acoustical Society of America* 105, no. 6 (1999): 3563–74. doi:10.1121/1.424680.

Thelen, Esther. "Motor Development: a New Synthesis." *American Psychologist* 50, no. 2 (1995): 79–95. doi:10.1037/0003-066X.50.2.79.

Uhlig, Marie, Merle T. Fairhurst, and Peter E. Keller. "The Importance of Integration and Top-Down Salience When Listening to Complex Multi-Part Musical Stimuli." *NeuroImage* 77, no. 8 (2013): 52–61. doi:10.1016/j.neuroimage.2013.03.051.

Vesper, Cordula, Robrecht P. R. D. van der Wel, Günther Knoblich, and Natalie Sebanz. "Making Oneself Predictable: Reduced Temporal Variability Facilitates Joint Action Coordination." *Experimental Brain Research* 211 (2011): 517–30. doi:10.1007/s00221-011-2706-z.

Voss, Patrice, Bruce G. Pike, and Robert J. Zatorre. "Evidence for Both Compensatory Plastic and Disuse Atrophy-Related Neuroanatomical Changes in the Blind." *Brain* 137, no. 4 (2014): 1224–40. doi:10.1093/brain/awu030.

Williamson, Victoria J., and Michael Bonshor. "Wellbeing in Brass Bands: the Benefits and Challenges of Group Music Making." *Frontiers in Psychology* 10 (2019): 1176. doi:10.3389/fpsyg.2019.01176.

Wright, Shannon E., and Caroline Palmer. "Physiological and Behavioral Factors in Musicians' Performance Tempo." *Frontiers in Human Neuroscience* 14 (2020): 2724. doi:10.3389/fnhum.2020.00311.

Young, Julian. *Heidegger's Philosophy of Art*. Cambridge: Cambridge University Press, 2001.

Zahavi, Dan. "Second-Person Engagement, Self-Alienation, and Group-Identification." *Topoi* 38 (2016): 251–60. doi:10.1007/s11245-016-9444-6.

Part IV

THE POWER OF MUSIC

Chapter 14

Somewhere between Plato and Pinker

A Heideggerian Ontology of Music[1]

Casey Rentmeester

The question as to the nature and power of music is posed by Aristotle at the end of his *Politics*. Noting explicitly that it is difficult to determine the power (δύναμις) of music (μουσική), Aristotle provides three general options: it could exist for the sake of amusement, could simply be a leisurely but potentially noble pursuit, or could contribute to virtue (ἀρετή) and thus have an effect on the soul (ψυχή) (1339a10-27).[2] In the end, Aristotle argues that all three seem to have some truth to them. Utilizing Aristotle's analysis as a launching pad, we can craft a spectrum of the ontology of music. At one end of the spectrum are theories like those of Steven Pinker, a contemporary evolutionary psychologist who believes music is merely amusement, and at the other end are theories like those of Plato, Aristotle's mentor, who believes music has a powerful and potentially dangerous effect on the soul. Pinker is right in pointing out that music can be pleasant to the senses, but his labeling of music as merely "auditory cheesecake"[3] surely doesn't do justice to the power of music. At the same time, Plato's argument that music's "rhythm and harmony permeate the inner part of the soul more than anything else" (401d),[4] prompting him to argue for state censorship over music, is far too extreme. After chronicling both ends of the spectrum, I use Martin Heidegger's philosophy to craft an ontology of music that lies somewhere between these two extremes. As a form of art, music has the ability to gather together meanings for persons and thus open up new worlds. A Heideggerian ontology of music overcomes the problems of Pinker's analysis, which is geared too single-mindedly toward the scientific point of view, and simultaneously avoids some of the pitfalls in Plato's analysis, particularly the view that the state should censor music. In the end, I argue that Heidegger provides insight as to how music can create new understandings of reality by opening new worlds, but he also helps us to understand how this world-building capacity is threatened with the onset of the digital age of music wherein music becomes mere material on hand to be consumed.

AUDITORY CHEESECAKE OR SOUL SHAPER?

In 1997, Steven Pinker published *How the Mind Works*, which provides an analysis of how the mind functions from an evolutionary perspective. Near the end of the work, Pinker attempts to understand the significance of music, admitting immediately that music is an enigma.[5] He provides several possible explanations for the evolutionary value of music such as the bonding of the social group, the enhancement of ritual, and the releasement of tensions, but he does not think any of these explanations provides a clear account as to the ultimate significance of music. From an evolutionary perspective wherein the only measures of success are survival and reproduction, music does not seem to have a significant role to play. Pinker puts the point this way: "As far as biological cause and effect are concerned, music is useless. . . . Compared with language, vision, social reasoning, and physical know-how, music could vanish from our species and the rest of our lifestyle would be virtually unchanged."[6] He does note that music seems to be culturally universal and that certain rhythmic sounds seem to provide listeners with pleasure, but he ultimately argues that music is unable to confer any clear survival advantage. He therefore concludes by famously stating that "music is auditory cheesecake, an exquisite confection crafted to tickle the sensitive spots [of the mind]."[7] From Pinker's perspective, then, music exists simply for the sake of amusement.

The problem with Pinker's account is that he looks at things from the myopic focus of a Darwinian evolutionary scientist. In his *Origin of Species*, Charles Darwin provides one general law that leads to the advancement of all organic beings: "multiply, vary, [and] let the strongest live and the weakest die."[8] From an evolutionary perspective, only aspects of life that are related to survival and reproduction are valuable. Survival and reproduction are clearly important, but reducing all significance to survival and reproductive value leaves out so many things that make life worth living. While we may not want to wholeheartedly agree with someone like Friedrich Nietzsche, who claims that "without music life would be an error,"[9] we do want to say that music is one of the things that makes life worth living. Music adds significance to our lives, and not simply because it induces pleasure. Indeed, despite Pinker's cursory dismissal, one cannot deny that music plays an integral role in many social rituals, has the power of inspiring and uniting people together, and can be deeply attuned to a range of emotions beyond simply the feeling of pleasure. As Andrew Bowie argues, "Music is world-disclosive: the world itself can take on new aspects because of it."[10] Music can change the way we look at the world, and the way we live in it.

From a Heideggerian perspective, Pinker's account of music can be leveled with a charge of scientism, which is the view that science provides the only legitimate picture of reality. In his 1954 lecture, "Science and Reflection," Heidegger states, "For a long time, ever more decisively and at the same time ever more unobtrusively, the sciences have been intersecting in all . . . forms of modern life."[11] While the scientific perspective is one way of framing reality, Heidegger makes it clear that it is not the *only* way, and that certain aspects of life are clearly not amenable to proper elucidation when approached from the scientific point of view. Heidegger argues that art is clearly one of those things that cannot be properly analyzed using a scientific perspective.[12] Thus, when posed with the nature of music, we can paraphrase Heidegger and say that "with our question we stand outside the sciences, and the knowledge for which our question strives is neither better nor worse but *totally different*."[13] Approaching music from the narrow lens of science is akin to bringing a hammer to a cookout: it is simply the wrong tool for the task at hand. If this Heideggerian critique is correct, we can say that Pinker provides part of the story in labeling music as pleasure-inducing, but certainly not the heart of the story.

We might be tempted, then, to adopt the other extreme on our spectrum of the ontology of music and agree with Plato, who argues that music has the capacity to mold our souls in deep and powerful ways. Before analyzing Plato's understanding of the ontology of music, though, we should note that Plato explicitly criticizes the view that music's sole value is to induce pleasure in the *Laws*, thus showing us how different Plato's perspective is when contrasted with Pinker's point of view. Just as some food and drinks may be pleasant to eat or drink but not actually produce health, some music may be pleasant to the ears but should not be judged by its pleasure-inducing capacity (668b).[14] For Plato, music is pleasant, but its fundamental power is far greater than its ability to create pleasure.

Plato argues that music familiarizes the soul with either well-ordered or ill-ordered emotions (659d-e).[15] We can recognize in music different types of emotional movements such as "moderation, courage, frankness, high-mindedness, and all of their kindred, and their opposites, too" (402c).[16] To understand what Plato had in mind, let us consider a contemporary example. Many listeners of John Lennon's 1971 song "Imagine" have sensed the way in which music elicits emotional movements. The graceful melody not only may leave the listener with a sense of pleasure, but may also evoke a serene sense of hope and faith that humanity can realize a better and more just world. Lennon's soothing vocals are matched beautifully by his piano play, and the listener is left with an explicit invitation to create the utopic vision he lays out through the iconic lyrics "I hope some day you'll join us." The person who has carefully listened to "Imagine" just might come out of the experience as not only in a better mood, but as a more hopeful person. If this were to happen, we could see why Plato would say that the exposure to music can lead to a molding of the soul; indeed, Plato thinks that music's "rhythm and harmony permeate the inner part of the soul more than anything else" (401d).[17] Mary Schoen-Nazzaro explains this process as follows:

> Music naturally forms the soul according to its own image in a subtle and powerful way. It penetrates deeply and directly, pushing its way into the soul of the listener, moving his emotions and giving them its shape. The music departs, but it leaves its mark on the listener.[18]

Plato argues that this soul-shaping capacity is so powerful that it can force persons to lose themselves. In his *Ion*, for example, he speaks of persons whose souls "fall under the power of music and meter" and thus become possessed to such an extent that they are out of their minds (354a).[19] Again, to provide a contemporary example, one can think of those who lose control during a mosh pit at a Metallica concert. The music in such a context can elicit frenzied and aggressive behavior, which may be dangerous for participants. Thus, due to music's ability to tap into one's emotions and penetrate the soul, Plato thinks that music is a powerful and potentially dangerous force.

This is why Plato famously argues in both the *Laws* and the *Republic* for the state censorship of music. The wild and free feelings that music can create through its pleasure-inducing capabilities is explained most vividly in the *Laws*. Here, Plato speaks of musicians who "were ignorant of what was just and lawful in music . . . [and], being frenzied and unduly possessed by a spirit of pleasure . . . blended every kind of music with every other"[20] (700d), which led the populace (οἱ πολλοί)[21] to believe that the best criterion of music is its ability to induce pleasure. In doing so, they "bred in the populace a spirit of lawlessness in regard to music" (700e),[22] which led to them audaciously thinking they can judge for themselves freely as to what is good and bad in music. This taste of freedom then crept into their lives in general, and they began to disregard the laws, thinking they could do as they please and judge as they please with all matters concerning right and wrong. The result, so argues Plato, would be citizens who no longer respected rulers, parents, elders, or gods (700e–701d).[23] Thus, Plato argues that the state must censor any and all music that is to be allowed in society to stave off lawlessness and disorder, a claim that he also makes in the *Republic* (424b).[24]

How are we to approach Plato's argument as to music's penetrating power on a person's soul? One clear critique has to do with the stunning lack of autonomy that Plato ascribes to persons "under the influence" of music.

At times, it seems Plato speaks of the soul as if it were a merely passive receptacle of the imprints gained from rhythmic and harmonic sounds. As Francesco Pelosi notes in his analysis of Plato and music, "The role of the soul, malleable *material* under the influence of rhythm and harmony, seems entirely passive."[25] Part of this undoubtedly has to do with the fact that Plato is speaking primarily of the role that music plays in childhood education, which he refers to as the early stages of enculturation (παιδεία).[26] For Plato, before humans reach the point of rationality, their characters are extremely plastic and thus moldable, thereby lending them to potential corruption from the power of music. However, Plato seems to think that music's power and influence can penetrate the souls of anyone whomsoever, as evidenced by his commentary in *Ion*. Although some music is extremely powerful, we surely do not want to say that humans have no control as to how they are affected by it. Moreover, Plato's argument in the *Laws* that an improper initiation into music leads to social and political lawlessness may be leveled with a slippery slope fallacy. Just because a song can cause someone to feel wild and free does not mean that this taste of freedom will spark any such political rebellion. For example, certain people who heard Lennon's "Imagine" surely sought to create the utopic world that he outlines so beautifully, but there were plenty of others, of course, who simply did not. Similarly, the rebellious and aggressive behavior that occurs in a mosh pit does not necessarily bleed into the everyday lives of those who have experienced it.

A HEIDEGGERIAN ONTOLOGY OF MUSIC

In summary, Pinker's perspective on the nature of music proves to be too minimalistic, while Plato confers too much power on the nature of music. Heidegger's 1935 lecture titled "The Origin of the Work of Art" provides us with a foundation from which we can craft an ontology of music that lies somewhere in between these two extremes. Here, Heidegger argues that a work of art is able to set up a world: "the work opens up a *world* and keeps it abidingly in force."[27] Before we can understand what he means by "world" in this later work, we need to examine his analysis of this concept in his *magnum opus*, *Being and Time*. Here, Heidegger defines world as "that '*wherein*' a factical Dasein as such can be said to 'live.'"[28] Essentially, the world is the relational context of meanings wherein Dasein—the human being—dwells.[29] In "The Origin of the Work of Art" and onward, Heidegger regularly speaks of the worlding of the world to express how vibrant the various relational meanings can be.[30] Thus, the concept is similar to what we find in *Being and Time*, but his explicit shift from the noun "world" to the verb "worlding" points to an emphasis on the relationality of the concept. Heidegger interprets

Vincent Van Gogh's 1886 painting *A Pair of Shoes* as an artwork that exemplifies the worlding of the world. The worn-out, haggard shoes depicted in the painting reveal what it means *to be* a peasant woman working in the fields. Heidegger's detailed account of Van Gogh's artwork provides us with an example of how meaning-packed a work of art can be:

> From the dark opening of the worn insides of the shoes the toilsome tread of the worker stares forth. In the stiffly rugged heaviness of the shoes there is the accumulated tenacity of her slow trudge through the far-spreading and ever-uniform furrows of the field swept by a raw wind. On the leather lie the dampness and richness of the soil. Under the soles stretches the loneliness of the field-path as evening falls. In the shoes vibrates the silent call of the earth, its quiet gift of the ripening grain and its unexplained self-refusal in the fallow desolation of the wintry field. This equipment is pervaded by uncomplaining worry as to the certainty of bread, the wordless joy of having once more withstood want.[31]

As a great work of art, Van Gogh's shoes are not merely a representation of the farmer's shoes. Rather, the painting opens us up to the world of the peasant who wore them and thereby shows us what it means *to be* in her shoes in both the literal and figurative senses.[32]

From a Heideggerian perspective, art does not simply open up already existing worlds. Rather, Heidegger argues that "art lets truth originate."[33] In other words, great artworks can literally *create* new worlds by showing us new ways to be. Hubert Dreyfus provides us with some Heideggerian insight as to how music, as an art form, can reveal new worlds to people in his interpretation of the significance of music from the late 1960s and the 1969 music festival, Woodstock:

> [Some] rock groups became for many the articulators of a new understanding of what really mattered. . . . People actually lived for a few days in an understanding of being in which mainline contemporary concerns with order, sobriety, willful activity, and flexible, efficient control were made marginal and subservient to certain pagan practices, such as enjoyment of nature, dancing, and Dionysian ecstasy, along with neglected Christian concerns with peace, tolerance, and nonexclusive love of one's neighbor.[34]

Marketed as "three days of peace and music," Woodstock was a climactic event for the countercultural movement of the late 1960s: the hippies. The festival featured some of the most iconic acts of that generation of music, including the Grateful Dead, Creedence Clearwater Revival, Janis Joplin, The Who, The Band, Crosby Stills, Nash & Young, and Jimi Hendrix, among others. During the event, roughly 500,000 persons came together to celebrate and embody the hippie culture of peace, tolerance, communal living, free love, the exploration of altered states of consciousness through recreational drug use, and, of course, psychedelic music.

In the waning hours of the festival, Woodstock featured perhaps the most famous rendition of "The Star Spangled Banner" of all-time when Jimi Hendrix played a version of the traditional song that has come to be regarded as the defining moment in the countercultural movement.[35] As the official national anthem of the United States, one would be hard-pressed to find a song more ensconced in bureaucracy, as it is regularly played in military settings, national and local festivals, and sporting events. In most renditions of the anthem, citizens take their hats off and direct their attention toward the U.S. flag as a sign of respect for their country. This, however, was not the sort of response that was elicited by Hendrix's performance. Having already established himself as the driving force behind the psychedelic rock movement, Jimi Hendrix was the perfect embodiment of the counterculture that was the hippie movement.[36] He came on stage decked out in appropriate hippie garb: a blue-beaded leather fringe jacket, blue jeans, and his signature head scarf. Upon flashing a "peace" sign to the crowd, Hendrix went on to perform an interpretive version of "The Star Spangled Banner" that was anything but bureaucratic. While demonstrating his mastery of the electric guitar, Hendrix utilized distortion and amplifier feedback to create sounds that mimicked rockets and bombs to signify the violence that had been occurring in the heavily protested Vietnam War. The rendition—a heart-wrenchingly masterful embodiment of the anti-establishment mentality that drove the counterculture movement—was welcomed by an audience who celebrated and were left mesmerized by the performance. Indeed, the image of Hendrix's "Star Spangled Banner" became the iconic emblematic performance of the hippie movement. Charles Shaar Murray sums this up as follows: "One man with a guitar said more in three and a half minutes about that peculiarly disgusting war and its reverberations than all the novels, memoirs and movies put together."[37] Hendrix, of course, was not merely commenting on the Vietnam War, but simultaneously engraining an entirely new understanding of the national anthem—and the nation itself—to those who witnessed the performance. As Mark Clague has argued persuasively, more than simply an anti-war artistic demonstration, "Hendrix's Banner . . . is a celebration of possibility inspired by the Woodstock festival itself."[38] Hendrix shows us what it means *to be* part of the countercultural movement, and what a new hippie-inspired vision of the United States might look like that could be driven by peace, love, and music, a place where all persons—even a black man who grew up in abject poverty in the streets of Seattle like Hendrix—can speak their minds freely and openly.

From a Heideggerian point of view, we can say that Hendrix artistically utilized a traditionally bureaucratic song that exemplified patriotism as a medium to open up a new world of possibilities for members of the counterculture movement. Heidegger argues that any authentic establishment of a new way of being is an enactment of "a possibility which [Dasein] has inherited and yet has chosen."[39] Commenting on this, Charles Guignon explains: "because Dasein is historical in the primordial sense of being a happening, it is always taking up the possibilities of the heritage into which it is thrown."[40] When a new world is opened up, it does so against the horizon of the possibilities that comes from one's heritage. In the case of Hendrix, he takes perhaps the most patriotic song for U.S. citizens that at the time had highly formal connotations and playfully bended it to voice the anti-establishment mentality of the countercultural movement and, in doing so, simultaneously opened up a new understanding of what it means to be patriotic. This aligns well with Heidegger's claim that "in setting up a world . . . [the artwork] causes [entities] to come forth for the very first time and to come into the open region of the work's world."[41] Hendrix's "Star Spangled Banner" opens up a new perspective on what it meant for the United States to be engaged in the Vietnam War, but also what a new world could look like if we were to take up the values of the participants at Woodstock.

Dreyfus argues that "if enough people had recognized in Woodstock what they most cared about and recognized that many others shared this recognition, a new understanding of being might have been focused and stabilized."[42] As it turned out, the hippie dream that Hendrix and others embodied so well died as the decade of the 1970s unfolded, as did some of the visionaries who personified that dream. Hendrix was dead by October of 1970, and fellow countercultural musical giants Janis Joplin and Jim Morrison followed soon thereafter. Nevertheless, Hendrix at Woodstock provides an example of the way in which music can open new worlds. Dreyfus helpfully uses Thomas Kuhn's language of paradigms to explain the shifts that can occur in music and other venues. Kuhn spoke of paradigms as "models from which spring particular coherent traditions of scientific research."[43] Just as Isaac Newton's *Principia Mathematica* established a paradigm as to what constituted good science for several generations of scientists before the paradigm was overtaken by Einsteinian science, works of art similarly can be understood from the lenses of paradigm establishment and entrenchment. To differentiate them from scientific paradigms, Dreyfus uses the language of "cultural paradigms." He states, "A cultural paradigm collects the scattered practices of a group, unifies them into coherent possibilities for action, and holds them up to the people who can then act and relate to each other in terms of that exemplar."[44] The hippie movement, embodied brilliantly by Hendrix's "Star Spangled Banner," was a new understanding of what mattered to those who participated in the countercultural movement. Since then, music has sparked the establishment of various different worlds, including the even more vigorous anti-establishment mentalities that come from punk rock in the mid-1970s and rap music in the 1980s. However, I will argue in the next section that this world-building capacity is more difficult to cultivate in the digital era of music.

THE DIGITIZATION OF MUSIC

If we agree with a Heideggerian understanding of music, we will agree with people like the musicologist Simon Frith, who argues that "music, the experience of music for composer/performer and listener alike, gives us a way of being in the world, a way of making sense of it."[45] For Frith, "the issue is not how a particular piece of music or a performance reflects the people, but how it produces them."[46] Truly great musical performances have the capacity of opening up new worlds, as we have seen with our analysis of Hendrix's performance at Woodstock. At the same time, however, the ways in which we experience music can hide music's world-building capacity. In his later thought, Heidegger argues that what an entity *is*, that is, its being, is historical in nature, and his doctrine of ontological historicity captures his idea that "even humanity's most fundamental sense of reality changes, and so needs to be understood in terms of its history."[47] This means that what matters to persons differs in various historical periods and contexts. Also, the way in which entities show up *as* the entities that they are is historical in nature. Keeping this in mind, in general, we can say that music festivals like Woodstock are moments of gathering in at least two different senses. Not only do persons gather together to celebrate and enjoy the festivities, but the festival allows for the gathering together of shared meanings, which thereby open up new worlds.[48] In the remaining part of this chapter, I will argue that the digitization of music threatens music's meaning-gathering and world-building capacity by turning music into mere material on hand to be consumed, which Heidegger refers to as *Bestand*.

In 1955, Heidegger was asked to speak at a public gathering to commemorate the 175th birthday of the composer Conradin Kreutzer in his hometown of Messkirch, Germany. Here, Heidegger critiques the seemingly ubiquitous thoughtlessness that has accompanied the onset of the modern world: "nowadays we take in everything in the quickest and cheapest way, only to forget it just as quickly, instantly. Thus one gathering follows on the heels of another."[49] In particular, Heidegger is worried about the ways in which modern technology changes our relationship to entities. Entities become mere material on hand that are seamlessly aligned with human interests. He states, "The power concealed in modern technology determines the relation of man to that which exists. It rules the whole earth."[50] Heidegger recognized that technological advancements in particular had the power to change our relationships with entities and he laments the loss of rootedness (*Bodenständigkeit*) that has accompanied the modern world where "everything present is equally near and equally far," as he puts it in his late essay "The Thing."[51]

Music is not exempt from the changes in the ways entities present themselves in the modern age of technology. Historically, music was bound to certain constraints and was heavily intertwined with local culture. Today, however, we are in the midst of the digital age of music wherein the communal aspects of music are falling to the wayside. Instead of local concerts that celebrate and generate communal identities and values, music is on the brink of becoming mere material on hand to be consumed. Albert Borgmann explains this shift as follows:

> In a premodern setting [persons] depended on communal cooperation for entertainment and celebration. But with the rise and progressive articulation of modern prosperity and liberty, these communal ties came to be seen as burdens and have since been removed to make room for commodious individualism, the unencumbered enjoyment of consumption goods or commodities.[52]

One could argue that the shift in the being of music from a communal celebration to an instantiation of commodious individualism on a mass scale likely began in the late 1970s and early 1980s with the introduction of the Walkman, a portable cassette player that individualized the music listening experience.[53] Prior to the Walkman, the music listening experience still held communal aspects, whether it occurred at music concerts, festivals, or consisted of family members huddled around the communal radio or record player. The introduction of the Walkman greatly individualized music for listeners by allowing individuals to "tune out" one's surroundings and "tune in" to the music coming from their headphones. The Walkman, of course, was followed by similarly significant shifts that helped to further individualize the music listening experience with the introduction of the iPod in 2001 and, most recently, smartphones and smart speakers that are able to tap into broad and diverse musical databases. From a Heideggerian perspective, it is not the specific technological devices themselves that deserve a thorough philosophical elucidation, but rather the way in which these technological devices reveal the music that is generated by them.

In his 1954 essay "The Question Concerning Technology," Heidegger states that "technology is not equivalent to the essence of technology."[54] Whereas technology refers to individual technological devices like the Walkman and the iPod, as well as the manufacturing and utilization of these devices, the essence of technology refers to the ways in which this said technology reveals entities to humans. Heidegger argues that modern technology reveals entities as mere material on hand to be consumed: "Everywhere everything is ordered to stand by, to be immediately at hand, indeed to stand there just so that it may be on call for a further ordering. Whatever is ordered about in this way has its own standing. We call it the standing-reserve."[55] For Heidegger, the essence of modern technology, which he refers to as enframing (*Gestell*), reveals entities *as* standing-reserve (*Bestand*), that is, as mere material on hand to be consumed.

How does music show up to us in the age of modern technology? I believe that the experience of music has changed drastically with the digitization of music. Whereas festivals like Woodstock were a way of gathering together new ways of being for persons who experienced them, smart speakers reveal music as *Bestand*. Voice-controlled speakers with virtual assistants—think Alexa in the Amazon Echo format—allow listeners to play music from a vast database of millions of songs without even a touch of a button, but merely through an audio directive. The music "stands by," as it were, ready to be activated by a person's voice. The virtual assistant that activates the voice commands is there to fulfill the requests of the person, and in such a setup, the music becomes *Bestand*, in that the music doesn't *teach us* ways to be but rather *we tell the music* whether or not it can be manifested. If we ask the voice-controlled speaker to play a playlist and we do not like the song, we quickly discard that musical experience and seek another, more *pleasant* one. In this format of imminent disposability and discontinuity, we have come to a point in which music shows up merely as auditory cheesecake. There is no longer a genuine force to the music when emanated from a smart speaker, since there is no genuine commitment to fully participate in the musical experience.

In such a format, we can see why Heidegger claimed that "enframing blocks the shining-forth and holding-sway of truth."[56] At the same time, however, Heidegger saw a glimmer of hope in the human ability to remain open to new worlds through art.[57] As art, music still has a world-building capacity, but this capacity must be located and nurtured if we are to let it shine. Taking a cue from Albert Borgmann, I think that the mode of delivery makes a discernable difference in allowing for the possibility of heeding the world-building capacity of music. In his *Crossing the Postmodern Divide*, Borgmann speaks of focal realities, which can be defined as things or events that center our lives by revealing truths about life, which thereby occasion us to encounter and possibly affirm new worlds.[58] Focal realities can be distinguished from what Borgmann refers to as "the device paradigm" in which humans surround themselves with devices primarily for the sake of convenience.[59] Whereas music can show up as *Bestand* when emanating from smart speakers and thus lose its force, there are alternative modes of musical delivery that allow us to have a genuine encounter with the music, as the music shows up as a focal reality. The prime example of this is a live concert in a fitting venue wherein the listener is more likely to be committed to the world-building capacity of music.[60] Here, the music is less likely to show up as disposable as there is a commitment on the part of the listener regarding the musical experience that is less likely to be present when accessing music from the vast databases in smart speaker formats where it is so easy to move on from an unpleasant sound through an audio directive. Moreover, the concert format allows for the elicitation of the communal feel of music that was found in pre-digital contexts that is much harder to create in digital settings. Borgmann puts the point the following way: "Real music [is] a matter of living persons gathering here and now with their tangible instruments, playing together."[61] I don't necessarily think that it is impossible to allow the world-building capacity of music to shine forth in digital formats (think, for instance, of some of the creative collaborations musicians achieved during the COVID-19 pandemic in which gathering together physically was not an option), but it certainly seems to take an intentional stance to do so, a stance that Dreyfus and Sean Kelly might refer to as a "choice to experience the world as sacred and meaningful,"[62] rather than as immanently disposable.

CONCLUDING THOUGHTS

One of Heidegger's oft-quoted bits of poetry from his favorite poet, Friedrich Hölderlin, reads: "But where there is danger, there grows also the saving power."[63] I have tried to show how the digital age of music threatens music's world-building capacity in that music has begun to reveal itself as mere material on hand to be consumed in certain contexts. If my Heideggerian understanding of the ontology of music is plausible, then music can change not only our understanding of the world but our way of being in the world. The first step in saving music's world-building capacity is to recognize the danger of music becoming *Bestand* and cultivating contexts in which music can still "open up a *world* and keep it abidingly in force."[64]

NOTES

1. This chapter is dedicated to Charles Guignon and Martin Schönfeld, both of whom served as influential mentors for me philosophically and who passed away in 2020. I presented this chapter at the University of South Florida's philosophy conference held in their memory in 2021 and am indebted to comments by participants in the audience, especially from Kevin Aho, Megan Altman, and Michael Thompson.

2. Aristotle, *Politics*, trans. C. D. C. Reeve (Indianapolis and Cambridge: Hackett Publishing Company, 1998), 232–233. Bekker numbers are provided in the text for

those referencing alternative translations. In ancient Greece, μουσική referred broadly to music, poetry, and the fine arts.

3. Steven Pinker, *How the Mind Works* (New York: W. W. Norton & Company, 1997), 534.

4. Plato, *Republic*, trans. G. M. A. Grube and C. D. C. Reeve (Indianapolis and Cambridge: Hackett Publishing Company, 1992), 78. Stephanus numbers are provided in the text for those referencing alternative translations. As many Plato commentators point out, it is difficult to ascribe an actual view to Plato per se as he often utilizes characters—most prominently the character of Socrates—as mouthpieces to voice philosophical perspectives. Thus, we should understand Plato's philosophy of music as not so much "his theory" but rather a viewpoint he at least discussed.

5. Pinker, *How the Mind Works*, 528.

6. Pinker, *How the Mind Works*, 528.

7. Pinker, *How the Mind Works*, 534.

8. Charles Darwin, *The Origin of Species*, ed. Gillian Beer (Oxford and New York: Oxford University Press, 1996), 198. Darwin spends a surprising amount of time writing on the evolutionary value of music in his *Descent of Man and Selection in Relation to Sex*, but ultimately states that the human musical faculty "must be ranked among the most mysterious with which he is endowed" (Princeton: Princeton University Press, 1981), 33.

9. Friedrich Nietzsche, *Twilight of the Idols or How to Philosophize with the Hammer*, trans. Richard Polt (Indianapolis and Cambridge: Hackett Publishing Company, 1997), 10.

10. Andrew Bowie, *Music, Philosophy, and Modernity* (Cambridge: Cambridge University Press, 2007), 27.

11. Martin Heidegger, "Science and Reflection," in *The Question Concerning Technology and Other Essays*, trans. William Lovitt (New York: Harper & Row, 1977), 157.

12. Cf. Martin Heidegger, "The Origin of the Work of Art," in *Basic Writings*, ed. David Farrell Krell (New York: HarperCollins, 1993), 143–212. There may be situations in which art is best approached from a scientific perspective as in, for instance, art restoration. However, for the most part, the scientific lens is concealing, as opposed to revealing, when it comes to art.

13. Martin Heidegger, *What is a Thing?* trans. W. B. Barton, Jr. and Vera Deutsch (Chicago: Henry Regnery Company, 1967), 10 (my emphasis).

14. Plato, *Laws*, trans. R. G. Bury (Cambridge and London: Harvard University Press, 1926), 139. Qinghua Zhu discusses Plato's views on music and pleasure in his chapter of this volume.

15. Plato, *Laws*, 109–111.

16. Plato, *Republic*, 78.

17. Plato, *Republic,* 78.

18. Mary B. Schoen-Nazzaro, "Plato and Aristotle on the Ends of Music," *Laval théologique et philosophique* 34, no. 3 (1978), 263.

19. Plato, *Ion*, trans. Benjamin Jowett (Cabin John, Maryland: Polit Press, 2018), 9.

20. Plato, *Laws*, 247.
21. The term οἱ πολλοί has a negative connotation in ancient Greek and refers derogatorily to the masses.
22. Plato, *Laws*, 247.
23. Plato, *Laws*, 248.
24. Plato, *Republic*, 99.
25. Francesco Pelosi, *Plato on Music, Soul and Body*, trans. Sophie Henderson (Cambridge and New York: Cambridge University Press, 2010), 20.
26. As Heidegger notes, "The German word *Bildung* ['education,' literally 'formation'] comes closest to capturing the word παιδεία, but not entirely" in "Plato's Doctrine of Truth," in *Pathmarks*, ed. William McNeil (Cambridge and New York: Cambridge University Press, 1998), 166.
27. Heidegger, "The Origin of the Work of Art," 169.
28. Martin Heidegger, *Being and Time*, trans. John Macquarrie and Edward Robinson (New York: Harper & Row, 1962), 93.
29. I realize that "human being" is not a perfect translation for Dasein, but it works for our purposes. For a more detailed elucidation of Dasein, see Pio's chapter in this volume.
30. Heidegger also changes the noun "world" to the verb "worlding" in his earliest lectures from 1919. Cf. "The Idea of Philosophy and the Problem of Worldview," in *Towards the Definition of Philosophy*, trans. Ted Sadler (London and New York: Continuum, 2000), 6–99.
31. Heidegger, "The Origin of the Work of Art," 159. Savage discusses Heidegger's interpretation of Van Gogh's painting in the next chapter. Stahl also touches upon it in the last chapter of this volume. On an extended commentary on "The Origin of the Work of Art" and music, see Richter's chapter in this volume.
32. As most commentators point out, we now know that Van Gogh's painting is actually of his own shoes, not those of a peasant woman's, as Heidegger believed. I think Heidegger's conceptual point, however, remains convincing, as it highlights the worlding-opening capacity of art well.
33. Heidegger, "The Origin of the Work of Art," 202.
34. Hubert Dreyfus, "Heidegger on the Connection Between Nihilism, Art, Technology, and Politics," in *The Cambridge Companion to Heidegger*, ed. Charles Guignon (Cambridge: Cambridge University Press, 1993), 311.
35. Mark Daley, "Jimi Hendrix: Woodstock Festival, 1969," in *Performance and Popular Music: History, Place and Time*, ed. Ian Inglis (Hampshire, England and Burlington, VT: Ashgate, 2006), 57.
36. It matters, of course, that Hendrix was black, but this curiously doesn't get emphasized as much as it does for other black musicians like, for instance, Muddy Waters. This may be partially due to the fact that the free concert he held at the Harlem Street Fair on September 5, 1969 (just weeks after Woodstock) for "his people," that is, for black people, was not met with the same praise he received at Woodstock. On Hendrix and "blackness," see Steve Waksman's chapter "Black Sound, Black Body: Jimi Hendrix, the Electric Guitar, and the Meanings of Blackness," in *Instruments*

of Desire: The Electric Guitar and the Shaping of Musical Experience (Cambridge: Harvard University Press, 2001).

37. Charles Shaar Murray, *Crosstown Traffic: Jimi Hendrix and the Post-War Rock 'n' Roll Revolution* (New York: St. Martin's Press, 1991), 24.

38. Mark Clague, "'This is America': Jimi Hendrix's Star Spangled Banner Journey as Psychedelic Citizenship," *Journal of the Society of American Music* 8, no. 4 (2014): 461.

39. Heidegger, *Being and Time*, 435.

40. Charles B. Guignon, *Heidegger and the Problem of Knowledge* (Indianapolis: Hackett Publishing Company, 1983), 214.

41. Heidegger, "The Origin of the Work of Art," 171.

42. Dreyfus, "Heidegger on the Connection Between Nihilism, Art, Technology, and Politics," 311.

43. Thomas Kuhn, *The Structure of Scientific Revolutions*, 2nd ed. (Chicago: The University of Chicago Press, 1970), 10. Rinat Nugayev and Tanzila Burganova have argued that Kuhn's philosophy was indirectly influenced by Heidegger in "Heideggerian Epistemology as a Source of Kuhn's Concept of the Growth of Knowledge," *Italian Science Review* 1, no. 34 (2016): 156–167.

44. Dreyfus, "Heidegger on the Connection Between Nihilism, Art, Technology, and Politics," 298.

45. Simon Frith, "Music and Identity," in *Questions of Cultural Identity*, ed. Stuart Hall and Paul du Gay (Thousand Oaks, CA: Sage Publications, 1996), 114.

46. Frith, "Music and Identity," 109.

47. Iain Thomson, *Heidegger on Ontotheology: Technology and the Politics of Education* (Cambridge and New York: Cambridge University Press, 2005), 9.

48. As Jeff R. Warren notes, these shared worlds also entail ethical relationships among persons who dwell in them. See his excellent *Music and Ethical Responsibility* (Cambridge and New York: Cambridge University Press, 2014).

49. Martin Heidegger, "Memorial Address," in *Discourse on Thinking*, trans. John M. Anderson and E. Hans Freund (New York: Harper & Row, 1966), 45.

50. Heidegger, "Memorial Address," 50.

51. Martin Heidegger, "The Thing," in *Poetry, Language, Thought*, trans. Albert Hofstadter (New York: Harper & Row, 1971), 177.

52. Albert Borgmann, *Crossing the Postmodern Divide* (Chicago and London: The University of Chicago Press, 1992), 43.

53. On how the Walkman changed the relationship to music for consumers, see Paul Du Gay, Stuart Hall, Linda James, Anders Koed Madsen, Hugh Mackay, and Keith Negus, *Doing Cultural Studies: The Story of the Sony Walkman*, 2nd ed (London: Sage, 2013).

54. Martin Heidegger, "The Question Concerning Technology," in *The Question Concerning Technology and Other Essays*, trans. William Lovitt (New York: Harper & Row, 1977), 4.

55. Heidegger, "The Question Concerning Technology," 17.

56. Heidegger, "The Question Concerning Technology," 28.

57. Heidegger, "The Question Concerning Technology," 35.

58. Borgmann, *Crossing the Postmodern Divide*, 78–147. Harper-Scott elaborates on Borgmann's concept of focal realities in his chapter of this volume.

59. Albert Borgmann, *Technology and the Character of Contemporary Life: A Philosophical Inquiry* (Chicago and London: The University of Chicago Press, 1984), 40–47.

60. Even in such settings, though, listeners should heed to the possibility that music becomes a mere commodity. For instance, many of the large music festivals have now been commodified in a way that simply was not the case at Woodstock.

61. Borgmann, *Crossing the Postmodern Divide*, 93.

62. Hubert Dreyfus and Sean Dorrance Kelly, *All Things Shining: Reading the Western Classics to Find Meaning in a Secular Age* (New York: Free Press, 2011), 40. We should not interpret "the sacred" in this context to necessarily be religious in nature. Rather, music can open us up to a secular sense of the sacred.

63. Quoted in Heidegger, "The Question Concerning Technology," 34; see also Heidegger, "The Thing," 118.

64. Heidegger, "The Origin of the Work of Art," 169. I thank Richard Polt, Gregory Fried, Jeff R. Warren, Tony Olson, and Tyson Kratz for comments on earlier drafts of this chapter.

BIBLIOGRAPHY

Aristotle. *Politics*. Translated by C. D. C. Reeve. Indianapolis and Cambridge: Hackett Publishing Company, 1998.

Borgmann, Albert. *Crossing the Postmodern Divide*. Chicago and London: The University of Chicago Press, 1992.

Borgmann, Albert. *Technology and the Character of Contemporary Life: A Philosophical Inquiry*. Chicago and London: The University of Chicago Press, 1984.

Bowie, Andrew. *Music, Philosophy, and Modernity*. Cambridge: Cambridge University Press, 2007.

Clague, Mark. "'This is America': Jimi Hendrix's Star Spangled Banner Journey as Psychedelic Citizenship." *Journal of the Society of American Music* 8, no. 4 (2014): 435–478.

Daley, Mark. "Jimi Hendrix: Woodstock Festival, 1969." In *Performance and Popular Music: History, Place and Time*, edited by Ian Inglis, 52–58. Hampshire, England and Burlington, VT: Ashgate, 2006.

Darwin, Charles. *Descent of Man and Selection in Relation to Sex*. Princeton: Princeton University Press, 1981.

Darwin, Charles. *The Origin of Species*. Edited by Gillian Beer. Oxford and New York: Oxford University Press, 1996.

Dreyfus, Hubert L. "Heidegger on the Connection Between Nihilism, Art, Technology, and Politics." In *The Cambridge Companion to Heidegger*, edited by Charles Guignon, 289–316. Cambridge: Cambridge University Press, 1993.

Dreyfus, Hubert and Sean Dorrance Kelly. *All Things Shining: Reading the Western Classics to Find Meaning in a Secular Age*. New York: Free Press, 2011.

Du Gay, Paul, Stuart Hall, Linda James, Anders Koed Madsen, Hugh Mackay, and Keith Negus. *Doing Cultural Studies: The Story of the Sony Walkman*, 2nd ed. London: Sage, 2013.

Frith, Simon. "Music and Identity." In *Questions of Cultural Identity*, edited by Stuart Hall and Paul du Gay, 108–127. Thousand Oaks, CA: Sage Publications, 1996.

Guignon, Charles B. *Heidegger and the Problem of Knowledge*. Indianapolis: Hackett Publishing Company, 1983.

Heidegger, Martin. *Being and Time*. Translated by John Macquarrie and Edward Robinson. New York: Harper & Row, 1962.

Heidegger, Martin. "The Idea of Philosophy and the Problem of Worldview." In *Towards the Definition of Philosophy*, translated by Ted Sadler, 6–99. London and New York: Continuum, 2000.

Heidegger, Martin. "Memorial Address." In *Discourse on Thinking*, translated by John M. Anderson and E. Hans Freund, 43–57. New York: Harper & Row, 1966.

Heidegger, Martin. "The Origin of the Work of Art." In *Basic Writings*, edited by David Farrell Krell, 143–212. New York: HarperCollins, 1993.

Heidegger, Martin. "Plato's Doctrine of Truth." In *Pathmarks*, edited by William McNeil, 155–182. Cambridge and New York: Cambridge University Press, 1998.

Heidegger, Martin. "The Question Concerning Technology." In *The Question Concerning Technology and Other Essays*, translated by William Lovitt, 3–35. New York: Harper & Row, 1977.

Heidegger, Martin. "Science and Reflection." In *The Question Concerning Technology and Other Essays*, translated by William Lovitt, 155–182. New York: Harper & Row, 1977.

Heidegger, Martin. "The Thing." In *Poetry, Language, Thought*, translated by Albert Hofstadter, 163–186. New York: Harper & Row, 1971.

Heidegger, Martin. *What is a Thing?* Translated by W. B. Barton, Jr. and Vera Deutsch. Chicago: Henry Regnery Company, 1967.

Kuhn, Thomas. *The Structure of Scientific Revolutions*, 2nd ed. Chicago: The University of Chicago Press, 1970.

Murray, Charles Shaar. *Crosstown Traffic: Jimi Hendrix and the Post-War Rock 'n' Roll Revolution*. New York: St. Martin's Press, 1991.

Nietzsche, Friedrich. *Twilight of the Idols or How to Philosophize with the Hammer*. Translated by Richard Polt. Indianapolis and Cambridge: Hackett Publishing Company, 1997.

Nugayev, Rinat and Tanzilia Burganova. "Heideggerian Epistemology as a Source of Kuhn's Concept of the Growth of Knowledge." *Italian Science Review* 1, no. 34 (2016): 156–167.

Pelosi, Francesco. *Plato on Music, Soul and Body*. Translated by Sophie Henderson. Cambridge and New York: Cambridge University Press, 2010.

Pinker, Steven. *How the Mind Works*. New York: W. W. Norton & Company, 1997.

Plato. *Ion*. Translated by Benjamin Jowett. Cabin John, MD: Polit Press, 2018.

Plato. *Laws*. Translated by R. G. Bury. Cambridge and London: Harvard University Press, 1926.

Plato. *Republic*. Translated by G. M. A. Grube and C. D. C. Reeve. Indianapolis and Cambridge: Hackett Publishing Company, 1992.

Schoen-Nazzaro, Mary B. "Plato and Aristotle on the Ends of Music." *Laval théologique et philosophique* 34, no. 3 (1978): 261–273.

Thomson, Iain. *Heidegger on Ontotheology: Technology and the Politics of Education*. Cambridge and New York: Cambridge University Press, 2005.

Waksman, Steve. *Instruments of Desire: The Electric Guitar and the Shaping of Musical Experience*. Cambridge: Harvard University Press, 2001.

Warren, Jeff R. *Music and Ethical Responsibility*. Cambridge and New York: Cambridge University Press, 2014.

Chapter 15

Touched by Music
Affective Expression as Measure-Taking
Roger W. H. Savage

In his essay ". . . Poetically Man Dwells . . . ," Martin Heidegger gives an account of poetry's worlding power based on his reading of Friedrich Hölderlin's poem *Der Ister*. By building up a world to which it gives its own distinct expression, poetry, according to this reading, takes the measure of our being. For Heidegger, writing "poetry is measure-taking"[1] not in the sense of providing a system of objective coordinates but rather in the way that poetry reveals otherwise hidden dimensions of our manner of inhering in the world. The poetic measure-taking of the breadth of our being thus springs from the way that poetry, like music, fiction, and works of art, searches out those possibilities that it uncovers. Poetry's worlding power, we might therefore say, is the wellspring of the truth to which it singularly lays claim.

By suggesting that music touches us in distinctively unique ways, I intend in this chapter to explore how Heidegger's philosophical interpretation of poetry adds to our understanding of music's affective power. By giving voice to feelings and moods that it alone possesses, music, I will say, opens us to the world and the world to us anew. Heidegger's hierarchization of the levels of temporality offers a unique vantage point from which to consider the power that music has in staking out the borderlines between time and eternity. In the course of the following discussion, I therefore propose to weave together a commentary on Heidegger's claim that poetry takes the measure of the dimension of our being with a hermeneutical reflection on music's significance in light of the aporia of time's ultimate inscrutability.

WORLDING AS MEASURE-TAKING

Heidegger's account of the origin of the work of art offers a welcome insight into the inimitable relation between a work's worlding power and its ontological vehemence, by which I mean the impact a work has through affecting our ways of thinking, feeling, and acting. For him, the world is "never an object that stands before us"[2] as an entity from which we set ourselves at some remove. Consequently, the world is neither merely the collection and assemblage of things in it nor the conceptual or metaphysical framework of a composite system into which this collection and assemblance of familiar and unfamiliar entities fit. Rather, the world, Heidegger tells us, "is the ever-nonobjective to which we are subject"[3] as mortally finite human beings. Stones, plants, and animals, he insists, have no world.[4] Conversely, the peasant woman whose work-worn shoes are the subject of Van Gogh's painting has a world, since in the painting we apprehend as if for the first time a manner of dwelling on the earth that the painting itself renders uniquely visible.[5]

Art, Heidegger accordingly maintains, "is truth setting itself to work."[6] The depiction of the peasant shoes in Van Gogh's painting is therefore no mere reproduction of the image of material objects that captures, so to speak, their exact likeness. On the contrary, the painting is a faithful rendering of the shoes only to the extent that it breaks with the principle of verisimilitude by disclosing a world that the painting itself builds up. The painting's representation of the shoes is consequently not a copy or imitation of some real existing thing. Rather, this mimetic representation acquires its own tangible reality through revealing dimensions of being-in-the-world that only this painting uncovers.

By insisting that the work of art has its origin in setting truth to work, Heidegger brings to the fore the paradox of all poetic creation. The reality of the work, he maintains, "is defined by that which is at work in the work."[7] The reality of the work is therefore indistinguishable from the "happening of truth."[8] Hans-Georg Gadamer reminds us that, through occasioning an experience that it alone affords, the work addresses us in a singularly unique way. If, as Heidegger says, "[w]e think of all creation as a bringing forth"[9] of something that previously was hidden or did not exist, the distinction he draws between the work-being of the work and the craftsmanship required to produce it sets the happening—better, the eventing—of truth in relief. What, then, Heidegger asks, is truth? For Greek thought, he explains, "the nature of knowledge consists in *aletheia*, that is, in the uncovering of beings."[10] This "unconcealedness of beings (being) puts us into such a condition that in our representation we always remain installed within and in attendance"[11] upon it. Since human being is always *in medias res*, truth for Heidegger therefore inheres in the conflict in which that which reveals itself as being shines forth, while that which hides itself withdraws. The "openness of this Open,"[12] which Heidegger stresses is won through this conflict, is *in fine* truth only insofar as this openness admits a place for beginning something new. Every genuine beginning is the source of an excess or superabundance of meaning that shatters congealed expectations, horizons, and habits of thought. As such, every genuine beginning holds in readiness as yet undisclosed possibilities that refashion the real anew. By setting truth to work, art, like poetry, thus renews our manner of inhering in the world in accordance with the worlds projected by it.[13]

In view of the idea that the work of art brings a meaning intended by it to a stand through setting truth to work, we might wonder if a conception of truth as manifestation (*aletheia*) such as Heidegger espouses fully does justice to the experiences occasioned by music, poetry, fiction, paintings, and the like. Art, he tells us, "lets truth originate."[14] Hence art is itself an origin inasmuch as the truth to which the work singularly attests shines forth in the way that the work presents itself. This coming into being of truth constitutes the event occasioned by the work through the manner in which it unfolds.[15] This event consequently springs from the way that the truth of the work makes its appearance in the world. This event is the source of the work's worlding power. By setting the truth to which the work lays claim to work, this worlding power thus achieves its practical import each time the experience occasioned by the work brings about an increase in being through augmenting the reader, listener, or spectator's ways of thinking, feeling, and acting.

How, then, might the worlding of the work take the measure of the breadth of the being that we are? By turning to music, I propose to relate Heidegger's philosophical commentary on Hölderlin's poem to the ways that eternity experiences in music refigure time's ultimate unrepresentability. In *Music, Time, and Its Other*, I explained how, by meting out the difference between time and eternity, limit experiences afforded by music take the measure of the being and the non-being of time.[16] Music figures among the ways of speaking of time that surpass the narrative art, which Paul Ricoeur emphasizes approaches its internal limit in attempting to draw near time's inscrutable character.[17] The presentiment of abiding grace in J. S. Bach's Andante from his *Sonata for Flute and Continuo* (BWV 1034), for example, places its note of sanction on the part we have in being in answer to time's ontological deficiency. In a markedly different vein, the transvaluation of the traditional cadential closing in the finale of Philip Glass's *Einstein on the Beach* gives rise to a postmodern simulacrum of a mythic return to a time *in illo tempore*. In each case, the ways that these works explore the boundaries between time and eternity take the measure of time and its other through refiguring time's ultimate unrepresentability.

The notion that, by building up a world, poetry metes out the dimension in which we have our being leads me to ask whether music's refiguration of time's ultimate unrepresentability bears out Heidegger's claim that "poetry first causes dwelling to be dwelling."[18] For him, when Hölderlin speaks of dwelling in his poem, *Der Ister*, "he has before his eye the basic character of human existence."[19] This basic character, Heidegger remarks, appears only to poets who shut their eyes to that which in actuality exists. Hence, instead of acting, he says, "poets dream."[20] These works of imagination are made in the fashion of *poiesis*. Every such making is therefore also a creation that brings something new into the world. If, with Heidegger, we think of poetry and dwelling in terms of what he describes as their essential nature, we have to admit that this creation is no mere copy of some existing thing, as I indicated previously. Hence, with him, we have also to acknowledge that the poetic does not "exhaust itself in an unreal play"[21] but instead intends being through the way that poetry, for instance, builds up a world in which we can dwell. We might wonder whether the distinction Heidegger draws between the reproduction of an existing entity and the "reproduction of the thing's general essence"[22] by the work passes over too quickly the full import of a creative imitation in which the power of imagination is set to work. Nevertheless, his commentary on the way that, in Hölderlin's poem, spanning "the between of sky and earth"[23] metes out the dimension of our mortal dwelling provides a fecund point of access for exploring the inner connection between music's temporal characteristics and its affective power.

SPANNING THE BETWEEN

The sense of alterity that in Heidegger's reading of Hölderlin's poem suffuses the measure taken by poetry of the dimension in which we have our being is the touchstone for my own reflections on the way that music refigures time's unrepresentability in answer to the aporia of its ultimately inscrutable character. Time's deficiency in relation to its other, which in the cases to which I just referred elicits a response that can be described variously as evoking a presentiment of abiding grace or as simulating a mythic time *in illo tempore*, marks the difference between the being and the non-being of time. By indicating an order that, surpassing our capacity to constitute it, exceeds our will to mastery, the aporia of time's ultimate inscrutability consequently calls for the poetic riposte that in eternity experiences in music refigures time's ultimate unrepresentability. Hence, like the radiance of the sky's inestimable height, the alterity of an order that everywhere envelops us also hides itself in the "darkness of its all-sheltering breadth."[24]

By maintaining that music in which time is surpassed by its other marks out the boundaries between time and its other, I want to draw out how listening for the *One* that for the poet is the measure of this all-sheltering breadth acquires its unique specificity in music in answer to the aporia of time's inscrutability. Hölderlin, Heidegger tells us, "is perplexed by the exciting question: how can that which by its very nature remains hidden ever become a measure?"[25] According to him, for Hölderlin, it is only as this self-concealing other that God is the measure of our being. How, then, can we gauge this measure when the "god who remains unknown . . . must appear as the one who remains unknown"[26] in order to show "*himself* as the one who he is"?[27] How, in other words, can the sky's radiant height, turned as it is to the earth to which the upward glance is bound, give the measure of our manner of inhering in the world when the sight of the sky, which "remains alien to the god,"[28] is all that is familiar and accessible to us?

Heidegger's hierarchization of the levels of temporality provides a privileged point of access for a reflection on music's singular significance in refiguring the ultimate unrepresentability of time in this regard. By carrying over the familiar Augustinian problem of the threefold present, the temporalization of temporality reintroduces the enigma of the *distentio animi* via the unification and diversification of the three temporal ecstases while raising it to a higher degree of virulence. Ricoeur points out that, for Augustine, the thought of eternity functions as a limiting idea "against the horizon of which the experience of the *distentio animi* receives, on the ontological level, the negative mark of a lack or a defect in being."[29] The thought of eternity consequently highlights time's ontological deficiency by placing speculations on time "within the horizon of a limiting idea that forces us to think at once about time and about what is other than time."[30] Augustine's question, "What, then, is time?"[31] accordingly inaugurates a type of discourse for which every inquiry into the being of time operates under the aegis of the thought of time's other.

By succeeding in pointing to time's ultimately inscrutable character, the process of temporality's hierarchization brings to the fore the ontological difference that in Heidegger's thinking alongside Hölderlin's poem lies at the heart of the dimension on which the vis-à-vis of sky and earth depends. Having hierarchized the levels of temporality (within-time-ness, historicity, temporality), Heidegger raises the problem of temporalization as making possible the unity of the three temporal ecstases.[32] The dehiscence of the temporal ecstases (future, past, present) undermines this unity from within, thereby returning, so to speak, to the Augustinian paradox of the soul that distends itself across the present of the present, the present of the past, and the present of the future (*distentio animi*). What, Ricoeur then asks, do we "understand when we say with Heidegger that the 'most original temporalizing of temporality as such is Temporality'?"[33] Nothing, he says, unless we are "able to link the distinction between temporal and temporalizing to the ontological difference"[34] that in Augustine's meditations is the sign of the deficiency or lack that strikes at the heart of our experiences of time. Ricoeur accordingly adds that, by itself, "the distinction between temporal-being and temporality no longer designates a phenomenon accessible to hermeneutic phenomenology as such."[35]

By summing up our failure when it comes to thinking about time, the mutual occultation of phenomenological time, that is, the internal consciousness of the experience of time, and cosmological time, that is, time that is measured by the movement of external bodies and hence is conceived as an infinite succession of instantaneous "now" points, consequently sets the aporia of time's ultimate inscrutability in relief. When, in the process of recovering time's genuine constitution as regards the "primordial unity of the structure of care,"[36] Heidegger's analysis fails to abolish the ordinary representation of time, this aporia once again surges forth. The appeal to temporality's authentic structure (the highest of the three levels in the process of time's hierarchization) serves as guarantor of this analysis' primordial character. The aspect of the stretching along of a life between birth and death as constituted by Dasein accordingly belongs to the second level, historicity. The third level, within-time-ness, completes the structure of historicity from which it is also derived. Reckoning with the time of everyday affairs thus represents a leveling off of the most authentic level of temporality for Heidegger while remaining a feature of care.[37]

Asking whether Heidegger's quest for authenticity can "be carried out without a constant appeal to the testimony of the existentiell"[38] opens a space for exploring how the failure to which the aporia of time's inscrutability attests has a productive counterpart in the ways in which fiction, poetry, and music, for example, multiply our experiences of eternity. Ricoeur questions whether Heidegger's analysis is bound over to a personal conception of authenticity "on a level where it competes with other existentiell conceptions, those of Pascal or Kierkegaard—or that of Sartre—to say nothing of that of Augustine."[39] As the "supreme test of authenticity,"[40] resoluteness in being-toward-death bears the stamp of an ethical configuration borne out by the structure of care. Placing the thought of time under the limit of death as our ownmost possibility thus sets its own distinctive seal on the entire analysis that, "heavily influenced by the recoil-effect of the existentiell on the existential,"[41] imposes its own constraints.

The diversity of works that multiply our experiences of eternity stand as proof, so to speak, of the different ways in which music stakes out the boundaries between time and its other in answer to the aporia of time's ultimately inscrutable character. The eternity of the instant that in Arnold Schoenberg's *Erwartung* violently arrests the normative expectation of dissonance's resolution speaks not of the non-being of time but rather is an aesthetic harbinger of the temporal ecstases' radical dispersion. Berthold Hoeckner argues that the temporal paradox that in *Erwartung* springs from Schoenberg's emancipation of dissonance converts the *Eroica*'s "heroic fusion of an expansive reality into the eternal moment of the [Hegelian] 'good infinity'"[42] into its opposite. *Erwartung*'s ethos of anxious foreboding is no mere musical doubling of Marie Pappenheim's text, which Theodor W. Adorno regards as "dilettante in its language and structure."[43] On the contrary, through giving voice to a moment in which the tensive relation between future, past, and present is placed radically into suspense, *Erwartung* in its own way metes out the difference between the unity of the three temporal ecstases and their fragmentation and dispersion.

The two examples to which I previously referred, the Andante from Bach's *Sonata for Flute and Continuo* in E minor and the closing cadential formula of the finale in Glass's *Einstein on the Beach*, are markedly different in the ways that, like Schoenberg's *Erwartung*, they sound out the difference between time and its other. The crowning note of joy that in Bach's Andante gives voice to the presentiment of an abiding grace draws close to the threshold of religious aesthetics. The feeling of height that in religious experience attests to the glory of the infinite in the Andante sublimates the deficiency that places its stamp on our experiences of time. Bach's conviction that music's sole purpose was for the glory of God alone—*Soli Deo Gloria*—tasks music with this sublime vocation. The experience of "sin as *Angst*,"[44] which Jaroslav Pelikan remarks fuels Pietism's preoccupation with sin and death, has its existential root in the ontological difference between being and beings. Hence, only joy attests that, this difference notwithstanding, we have a part in being.[45] In contrast, anxiety is the affective sign of the deficiency that places its seal on the lack we feel in the face of the disproportion between the span of our mortal lives and an order of time that envelops it. The presentiment of abiding grace that in Bach's music replies to the Pietistic experience of sin gives voice to the anteriority, exteriority, and height of the Other that is the object of praise. Under the aegis of the glory of the infinite, this presentiment of abiding grace refigures time's ultimate unrepresentability in response to the ontological deficiency that places its seal on our temporally finite existence.

The music of the finale with which Glass's *Einstein on the Beach* concludes replies to the aporia of time's ultimate inscrutability in a distinctly different way. The contra-finality of the concluding cadential pattern transfixes the "time-honored closing"[46] that imposes a sense of temporal unity on traditional tonal works. Unlike Schoenberg's *Erwartung*, where the emancipation of dissonance places the normative expectation of dissonance's resolution radically into question, this recurring "cadential" formula transforms the traditional sense of closure into an endless ending. The recurring "cadential" formula, $f - D^b - B^{bb}/A - B - E$, begets its cyclic repetition by resolving a half-step below the harmony on which it begins. By consigning memory and anticipation to oblivion, the "apocalyptic grand finale"[47] in the concluding Spaceship scene bids farewell to all earthly bound existence. It is as though, by putting "forward the unpresentable in presentation itself"[48] in a manner that Jean-François Lyotard insists is the hallmark of the postmodern sentiment of the sublime, the contra-finality of this closing temporal gesture evokes the archaic rhythm of an immemorial beating that heralds the passage beyond.

This postmodern simulacrum of a time *in illo tempore* far from vacates the ontological difference to which the distinction between temporal being and the temporalizing of temporality points. For what sense could we make of this evocation of a "time beyond time" apart from the way that this temporal configuration of an endless ending refigures time's ultimate unrepresentability through staking out the borderlines between time and eternity? Eternity experiences that evoke a feeling of being "out of" or "beyond time" are accordingly no mere repetition or reduplication of an order the alterity of which is wholly alien to our experiences of it. On the contrary, like the god who in Hölderlin's poem Heidegger tells us "must by showing *himself* as the one he is, appear as the one who remains unknown,"[49] the alterity of an order that, like this god's manifest appearance makes itself felt only through ciphers and signs, remains mysterious in itself. Lyotard contends that, in contrast to the modernist nostalgia for reconciliation, the postmodern imparts a true sentiment of the sublime more violently through presenting the unpresentable. For him, the pure matter of sound thus reaches the subject only at the price of "surpassing, or 'sub-passing,' its capacity for synthetic activity."[50] We might wonder, however, whether the imagination's failure in the face of an order that exceeds its power to provide an adequate representation of it is in the end the sign of the subject's extinction. This negative judgment regarding the possibility of a subject "constituted according to the model of the *Ich denke* and the temporality required for theoretical thinking"[51] lays bare the abyss over which Nietzsche recommends casting an Apollonian veil. Lyotard's inversion of Kant's concept of the sublime privileges the excess that for Kant is initially contra-purposive with respect to the imagination's power to provide an adequate representation of its object. The subreption that for Kant replaces the idea of the humanity in us with a respect for the sublime object in nature consequently has its negative counterpart in the aestheticizing dissolution of the subject's capacity to draw a meaningful figure from tones, harmonies, timbres, and the like sounding in succession. The idea of "pure, punctual presence"[52] that for Lyotard vacates the imagination's schematizing power has its distinctive exemplar in the music that allegedly embodies itself as a "pure sound-event."[53] By evoking the sempiternal presence of an instant of time without past or future, the contra-finality of an ending without ending thus places its stamp on the crisis of time in accordance with the way that the feeling of being "out of" or "beyond" time expressed by it refigures time's ultimate unrepresentability.

By suggesting that music's refiguration of time's ultimate unrepresentability takes the measure of our temporal condition in answer to the aporia of time's inscrutable character, I want finally to highlight how Heidegger's thinking alongside Hölderlin's poem admits a place for poetry, music, fiction, and in general the work of art's power to transcend the given order of existence from within. The measure that poetry takes of the dimension meted out by spanning the "'on the earth' and the 'beneath the sky'"[54] acquires its significance and force through the way poetry builds up a world. This building up, however, is meaningful only because the world projected by the work renews our manner of thinking, feeling, and acting in accordance with itself. The truth to which the work lays claim through bringing forth a world expressed by it gives the measure of our mortal dwelling in this regard. This truth, I indicated previously, acquires it ontological vehemence only by reason of the work's worlding power. Only the measure consisting in the way that the sky reveals the god who remains unknown, Heidegger tells us, gauges our ownmost nature vis-à-vis the brevity of our stay on earth. By staking out the borderlines between time and eternity, music in which time itself is surpassed by its other gives the measure of the time on which the deficiency of the part we have in being places its seal.

AFFECTIVE RESONANCES

By asking how the measure that in eternity experiences in music marks out the difference between time and its other makes itself felt, I propose now to draw out the connection between music's temporal features and its affective power. The primordial attribute that Heidegger attributes to mood in revealing a manner of being "prior to all cognition and volition, and *beyond* their range of disclosure"[55] has its poetic counterpart in music, poetry, fiction, painting, and, indeed, all artworks' affective tonalities. The listener, reader, or spectator's pre- or hyper-predicative apprehension of the moods or feelings expressed by a tune, song, or piece of music has its corollary counterpart in the way in which tones, harmonies, and timbral combinations sounding in succession, for example, engender a melodic figure, a harmonic progression, or a rhythmic pattern's distinctive character. The building up of a world that in poetry takes the measure of our inherence in the world in music consequently brings to the fore the configuring operation from which, in a sense that I will explain, music's temporal features and affective attributes both spring.

In *Music, Time, and Its Other*, I noted how, for Alfred Schutz, the Eleatic paradox serves as a foil for the idea that music's temporal flux is irreducible to the ordinary representation of time as an infinite series of instantaneous "now" points.[56] For Schutz, the paradox—that, by reducing the trajectory of an arrow to a sequence of successive points, the arrow no longer flies—illustrates the weakness of representing music's temporal character through spatializing projections. The logical space of possible tonal relationships that Robert Morgan maintains comprises the "framework within which, and through which, the actual sequence of events is shaped"[57] privileges the concept of tonal space by reversing the order of priority between the configurating operation that in the experience of a work draws an expressive figure from a sequence of tones, for example, and the methodological abstraction of sets of tonal relations in this regard. Accordingly for Schutz, the "dimension of time in which the work of music exists"[58] is built up polythetically, as each successive impulse adds to shaping the temporal unity of music's ongoing temporal flux. The enigma of tonal motion that leads Carl Dahlhaus to set the "stretchings and shortenings of experienced time"[59] against a "fixed" temporal backdrop brings to the fore the seeming incommensurability of an external order of time as measured by the movement of the heavenly bodies (cosmological time) and the internal consciousness of the experience of time (phenomenological time) in this regard. By refusing to identify the inner time of the stream of consciousness as structured by music's ongoing flux with any spatial extension, Schutz rescinds time's dependence upon external movement. Conversely, by drawing upon Henri Bergson's concepts of *temps durée* and *temps espace*, Dahlhaus tries to resolve the enigma of the feeling of temporal motion by setting the *temps durée* against the *temps espace*, where time is imagined as being extended spatially, in order to account for a sense of movement, continuity, and change.

How, then, does a sequence of tones sounding in succession, for example, elicit the sensation of movement? And how does this succession of tones evoke a feeling or mood that a melody or tune, for instance, possesses? Schutz's remark that in listening to music we have the sense that a certain configuration structures music's ongoing flux is decisive in this regard.[60] A sequence of tones is one thing; a melodic figure is another. This figure is drawn from a sequence of tones sounding in succession by a listener who apprehends the fit of the melody or the tune. It is not by chance that the Oxford English Dictionary gives as one of the archaic definitions of the word "fit" a "piece of music; [or] a strain," where a strain is defined as a "musical sequence of sounds; a melody, a tune." By drawing a figure from a sequence of tones, the listener resolves the paradox stemming from the fact that tones that follow one another in succession do not move each time she hears the tune expressing its own distinctive character. A poem, Ricoeur reminds us, "is like a work of music in that its mood is exactly coextensive with the internal order of symbols articulated by its language."[61] Poetic language inverts the referential direction of ordinary language in giving a figure and a body to the mood that the poem. Accordingly, the retreat from the real that for romantic sensibilities was the sign of music's metaphysical dignity and for social critics was the cipher of the bourgeois cult of *Bildung* and its privileged life of ease is the condition of power to give voice to feelings and moods that only it possesses. Music, I will therefore maintain, expresses feelings and moods that are unique to it by exemplifying them.

Heidegger's claim that in "poetical discourse, the communication of the existential possibilities of one's state-of-mind can become an aim in itself, and [that] this amounts to a disclosing of existence"[62] lends support to the idea that music renews our manner of inhering in the world through exemplifying feelings and moods to which it gives voice. We might therefore wonder if Heidegger excludes "feeling from world-disclosure,"[63] as Andrew Bowie remarks. Bowie himself finds this alleged exclusion implausible, arguing that Heidegger's idea of mood would be better characterized as "'attunedness' (*Gestimmtheit*) . . ., which makes the musical connotation more explicit,"[64] as he remarks Heinrich Bessler maintains. For Heidegger,

> Only because the "senses" [*die Sinne*] belong ontologically to an entity whose kind of being is being-in-the-world with a state-of-mind, can they be "touched" by anything or "have a sense for" [*Sinn haben für*] something in such a way that what touches them shows itself in an affect.[65]

The primacy of hearing over seeing for which Hans-Georg Gadamer argues in defining the "idea of belonging (*Zugehörigkeit*) as accurately as possible"[66] has a corollary counterpart in the way that feelings and moods expressed by music augment affective dimensions of our experiences in this regard. Listening to a work and hearing this temporally sounding phenomenon as expressing the properties that the work itself possesses bears out the latter's phenomenological priority. Heidegger accordingly stresses that "Dasein hears because it understands."[67] Hence for him, "it requires a very artificial and complicated frame of mind to 'hear' a 'pure noise.'"[68] More crucially still, by delivering Dasein over to the manner in which it is disclosed as already there in the world, moods manifest the state in which it finds itself. These moods are the ontic signatures of a "state-of-mind."[69] As such, moods constitute the fundamental structure of our being-attuned to the world. Thrownness, Heidegger explains, refers to the "facticity of its [Dasein's] being delivered over"[70] to its being-in-the-world. Consequently, "Dasein is always brought before itself, and has always found itself . . . in the sense of finding itself in the mood that it has."[71]

Could we then say that, by building up a world that is unique to it, a musical work augments the range of possibilities of being-attuned to the world in accordance with the properties it possesses? Moods, Heidegger emphasizes, assail us. As such, a mood "makes it possible first of all to direct oneself toward something."[72] If, as he maintains, a mood "comes neither from 'outside' nor from 'inside,' but arises out of being-in-the-world, as a way of such being,"[73] the act of bringing forth something that previously did not exist takes on a distinctively unique significance when it comes to the affective attributes of music, poetry, fiction, and works of art, broadly conceived. No work expresses a world without also exemplifying a feeling or atmosphere emanating from and illuminating that world, as Mikel Dufrenne has told us.[74] Music is exceptional in this respect. By drawing together tones, harmonic sonorities, impulses, timbral combinations, and the like, music's temporal configuration of melodic lines, harmonic progressions, rhythmic articulations, and changing colors gives a body to properties that have only feelings and moods as their referents. Ricoeur's account of feeling's intentional structure provides a helpful guide in this regard. Feeling, he explains, "designates qualities felt *on* things, *on* persons, *on* the world"[75] at the same time that it manifests the way in which we are inwardly affected by them. Feeling's intentional correlates are consequently qualities founded on the objects on which they appear. These intentional correlates "cannot be separated from the representative moments"[76] of the thing since they are floating qualifiers without any autonomy of their own. The poetic metamorphosis that elevates everyday feelings in poetry and fiction, for example, in music accordingly sounds out possibilities for our manner of inhering in the world in its purest state. The affective tonality that a work establishes in us, so to speak, through the experience occasioned by it thus touches us by affecting us inwardly as a coloring of the soul. The communicability of feelings and moods exemplified through the manner in which a work's constitutive elements cohere in this way fulfills the aim of poetic discourse, as Heidegger tells us, through disclosing possibilities of states-of-mind that attune us to the world in ways that only the work itself can.

Could we then say that, at the limit, music opens us to the world and us to the world anew in answer to the aporia of time's ultimate inscrutability? By taking the measure of the dimension in which our temporal existence stands in marked contrast to the alterity of an order that, escaping our will to mastery, exceeds our capacity to think about time, eternity experiences in music refigure time's ultimate unrepresentability in answer to the ontological difference between being and our part in it. Every work that evokes time's surpassing by its other has its mood. Music's refiguration of its ultimate unrepresentability thus touches the heart of our mortal existence through coloring time with a feeling or mood. "Dasein's openness to the world," Heidegger tells us, "is constituted existentially by the attunement of a state-of-mind."[77] The role moods play in bringing "Dasein before the 'that-it-is' of its 'there'"[78] thus has its distinctive vis-à-vis in music's express exemplification of feelings and moods that augment the primordial feature of Dasein's manner of inhering in the world.

CONCLUSION: TOUCHED BY MUSIC

I would like in conclusion to offer a few further remarks in reference to the title of my chapter regarding the significance of Heidegger's philosophical investigations for our understanding of music's affective power. Previously, I noted how, for him, the capacity to sense something and be touched by it is the condition of Dasein's being-in-the-world. Moreover, having the sense for something and being touched by it manifests itself in an affect that inclines us to act. Touch, Jean-Luc Nancy tells us, "sets something in motion."[79] Through touch, we are assured of the certainty of our own existence as much as that of the external world, people, and things in it. Ricouer accordingly stresses that touch reveals the flesh's characteristic aptitude for feeling. One's flesh, he therefore explains, "is most originally mine and of all things that which is closest"[80] as one's own. An ontology for which the otherness of the flesh is indicative of the flesh's primordiality with respect to our projects, plans, and designs highlights the distinction between flesh and body. The capacity for being affected through touch is consequently inscribed in the mode of our incarnation in the world. Richard Kearney emphasizes that touching things and people in the world and being touched by them are reciprocally related, binding together the act directed toward an object or person and the way in which the self is inwardly affected.[81] For him, the chiasma of the flesh is therefore "an ontological 'element' in which we already find ourselves—sensing and sensed, speaking and spoken at once,"[82] where the crossings between the act of reaching out, touching, and embracing others and the world and one's ownmost intimate (self-)affection occur.

The capacity for being affected, which I just indicated is characteristic of the flesh's aptitude for feeling, is accordingly the *conditio per quam* of music's affective force. By liberating the lived body from objectifying representations, an ontology of the flesh thus brings to the fore the fundamental experience at the root of music's expressive power. The modalities of passivity that for Ricoeur attest to the otherness of the other in the first instance spring from the intimacy of the experience of one's own body.[83] By registering the nuance of things, feelings reveal how we are affected by the world and people and things in it through being attuned to them. Music is most profoundly human when, in taking the measure of our temporal condition, it touches the fundament of our mortal existence. In answer to the aporia that springs forth at the moment that our effort to constitute time runs up against an order that outstrips it, music reverberates with feelings that resonate with the manner in which we rediscover as if for the first time our inherence in the world. In this way, music's refiguration of time's ultimate unrepresentability takes the measure that Heidegger tells us poetry takes stands as a riposte to the deficiency that strikes at the heart of our experiences of time. Touched by music, feelings and moods evoked in us are the ciphers of the avowal that, despite the ontological difference that separates us from being, we have a part in it through the givenness—the gift—of existence.

NOTES

1. Martin Heidegger, *Poetry, Language, Thought*, trans. Albert Hofstadter (New York: Harper and Row, 1971), 221–222.
2. Heidegger, *Poetry, Language, Thought*, 44.
3. Heidegger, *Poetry, Language, Thought*, 44.
4. Cf. Martin Heidegger, "Letter on Humanism," in *Basic Writings*, ed. David Farrell Krell (New York: HarperCollins, 1993), 230.
5. Rentmeester discusses Heidegger's interpretation of Van Gogh's shoes in the previous chapter.
6. Heidegger, *Poetry, Language, Thought*, 39.
7. Heidegger, *Poetry, Language, Thought*, 57.
8. Heidegger, *Poetry, Language, Thought*, 57.
9. Heidegger, *Poetry, Language, Thought*, 58.
10. Heidegger, *Poetry, Language, Thought*, 59.
11. Heidegger, *Poetry, Language, Thought*, 52.
12. Heidegger, *Poetry, Language, Thought*, 61. Heidegger explains that "[c]learing of openness and establishment in the Open belong together. They are the same single nature of the happening of truth" (61).
13. See Heidegger, *Poetry, Language, Thought*, 76; cf. Paul Ricoeur, François Azouvi, and Marc de Launay, *Critique and Conviction: Conversations with François Azouvi and Marc de Launay*, trans. Kathleen Blamey (New York: Columbia University Press, 1998), 173–174.
14. Heidegger, *Poetry, Language, Thought*, 77.
15. See Hans-George Gadamer, *Truth and Method*, 2nd rev. ed., trans. Joel Weinsheimer and Donald G. Marshall (New York: Crossroad, 1989), 110–113.
16. Roger W. H. Savage, *Music, Time, and Its Other: Aesthetic Reflections on Finitude, Temporality, and Alterity* (Abingdon, Oxon: Routledge, 2018).
17. Paul Ricoeur, *Time and Narrative*, vol. 3, trans. Kathleen Blamey and David Pellauer (Chicago: University of Chicago Press, 1988), 271.
18. Heidegger, *Poetry, Language, Thought*, 215.
19. Heidegger, *Poetry, Language, Thought*, 215.
20. Heidegger, *Poetry, Language, Thought*, 214.
21. Heidegger, *Poetry, Language, Thought*, 214.
22. Heidegger, *Poetry, Language, Thought*, 37.

23. Heidegger, *Poetry, Language, Thought*, 220.
24. Heidegger, *Poetry, Language, Thought*, 226.
25. Heidegger, *Poetry, Language, Thought*, 222.
26. Heidegger, *Poetry, Language, Thought*, 222.
27. Heidegger, *Poetry, Language, Thought*, 222.
28. Heidegger, *Poetry, Language, Thought*, 225.
29. Paul Ricoeur, *Time and Narrative*, vol. 1, trans. Kathleen McLaughlin and David Pellauer (Chicago: Chicago University Press, 1984), 26.
30. Ricoeur, *Time and Narrative*, vol. 1, 22.
31. Saint Bishop of Hippo Augustine, *Confessions*, trans. R. S. Pine-Coffin (New York: Penguin Books, 1961), 264.
32. Ricouer, *Time and Narrative*, vol. 3, 255.
33. Ricoeur, *Time and Narrative*, vol. 3, 270; see Martin Heidegger, *The Basic Problems of Phenomenology*, rev. ed., trans. Albert Hofstadter (Bloomington, IL: Indiana University Press, 1982), 302.
34. Ricoeur, *Time and Narrative*, vol. 3, 270.
35. Ricoeur, *Time and Narrative*, vol. 3, 270.
36. Martin Heidegger, *Being and Time*, trans. John Macquarrie and Edward Robinson (New York: Harper and Row, 1962), 375. Original in italics.
37. See Ricoeur, *Time and Narrative*, vol. 3, 80 ff.
38. Ricoeur, *Time and Narrative*, vol. 3, 65. The distinction between the existentiell and the existential is critical to Heidegger's phenomenological investigation into Dasein as that entity that asks into the meaning of its own existence. Whereas the analysis of the existentiell relies on ontic determinations of experience, the analysis of the existential seeks to uncover the fundamental structures underlying these determinations. See Heidegger, *Being and Time*, 33; 312ff.
39. Ricoeur, *Time and Narrative*, vol. 3, 67.
40. Ricoeur, *Time and Narrative*, vol. 3, 67.
41. Ricoeur, *Time and Narrative*, vol. 3, 67.
42. Berthold Hoeckner, *Programming the Absolute: Nineteenth-Century German Music and the Hermeneutics of the Moment* (Princeton, NJ: Princeton University Press, 2002), 198.
43. Theodor W. Adorno, *Prisms*, trans. Samuel and Shierry Weber (Cambridge, MA: MIT Press, 1967), 163.
44. Jaroslav Pelikan, *Bach Among the Theologians* (Eugene, OR: Wipf and Stock, 1986), 61; see Paul Ricoeur, *Freedom and Nature: The Voluntary and the Involuntary*, trans. Erazim V. Kohák (Evanston, IL: Northwestern University Press, 1966), 462.
45. See Paul Ricoeur, *Fallible Man*, trans. Charles A. Kelbley (New York: Fordham University Press, 1986), 106.
46. Philip Glass, *Music by Philip Glass*, ed. Robert T. Jones (New York: Harper and Row Publishers, 1987), 60.
47. Glass, *Music by Philip Glass*, 33.
48. Jean-François Lyotard, *The Postmodern Condition: A Report on Knowledge*, trans. Geoff Bennington and Brian Massumi (Minneapolis: University of Minnesota Press, 1984), 81.

49. Heidegger, *Poetry, Language, Thought*, 222.

50. Jean-François Lyotard, *The Inhuman: Reflections on Time*, trans. Geoffrey Bennington and Rachel Bowlby (Cambridge: Polity Press, 1991), 156.

51. Jean-François Lyotard, *Lessons on the Analytic of the Sublime: (Kant's Critique of Judgement §§23–29)*, trans. Elizabeth Rottenberg (Stanford: Stanford University Press, 1994), 23; see Lyotard, *The Postmodern Condition*, 21–22.

52. Lyotard, *The Inhuman*, 156; Lyotard, *The Postmodern Condition*, 21.

53. Philip Glass, cited in Wim Mertens, *American Minimal Music: La Monte Young, Terry Riley, Steve Reich, Philip Glass*, trans. J. Hautekiet (London: Kahn and Averill, 1983), 88.

54. Heidegger, *Poetry, Language, Thought*, 223.

55. Heidegger, *Being and Time*, 175.

56. Savage, *Music, Time, and Its Other*, 29–30.

57. Robert P. Morgan, "Musical Time/Musical Space," *Critical Inquiry* 6, no. 3 (1980): 529.

58. Alfred Schutz, "Fragments on the Phenomenology of Music," ed. Fred Kersten, *Music and Man* 2 (1976), 31.

59. Carl Dahlhaus, *Esthetics of Music*, trans. William Austin (New York: Cambridge University Press, 1982), 74–75.

60. Schutz, "Fragments," 31; see Roman Ingarden, *The Work of Music and the Problem of Its Identity*, trans. Adam Czerniawski (Berkeley: University of California Press, 1986), 90 ff.

61. Paul Ricoeur, *Interpretation Theory: Discourse and the Surplus of Meaning* (Fort Worth, TX: Texas Christian University Press, 1976), 59.

62. Heidegger, *Being and Time*, 205.

63. Andrew Bowie, *Music, Philosophy and Modernity* (Cambridge: Cambridge University Press, 2007), 303.

64. Bowie, *Music, Philosophy and Modernity*, 297.

65. Heidegger, *Being and Time*, 176–177.

66. Gadamer, *Truth and Method*, 462.

67. Heidegger, *Being and Time*, 206.

68. Heidegger, *Being and Time*, 207.

69. See Heidegger, *Being and Time*, 172.

70. Heidegger, *Being and Time*, 174. Original in italics.

71. Heidegger, *Being and Time*, 174.

72. Heidegger, *Being and Time*, 176. Original in italics.

73. Heidegger, *Being and Time*, 176.

74. Mikel Dufrenne, *The Phenomenology of Aesthetic Experience*, trans. Edward S. Casey et al. (Evanston, IL: Northwestern University Press, 1973).

75. Ricoeur, *Fallible Man*, 84.

76. Ricoeur, *Fallible Man*, 84.

77. Heidegger, *Being and Time*, 176.

78. Heidegger, *Being and Time*, 175.

79. Jean-Luc Nancy, "Rethinking Corpus," in *Carnal Hermeneutics*, trans. Richard Kearney and Brian Treanor (New York: Fordham University Press, 2015), 85.

80. Paul Ricoeur, *Oneself as Another*, trans. Kathleen Blamey (Chicago: University of Chicago Press, 1992), 324.

81. Richard Kearney, "The Wager of Carnal Hermeneutics," in *Carnal Hermeneutics*, ed. Richard Kearney and Brian Treanor (New York: Fordham University Press, 2015), 15–56.

82. Kearney, "The Wager of Carnal Hermeneutics," 38.

83. See Ricoeur, *Oneself as Another*, 319–329.

BIBLIOGRAPHY

Adorno, Theodor W. *Prisms*. Translated by Samuel and Shierry Weber. Cambridge, MA: MIT Press, 1967.

Augustine, Saint Bishop of Hippo. *Confessions*. Translated by R. S. Pine-Coffin. New York: Penguin Books, 1961.

Bowie, Andrew. *Music, Philosophy and Modernity*. Cambridge: Cambridge University Press, 2007.

Dahlhaus, Carl. *Esthetics of Music*. Translated by William Austin. New York: Cambridge University Press, 1982.

Dufrenne, Mikel. *The Phenomenology of Aesthetic Experience*. Translated by Edward S. Casey, Albert A. Anderson, Willis Domingo, and Leon Jackobson. Evanston, IL: Northwestern University Press, 1973.

Glass, Philip. *Music by Philip Glass*. Edited by Robert T. Jones. New York: Harper and Row Publishers, 1987.

Heidegger, Martin. *The Basic Problems of Phenomenology*. Revised Edition. Translated by Albert Hofstadter. Bloomington, IL: Indiana University Press, 1982.

Heidegger, Martin. *Being and Time*. Translated by John Macquarrie and Edward Robinson. New York: Harper and Row, 1962.

Heidegger, Martin. "Letter on Humanism." In *Basic Writings*, edited by David Farrell Krell, 217–265. New York: HarperCollins, 1993.

Heidegger, Martin. *Poetry, Language, Thought*. Translated by Albert Hofstadter. New York: Harper and Row, 1971.

Hoeckner, Berthold. *Programming the Absolute: Nineteenth-Century German Music and the Hermeneutics of the Moment*. Princeton, NJ: Princeton University Press, 2002.

Ingarden, Roman. *The Work of Music and the Problem of Its Identity*. Translated by Adam Czerniawski. Berkeley: University of California Press, 1986.

Kearney, Richard. "The Wager of Carnal Hermeneutics." In *Carnal Hermeneutics*, edited by Richard Kearney and Brian Treanor, 15–56. New York: Fordham University Press, 2015.

Lyotard, Jean-François. *The Inhuman: Reflections on Time*. Translated by Geoffrey Bennington and Rachel Bowlby. Cambridge: Polity Press, 1991.

Lyotard, Jean-François. *Lessons on the Analytic of the Sublime: (Kant's Critique of Judgement §§23–29)*. Translated by Elizabeth Rottenberg. Stanford: Stanford University Press, 1994.

Lyotard, Jean-François. *The Postmodern Condition: A Report on Knowledge*. Translated by Geoff Bennington and Brian Massumi. Minneapolis, MN: University of Minnesota Press, 1984.

Mertens, Wim. *American Minimal Music: La Monte Young, Terry Riley, Steve Reich, Philip Glass*. Translated by J. Hautekiet. London: Kahn and Averill, 1983.

Morgan, Robert P. "Musical Time/Musical Space." *Critical Inquiry* 6, no. 3 (1980): 527–538.

Nancy, Jean-Luc. "Rethinking Corpus." In *Carnal Hermeneutics*, edited by Richard Kearney and Brian Treanor, 77–91. New York: Fordham University Press, 2015.

Pelikan, Jaroslav. *Bach Among the Theologians*. Eugene, OR: Wipf and Stock, 1986.

Ricoeur, Paul. *Fallible Man*. Translated by Charles A. Kelbley. New York: Fordham University Press, 1986.

Ricoeur, Paul. *Freedom and Nature: The Voluntary and the Involuntary*. Translated by Erazim V. Kohák. Evanston, IL: Northwestern University Press, 1966.

Ricoeur, Paul. *Interpretation Theory: Discourse and the Surplus of Meaning*. Fort Worth, TX: Texas Christian University Press, 1976.

Ricoeur, Paul. *Oneself as Another*. Translated by Kathleen Blamey. Chicago: University of Chicago Press, 1992.

Ricoeur, Paul. *Time and Narrative*. Vol. 1. Translated by Kathleen McLaughlin and David Pellauer. Chicago: University of Chicago Press, 1984.

Ricoeur, Paul. *Time and Narrative*. Vol. 3. Translated by Kathleen Blamey and David Pellauer. Chicago: University of Chicago Press, 1988.

Ricoeur, Paul François Azouvi, and Marc de Launay. *Critique and Conviction: Conversations with François Azouvi and Marc de Launay*. Translated by Kathleen Blamey. New York: Columbia University Press, 1998.

Savage, Roger W. H. *Music, Time, and Its Other: Aesthetic Reflections on Finitude, Temporality, and Alterity*. Abingdon, Oxon: Routledge, 2018.

Schutz, Alfred. "Fragments on the Phenomenology of Music." Edited by Fred Kersten. *Music and Man* 2 (1976): 5–71.

Chapter 16

Remembering Air in Schilingi's Generative Music

Heideggerian Reflections on Argo *and* Terra

Jill Drouillard

Jacopo Baboni Schilingi's interactive musical compositions *Argo* and *Terra* play with time, space, and material sound to capture a symbiotic relationship between technology and the most intimate process fundamental to life: breathing. *Argo* reacts to the artist's respiration in "real time," generating an "infinite" sequence of diverse musical arrangements that question the relation between the human body and technology and contingency and programming. Noting the egotistical tendencies of artists, Schilingi likens himself to Odysseus, the master of *Argo*, the name given to his faithful technological invention. This theme of mastery is revisited in *Terra* where Schilingi's hands, covered in sensors, manipulate both the musical composition and the dance movements of a female body, a body whose fertile tension both emerges and withdraws in a battle akin to Heidegger's earth/world strife. This chapter provides a hermeneutic reading of *Argo* and *Terra* within a Heideggerian framework that does not, as Luce Irigaray has noted, forget air. Irigaray states, "Air does not show itself. As such, it escapes as (a) being. It allows itself to be forgotten."[1] Schilingi's generative music makes air visible and hauntingly audible, as the music can only be stopped when the artist's life comes to an end.

*AIR IS ALWAYS THERE, BUT MAN CAN
ONLY SEE WHAT HE CAN MASTER*

In *The Forgetting of Air in Martin Heidegger*, Luce Irigaray criticizes Heidegger for privileging language as the essential site disclosive of being. In referring to language as the "house of being,"[2] Heidegger forgets the sheltering agent of air, an element associated with the feminine in its inability to be properly thought. Throughout the body of her work, Irigaray has focused on the ontological concept of sexual difference and how *at least two* sexes are responsible for infinite becoming. Unfortunately, throughout the history of western philosophy, the feminine side of this dialectic has been silenced and assimilated to a universal masculine understanding of being. Air is everywhere and necessary for life, yet it largely remains invisible. The feminine, too, is a ubiquitous and necessary part of becoming, yet it is covered over insofar as we think the question of being can be answered by turning to language (*phallogocentrism*).[3] While I agree with Irigaray's critique of Heidegger, I also find aspects of his philosophy useful for trying to recover what has been silenced. Thus, in this chapter, while I reproach Heidegger for his "forgetting," I also apply his thought to a hermeneutic reading of Jacopo Baboni Schilingi's generative music projects, *Argo* (2018) and *Terra* (2018), to try to remember what air and the feminine can tell us about being.

Irigaray says that a man has erected *logos* in order to forget the mutuality of air. Western philosophers, Heidegger included, forget that air is prior to any discourse and is a prerequisite for the latter.[4] Like the mother tongue that precedes initiation into the law of the father, air has a quality that cannot be made visible. We can feel a gust of wind or become cognizant of our breathing pattern, but air is not something directly under our gaze as something easily objectifiable. Irigaray says because it cannot be grasped as an object of comprehension, it resists being controlled as part of the standing reserve (*Bestand*), Heidegger's term for the way we perceive beings in the world as an amalgam of resources ready to be calculated, ordered, and exploited for their future utility.[5] Air is always there, but man can only see what he can master. If the feminine is like air in its inability to be properly thought (and objectified), can the feminine likewise resist being mastered? Would being receptive to such a feminine presence allow us to rethink the question of being?

Throughout his work, Heidegger has posed the question of being through his thinking on temporality, affective states (moods), language (poetry), technology, and art. Although in *Being and Time* he tends to privilege the individual over the relational, referring to the former as capable of a more authentic being-in-the-*world*, in his later work, world is no longer a solitary concept but always thought alongside *earth*.[6] The tension of this duality and its relation to moods, technology, art, and language is apparent in *Argo* and *Terra*, as these works remember air and the feminine by making them visible and audible. While *Argo* explores the moods of the individual, *Terra*, whose subtitle is "a tribute to the status of woman," captures a tension akin to Heidegger's earth/world strife, an antagonism that does not neglect the sexuate nature of this relation. Thus, in this chapter, I read Heidegger alongside Schilingli's performance pieces, as there is a progression in both bodies of work to move from an individual account to a relational understanding of being. Moving in between Heidegger's early ontology and his later works and in between *Argo* and *Terra* opens space to uncover the feminine.

ARGO

In 2017, Schilingi began his performance art piece *Argo*, a generative music project that creates a non-repetitive infinite sequence of music, or at least until the artist stops breathing. Schilingli will wear a respiratory sensor[7] encircled around his torso every day until his death to capture his breathing patterns that are then translated into semantic functions, a form of code, that are calculated via programmed algorithms. These algorithms create diverse musical sounds, as daily breathing patterns are never repeatable and produce a visual display of aleatory intricate webs (see figure 16.1). These webs appear as a 3D spheroid representing the perpetual movement of the artist's body and breath. According to Schilingi, *Argo* questions the relationship between man and the machine, between the human body and that of robots, and between contingency and programming.[8]

Figure 16.1 Still Image from the Film by Claude Mossessian, "Jacopo Baboni Schilingli Argo." *Source:* Directed by Claude Mossessian *Jacopo Baboni Schilingli Argo* Grand Palais, June 19, 2018.

Argo was first performed at the Grand Palais during an exhibition titled *Artistes et Robots*, an exposition that explored the relation between nature (*physis*) and technology *(techne)* and what we consider art during our current era when these lines so seldom blur. Given Heidegger's philosophy that questions this *physis/techne* distinction, particularly as it plays out in defining the artwork, any one of the pieces on display could lend themselves to his scrutiny, and yet, *Argo* "astounded" me.[9] While Heidegger is critical of technology and its ideology that treats the world as a standing reserve, he says a "saving power" may be found in technology if we view it as art. Such a view entails being astounded in such a way that invites questioning that reveals a certain truth (of being) outside of the mastery of the standing reserve.[10] Here, I present my interpretation of *Argo* and the questioning it evoked.

When I first encountered *Argo*, I immediately remarked the religious quality of its sound, ethereal, enlightening, yet ominous. A sound that at once makes you feel like a part of something larger and yet small. Schilingi's breathing is translated into sounds that reminded me of a choir at mass; there is a celestial sound that perhaps stems from a synthesizer, as well as waves of breathing, and the whistling of a flute. While not all sounds are immediately perceptible, they are all the result of some form of activity that requires breath. I could hear the music before any visible confirmation of where it was coming from. I had to climb the stairs of an actual palace with high-vaulted cathedral-like ceilings to locate the origin of the sound. What seemed like voices that conjured feelings of revelation and requiem were audible as I journeyed to find the origin of the artwork.

Heidegger ends "The Origin of the Work of Art" with a cautionary piece of poetry by Friedrich Hölderlin called "The Journey," including the line "that which dwells near its origin abandons the site."[11] I take this to be a critique of causality and the impossibility of locating any one cause. In "The Question Concerning Technology," one of Heidegger's main critiques of our technological era is that our calculating ideology favors a singular efficient cause, neglecting the co-responsibility of Aristotle's four causes (material, formal, efficient, final).[12] What this means is that rather than understand how matter, idea, producer, and purpose come together to create something—in this case the artwork—we immediately view the artist, the master, as that which is responsible for its being. Simply locating the origin of the sound and reading about the artist and his intentions cannot tell all regarding the artwork. There is a certain givenness of the artistic material, as well as a specific reception on the part of the one who becomes "astounded" by it. So, while I do at times reference statements made by the artist, what I present here details my own reception of the artwork.

Argo is so named after *Argos*, the loyal dog of Odysseus. Explaining the reasoning behind this title, Schilingi highlights the "egotistical tendencies of artists."[13] Schilingi is Argo's master who travels around the world while his faithful technology awaits at home recording his every breath. The narcissistic nature of the creator is once again referenced during a question and answer session when an audience member asks Schilingi why he describes *Argo* and *Terra* as projects that generate music sequences "forever."[14] Forever insinuates that the artist will never die, once again pointing to the invincible nature of the master. Is *Argo* a testament to man's will to mastery, to create something in his own image to last forever? Does Schilingi succeed in making visible that which stubbornly refuses to show itself (air)? I read *Argo* as a display of man's grappling with his mortality, as a longing to preserve that which will surely one day run out: breath. I will argue that *Argo*, like Heidegger's initial question of being, is very individualized and not yet ready to breach the unthought feminine.

Schilingi describes *Argo* as an homage to breathing, noting respiration is significant in revealing aspects of human identity. *Argo* is a surrogate for his moods, creating an array of sequences based on whether he is stressed, curious, or calmly drinking tea. Every mood conjugates to a breathing pattern that is registered and translated into a musical arrangement. One can thus hear and see heightened states of agitation and calm. According to Heidegger, moods are revelatory of our being-in-the-world. They are part of the existential constitution of our factical "being there" and of our thrownness.[15] Heidegger asserts that "mood makes manifest 'how one is, and how one is faring' [*wie einem ist und wird*]. In this 'how one is,' having a mood brings Being to its 'there.'"[16] Dasein always has a mood and orients itself in the world accordingly. That is, things matter to us and disclose themselves to us as such based on our affective state. By visually mapping and musically translating his moods, can *Argo* tell us anything ontologically disclosive about Schilingi's being? Coincidentally, the mood has been translated from the German *Stimmung*, which originally means the tuning of a musical instrument.[17] Like an instrument that must be "in tune" to be properly translated, Heidegger argues that our understanding of the world must be perceived from a certain state of "attunement." My understanding of the world is in harmony with my affective state, so a mood of sadness may adversely affect my experience of being-in-the-world. This means that *Stimmung* has a relational aspect. When my musical instrument is in tune, I am at a pitch that allows me to accord with other instruments. On the one hand, Heidegger recognizes this interdependence as he notes that our being-in-the-world is always a being-with-others, and yet he still seeks a more "authentic" mood of understanding that can only be realized as an individual. This "individualized" mood is experienced as anxiety whereby I am held out to the nothingness of my death.

The sound of *Argo* has a haunting quality and invites its audience to contemplate their mortality, that which produces the most "authentic" being-in-the-world. Likewise, the spheroid visual that accompanies the audio plays on the contingency of life with its constant unrepeatable patterns. Furthermore, at a certain moment, the webs on the screen appear to morph into hourglass shapes, representing the very notion of time. Schilingi says *Argo* is an homage to breathing, a praise of respiration. As an homage, does it recognize air as the element most fundamental to life? Does Schilingi try to represent air in an attempt to master it? By saying that *Argo* generates music *forever*, is he revealing his finitude or expressing a desire to achieve immortality? These questions will be answered once we turn to Heidegger's discussion of how the artwork is "set up" as a "praise," for insofar as *Argo* is a "praise" of respiration, inquiring into this praise will offer us insights into how this work of art is "set up."

Heidegger notes that when a work is brought into a collection or placed in an exhibition, we say that the artwork is "set up," yet such setting up only explains the display of the work in superficial terms. The artwork is not "set up" as mere "presence" but as a "praise." In setting up the work, "the holy is opened up as holy and the god is invoked into the openness of his presence."[18] The work, in its presence, opens up a world, the "ever-nonobjective to which we are subject as long as the paths of birth and death, blessing and curse keep us transported into being."[19] As the aptly titled "The Origin of the Work of Art" suggests, Heidegger is interested in what makes art an *art*, what makes it present itself as such. Heidegger's religious references of praise, holy, and the gods can be thought of in terms of an epiphany. *Aha!* I have an epiphany, and something comes to light. The Christian holiday Epiphany is the day when the three kings visited baby Jesus; it was only after this day that the birth of Christ was acknowledged, when that which was hitherto invisible was made visible. And so too, like an epiphany, the artwork in its presence, in "the reflected glory of this splendor there glows, i.e., there clarifies what we called the world."[20] The artwork thus tells us something about our world that before its "setting up" had remained unknown.

Heidegger says "art is the setting-into-work of truth" and "art lets truth originate"; yet the world that is revealed, that is made visible, cannot be said to reveal any truth in an absolute or originary way. Insofar as we think of origin as singular in nature, stemming from some sort of cause, there is no "origin" of the work of art. Art reveals the truth of our historical situation, and each era produces its own myths of creation, its own causal foundation. As Heidegger states,

> This foundation happened in the West for the first time in Greece. What was in the future to be called being was set into work, setting the standard. The realm of beings thus opened up was then transformed into a being in the sense of God's creation. This happened in the Middle Ages. This kind of being was again

transformed at the beginning and during the course of the modern age. Beings became objects that could be controlled and penetrated by calculation. At each time a new and essential world irrupted.[21]

Here we see how different periods of history present different causal explanations of being, and how these origin stories can be portrayed in the artworks of the time. In the Middle Ages, religion was viewed as the cause and this is reflected in visual displays of Christianity. In the modern era, the focus was replaced on the individual and rational thought, and this return to the humanism of the Ancient Greeks can be seen in pieces from the "renaissance" (rebirth). Our current technological era is ruled by an ideological framework that Heidegger calls enframing (*Gestell*) where we approach the world as an amalgam of resources ready to be exploited as part of the standing reserve (*Bestand*).[22] Nature is viewed in terms of its future utility, as its elements are stockpiled and on hold for later use. The sun is challenged forth for its heat and the Rhine provides the supply for a hydroelectric plant.[23] Does the art of our era reveal our ideology of enframing? Does it set up the truth of how our era conceives of being as that which can be known via calculations based on utility? *Argo* does disclose this way of thinking insofar as Schilingi tries to capture important aspects of human identity through calculating and translating his breathing into musical algorithms. Does representing air on a visual screen or via audible patterns allow Schilingi to feel like he understands that which resists grounding?

As previously mentioned, Irigaray argues that because of its inability to be comprehended as an object of inquiry, air resists being a part of the standing reserve. And yet, Schilingi makes air audibly and visually perceptible. Is everything, even the most elusive element, now enframed? That is, is air, one of the most natural of elements, only to be understood through technological intervention? One reading of *Argo* could view Schilingi as trying to "tame" or "master" air, catching that fluid element that is everywhere and yet impossible to grasp. Heidegger writes: "Being is the emptiest and at the same time a surplus, out of which all beings, those that are familiar and experienced as well as those unfamiliar and yet to be experienced, are granted their respective modes of being."[24] Being is everywhere in that everything "is," and yet qualifying what this "is" *is* requires turning being into an object. Because being cannot be objectified and such objectification is required for our understanding, being is empty, devoid of meaning. Air, too, is like this. It is everywhere, even when we perceive empty space.

Schilingi says air (*le souffle*) has been badly translated by Judeo-Christian religions to *anima/âme*, implying it is not the soul but breath that gives us existence (being).[25] This statement is much in line with Heidegger's point that each era has its own understanding of being and that such understanding is made visible in the artwork. In the Middle Ages, the body was thought to be animated by the soul and so the origin of our existence was depicted in religious artifacts. *Argo* is a product of a scientific era that can capture our last breath as we flatline. *Argo* could not have been possible in any other era of time, and so tells us something intimate about our historical situation, about the relation between man and machine.

Schilingi describes himself as the master of *Argo*, and yet he remains intricately bound to it; he literally wears a sensor that encircles his entire torso. *Argo* represents an aspect of his existence that he can never evade. While Schilingi muses that *Argo*'s musical arrangement lasts forever, this technology makes the artist's finitude hauntingly audible. On the one hand, the unpredictability of the musical arrangement highlights a contingency of existence that resists attempts at programming. On the other hand, such attempts highlight our will for necessity, for grounding, for something that endures. Schilingi's art uncovers something essential about human identity, about that which gives us existence, and what it reveals is that existence cannot be thought without the use of technology, or outside a technological mode of thought.

Irigaray begins *The Forgetting of Air* with a quote, or rather a question from Heidegger, "What are we meant to understand by this 'there is'?"[26] She says Heidegger is unable to properly think through this question insofar as he neglects the fluid reality of air, along with its symbolic entanglements of sexual difference. She asserts Heidegger will not overcome metaphysics until he gets his feet off the ground.[27] What she means is that Heidegger is too focused on our finitude and our dwelling on earth; he privileges solid grounding and mortality at the expense of air and infinite becoming.[28]

Schilingi's *Terra*, subtitled "a tribute to the status of woman," visually and audibly plays with this desire for grounding as it portrays attempts to master the earth and to keep silent the feminine. While Irigaray critiques Heidegger for thinking earth at the expense of air, reading *Terra* alongside his philosophy of earth/world strife allows us to remember this element. Argo is about human identity and the moods of an individual, but I read *Terra* as an acknowledgment that the individual does not breathe alone, and what's more, only breathes because of their sexuate nature. What begins as an homage to breathing (to air) carries over to a tribute to woman (the forgotten feminine). Schilingi's move from *Argo* to *Terra* may thus fill in the gaps that Irigaray accuses Heidegger of forgetting.

TERRA

Terra is a dance and music performance piece that once again uses respiratory sensors to translate breathing into a diverse array of musical arrangements. In contrast with *Argo*, however, sounds are generated by the counterpoint between *two* breaths, that of the female dancer and that of the male composer.[29] *Terra* was initially presented in 2018 at the *Grand Palais* in collaboration with PeiJu Chien-Pott, principal dancer of the Martha Graham Dance Company. Yet again playing upon the theme of mastery, the composer (Schilingi) wears sensory captors on his hands so that he may manipulate the production of sound, while also orchestrating the movements of the dancer. Schilingi is present in the performance piece but he takes on a role akin to a sculptor who controls and molds the female body. *Terra*, usually translated as earth, is later described by Schilingi as the "planetary image of fecundity."[30] *Terra*'s subtitle is "a tribute to the status of woman," and so the aim of this section is to provide a hermeneutic reading of how earth, world, fecundity, sexual difference, and air are "set up" in such praise. I argue that the interplay between the male composer and female dancer plays out in a battle akin to Heidegger's earth/world strife, a conflict where breath (air) is omnipresent in the background (as audio and visual).

At the beginning of the performance, both composer and dancer face each other, eyes closed, as two screens appear in the background, one behind the composer and one behind the dancer. Like *Argo*, these screens display a visual web of breathing patterns, that of the female and that of the male. As their eyes open, they each fixate in a gaze. While the female clearly focuses her eyes on the composer, her male counterpoint looks aloof, seemingly transfixing his eyes not on her, but on the visual display of her breathing pattern. He then raises his hands, and the dancer, who wears a semi-opaque black cloth around her waist, lifts the fabric over her body to conceal herself. The composer continues moving his hands as the dancer is molded into a position that is reminiscent of the act of giving birth. The female's arms are stretched in the air, as if making the letter "V," as her head emerges, pushing through the cloth at the crux of this "V-shape" (see figure 16.2). The fabric is transparent enough to see her form, yet opaque enough to still remain elusive.

All of a sudden, the artist speeds up the rhythm of his hands, and the dancer chaotically moves toward him, her movements being inhibited by the cloth. The music that was once ethereal turns sharp like chains and metal. He then slowly lowers his hands as the female assumes a passive position, like clay ready to be sculpted. His hands appear to have tools that manipulate the material to his liking. Once again, he speeds up the rhythm of his hands, choreographing a series of confusing movements. It appears that the female is unsure what form to take until he slows his movements and her body transforms into what looks almost like an hourglass in its top/bottom symmetry. The "V" gesture of her arms is mirrored by her legs, where triangle and inverted triangle meet at her torso (see figure 16.3). The sound of scratching metal returns as hands speed up and manipulate the unruly dancer before once

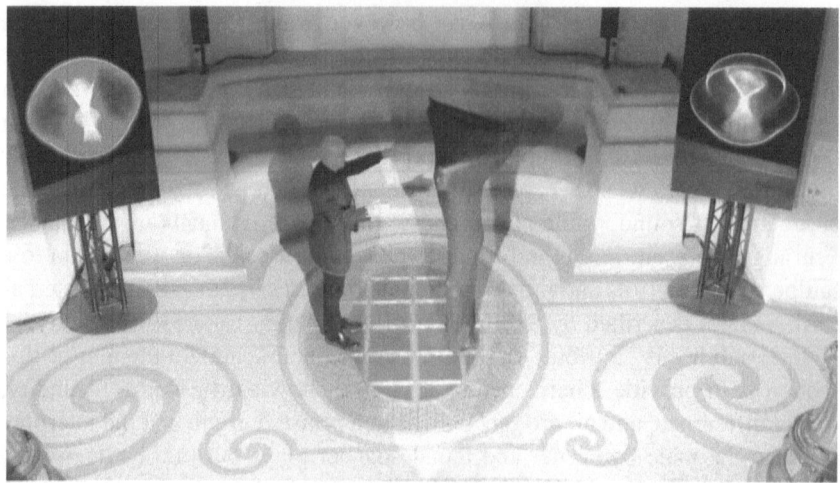

Figure 16.2 Still Image from the Film by Claude Mossessian, "Jacopo Baboni Schilingli Terra." *Source:* Directed by Claude Mossessian, *Jacopo Baboni Schilingli Terra* Grand Palais, June 19, 2018.

again making her a docile malleable body. He yet again sculpts her before grabbing her hands through the fabric, turning her body, and withdrawing from the scene.

As he withdraws, she frees herself from the cloth, and though a faster metallic sound emerges, it is not a heavy scratching but light fluid drops. Her movements are at first a bit forced, at times feeling compelled to walk in the direction of the composer, but soon she becomes more confident and

Figure 16.3 Still Image from the Film by Claude Mossessian, "Jacopo Baboni Schilingli Terra." *Source:* Directed by Claude Mossessian, *Jacopo Baboni Schilingli Terra* Grand Palais, June 19, 2018.

versatile. We are then left with the intense sound of her breathing, not just her breathing translated into music, but the bare breath that supersedes that of the electronic arrangement. The composer then re-emerges on the scene and she once again steps into the cloth and ties it around her waist.

I read *Terra* as a performance piece that captures the tension between world and earth that Heidegger illustrates in his "Origin of the Work of Art." As previously noted, the world is defined as the "ever-nonobjective to which we are subject as long as the paths of birth and death, blessing and curse keep us transported into being."[31] Heidegger also states that "world demands its decisiveness and its measure and lets beings attain to the open regions of their paths."[32] World, in demanding its decisiveness, insists on a ground, a foundation of truth. World is that viewpoint through which each era conceives of being, and our modern era is that of *Gestell*. Though *Gestell* is usually translated as enframing, perhaps Andrew Mitchell's term "positionality" more accurately captures the active element of this mode of thought. The word "enframing" risks viewing our current ideology as something that has come from the outside, like borders of a picture frame encasing its inside elements. Mitchell asserts:

> We cannot think positionality as some kind of framework or scaffolding thrown over the world. To do so is to persist in the belief that this incursion of the technological would be something that came to us from the outside, that it would remain somehow extrinsic to all that is . . . It is to believe, for example, that nature would still exist outside of technology, even if only as the source from which it draws its materials.[33]

Positionality suggests that nature is not something passive that has been independently mastered from the outside. Viewing nature in this way would suggest that it is objectifiable in a way that grounds its truth. Yet, there is no ground, as being is approached in relation to one's position. Thus, as the "ever non-objective," world does not stand over against nature and the materials from which it emerges. World only arises out of the seclusion of the earth. Heidegger states,

> Upon the earth and in it, historical man grounds his dwelling in the world. In setting up a world, the work sets forth the earth . . . To set forth the earth means to bring it into the open region as the self-secluding.[34]

World and earth are thus in constant interplay, yet as one presences, the other withdraws. *Terra* visually captures this antagonism with the male composer representing world and the female dancer symbolizing the earth. The performance illustrates the inextricability of this relation while also highlighting that despite the co-dependency of these notions, we are only able to properly think one side at a time. As one comes to presences/emerges, the other absences/self-secludes. The union of this relation is set to music as the counterpoint of their breathing patterns. The performance relies on the element that is most fundamental to human existence, air, and yet the truth of this is only realized through its being challenged forth, through *Gestell*.

Heidegger argues that our current era only conceives the world as a standing reserve, and this mode of thinking that "challenges forth" nature is made clear from the onset of the performance. The male composer opens his eyes, yet instead of gazing at the female dancer, he fixates on the technology that makes her breathe visible. The female dancer (earth) cannot be known in and of itself but only through the technological thought of *Gestell*. This is not to say that the female dancer has an unchanging "in itself" that would emerge without world, though by only seeing the female (earth) through a lens of technical know-how, a part of her is forgotten.

At first, Schilingi's male composer (world) does not "see" the female dancer (earth). All he sees is nature ready to be made in his own image, or as Irigaray would say, ready to appropriate through his *logos*. As Helen Fielding asserts:

> [For Heidegger] there is no recognition of air that precedes language, and gives life; there is, however, a nostalgic mourning for the indivision that preceded that first cry before separation. He mourns the loss of this first wholeness from which he is thrown into the world, but it is a loss he does not think through (FA, pp.77/72). Because it is not acknowledged in a recognition of the gift of the maternal-feminine, the "mourning consists in re-appropriating absence—she who is absent—for himself . . ." (FA, pp. 44/44). He assimilates her into the *Gestell*.[35]

What this mourning of being "thrown into the world" entails is being born on the basis of a "nullity," that is, being born without ground. In our thrownness, we seemingly come from nowhere, without causal explication, without requesting to be here. The realization of our thrownness and the recognition of our factical "being there" produces a certain affective state whereby we are disclosed to an understanding of being; being born from "nothing," we long for answers, for "wholeness." Yet, as Fielding points out in her assessment of Irigaray, Heidegger will not receive such answers, so long as he is unable to acknowledge the "maternal-feminine," the body of which I was a part before I drew my first breath, before my thrownness. While the mother's body may not be an original cause that explains all of existence, her matter matters in the separation prior to my existence as an individual.[36] For Heidegger, this first breath and its association with the feminine is erased, and the question of being becomes a linguistic undertaking. Heidegger perceives language, and poetry more specifically, as a space disclosive of being; yet, Irigaray views language as another appropriating technique, a mode of *Gestell*.

In *Terra*, the absence of the feminine is highlighted by her being covered in a semi-opaque black fabric. Furthermore, the presence of the composer manipulates both the movements of her body and the music of her breathing patterns, mimicking a sculptor as she is set up like clay being shaped to his liking. The female dancer is viewed as passive matter, the material on which the "active" male will plant his seed (according to Aristotle's view on sexual difference and generation) but so too does she harbor an intrinsic possibility to be other than what she is.

In the beginning of the performance, the male slowly moves his hands to choreograph the movements of the female dancer, a body that takes form as the "act of birthing" incarnate. The music in the background has a religious quality to it and one can almost hear "spatiality" like an echo filling up a large cathedral: "the holy is opened up as holy and the god is invoked into the openness of his presence."[37] As the gestures of the composer speed up, the music becomes sharp, and the dancer chaotically tries to resist before being turned into matter ready to be sculpted by the composer. While at times made docile by (world), earth "shatters every attempt to penetrate it. It causes every merely calculating importunity upon it to turn into a destruction."[38] The female dancer as earth cannot be penetrated to reveal "what it is" because it is as possibility, as air, as fluid becoming. At one moment, the dancer takes an almost "hourglass stance," her body transforming into what appears a triangle and inverted triangle. We notice that her body resembles the webs displayed on the screens in the background that visually represent their breathing patterns; she becomes the very image symbolic of breath itself. The female transforms into air. The two triangles may also represent male and female, the sexual difference responsible for becoming. While the maternal-feminine is symbolic of air in its inability to be thought, Irigaray does not invert Aristotle's theory of generation and try to privilege the female, as she notes the becoming of nature is "at least two." In my reading of *Argo*, I previously interpreted the hourglass as being symbolic of time. For Heidegger, temporality is intricately linked to an understanding of being, hence his eponymously titled opus, *Being and Time*. Heidegger notes that our current understanding of "what is" (being) as "presence" (temporality as a series of now moments) has led to a forgetting of being (*Seinsvergessenheit*). Irigaray understands being as an infinite becoming intrinsically linked to sexual difference. She notes our inability to think outside the masculine economy of language and our incapacity to think that which is everywhere but made absent is a forgetting of air.

As a tribute, does *Terra* try to think of the forgotten feminine? Does Schilingi show a resistance at attempts to exploit the female as docile matter?

Though the composer leaves the scene and his hands no longer inhibit the movement of the female, it is not as if she is free from the constraints of technology, or rather technological thought. As she freely dances, the music turns electronic, almost robotic, yet versatile like metallic pin drops. As Mitchell illustrates in his translation of *Gestell* as positionality, nature is never outside of technology. The sensors on the composer's hands may no longer be visible, but world is still there. As an interplay of presence/absence, emerging/withdrawal, *Terra* performs the tension between earth and world that is responsible for truth, and the truth of our era is *Gestell*.

In conclusion, by offering a hermeneutic reading of Schilingi's generative music projects *Argo* and *Terra*, I've tried to show how Heidegger's philosophy can be read in a way that fills in the gaps of Irigaray's critiques. While I agree with Irigaray that Heidegger is unable to think the forgotten feminine by focusing too much on language, I've tried to show how aspects of his philosophy can be read in such a way as to remember. Like Heidegger's early work, Schilingi's first performance piece, *Argo*, focuses mainly on individual existence; however, similar to Heidegger's later work, his second piece, *Terra*, lends itself to a relational understanding of being. Reading Heidegger's philosophy alongside Schilingi's music projects allow us to think the forgotten concepts of air and the feminine, while also questioning whether they can ever be thought outside of technological appropriation.

NOTES

1. Luce Irigaray, *The Forgetting of Air in Martin Heidegger*, trans. Mary Beth Mader (Austin, TX: University of Texas Press, 1999), 4.

2. Heidegger refers to language as the "house of being" in "Letter on Humanism." He states, "Rather, language is the house of Being in which man ek-sists by dwelling, in that he belongs to the truth of Being, guarding it." Martin Heidegger, "Letter on Humanism," in *Basic Writings*, ed. David Farrell Krell (San Francisco: Harper Collins, 1993), 237.

3. Jacques Derrida first coined the term "phallogocentrism" in 1972 to highlight how human males have historically dominated the meaning and sense of language. See Derrida, *Marges de la philosophie* (Paris: Éditions de minuit, 1972). In 1974, Luce Irigaray uses the term to theorize sexual difference. See Irigaray, *Speculum. De l'autre femme* (Paris: Éditions de minuit, 1974).

4. Luce Irigaray, *L'oubli de l'air* (Paris: Éditions de minuit, 1983), 84–85. Highlighting how man uses language to create a world of his own making, she states the following on page 85: "Le langage serait la technique—l'architechnique, l'architectonique—de l'homme façonnant le vivant selon son project sexuel."

5. Heidegger asserts that each era approaches being through a certain ideological framework; our current era is ruled by a mode of thought called enframing (*Gestell*).

Such technological thinking views the world as a standing reserve (*Bestand*), as an amalgam of resources ready to be calculated and put on reserve for future utility. Cf. Martin Heidegger, "The Question Concerning Technology," in *Basic Writings*, ed. David Farrell Krell (San Francisco: Harper Collins, 1993), 311–341.

6. In "The Origin of the Work of Art," Heidegger introduces earth as a complement to world where this duality is responsible for the coming to be of the artwork. He will, however, later abandon this world/earth duality in favor of the fourfold (earth, mortals, divinities, skies), but I believe this is just another way of formulating the dialectic as mortals/earth and divinities/skies. See Martin Heidegger, "The Origin of the Work of Art," in *Basic Writings*, ed. David Farrell Krell (San Francisco: Harper Collins, 1993), 143–203.

7. This respiratory sensor is called *AirGo* and was produced by the society *MyAir* by David Kuller.

8. Schilingi describes *Argo* as such in the catalog *Artistes et Robots*, a 2018 exhibition where his work was presented in the Grand Palais. *Artistes et Robots*, Grand Palais, Galeries nationales 5 avril–9 juillet 2018, ouvrage sous la direction de Laurence Bertrand Dorléac et Jérôme Neutres, « Argo » de Jacopo Baboni Schilingi, 106.

9. Heidegger states, "Whether art may be granted this highest possibility of its essence in the midst of the extreme danger, no one can tell. Yet, we can be astounded by it." See Heidegger, "The Questioning Concerning Technology," 340.

10. Heidegger, "The Question Concerning Technology," 311–341.

11. Heidegger, "The Origin of the Work of Art," 203.

12. Heidegger, "The Question Concerning Technology," 311–316.

13. Jacopo Baboni Schilingi, "Argo" Exposition Artistes & Robots, Grand Palais, Paris, France (version longue), a short film by Claude Mossessian. https://vimeo.com/264075872.

14. Jacopo Baboni Schilingi, « A propos d'Argo et de Terra 18 juin 2018, » https://www.youtube.com/watch?v=PMD5jYeXBc4.

15. Heidegger states, "The character of Dasein's being—this 'that it is'—is veiled in its 'whence' and 'wither,' yet disclosed in itself all the more unveiledly; we call it the '*thrownness*' *[Geworfenheit]* of this entity into its 'there'; indeed, it is thrown in such a way that, as Being-in-the-world, it is the 'there'" in Martin Heidegger, *Being and Time*, trans. John Macquarrie & Edward Robinson (New York: Harper & Row, 1962), 174.

16. Heidegger, *Being and Time*, 173.

17. On page 172 of the Macquarrie and Robinson translation of *Being and Time*, the translators offer the following footnote, "'die Stimmung, das Gestimmtsein.' The noun 'Stimmung' originally means the tuning of a musical instrument, but it has taken on several other meanings and is the usual word for one's mood or humour." Babich also speaks of the musical sense of *Stimmung* in her chapter of this volume.

18. Heidegger, "The Origin of the Work of Art," 169.

19. Heidegger, "The Origin of the Work of Art," 170.

20. Heidegger, "The Origin of the Work of Art," 169.

21. Heidegger, "The Origin of the Work of Art," 201.

22. Heidegger, "The Question Concerning Technology," 311–341.
23. Heidegger, "The Question Concerning Technology," 321.
24. Martin Heidegger, *Basic Concepts*, trans. Gary E. Aylesworth (Bloomington & Indianapolis: Indiana Univ. Press, 1993), 42.
25. Jacopo Baboni Schilingi, « A propos d'Argo et de Terra 18 juin 2018 ».
26. Irigaray, *L'oubli de l'air*, 9.
27. Irigaray, *L'oubli de l'air*, 10. She states, "Tant qu'Heidegger ne quitte pas la 'terre', il ne quitte pas la métaphysique."
28. Anne O'Byrne highlights Heidegger's privileging of finitude at the expense of natality in her aptly titled book *Natality and Finitude* (Bloomington: Indiana Univ. Press, 2010). Trish Glazebrook who has worked on ecofeminist approaches to Heidegger made a reference to air and the forgotten feminine at the 2019 Heidegger Circle when she was on a book panel for Susan Dawn Claxton's *Heidegger's Gods: An Ecofeminist Perspective* (London and New York: Rowman & Littlefield International, 2017). Quoting lyrics from an Ani Difranco song, she asserted, "These businessmen got the money. They got the instruments of death. But I can make life. I can make breath." The lyrics come from DiFranco's song "Blood in the Boardroom," track 7 on the album *Puddle Dive*.
29. For the initial performance at the Grand Palais, see: http://www.baboni-schilingi.com/index.php/music/performances/20-performances/79-terra?tmpl=modal.
30. Jacopo Baboni Schilingi, « A propos d'Argo et de Terra 18 juin 2018 ».
31. Heidegger, "The Origin of the Work of Art," 170.
32. Heidegger, "The Origin of the Work of Art," 188.
33. Andrew J. Mitchell, *The Fourfold: Reading the Late Heidegger* (Evanston: Northwestern Univ. Press, 2015), 50. For Mitchell, positionality is inseparable from the fourfold that Heidegger later describes in "Building, Dwelling, Thinking" as the oneness of earth, sky, divinities, and mortals. Heidegger states, "In saving the earth, in receiving the sky, in awaiting the divinities, in initiating mortals, dwelling propriates as the fourfold preservation of the fourfold" in "Building, Dwelling, Thinking," in *Basic Writings*, ed. David Farrell Krell (San Francisco: Harper Collins, 1993), 353. Though "The Origin of the Work of Art" is prior to "Building, Dwelling, Thinking," Heidegger will go on to drop the element of "world" in the fourfold. The tension between earth/world and the being of the artwork that emerges through this interaction as a "founding preserving" is similar to the "dwelling" that Heidegger describes in the fourfold.
34. Heidegger, "The Origin of the Work of Art," 172–173.
35. Helen Fielding, "Questioning Nature: Irigaray, Heidegger, and the Potentiality of Matter," in *Continental Philosophy Review* 36, no. 1 (2003): 14. When Fielding cites *FA*, she is referencing the English translation of Irigaray's *The Forgetting of Air in Martin Heidegger*, trans. Mary Beth Mader (Austin: University of Texas Press, 1999).
36. I say matter matters as a double tip of the hat to Karen Barad and Carol Bigwood. In "Posthumanist Performativity: Toward an Understanding of How Matter Comes to Matter," Barad criticizes how language has been given too much power, while looking at the "intra-active" quality of materiality. Carol Bigwood offers a direct critique of Heidegger and western metaphysicians in general who neglect

or inferiorize the maternal body. A chapter of her book *Earth Muse: Feminism, Nature, and Art* is titled "Mother Doesn't Matter." See Karen Barad, "Posthumanist Performativity: Toward an Understanding of How Matter Comes to Matter," *Signs: Journal of Women in Society and Culture* 28, no. 3 (2003): 801–831; and Carol Bigwood, *Earth Muse: Feminism, Nature, and Art* (Philadelphia: Temple University Press, 1993).

37. Heidegger, "The Origin of the Work of Art," 169.
38. Heidegger, "The Origin of the Work of Art," 172.

BIBLIOGRAPHY

Artistes et Robots. Grand Palais, Galeries nationales 5 avril- 9 juillet 2018, ouvrage sous la direction de Laurence Bertrand Dorléac et Jérôme Neutres, « Argo » de Jacopo Baboni Schilingi, 106.

Barad, Karen. "Posthumanist Performativity: Toward an Understanding of How Matter Comes to Matter." *Signs: Journal of Women in Society and Culture* 28, no. 3 (2003): 801–831.

Bigwood, Carol. *Earth Muse: Feminism, Nature, and Art*. Philadelphia: Temple Univ. Press, 1993.

Claxton, Susanne. *Heidegger's Gods: An Ecofeminist Perspective*. London and New York: Rowman & Littlefield International, 2017.

Derrida, Jacques. *Marges de la philosophie*. Paris: Éditions de minuit, 1972.

Fielding, Helen. "Questioning Nature: Irigaray, Heidegger, and the Potentiality of Matter." *Continental Philosophy Review* 36, no. 1 (2003): 1–26.

Heidegger, Martin. *Basic Concepts*. Translated by Gary E. Aylesworth. Bloomington & Indianapolis: Indiana University Press, 1993.

Heidegger, Martin. *Being and Time*. Translated by John Macquarrie and Edward Robinson. New York: Harper & Row, 1962.

Heidegger, Martin. "Building, Dwelling, Thinking." In *Basic Writings*, edited by David Farell Krell, 347–363. San Francisco: Harper Collins, 1993.

Heidegger, Martin. "Letter on Humanism." In *Basic Writings*, edited by David Farrell Krell, 217–265. San Francisco: Harper Collins, 1993.

Heidegger, Martin. "The Origin of the Work of Art." In *Basic Writings*, edited by David Farrell Krell, 143–203. San Francisco: Harper Collins, 1993.

Heidegger, Martin. "The Question Concerning Technology." In *Basic Writings*, edited by David Farrell Krell, 311–341. San Francisco: Harper Collins, 1993.

Irigaray, Luce. *The Forgetting of Air in Martin Heidegger*. Translated by Mary Beth Mader. Austin, TX: University of Texas Press, 1999.

Irigaray, Luce. *L'oubli de l'air*. Paris: Les Éditions de minuit, 1983.

Irigaray, Luce. *Speculum. De l'autre femme*. Paris: Éditions de minuit, 1974.

Mitchell, Andrew J. *The Fourfold: Reading the Late Heidegger*. Evanston: Northwestern University Press, 2015.

O'Byrne, Anne. *Natality and Finitude*. Bloomington: Indiana University Press, 2010.

Chapter 17

The Working of Aural Being in Electronic Music

Gerry Stahl

Heidegger's exploration of how things are disclosed (his ontology or philosophy of being) provides innovative ways of understanding many phenomena, including works of art. Although Heidegger did not write directly about music, he discussed the working of other art forms, including painting, pottery, and sculpture. To discuss the implications of Heidegger's philosophy for understanding the nature of music, we can consider his analyses of these different art forms and adapt them to music. This chapter will extend Heidegger's approach to art by applying it to the development of electronic music in the mid-twentieth century to elucidate both his philosophy and that intriguing movement in music.

Heidegger is concerned with the way things come into being, their forms of being, or how their being is worked out. The *being* of something centrally involves how it presents or discloses itself in its specific form. This chapter will explore the being of works of a certain genre of music, *e-music*—that is, how works of electronic music are structured to disclose worlds of sound in certain ways.

"E-music" is here coined to refer to a particular vision of electronic music as it developed in the 1950s and 1960s.[1] E-music grew out of the serial music of Arnold Schoenberg and others, and featured composers such as Edgard Varèse, Karlheinz Stockhausen, Pierre Boulez, and Iannis Xenakis. It had broad influences on classical, jazz, fusion, acid rock, rap, new-age trance, and disco-dance music. Integral to e-music's compositional experimentation was the concomitant development of analog and digital technologies of sound production, including tape splicing, sound sampling, sequencers, and synthesizers. We will consider e-music specifically as exemplified by paradigmatic works and reflections of Stockhausen,[2] which defined an approach to composition with striking parallels to Heidegger's philosophy.

My aim is to view the being of works of e-music from the perspectives of four identifiable approaches by Heidegger to analyzing how works of art and other beings are disclosed:

(a) Available beings like tools are disclosed as *understood* within the nexus of beings that form one's world as one pursues human concerns.[3]
(b) Works of art like paintings disclose by setting truth into work—that is, disclosing a *world* created by the working of the artwork.[4]
(c) Things like handcrafted jugs are disclosed in accordance with their historic *epoch* of being, such as the antique, medieval, mechanical, or digital era.[5]
(d) Works like sculpture disclose *relations of form, space, and time*—thereby creating material, moments, and places for people to dwell.[6]

We will explore how to apply each of these four ontological approaches to works of music through an investigation of e-music as it emerged in the 1960s. The following characteristics of e-music relate to Heidegger's philosophy:

(a) E-music illustrates how one hears *interpreted* sound versus noise.
(b) Works of e-music open sonic *worlds* in which novel aural phenomena are set into work.
(c) E-music is produced with innovative *technologies*—such as the use of digital synthesizers or computers to manipulate sound parameters—which are explored by e-music compositions.
(d) Works of e-music establish *relations of form, space, and time* among sounds through the explicit, controlled composition of these dimensions.

While Heidegger offers a transformative way of viewing art, his conception of historical change is open to critique. In addition to illustrating the power of Heidegger's innovative insights, we will also note their limitations—primarily from the viewpoint of Marx's sociohistorical philosophy, which Heidegger failed to appreciate[7]:

(a) Heidegger's view of authentic man is ideological and individualistic, while his analysis of tools like e-music technologies downplays their ties to modes of production and consumption.[8]
(b) Heidegger's analysis of art ignores the complexity of the labor involved in making a film, a jug, or a musical composition, and how that work is socially and historically mediated.[9]
(c) Heidegger's account of history ignores its social structuration, whereby history is not just given but is produced, reproduced, and transformed by works, including works of music.[10]

(d) Heidegger's characterization of sculpture imposes his conceptualizations of space and time, rather than developing them from how they are disclosed in the work of sculptors and composers.[11]

Heidegger sees the revelation of truth in the working of the work of art. Marxists see the production of art as creative labor mediated by technological means and social processes. Although neither Heidegger nor Marx explicitly considered music at length, analysis of the technology and history of e-music can provide an increased understanding of the insights and the limitations of both philosophies. The following sections discuss e-music and other art forms from the perspectives of Heidegger's four successive approaches to the being of artworks, raising concerns about the adequacy of those views. Examples from the development of e-music—and observations from painting, pottery, and sculpture—are used to extend Heidegger's philosophy. These instances should render Heidegger's abstruse ontological theories more tangible and comprehensible, as well as suggest how aspects of the production process and sociohistorical context should be incorporated in the origin of the being of works of art.

BEINGS IN THE WORLD

Heidegger's most important publication—which argued for the need to understand the being of beings in terms of how they are disclosed—was *Being and Time*.[12] Here he rejected the traditional view that people exist within an objective, value-free environment, surrounded by material objects upon which they impose meanings. In contrast, he proposed that human existence discloses a network of meaningful beings, whose significance is tentatively suggested from the start in terms of one's concerns, expectations, and pre-judgments. The world around us is always already understood; Heidegger's analysis is a philosophy of just how the world is pre-interpreted—and how this understanding may subsequently be made explicit and further articulated.[13]

Heidegger illustrates the pre-interpretation of the world in terms of how we hear sounds: "Initially we never hear noises and complexes of sounds, but the creaking wagon, the motorcycle. We hear the column on the march, the north wind, the woodpecker tapping, the crackling fire. It requires a very artificial and complicated attitude in order to 'hear' a 'pure noise.'"[14] In perceiving a sound, we perceive it *as* something, as the sound of a certain object, instrument, or process, or as a certain kind of sound.

This can be directly applied to how we hear music. We do not first or primarily hear music as uninterpreted raw sounds that we must then interpret. Rather we hear the bowing of a violin, the ringing of a bell, the strumming of a guitar. We hear the solemnity of a requiem, the joy of a jig, or the romance of a love song. We may also hear the expressive communication of a performer or the emotional intention of a composer. According to Heidegger, these initial forms of being of the sounds are determined by our culture, by how "one" interprets them. Once something is initially disclosed in a certain way, we can develop our interpretation of it through explicitly building upon possibilities opened by how it was disclosed.

While Heidegger is focused on describing the experiential phenomena of pre-interpretation, it is easy to see that there are social mechanisms at work there. For instance, pop music prejudices are systematically manufactured by a powerful culture industry, which produces, promotes, hypes, and sells musical concerts and recordings.[15] More subtly, composers adopt mechanisms that contribute to pre-understanding. The system of Western classical tonality is one example. Although music theory defines twelve tones to the octave, virtually every classical musical piece focuses on a subset of those twelve tones. For instance, a piece in the C-Major scale primarily uses the seven notes of the octave that are white keys on a piano. Different scales produce different pre-understandings of mood for listeners.

The alternative twelve-tone approach of serial composers like Schoenberg was an attempt to avoid the pre-understanding fostered by tonal composition. Schoenberg arranged all twelve tones of the octave in a series, and his serial pieces ran through their series before repeating any tone.[16] That eliminated the suggestion of an emphasized key and removed corresponding prejudices about the piece for the audience. The audience then had to overcome the consequent feeling of disorientation and search for other interpretive features of the music. Although he sometimes rejected the tonality of traditional keys, Schoenberg retained the timbres of orchestral instruments and the emotionality of standard patterns of loudness (amplitude) and speed (tempo).

The pioneers of e-music extended Schoenberg's rejection of classical tonality to other parameters of sound in their compositions. Anton Webern— still within the Schoenberg school—integrated loudness into the serialization process, emphasizing silence at one end of that parameter's scale. Silence was transformed from just an implicit rest to slow down notes, into an explicit (disclosed, hearable) composed element.

The vision of e-music was influenced by Varèse and others who foresaw the possibility of composing with arbitrary timbres, not just the characteristic sounds of traditional physical instruments. The new science of acoustics and the developing technologies of electronic sound production suggested creating sounds with any desired characteristics. In theory, the sound of a note played on a piano, organ, guitar, or violin—while quite complex—could be scientifically analyzed in terms of its pitch (frequency), timbre (overtones or waveform), and the attack, sustaining and decay of its loudness (amplitude envelope). Sounds could be produced and manipulated by electronic devices (oscillators, controllers, filters, modulators, etc.), creating radically new sonic material through the total organization of the sound parameters.[17] Subsequently, it was possible to define a sound digitally by specifying with a computer its amplitude at each of thousands of microseconds. These individually constructed sounds could then be combined into a sound composition by splicing tape recordings of fabricated and/or "found" (recorded) sounds, playing them sequentially on a synthesizer (figure 17.1) or aggregating them with a sequencer.

E-music eliminated many of the familiar aural clues that provided a preinterpretation to an audience. Historical developments in musical composition met resistance from changes in the audience of music. The reproduction of music through radio and records had created a huge audience for music. However, much of that audience did not have the cultural background to understand and appreciate classical music, such as Schoenberg's serial music. To people who were not oriented to exploring the new potentials of sound production, works of e-music could sound like "just noise"—incomprehensible sounds.[18] However, as discussed below, e-music opened up a world in which the nature of noise was itself disclosed as interpretable through a technological understanding of its being.

Figure 17.1   A 1975 Moog Synthesizer. *Source:* Photo retrieved from https://en.wikipedia.org/w/index.php?title=Electronic_music&oldid=998812023.

THE WORKING OF THE WORK OF ART

In an essay central to his middle period, Heidegger focused on the being of art. "The Origin of the Work of Art" proposes that an artwork can disclose a world in which people may encounter the being of tools.[19] For instance, Vincent van Gogh's painting of a peasant woman's shoes (figure 17.2) discloses the being of her shoes as embedded in the peasant's world:

> Van Gogh's painting is an opening-up of that which the tool, the pair of farmer's boots, in truth *is*. This being steps out into the unconcealment of its being. . . . There is a happening of truth at work in the work, if an opening-up of the being happens here in that which is and how it is.[20]

Heidegger proposes that the oil painting of the shoes discloses the nature of the shoes as serviceable and reliable tools in the peasant's world. This represents a reversal of perspective from *Being and Time*, in which the being-there (*Da-Sein*) of the viewer discloses the painting within its relations in the viewer's and peasant's networks of tools and concerns. Here, being is disclosed by artworks as well as by human Dasein.

Figure 17.2 Van Gogh's Painting of a Pair of Shoes. *Source:* Van Gogh Museum, Amsterdam. Photo by author.

In Heidegger's consideration of art, the opening of being can take place through a work, such as a painting, jug, sculpture, or poem. Such works disclose meaningful worlds. A tension (struggle) exists in these works between disclosing (world) and concealing (earth). For instance, by opening access to the world of shoes, van Gogh's painting conceals its own earthy materiality as paint on canvas. Heidegger refers to this tension as a *Riss*, which in German means tearing apart, but also the design, outline, or boundary. This boundary is particularly apparent in sculpture: A wood carving opens the space around and between the surfaces of the wooden forms that make up the sculpture's design, while the wood itself lies hidden below the surfaces.

Heidegger argues that van Gogh's painting discloses the nature of the shoes. However, this analysis only works because the painting is representational. Heidegger misses the painting's deeper art-historical importance: the relationship to impressionist revelations about light and shadow, or van Gogh's own exploration of brushstroke as an element of the materiality of paint. The significance of van Gogh's paintings does not primarily have to do with how they disclose the lives of the people or the being of the tools represented in the worlds of the paintings. More important are his techniques of applying paint to the canvas, leading to the emergence of abstract art as an exploration of the materials, geometry, light, and texture of oil painting. By focusing on the painting's representational function, Heidegger misses much of its historical import.

The year after Heidegger's essay on art was written, the Marxist literary critic Walter Benjamin published *The Work of Art in the Age of Mechanical Reproduction*.[21] This essay can be read as a (possibly intentional) response to Heidegger, who does not acknowledge the historic changes in art. Benjamin reflects on the essential transformation from painting to mechanically reproducible forms of imaging, such as lithography, professional photography, silent film, and sound movies. He delves particularly into what takes place in historic transitions due to reproducibility, such as the transformation from live theater to film. In a play on stage, the actors take on the roles of human characters and present them in a unique setting. By contrast, in the production of a movie, the actors are treated more like props, who adopt isolated poses, which are later edited together by a complex process involving many professionals and technical processes. The produced movie—having lost the "aura" of the unique occurrence—may then be seen by viewers anywhere and at any time. What formerly opened an innovative world is now constrained as a commodity for mass consumption.

Theodor Adorno, a music critic and friend of Benjamin, extends the analysis to music and the "culture industry."[22] He argues that commercial pop music and big-band jazz represent trends in music resulting from its popularization through mechanical reproduction in recordings, similar to that of film.[23]

Adorno discusses the dialectic of enlightenment, in which social progress toward increasing knowledge and morality has always been accompanied by regress. Benjamin's examples of mechanical reproduction of artworks illustrate this: the increasing democratization, popularization, and accessibility of art due to technological progress in means of production have been accompanied throughout history by regression in the innovation of popular works and the depth of understanding by the audience. While Adorno's dialectic of culture parallels Heidegger's abstract notion of the *Riss* as a conflict in art's impact, Adorno and his critical-social-theory colleagues such as Benjamin, Max Horkheimer, Herbert Marcuse, and Jürgen Habermas delve into the social and historical processes through which this tension occurs. The history of e-music illustrates the decline in the public's musical understanding in the following sections, as the ontological vision of e-music is gradually lost in the commercialism of pop music using electronic technologies.

ART IN THE AGE OF TECHNOLOGY

In a late essay, Heidegger returned to the project of *Being and Time* with a discussion of *Time and Being*.[24] Here, he maintains that the disclosure of being is given by successive "epochs of being" throughout history. For instance, things were disclosed as creations of God during medieval times and now they are given as material for, or products of, technological manipulation. This is Heidegger's approach to integrating history into his ontology. The question is whether this is an adequate comprehension of the role of history, particularly in the working of artworks.

According to Heidegger, works of art set truth into work as the disclosure of being, where being is always disclosed in accordance with the prevailing epoch of being. Consider how this applies to music. Works of music open worlds—acoustic landscapes of meaningful sound. When the music is self-consciously technological, such as Stockhausen's *Kontakte*,[25] the sonic world is opened and understood as a technological product, and the technical parameters may be made perceptible (heard as such). The nature of the sound is itself disclosed, rather than appearing as a presence of some other being (instrument, performer).

E-music provides a propitious example of a technological being. E-music treats sound from a technological perspective (figure 17.3): as technically defined in an objective, measurable terms of frequency and amplitude and as material for production and manipulation by technological means.[26] Even individual notes can be composed out of sound parameters—generating new kinds of sounds. Works of e-music often evoke reflections on our technological age, such as images of space travel or video games. At the same time,

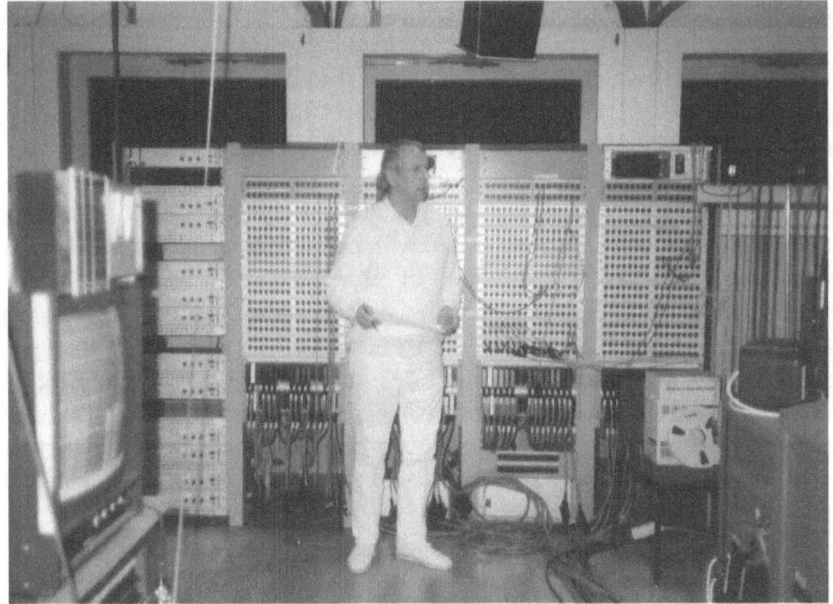

Figure 17.3   Karlheinz Stockhausen in the Electronic Music Studio of WDR, Cologne, in 1991. *Source:* Photo by Kathinka Pasveer, retrieved from https://commons.wikimedia.org/w/index.php?curid=8385683.

they are frequently heard as noise—either the din of mechanical and technical contrivances or the incomprehensibility of strange sounds.

Within a Heideggerian viewpoint, noise is sound that is not pre-interpreted: It makes no sense to the listener; it is not disclosed as meaningful.[27] The pioneers of e-music had to explain to the listening public what they were trying to do with sounds that seemed to *be* just noise. Verbal descriptions of the aims and methods of e-music works supported understanding, helping the music to be disclosed in a way that would not be rejected as incomprehensible noise but could be interpreted within a context (world) of aural being (explorations of sound). Rigorous theoretical considerations by e-music composers abounded in the 1960s: Stockhausen's *Texte*, Xenakis' *Formalized Music*, Boulez' *Boulez on Music Today*, and articles in *Die Reihe* and *Perspectives of New Music*.[28] In this way, the composers acted as ontologists, elucidating the hermeneutics of e-music. For Heidegger, ontology is simply the explication or radical interpretation of everyday understanding, which was particularly urgent for e-music, given the extent to which it rejected many of the traditional crutches of music appreciation.

The working of an e-music composition discloses something of the ontology of sound. In being crafted by a composer, performed by a musician, appreciated by a listener, and analyzed by a critic, the work makes something of its sonic ontology visible to each of these audiences. They each articulate a different narrative of their interpretations, based on their concerns, expectations, and pre-judgments. However, a successful work must connect these communities within the shared world opened by the e-music work.

Even *noise*—which is generally taken to be a rejection of understandability—can be interpreted through a technological approach to sound and its theory. E-music analyzed and worked with noise. In technical terms, "white" noise is a mixture of all frequencies of sound. It can, for instance, be digitally generated with a random-number generator specifying all frequencies stochastically. White noise can then be manipulated with filters and amplitude envelops to produce musically interesting noise sounds within selected pitch ranges. Controlled noise can be integrated into music to add depth, as rock musicians did with feedback from speakers and electronic distortion of their instruments, but now manipulated across the spectra of its technical parameters.

The way in which a new understanding of noise arises through the composition of e-music suggests that Heidegger's analyses inadequately appreciate the role of the artist's productive labor that makes the work of art what it is. The artist does not merely bring forth a work whose being is given by history, but rather structures the details of the work's being through the artist's creative labor (working). This may point to a general problem with Heidegger's ontology. While providing a brilliant phenomenological description of how beings are disclosed, he does not describe how an individual being (whether thing, tool, work, or Dasein) comes to be disclosed not only as the kind of being it is but also as the unique being it is. Even if one focuses on the artwork's being, it is necessary to analyze how that being becomes specified.

What is the relation of an artwork's working to the artist's historically situated work? Perhaps what Heidegger discusses as the *Riss* between earth and world in the being of van Gogh's painting was set into the artwork by van Gogh's artistic working with earth and world in creating the painting, as they interacted within the play of van Gogh's historical world. How is his painting's earth related to the artist's brushstroke style and how is the painting's world related to the life of contemporary farmers? How is the working of noise in e-music structured by the composer's work in creating the music?

In his essay on "The Thing," Heidegger considers the example of a jug to discuss in general how things are disclosed.[29] He suggests that the being of the jug is centered on its interior void, which can be filled with water or wine and can offer it for pouring and imbibing. Heidegger seems to have in mind a handcrafted ancient Greek jug, which functioned with the "aura" of a unique thing in the here and now—not an interchangeable jug from a factory assembly line in the technological era. However, he does not describe how an individual jug concretely comes to be what it is—with its unique character and aura as well as with its particular, functional shape—through the potter's effort, rather than through a factory's production.

Learning to make traditional pottery involves skills and knowledge to be able to produce jugs that can fulfill a well-functioning jug's tasks. An artist does not simply impose a pre-conceived template on some physical material (e.g., clay, wood, pigment, sound, etc.). There is an interplay between creator and created, between mind and eye, between disclosing and concealing, between enlightenment and regress. This interplay during creation is then established in the work of art as its specific working or unique being.

In "The Origin of the Work of Art," Heidegger writes about the connection of the work to its creator:

> Although the work of art becomes actual only in the carrying out of the creating, and thus depends upon this act for its reality, the nature of creating is thereby dependent upon the nature of the work. . . . From the perspective of the achieved outlining of the nature of the artwork—according to which, in the work the happening of truth is at work—we can characterize creating as a letting something emerge as something brought forth. The work's becoming a work is a way in which truth becomes and happens.[30]

Here, Heidegger acknowledges the craft of the artist but subordinates it to the working of the work itself that opens a world and reveals something. Heidegger's shift from the artist to the work as the primary creative agent is central to his philosophic contribution, overcoming the subjectivism of previous philosophy and aesthetic theory. However, his presentations lack adequate concreteness and tend to leave underlying processes vague and mysterious. He does not recognize the ontological role of the artist in shaping how the individual work that is brought forth becomes what it is as a particular work with a unique way of working. While it is true that the potter's work is guided by the nature of jugs, each jug is different in detail due to the specifics of the potter's work.

The creation of art is always a historically mediated process, reaching back to the stone age for pottery, painting, music, sculpture, and poetry—while innovating into the future. The artist pushes previous inquiries further, confronting issues that arose in past works and adopting techniques that have been developed by earlier artists. For instance, the potter, in creating a jug that will open a world that discloses people enjoying the fruits of the earth and skies, explores how best to accomplish that, given the historically prevailing conditions and technologies. The potter selects the right clay and glazes. She experiments with how different construction techniques, various spouts, and specific handle curves contribute to how the unique created jug works to open a specific world, in which the jug can work effectively as desired. The potter's craft, worked out on a specific, concrete piece of work, refines the being of that work, deciding how it will work, that is, how it will be.

Only through the historically situated labor of the artist is the work of art established the way that it is (its being) in the world that it opens—not just through historical change writ large, but through the concrete application of specific production technologies under particular socioeconomic conditions. This process is suggested by Heidegger, but not investigated in sufficient social and historical detail. Benjamin's studies of mechanical reproduction and Adorno's writings on the culture industry provide important extensions and correctives to Heidegger, showing that in addition to the artistic and craft-related explorations of the artist, the current forces of production (e.g., mechanical reproduction) and the prevailing social/economic relations (e.g., commodification by the culture industry) affect the way a work opens (and conceals) its world.

The development of e-music illustrates the complexity of historic processes of progress and regress. We have already seen how the composers of e-music explored innovative ways to open acoustic worlds. However, there is also a retrograde movement: Technology enables new sounds but removes compositions of these sounds further from the comprehension of an audience. The origins of music in the human body (heartbeat, breathing), dance and the physicality of playing physical instruments are replaced in e-music by technical tasks that manipulate abstract parameters on machines. For instance, Stockhausen often computes the timing and other parameters of sounds mathematically rather than through bodily movements.[31] Live, responsive performance is supplanted by methodical efforts in electronic laboratories far removed from potential audiences (see, again, figure 17.3).

The issues of performance and audience raised by e-music had to be addressed. They led to the incorporation of sounds and techniques pioneered by e-music being integrated into and co-opted by more popular musical forms. This brought in live performance, reintroducing and even accentuating the movement of the human body as a basis of repetitive rhythm.[32] The electronic synthesizer, the sequencer of recorded sounds, and even the computer-generated tape became additional musical instruments, eventually often subordinated to traditional instruments (piano, guitar) and practices (tonality, common tempo).[33] New genres also appeared, incorporating and concealing e-music techniques: electro-acoustics combining synthesizers, tape, and instruments; rap mixing drum machines and recorded sounds; trance-music exploiting ethereal resonances and mechanized repetition. These hybrids were easier to market as cultural commodities and they frequently lost their aura of innovative openings to worlds of sound as disclosed in e-music. Electronic music had a profound impact on the history of music. It fueled a diverse array of new genres, enabling innovative ways for music to be and work. Simultaneously, the technologies of electronic music were co-opted by the pop music culture industry, slightly modifying commercial music, but ignoring the e-music vision of opening worlds that disclosed the nature of sound. This history of e-music is much richer than suggested in Heidegger's simplified history of being.

RELATIONS OF ARTISTIC FORM

One of Heidegger's last publications, "Art and Space,"[34] is associated with his contact with sculptors.[35] Here, Heidegger rejects the traditional view of sculpture as a formed matter within an objective, pre-existing extended space. Although he does not discuss any specific example of sculpture, he considers how sculptures define "places" in relation to each other. Heidegger resorts to his critique in *Being and Time* of Newtonian space in favor of human places, now expressed in his later terminology. He writes that sculpture does not passively occupy homogeneous three-dimensional space, but opens up regions in which people can meaningfully live: "Sculpture [is] the embodiment of places. Places, in preserving and opening a region, hold something free gathered around them which grants the tarrying of things under consideration and a dwelling for man in the midst of things."[36] Sculpture, as a form of artwork, can reveal spatial being. Henry Moore's *Three-Piece Sculpture* (figure 17.4) illustrates a region of places opened up and embodied by a sculpture. The

Figure 17.4 Henry Moore, Three-Piece Sculpture: Vertebrae, 1968–1969. Bronze, approx. 3' × 8' × 4'. *Source:* Hirschhorn Sculpture Garden, Washington, DC. Photo by author.

massive bronze forms of bonelike knobs and points of Moore's sculpture define multiple *places* in relationship to each other. They reflect each other as related, but each is unique. The interconnected forms press upon one another and support each other, creating a complex of places that defines a structured region.

As a work, a sculpture opens a devoted area around itself, structured by the sculpture's massed forms, which extends out from that work. The surfaces of the forms are revealed, but they simultaneously conceal what lies below, behind, or beyond the surface: the interior of the wood, stone, bronze, or other material, as well as the voids, hidden surfaces, and surroundings. Through such elements of the work's design, the interior is opened up, but then simultaneously closed along the new surfaces (outline or *Riss*).

Sculptors like Moore explore materials, sizes, shapes, representations, and topologies that allow their sculptures to work to open worlds, places, and regions for human tarrying. Through their sculpting, they pursue ontological investigations of how to let works be, so that they open certain sorts of worlds. Moore's sculpture of vertebrae incorporates his lifetime of sculptural studies of boney forms, reclining human figures, and multi-piece interactions.

Analogous to sculpture, e-music can be heard as sequences of sculpted moments of sound, often delimited and individuated by silences. In a lecture, "The Four Criteria of Electronic Music," Stockhausen specified that e-music was characterized by its focus on composing relations among times, tones, spaces, and noise. His defining features of e-music were:

1. Unified time structuring
2. Splitting of the sound
3. Multilayered spatial composition
4. Continuum of tone and noise[37]

His composition *Kontakte* was structured by decomposing sound into its parameters of temporal duration, timbral components, spatial location, and noise band, as well as pitch and loudness—each defined along scales. Here, Stockhausen extended the intervallic serialization he learned from Schoenberg and Webern to all the parameters of sound, creating tones that had not been composed before, in more complex relationships, opening new possibilities of acoustic places and moments layered upon each other to create temporal structures.

Music, more explicitly than other art forms, creates temporal forms. The being of a musical work according to Heidegger's analysis of art is its working, which is a process that necessarily unfolds in time. The character, being or origin of a work of music, is not an attribute of its immediate presence but is disclosed through its manner of opening a sonic world temporally. Specifically, e-music harnessed electronic and digital technologies to control the timing of individual sounds, of phrases, and of overall compositions. E-music explored innovative timings of sound waveforms, envelopes, sequences, and movements. It not only replaced traditional timings but developed a wholly new systematic approach to temporality as a central dimension of control and composition.

Stockhausen methodically explored the being of sound and how works of music open acoustic worlds. He shifted the science of acoustics into a philosophy and ontology of sound by investigating the effects of the various parameters of sound on the working of e-music compositions to achieve musical works with innovative being. Many of Stockhausen's major pieces of e-music were designed, defined, composed, and refined by him to disclose selected aspects of the being of sound through the working of the musical work. For example, his composition *"Beethoven Opus 1970"* electronically transformed moments from Beethoven's oeuvre to re-disclose the acoustic being of Beethoven's sounds in the technological era. His monumental *"Hymnen"* manipulated sound samples from national anthems to disclose how they opened nationalist worlds, just as Hendrix's distorted electric guitar version of "Star-Spangled Banner" opened a politically construed world for his audience at Woodstock during the Vietnam War.[38]

As part of its working, a work of art functions as a communication between its creator and its recipients. It discloses to the listener/viewer/preserver what is rendered perceptible in the work—an opening of worlds that can be shared. Heidegger notes about the audience role:

> Preserving the work does not individualize people to their life-experiences, but draws them into their belonging to the truth that happens in the work, and thereby grounds their being-for and being-with-one-another as the historical standing-out of being-there (Da-Sein) in relation to unconcealedness.[39]

Thus, the work functions to build historically situated inter-subjectivity, grounded in the work. It opens ontological understanding: a shared understanding of the being of the sounds, work, and world.

An artwork brings a work into the world, opening a space for it to do its work in its historical social setting. Of course, a work of music, painting, pottery, or sculpture does not appear *sui generis*, on its own, as Heidegger's presentation might lead one to believe. Just as the clay jug, van Gogh's painting or Moore's sculpture required a complex crafting, based on culturally developed and passed-down practices, Stockhausen's compositions called upon the skill and intellectual effort of a world-class artist and drew upon the state-of-the-art technical world to compose works with the proper being.

While Heidegger's focus on the being of the work is central to his contribution, it is also necessary to consider the role of the artist and the audience in not just passively dwelling in the world opened by the work, but also in actively determining the concrete and specific way a work, as a unique being, works. Talented artists are ontologists, sculpting the being of their works, as evidenced by the historically innovative forms of disclosure of the worlds they open.

Heidegger's philosophy of being, as it evolved through his life's work, provides useful ways of considering the nature of music and other art forms. Conversely, considerations of sociohistorical aspects of artistic production provide important correctives to Heidegger's incomplete analyses. E-music offers an example of musical development—contemporaneous with Heidegger's writings—that opens a view that can both confirm and extend his insights.

NOTES

1. Cf. David Dunn, *Eigenwelt Der Apparatewelt: Pioneers of Electronic Art* (Linz, Austria: Ars Electronica Exhibition, 1992); and Herbert Eimert, "What Is Electronic Music?" *Die Reihe* 1 (1957): 1–10.

2. Karlheinz Stockhausen, "The Concept of Unity in Electronic Music," *Perspectives of New Music* 1, no. 1 (1962): 39–48; Karlheinz Stockhausen, "Four Criteria of Electronic Music," (1972), https://www.youtube.com/watch?v=7xyGtI7KKIY.

3. Martin Heidegger, *Being and Time: A Translation of Sein und Zeit*, trans. Joan Stambaugh (Albany, NY: SUNY Press, 1927/1996).

4. Martin Heidegger, "The Origin of the Work of Art," in *Philosophies of Art and Beauty*, ed. Albert Hofstadter and Richard Kuhns (New York, NY: Modern Library, 1935/1964), 647–701.

5. Martin Heidegger, *On Time and Being* (New York, NY: Harper & Row, 1962/1972).

6. Martin Heidegger, "Art and Space," *Man and World* 6, no. 1 (1969/1973): 3–8.

7. Cf. Gerry Stahl, "Marxian Hermeneutics and Heideggerian Social Theory: Interpreting and Transforming Our World," (Ph.D. Dissertation, Northwestern University, 1975); and Jürgen Habermas, "Work and Weltanschauung: The Heidegger Controversy from a German Perspective," in *Heidegger: A Critical Reader*, ed. Hubert Dreyfus and Harrison Hall (Oxford, UK: Blackwell, 1992).

8. Theodor W. Adorno, *The Jargon of Authenticity* (Evanston, IL: Northwestern U. Press, 1964/1973).

9. Cf. Walter Benjamin, "The Work of Art in the Age of Mechanical Reproduction," in *Illuminations*, ed. Hannah Arendt (New York, NY: Schocken Books, 1936/1969), 217–51.

10. Cf. Anthony Giddens, *The Constitution of Society* (U of California Press, 1984), 1–40; and Pierre Bourdieu, *Outline of a Theory of Practice* (Cambridge, UK: Cambridge University Press, 1972/1995), 72–95.

11. Cf. Andrew Mitchell, *Heidegger among the Sculptors: Body, Space and the Art of Dwelling* (Stanford, CA: Stanford University Press, 2010).

12. Heidegger, *Being and Time*.

13. Cf. Gerry Stahl, "Interpretation in Design: The Problem of Tacit and Explicit Understanding in Computer Support of Cooperative Design," (Ph.D. Dissertation, University of Colorado, 1993); and Stahl, "Marxian Hermeneutics and Heideggerian Social Theory."

14. Heidegger, *Being and Time*, 163, 153. See also Martin Heidegger, "Der Ursprung Des Kunstwerkes," in *Holzwege*, ed. M. Heidegger (Frankfurt am Main, Germany: Klostermann, 1935/1963), 15, 656. Citations of German publications list publication/translation year, with German/English pagination.

15. Theodor W. Adorno and Max Horkheimer, *The Dialectic of Enlightenment* (New York, NY: Continuum, 1947/1972).

16. Theodor W. Adorno, *Philosophy of Modern Music* (New York, NY: The Seabury Press. 1948/1973).

17. Cf. Eimert, "What Is Electronic Music?"

18. Ben Neill, "Pleasure Beats: Rhythm and the Aesthetics of Current Electronic Music," *Leonardo Music Journal* 12 (2002): 3–6.

19. Heidegger, "The Origin of the Work of Art," and Heidegger, "Der Ursprung Des Kunstwerkes."

20. Heidegger, "Der Ursprung Des Kunstwerkes," 25, my translation. Rentmeester and Savage discuss Heidegger's interpretation of Van Gogh's painting in their respective chapters of this volume.

21. Benjamin, "The Work of Art in the Age of Mechanical Reproduction."

22. Adorno and Horkheimer, *The Dialectic of Enlightenment*.

23. Dunn, "A History of Electronic Music Pioneers."

24. Martin Heidegger, *On Time and Being* (New York, NY: Harper & Row, 1962/1972).

25. Stockhausen, "The Concept of Unity in Electronic Music."

26. Cf. Miller Puckette, *Theory and Techniques of Electronic Music* (Singapore: World Scientific Publishing Company, 2007); and Peter Manning, *Electronic and Computer Music* (Oxford: Oxford University Press, 2004).

27. Gerry Stahl, "Attuned to Being: Heideggerian Music in Technological Society," *Boundary 2* IV, no. 2 (1976).

28. *Die Reihe* was a music academic journal published in Vienna from 1955 to 1962 that was co-edited by Stockhausen; *Perspectives of New Music* is an academic journal that has been published in the United States since 1962.

29. Martin Heidegger, "Das Ding," in *Vorträge Und Aufsätze II*, ed. Friedrich-Wilhelm von Herrmann (Pfullingen, Germany: Neske, 1950/1967), 37–60.
30. Heidegger, "Der Ursprung Des Kunstwerkes," 48f/683f, my translation.
31. Neill, "Pleasure Beats."
32. Richard Glover, "Minimalism, Technology and Electronic Music," in *Ashgate Research Companion to Minimalist and Postminimalist Music*, ed. Keith Potter, Kyle Gann, and Pwyll Ap Sion (Farnham, UK: Ashgate, 2013), 161–80.
33. Cf. Neill, "Pleasure Beats"; and Dunn, Eigenwelt Der Apparatewelt.
34. Heidegger, "Art and Space," 3–8.
35. Mitchell, *Heidegger among the Sculptors*.
36. Heidegger, "Art and Space," 7.
37. Stockhausen, "Four Criteria of Electronic Music."
38. Rentmeester analyzes the world-building aspect of this performance in his chapter of this volume.
39. Heidegger, "Der Ursprung Des Kunstwerkes," 55/690, my translation.

BIBLIOGRAPHY

Adorno, Theodor W. *Philosophy of Modern Music*. New York, NY: The Seabury Press. 1948/1973.
Adorno, Theodor W. *The Jargon of Authenticity*. Evanston, IL: Northwestern University Press, 1964/1973.
Adorno, Theodor W. and Max Horkheimer. *The Dialectic of Enlightenment*. New York, NY: Continuum, 1947/1972.
Benjamin, Walter. "The Work of Art in the Age of Mechanical Reproduction." In *Illuminations*, edited by Hannah Arendt, 217–51. New York, NY: Schocken Books, 1936/1969.
Bourdieu, Pierre. *Outline of a Theory of Practice*. Cambridge, UK: Cambridge University Press, 1972/1995.
Dunn, David. *Eigenwelt Der Apparatewelt: Pioneers of Electronic Art*. Linz, Austria: Ars Electronica exhibition, 1992.
Eimert, Herbert. "What Is Electronic Music?" *Die Reihe* 1 (1957): 1–10.
Giddens, Anthony. *The Constitution of Society*. University of California Press, 1984.
Glover, Richard. "Minimalism, Technology and Electronic Music." In *Ashgate Research Companion to Minimalist and Postminimalist Music*, edited by Keith Potter, Kyle Gann, and Pwyll Ap Sion, 161–80. Farnham, UK: Ashgate, 2013.
Habermas, Jürgen. "Work and Weltanschauung: The Heidegger Controversy from a German Perspective." In *Heidegger: A Critical Reader*, edited by Hubert Dreyfus and Harrison Hall, 196–208. Oxford, UK: Blackwell, 1992.
Heidegger, Martin. "Art and Space." *Man and World* 6, no. 1 (1969/1973): 3–8.
Heidegger, Martin. *Being and Time: A Translation of Sein und Zeit*. Translated by Joan Stambaugh. Albany, NY: SUNY Press, 1927/1996.

Heidegger, Martin. "Das Ding." In *Vorträge Und Aufsätze II*, Edited by Friedrich-Wilhelm von Herrmann, 37–60. Pfullingen, Germany: Neske, 1950/1967.
Heidegger, Martin. "Der Ursprung Des Kunstwerkes." In *Holzwege*, edited by M. Heidegger, 649–701. Frankfurt am Main, Germany: Klostermann, 1935/1963.
Heidegger, Martin. *On Time and Being*. New York, NY: Harper & Row, 1962/1972.
Heidegger, Martin. "The Origin of the Work of Art." In *Philosophies of Art and Beauty*, edited by Albert Hofstadter and Richard Kuhns, 647–701. New York, NY: Modern Library, 1935/1964.
Manning, Peter. *Electronic and Computer Music*. Oxford: Oxford University Press, 2004.
Mitchell, Andrew. *Heidegger among the Sculptors: Body, Space and the Art of Dwelling*. Stanford, CA: Stanford University Press, 2010.
Neill, Ben. "Pleasure Beats: Rhythm and the Aesthetics of Current Electronic Music." *Leonardo Music Journal* 12 (2002): 3–6.
Puckette, Miller. *Theory and Techniques of Electronic Music*. Singapore: World Scientific Publishing Company, 2007.
Stahl, Gerry. "Attuned to Being: Heideggerian Music in Technological Society." *Boundary 2* IV, no. 2 (1976): 637–64.
Stahl, Gerry. "Interpretation in Design: The Problem of Tacit and Explicit Understanding in Computer Support of Cooperative Design." Ph.D. Dissertation, University of Colorado, 1993.
Stahl, Gerry. "Marxian Hermeneutics and Heideggerian Social Theory: Interpreting and Transforming Our World." Ph.D. Dissertation, Northwestern University, 1975.
Stockhausen, Karlheinz. "The Concept of Unity in Electronic Music." *Perspectives of New Music* 1, no. 1 (1962): 39–48.
Stockhausen, Karlheinz. "Four Criteria of Electronic Music." 1972. YouTube: https://www.youtube.com/watch?v=7xyGtI7KKIY.

Index

Page references for figures are italicized.

Abe, Masao, 98
Abgrund. See abyss
absolute nothingness (*mu*), 98, 103
absoluter Geist. See absolute spirit
absolute spirit (*absoluter Geist*), 98
abyss (*Abgrund*), 110, 113, 115–16, 128, 149, 181, 184–85, 260
acid rock, 289
Adams, John, 84
Adorno, Theodore, 58, 60, 98, 103, 127, 259; on commodification, 102; on the culture industry, 295, 300; on the dialectic of enlightenment, 296; interpretation of Hölderlin, 54, 63; on late style, 75; on rationalizing instinct, 91, 93; on subjectification in music, 93
Aeschylus, 54, 80, 174
Aesop, 56
African musical aesthetics, 143–54
AI. *See* artificial intelligence
alethēia, 92, 146–47, 153, 166, 200, 202, 254–55
Allen, Woody, 59
the Alps, 27–30
Anders, Günther, 58
Angst. See anxiety
anthropomorphism, 41–43

anxiety (*Angst*), 42, 44, 54, 259, 275
the Apollonian, 260
appropriation. *See Ereignis*
Arendt, Hannah, 148–49
aretē, 235
Aristotle, 77; on his four causes, 274; on his theory of generation, 283; on his theory of music, 235
Arnold, Matthew, 75
artificial intelligence, 118–19, 189
atopos, 56
attunement (*Stimmung*), ix, 6, 59, 61, 79, 117, 130, 183, 199, 206, 264, 275. *See also* mood
auditory cheesecake, 235–36, 245
Augustine, Saint, 54, 59, 257–58; on singing and time, 53, 63; on *voluptas aurium* (the pleasures of the ear), 76
authenticity (*Eigentlichkeit*), 12, 30, 40, 114, 216, 219, 223–24, 258; community as authentic, 8; Dasein's being as authentic, 43, 152, 181–82, 188, 213, 242, 272, 275, 290; language as authentic, 100
awe, 43

Bach, Johann Sebastian, 59, 76, 118, 255, 259

Baldwin, Dare, 215–16
The Band, 240
Barenboim, Daniel, 197–98
Bartók, Béla, 30
basho, 98
Basie, Count, 188
Bayreuth, Germany, 76, 81, 83, 103
Beethoven, Ludwig, 57–59, 75–78, 118, 303
Befindlichkeit. *See* situatedness
being-alongside (*Sein bei*), 213, 219–20
being-among-one-another (*Untereinandersein*), 213, 219–20
being-in-the-world (*In-der-Welt-sein*), 6–9, 11–14, 38–42, 46, 61, 94, 130, 164–69, 213–14, 218, 224, 254, 263–65, 272, 275–76
being-towards-death (*Sein-zum-Tode*), ix, 37–48
being-with (*Mitsein*), x, 60, 114, 213–15, 219–24, 275, 303
Benjamin, Walter, 58, 61, 300; on historical changes in art, 295–96; on translation, 94, 100
Bennett, H. Stith, 58, 61
Bergson, Henri, 262
Berlin, Germany, 30, 85
Berlioz, Hector, 60, 84
besinnliches Denken. *See* meditative thinking
Bestand. *See* standing-reserve
big-band music, 187–88, 295
Bizet, Georges, 78
The Black Forest, 19, 143
blood and soil (*Blut und Boden*), 30
Bodenständigkeit. *See* rootedness
Bohrer, Karl Heinz, 85
boredom, 38, 130
Borgmann, Albert, ix, 101, 244–46
Boulez, Pierre, 219, 289, 297
Bourdieu, Pierre, 58
Bowie, Andrew, 22, 209n57, 236, 263
British Columbia, 20–21, 31
Britten, Benjamin, ix, 92–100, 103

Bruckner, Anton, 85
Buddhism, 98, 103

Cage, John, 58–59, 115, 119
calculative thinking (*rechnendes Denken*), x, 179, 184, 203, 208n40
Calzabigi, Ranieri de', 84
Canada, 31
care (*Sorge*), 24, 26, 99, 151, 214–19, 222, 258
Cash, Johnny, 58
Cassirer, Ernst, 27
Celibidache, Sergiu, 196–97, 206
Cezanne, Paul, 196
Chien-Pott, PeiJu, 279
China, ix, 109, 112
Chopin, Frédéric, 118
Christianity, viii, ix, 92, 240, 276–77
classical music, 78, 81, 289, 292–93
the clearing (*die Lichtung*), 37, 40, 44–45, 58, 116, 148, 179, 217–18
Cohen, Leonard, 58, 61–62
Coltrane, John, 185, 187
Confucianism, 109, 112, 120n13
COVID-19, 187, 246
Creedence Clearwater Revival, 240
Crosby, Stills, Nash & Young, 240
the culture industry, 292, 295, 300–1

Dahlhaus, Carl, 61, 262
Damasio, Antonio, 144, 148, 151
dao. *See tao*
Daoism. *See* Taoism
Darwin, Charles, 236
Davis, Miles, 187
Davis, Richard, 180
Davos, Switzerland, 19, 27–28, 30
Debussy, Claude, 97
Derrida, Jacques, 58, 62, 78, 284n3
Deutsche Oper, 85
the device paradigm, 101–2, 245
dialectic of enlightenment, 296
the Dionysian, 85, 240
disco-dance music, 289

distraction, ix, 37–40, 45–48
divinities, 169, 173–75, 285n6. *See also*
  gods
doxa, 40
Doyle, Sir Arthur Conan, 28
Dresden, Germany, 81
Dreyfus, Hubert, 119, 240, 242, 246
dwelling (*wohnen*), x, 5, 20, 26–31, 102, 163–71, 175, 180, 254, 256, 261, 278, 281, 301, 304; tools of, ix, 20, 31

earth: as aspect of the fourfold, 116–17, 119, 169, 174–75, 285n6; as harmonious with *tian* (heaven), 110–11, 117; as juxtaposed with world, 58, 200, 218–19, 224, 271–72, 278–84, 285n6, 295, 298
Ehrenforth, Karl Heinrich, 8
eidos, 40
Eigentlichkeit. *See* authenticity
Einstein, Albert, 28, 242
ek-sistence, 147, 150
Electric and Musical Industries (EMI), 118
electronic music (e-music), xi, 22, 289–93, 296–302
Ellington, Duke, 188
EMI. *See* Electric and Musical Industries
e-music. *See* electronic music
enframing. *See* Gestell
entropy, 37, 40–48
Epiphany (Christian holiday), 276
equipmentality (*Zeugsein*), x, 163–71
Ereignis (appropriation; the event), x, 3, 14, 116–17, 163–64, 171, 181, 189, 199–202, 205–6
Essential thinking (*besinnliches Denken*). *See* meditative thinking
the event. *See* Ereignis
evolution, 45, 235–36
existential, 3–4, 12, 60, 258–59, 263–64, 267n38, 275

existentiell, 258, 267n38

facticity, 184, 189, 263
fallenness, 38, 40–41
the feminine, 120n8, 271–75, 278, 282–84
Florentine Camerata, 84
focal practices, 101–2
focal things, 101–2
forgetfulness, 144, 147; of being, ix, 91, 98, 186
the fourfold (*das Geviert*), 116–19, 169–75, 285, 286n33
fusion (musical genre), 189, 289

Gadamer, Hans-Georg, 19, 28, 59, 254, 263; on the function of philosophy, 56; on play, 171
gagaku music, 94
gathering, moment of, 8, 43–44, 46, 85, 116, 169, 243, 245–46
Gelassenheit (letting beings be; releasement), 12, 23, 86, 152, 184
George, Stefan, 53, 82
Georgiades, Thrasybulos, 82, 84, 174
Gerede, 100–2
Gestell (enframing; positionality), ix, 91–92, 101–3, 153, 179, 185–89, 245, 277, 281–84
das Geviert. *See* the fourfold
Geworfenheit. *See* thrownness
Glass, Philip, 84, 255, 259
Gluck, Christoph Willibald, 83–84
the god(s), 14, 103, 261, 276, 283; as an aspect of the fourfold, 116–17; fleeing of, 7; godding, 115–16, 122n51; godless age, 102, 202–3; the last, 12, 14; "only a god can save us," 101. *See also* deities
grand music, 109–12, 117, 119
Grand Palais, 274, 279
grand style, ix, 75–80, 82–83, 85–86
The Grateful Dead, 240
Greece, 30, 78, 80, 150, 247n2, 276

Gregorian music, 134
group music-making, 214, 221; benefits of, 223–24
Guignon, Charles, 242
Gustav III, King, 83

Habermas, Jürgen, 296
Haeffner, Johann Christian Friedrich, 83
handiness (*Zuhandenheit*). See ready-to-hand
Han period of China, 109
Hanslick, Eduard, 56–58
Harman, Graham, 23, 25
harmony, 54, 58, 92–94, 110–13, 128, 135, 235, 238–39, 260, 275; between heaven and earth, 110, 117; of the spheres, 174
Harnoncourt, Nikolaus, 196
Haydn, Joseph, 76
the hearable (*die Hörigkeit*), 4
hearing (*hören*), 5–6, 62, 114
heaven (*tian*), 120; as harmonious with di (earth), 110–11; music of, 109, 113
heavy metal, 21
Hegel, George Wilhelm Friedrich, 22, 77, 98, 259
Heidelberg, Germany, 27
das Heilige. See the holy
Heimat, 7
Hendrix, Jimi, 240–43, 248n36, 303
Heraclitus, 58–59
Herder, Johann Gottfried, 30, 53–54, 56, 204
hermeneutics, xi, 56, 59–60, 117, 128, 131, 171, 253, 258, 271–72, 279, 284, 297
Herrick, Robert, 55
Hindemith, Paul, 59
Hodges, Johnny, 188
Høffding, Simon, 218
Hofstadter, Douglas, 118
Hölderlin, Friedrich, 3, 5, 30, 116, 129–31, 136, 200–6, 253, 255–57, 260–61, 274; Heidegger's regard for, 53–54, 62–63; on his revival of the Greek world, 80, 82, 84; on the relationship between danger and the saving power, 246
the holy (*das Heilige*), 203, 206, 276, 283
hören. See hearing
Horkheimer, Max, 296
Husserl, Edmund, 43, 59, 62, 96, 215

iki, ix, 92, 95–97, 103
impressionism (art movement), 295
improvisation, x, 59–60, 163–66, 170–74, 181
International Davos Conference, 27
iPod, 244
Irigaray, Luce, xi, 271–72, 277–78, 282–84

Japan, ix, 92, 94–100, 103
Japonism, 97
jazz, x, 172, 179–90, 289, 295
Jochum, Eugen, 76
Joplin, Janis, 240
junzi (noble person), 110, 121n27

Kafka, Franz, 144, 149–50
Kant, Immanuel, 61, 98, 260
Kearney, Richard, 265
die Kehre. See the turn
Kelly, Sean, 246
Kern, Iso, 115
Kierkegaard, Søren, 258
Kitaro, Nishida, 98
Klee, Paul, 85
Kraus, Joseph Martin, 83–84
Kreutzer, Conradin, x, 243
Kuhn, Thomas, 242, 249n43
Kuki, Shūzō, ix, 92, 94, 96–99
Kurtág, György, 85
The Kyoto School, 98

Landowska, Wanda, 206
Laozi, 113, 117
leap (*Sprung*), 47, 181, 184–85; leap ahead, 222–24; leap in, 222
Lebewesen, 7

Lennon, John, 237, 239
letting beings be. *See Gelassenheit*
Levinas, Emmanuel, 27, 58
li, 120n13
die Lichtung. See the clearing
logos, 8, 117, 272, 282
Ludwig II, King, 83
Lyotard, Jean-François, 260

machination (*Machenschaft*), 76, 118
Mahler, Gustav, 85
das Man. See the they
Martha Graham Dance Company, 279
Marx, Karl, xi, 91, 101, 290–91; on the task of philosophy, 101
Marxism, 91, 291, 295
Massenet, Jules, 97
May, Reinhard, 91
Medieval Times, 76, 134, 290, 296. *See also* the Middle Ages
meditative thinking (*besinnliches Denken*), x, 179, 182, 184, 186–88, 208n40
Messkirch, Germany, x, 243
Metallica, 238
metaphysics, 77, 91, 98, 128–29, 188–89, 278. *See also* post-metaphysics
the Middle Ages, 6, 276–78. *See also* Medieval Times
Mitsein. See being-with
Monson, Ingrid, 180
mood (*Stimmung*), 4, 6, 14, 22, 24, 38, 42, 62, 111, 128–30, 135, 183, 185, 253, 261–66, 272, 275, 278, 292. *See also* attunement
Moog synthesizer, *293*
Moore, Henry, *301*, 301–3
Morrison, Jim, 242
Mossessian, Claude, *273, 280*
mountain biking, ix, 19–26, 31
Mozart, Wolfgang Amadeus, 58–59, 62, 76, 78, 199
mu. See absolute nothingness
Müller, Heiner, 84
Munich, Germany, 76, 80–81, 86
Murungi, John, ix, 143–53

musical multimedia, ix, 19–27, 31
musicking, 37, 60, 143–49, 151
music of the spheres, 6, 15n10, 57
myth of Er, 56
mythos, 8, 9; *mythos* horizon, 16n36

Nancy, Jean-Luc, 56, 213, 220–21, 265
National Socialism, 37, 79. *See also* Nazism
Naumann, Johann Gottlieb, 83–84
Nazism, 30. *See also* National Socialism
new-age trance music, 289
Newton, Isaac, 301
Nietzsche, Friedrich, ix, 54, 56, 58–59, 61–63, 75–80, 83–85, 127, 199–200, 260; on being as a vapor, 47–48; on his criticism of Socratism, 196; on the meaning of music, vii, 28, 236
Nono, Luigi, 85
nō theatre, 92
Nzewi, Meki, 143–45, 147–53

Orff, Carl, 76, 80–86, 199

paideia, 239
Palazzo Pitti, 75
Palestrina style, 134, 138n40
Paris, France, 84
Parker, Charlie, 188
Pärt, Arvo, 132–36
Pascal, Blaise, 196, 258
Petzet, Heinrich, 76, 81
phallogocentrism, 272, 284n3
phenomenology, 130, 258; of distraction, ix, 37; of music, xi, 54, 59; of reading, 56; of religious life, 76
physis, 44–47, 274
Pietism, 259
Pindar, 62
Pinker, Steven, x, 235–39
Plato, vii, x, 56–57, 59, 62, 77, 111–12, 146, 235, 237–39, 247n4; on Heidegger's translation of, 78
poiesis, 256
politics, vii, 37, 78–79, 111

Polt, Richard, 122n50
Pöltner, Günther, 201–2
popular music, 21, 59, 292, 295–96, 300–1
positionality. *See* Gestell
post-metaphysics, 209n57. *See also* metaphysics
post-serial music, 93. *See also* serial music
presence-at-hand (*Vorhandenheit*), 23, 167, 181, 217
Prinzregenten theater, 81
psychedelic music, 241
punk rock, 243
Pythagoras, 15n10, 174

radio, 76, 244, 293
rap music, 243
ready-to-handness (*Zuhandenheit*), 23, 25, 61, 115, 180, 186
rechnendes Denken. *See* calculative thinking
records, 186–87, 244, 293, 295
Rectorship Address of 1933, 181
Rede, 100, 102
releasement. *See* Gelassenheit
resoluteness, 258–59
resonance, 37, 43, 54, 300
the Rhine, 129, 277
Ricoeur, Paul, xi, 255–58, 262, 264–65
rift (*Riss*), 115, 295–96, 298, 302
Rihm, Wolfgang, 84–85
Rilke, Rainer Maria, ix, 53–56, 58–59, 62–63, 98
Riss. *See* rift
Romanticism, 29, 78
rootedness (*Bodenständigkeit*), 11, 79, 244

Said, Edward W., 75
Saint-Saëns, Camille, 97
Salzburg, Austria, 81
Sartre, Jean-Paul, 20, 24, 258
Schadewaldt, Wolfgang, 84

Schilingi, Jacopo Baboni, viii, xi, 271–79, *273*, *280*, 282–84
Schiller, Friedrich, 57
Schoenberg, Arnold, 258–59, 289, 292–93, 302
Schubert, Franz, 199
Schutz, Alfred, 261–62
Sciarrino, Salvatore, 85
serial music, 289, 293. *See also* post-serial music
Setiya, Kieran, 96
Sheehan, Thomas, 188
shengren, 112
shepherd of being, 150
silence, ix, 12, 44, 54, 58, 60, 63, 86, 113–16, 119, 127–28, 131–36, 180, 201, 204–6, 292
Silesius, Angelus, 62, 76
situatedness (*Befindlichkeit*), 165–66, 170–72, 183
Sjölin, Fredrik, 218
skepticism, 3, 11, 76
skiing, 19–29, 31
Small, Christopher, 60–61, 146
Smith, F. Joseph, 62
snowboarding, 22
Socrates, 56, 111, 247n4
Socratism, 196
Sophocles, 54, 63, 82, 84
Sorge. *See* care
Stambaugh, Joan, 39, 189
Stevens, Wallace, 55, 59
Stevenson, Robert Louis, 28
stillness (*die Stille*), 45, 59, 112, 114–19
Stimmung. *See* attunement; mood
Stockhausen, Karlheinz, 60, 289, 296–97, *297*, 300, 302–3
Strauss, Richard, 75, 97
Stravinsky, Igor, 81, 199

the sublime, 28, 260
tao (*dao*), 113, 117
Taoism (Daoism), 109, 112
techne, 38–39, 54, 57, 189, 274

the technique (*die Technik*), 3, 6, 11–14
the they (*das Man*), 39, 213
thrownness (*Geworfenheit*), 38, 41, 152, 184, 263, 275, 282, 285n15
tian. *See* heaven
tintinnabula, 129, 132
Todtnauberg, Germany, 30
topos, 164, 168. *See also atopos*
Trakl, Georg, 82, 136, 200
the turn (*die Kehre*), 37

Van Gogh, Vincent, 5, 240, 248n32, 254, *294*, 294–95, 298, 303
vapor, being as, 47–48
Varèse, Edgard, 289, 292
Vietnam War, 241–42, 303
vinyl records. *See* records
Vogler, Georg Joseph, 83–84
Vorhandenheit. *See* presence-at-hand

Wagner, Richard, 59, 76–78, 81, 83–84, 199, 206
the Walkman, 244, 249n53
Warring States Period of China, 109
Webern, Anton, 292, 302
welten. *See* worlding

white noise, 298
the Who, 240
Wittgenstein, Ludwig, 56
wohnen. *See* dwelling
wonder, 43, 150
Woodstock Music Festival, x, 240–43, 245, 303
worlding (*welten*), 128, 130, 174–75, 239–40, 248n30, 253–55, 261
World War II, 85

Xenakis, Iannis, 289, 297

yang, 110, 113, 120n8
yin, 111, 113, 120n8

Zahavi, Dan, 215
Zender, Hans, 196–97, 206
Zheng music, 112
Zhou Dynasty of China, 109, 119n1
Zhuangzi, 113; the book of *Zhuangzi*, 112–13
Zimmerman, Michael E., 23
Žižek, Slavoj, 102
Zuhandenheit. *See* ready-to-handness

About the Contributors

Babette Babich is a professor of philosophy at Fordham University in New York City, NY, USA, and currently Visiting Professor of Theology, Religion and Philosophy at the University of Winchester, England. A native New Yorker, she writes on philosophy of science, including technology, and classical and contemporary aesthetics as well as on music and, especially, musical covers. In addition to the Eberhard Karls Universität Tübingen, she also has taught at the Humboldt University in Berlin, Boston College, the University of California at San Diego, Stony Brook University, the Juilliard School, and so on. Books include *Günther Anders' Philosophy of Technology* (2021), *Nietzsches Plastik* (2021), *Nietzsches Antike* (2020), *The Hallelujah Effect* (2016 [2013]), and *Words in Blood, Like Flowers* (2006). Her recent edited collections include *Reading David Hume's 'Of the Standard of Taste'* (2020 [2019]) and *Hermeneutic Philosophies of Social Science* (2019 [2017]). She is the editor of *New Nietzsche Studies*.

Justin Christensen is a researcher, performer, and composer working as a postdoctoral researcher at the University of Saskatchewan in Canada. His research focuses on the temporal and interpersonal musical experience and has resulted in him writing a book titled *Sound and the Aesthetics of Play: A Musical Ontology of Constructed Emotions*. He has undertaken postdoctoral research at Aalborg University in Denmark, earned a PhD in music composition in the United Kingdom with the composer and pianist Michael Finnissy, and completed degrees in music composition and trumpet performance at the Koninklijk Conservatorium in the Netherlands and McGill University in Canada.

Jill Drouillard is an assistant professor of Philosophy at the Mississippi University for Women in Columbus, MS, USA. She received her PhD in Philosophy from the Université de Paris-Sorbonne IV. She has research interests in feminist philosophy, nineteenth- to twentieth-century Continental philosophy (especially Heidegger), reproductive ethics, and social philosophy in the United States and France. She has published in *Continental Philosophy Review, The International Journal of Feminist Approaches to Bioethics, The Journal of French and Francophone Philosophy, Implications Philosophiques, Bulletin Heideggérien,* and *The New Zealand Journal of French Studies*. She has forthcoming work on the hermeneutics of gender facticity of Dasein and time reckoning during labor.

Anthony Gritten was an organ scholar and research student at Cambridge University, writing his doctorate on Igor Stravinsky. He has worked at the University of East Anglia, the Royal Northern College of Music, and Middlesex University, and is currently head of Undergraduate Programmes at the Royal Academy of Music in London, England. His publications include essays on Adorno, Bakhtin, Balakirev, Cage, Debussy, Delius, Goehr, Holloway, Lyotard, Nancy, Roth, and Stravinsky, and numerous articles on issues in Performance Studies. Many of his publications can be downloaded from ram.academia.edu/AnthonyGritten.

J. P. E. Harper-Scott is a professor of Music History and Theory at Royal Holloway, University of London, and general editor of the Cambridge University Press series, "Music in Context." His work focuses on an examination of music's cultural, personal, and interpersonal significance since around 1800. It draws extensively on philosophical, cultural, and social theory and the explanatory resources of music theory, and espouses an explicitly Leftist perspective. He is the author of numerous books and articles, the latest of which is a book on the theoretical foundations of writing a history of music, *The Event of Music History* (2021).

Janeen Loehr is a cognitive neuroscientist whose research investigates the cognitive and brain mechanisms that allow people to coordinate complex actions with others, such as when playing in a musical ensemble. She completed her PhD at McGill University in Canada and a Marie Curie Postdoctoral Fellowship at the Donders Institute for Brain, Behaviour, and Cognitive Science in The Netherlands. She is now an associate professor in the Department of Psychology at the University of Saskatchewan, Canada.

Jeff Malpas is emeritus distinguished professor at the University of Tasmania, visiting distinguished professor at Latrobe University, and a fellow of the Australian Academy of Humanities. He publishes across several disciplines, including philosophy, but also architecture, geography, and the arts. His most recent book is *Rethinking Dwelling: Heidegger, Place, Architecture* (2021).

Sam McAuliffe is a a philosopher and a musician at Monash University in Melbourne, Australia. His research focuses on philosophical hermeneutics, place/topology, aesthetics, and music. He has had articles published in *Critical Horizons, Organised Sound, Jazz Perspectives*, and the *Journal of Aesthetic Education*. He also plays guitar and has curated sound installations for major Australian art festivals.

Agamenon de Morais is Master in Music Composition at the Graduate Program in Music of the Federal University of Rio Grande do Norte—UFRN—in Brazil. He has served as project coordinator at the UFRN Music School at Braille Musicography and Inclusion Support Office, is a member of the UFRN Research Group in Music Education, GRUMUS, and is a member of the UFRN Research Group in Music Education in Multiple Contexts, GPMUC. His research areas of interest include inclusive education, music composition, and aesthetics.

Frederik Pio is currently an associate professor at the University of Aarhus, Department of Education (DPU), and lives in Copenhagen, Denmark, with his wife, two kids, and a pet. He has authored several books on the philosophy of music education as well as the philosophy of general education. He is especially interested in music education, *Bildung*-theory, as well as phenomenological lines of thought within the field of education and teaching in general.

John Reid-Hresko is a first-generation settler on Sḵwx̱wú7mesh and ƛaʔuukʷiʔatḥ unceded territories, trained in environmental sociology, and is a faculty member at Quest University Canada, which is located in Squamish, British Columbia. His recent work explores how dynamics of settler colonialism, outdoor recreation, tourism, and Indigenous efforts toward reconciliation and resurgence intersect within the complicated landscapes of environmental politics in western British Columbia. As a settler, John focuses on how other settlers understand and make sense of their own relationships to landscapes, embodiment, indigeneity, and settler colonialism.

Casey Rentmeester is the director of General Education and associate professor of Philosophy at Bellin College in Green Bay, WI, USA. He is the author of the book *Heidegger and the Environment* (2016) and numerous peer-reviewed articles and book chapters on topics ranging from Continental philosophy, environmental philosophy, medical ethics, Chinese philosophy, social and political philosophy, comparative philosophy, and philosophy of music. He lives with his wife and three children in De Pere, WI.

Goetz Richter is a violinist and philosopher at the Sydney Conservatorium of Music in Australia. Goetz has appeared as a violin soloist, recitalist, and chamber musician in Australia, Asia, and Europe and has been a leader of several Australian Orchestras Symphony Orchestras before being appointed as associate professor at the Sydney Conservatorium of Music. Goetz is artistic director of the Kendall National Violin Competition and president of the Sydney Schubert Society. He has presented masterclasses and lectures internationally and in 2013 was appointed as a visiting professor at the Conservatorium in Wuhan, China. Born in Hamburg, Germany, Goetz studied violin performance in Munich and Berne before settling in Australia in 1985. He holds his PhD in philosophy from the University of Sydney and has published in philosophy, especially on Nietzsche and Plato and in the philosophy of music, musical performance, music education, and violin pedagogy. In 2019, he was appointed an honorary member of the Order of Australia.

Eve Ruddock taught music at schools in the several states of Australia before specializing in private studio teaching. Questions about Western music practice led her to undertake postgraduate research at the University of Western Australia. While writing a qualitative study of self-perceived non-musicians' perceptions of their musicality, she recognized that participant experiences exposed a learned distancing from instinctive musicality. This led her on a hermeneutic exploration of intrinsic human musicking that uncovered cultural (mis)conceptions that effect our capacity to *be* musical, which served as the focus of her doctoral thesis en route to her PhD in 2017. She has published several papers on this topic from a phenomenological and hermeneutical perspective.

Roger W. H. Savage is a professor in the Department of Ethnomusicology at the University of California, Los Angeles, USA, specializing in hermeneutics, aesthetics, and politics. His books include *Hermeneutics and Music Criticism*; *Music, Time, and Its Other: Aesthetic Reflections on Finitude, Temporality, and Alterity*; and *Paul Ricoeur's Philosophical Anthropology as Hermeneutics of Liberation: Freedom, Justice, and the Power of Imagination*. He also edited *Paul Ricoeur in the Age of Hermeneutical Reason: Poetics, Praxis, and Critique* and *Paul Ricoeur and the Lived Body*. Professor Savage is a founding member and past president of the Society for Ricoeur Studies.

Gerry Stahl followed the development of e-music while researching a philosophy dissertation on Heidegger and Marx in Germany and the USA in the

1960s and 1970s—and even experimented a bit in electronic and computer music, without success. His eventual career was in information science and research on computer support for group cognition and has authored several books on this topic (see http://GerryStahl.net). He retired as emeritus professor from Drexel University in the United States and now carves wood sculptures and promotes ecological preservation in Cape Cod, MA, USA.

Trevor Thwaites has been a music educator for the past forty-five years: twenty years as a head of department in New Zealand secondary schools and twenty-five years as a senior lecturer in teacher education, most recently (since 2006) at the University of Auckland where he was also head of the School of Visual and Creative Arts in Education and subsequently deputy head of the School of Arts, Languages and Literacies in Education. He was a project director for the development of a New Zealand curriculum for the Arts and has held leading roles in the development of assessment strategies in Music, including as national moderator for eight years. Journal articles by Trevor in which Heidegger is central to the argument have appeared in *Education, Philosophy and Theory*; *Action, Criticism, Theory for Music Education*; *Philosophy of Music Education Review*; *Research in New Zealand Performing Arts and Education*; and *Pacific Asia Journal of Education*. Trevor has also written Heidegger-informed book chapters, monographs, and he is a regular presenter at conferences of Philosophy of Education Society of Australasia (PESA), the Australasian Society of Continental Philosophy (ASCP), and the Australian and New Zealand Association for Research in Music Education (ANZARME). Committed to live music performances, Trevor is a busy jazz musician and is chairperson of both the Auckland Sinfonietta Trust and the Auckland Secondary Schools Music Festival Trust.

Peter Trawny is a professor of philosophy at Bergische Universität Wuppertal in Germany. He has authored numerous books and peer-reviewed articles on Heidegger and serves as the co-editor of the Martin-Heidegger-Gesamtausgabe.

Erik Wallrup is an associate professor of aesthetics at Södertörn University, Stockholm (*docent* in musicology) in Sweden. He has published widely on music, mood, and atmosphere—often in relation to Martin Heidegger— including the book *Being Musically Attuned: The Act of Listening to Music* (2015). In Swedish, he has written a book-length essay on Nietzsche's philosophy of listening (2002). He is a member of the Royal Swedish Academy of Music.

Jeff R. Warren is a professor of Music and Humanities at Quest University in Squamish, British Columbia. His book *Music and Ethical Responsibility*

(2014) examines the ethical implications of everyday musical experiences. Current research projects include musical multimedia and mountain biking culture; Christian congregational music; and the relationship between music, politics, and phenomenology using post-1968 Paris as a case study. His creative work includes sound recording, sound installations, and performance on double and electric bass.

Qinghua Zhu is the director of Western philosophy and professor of philosophy at Capital Normal University in Beijing, China. Having earned her PhD from Peking University in 2006, she has translated several of Heidegger's books from German to Chinese, including *Parmenides*, *Grundbegriffe der antiken Philosophie*, and *Sein und Wahrheit*. She has numerous peer-reviewed publications that reflect her interests in ancient Greek philosophy, phenomenology (especially Heidegger), comparative philosophy, and feminism.

www.ingramcontent.com/pod-product-compliance
Lightning Source LLC
Chambersburg PA
CBHW022009300426
44117CB00005B/96